Thomson, The Seasons and The Castle of Indolence

Clarendon Press Series

THOMSON'S SEASONS

AND

CASTLE OF INDOLENCE

LOGIE ROBERTSON

London
HENRY FROWDE

Oxford University Press Warehouse
Amen Corner, E.C.

Clarendon Press Series

THOMSON

THE SEASONS

AND

THE CASTLE OF INDOLENCE

EDITED

WITH BIOGRAPHICAL NOTICE, INTRODUCTIONS,
NOTES, AND A GLOSSARY

BY

J. LOGIE ROBERTSON, M.A.

EDITOR OF 'SELECTIONS FROM BURNS'

Oxford

AT THE CLARENDON PRESS

1891

𝔒𝔵𝔣𝔬𝔯𝔡

PRINTED AT THE CLARENDON PRESS

BY HORACE HART, PRINTER TO THE UNIVERSITY

PREFACE

—◆—

THOMSON has special recommendations as a British classic for the use of youth. Not only does he look upon Nature with the eye of a poet—and there is hardly an aspect of Nature that he has failed to note—but his descriptions possess such a power of freshness and fidelity, conveyed for the most part in language of astonishing felicity, that the heart must be dull indeed which they cannot inspire with interest and even rouse to enthusiasm. It is not too much to say that a love for Thomson's poetry in early life implies a permanent delight in the phenomena of rural Nature and an unfailing response to her restorative influences. It might be added that Thomson furnishes in The Seasons the best introduction to the study of Wordsworth's poetry,—if indeed the heart that has felt the charm of the earlier and more ingenuous poet be not satisfied to rest content with his teaching and to seek no farther. In The Castle of Indolence the same love of Nature and rural life which animates The Seasons is continually revealed in passages of exquisite beauty, and in the second Canto there is, more particularly, much sympathetic writing on the advantages of an open-air life of active industry which is surely very capable of inspiring and directing the energies of healthy youth.

The text of The Seasons adopted in the present edition is of course that of the year 1746, which was the last to receive the author's personal revision. At the same time the earlier texts have been examined, and it is believed that all the alterations of real interest, made in the first and subsequent texts before the completed poem at last settled into the shape in which we now have it, have been carefully recorded in the Notes—certainly to a much greater extent than will be found in any previous edition. For The Castle of Indolence the text of the second edition, published in octavo in 1748, the last year of Thomson's life, has been faithfully followed in the present edition.

Very special care has been taken in the preparation of the Notes. They have been written independently of, and are fuller and—it is hoped—not more diffuse than, those of any previous edition. Amongst other purposes they aim at making the author illustrate himself, by citing from his other poems passages parallel to those which happen to be under consideration. They are further intended to reveal the nature and extent of his indebtedness to his predecessors and contemporaries, and they at least indicate the manner in which he in his turn has influenced or suggested the poetical thought and work of others.

In regard to The Castle of Indolence, it may fairly be claimed that it is here for the first time fully annotated.

In writing the Biographical Notice I have had occasion to correct many faults which, having found their way into the early Lives of Thomson, have continued to infest his biography ever since. In this part of my task, more especially in dealing with the home life and youthful training of Thomson, I have received valuable aid—most courteously and generously given, and here gratefully acknowledged—from the Rev. John Mair, D.D., minister of the parish of Southdean, Roxburghshire.

J. LOGIE ROBERTSON.

LOCKHARTON TERRACE,
SLATEFORD, N.B.
7th July, 1891.

CONTENTS

CORRIGENDA

Page 15, l. 17, *for* Sir *read* Mr.

,, 31, l. 14, *for* ravished *read* ravaged

;, 61, l. 1110, *for* flames *read* aims

,, 98, l. 1232, *for* and nature smiles revived *read* yet weeping
from distress

,, 101, l. 1338, *for* fury *read* hurry

,, 119, l. 164, *for* stated *read* sated

,, 124, l. 338, *for* bank *read* banks

,, 129, l. 525, *for* dull *prefer* grave

,, 141, l. 949, *for* known *read* felt

,, 168, l. 569, *for* virtue *read* virtues

,, 186, l. 107, *for* breathes *read* spreads

,, 242, l. 5 from bottom, *for* Miller *read* Millar

,, 357, l. 6, *for* up *read* from 1730

,, 357, l. 7 from bottom, *for* (till 1738) *read* (1730–1738)

,, 358, l. 20, *after* earlier *insert* (1738)

,, 359, l. 9 from bottom, *add* (1730–1738)

,, 361, l. 5, *for* the original text *read* the first edition of The
Seasons, and indeed from 1724

,, 361, l. 12, *for* till after that of *read* from 1730 to 1738

,, 361, l. 17, *for* the early text *read* the first edition of The
Seasons

,, 361, l. 19, *after* earlier text *insert* (1730–1738)

,, 390, l. 3 from bottom, *for* 1726 *read* 1730

Thomson's Seasons

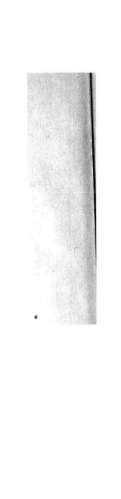

ERRATUM.

Page 353, line 15, *delete* Addison,

Thomson's *Seasons.*

BIOGRAPHICAL NOTICE.

In July of the year 1692, Mr. Thomas Thomson, son of a gardener in the employment of Mr. Edmonston of Ednam, was appointed minister of the parish of Ednam, an outlying district occupying the north-eastern corner of the pastoral county of Roxburgh. The law of patronage was then in abeyance, but the appointment was probably procured through the influence of Mr. Edmonston. The minister-elect was somewhere about twenty-five years of age. He seems to have entered upon the duties of the ministry with a mind entirely devoted to piety and the spiritual welfare of his people. His piety was not untinged with the terror of superstition—a dark feature of the religious feeling of his time; but in the execution of his sacred office he was undaunted by the powers of evil, seen or unseen, and earned a reputation for 'diligence in pastoral duty.' He was a man of quiet life, little, if at all, known beyond the bounds of his presbytery, and finding sufficient society in his flock, his family, and among a few of the local gentry. Long afterwards his illustrious son wrote of him as 'a good and tender-hearted parent.' Fifteen months after his settlement at Ednam, he married Beatrix, one of the daughters of Mr. Alexander Trotter, proprietor of the small estate of Widehope, or Wideopen, in the neighbouring parish of Morebattle. From her the poet inherited his sociality, his imagination, and his natural piety. To him, without any poetical exaggeration, she was 'the kindest, best of mothers.'

B

The Thomson household was a large one, including nine children in all, of whom four were born before the end of the century, and while the father was still in his first charge as minister of Ednam. Of these James was the fourth. Before him were born—Andrew, in 1695; Alexander, in 1697; and Issobell, in 1699. The birth of the poet, which almost certainly occurred in the manse of Ednam, is believed to have taken place on the 7th —his baptism was on the 15th—of September, 1700. About the time of his birth, his father's name for 'piety and diligence in pastoral duty' was so well established, that no fewer than three parishes, Southdean, Castleton, and Morebattle, were coveting the services of the minister of Ednam. Southdean, as represented by its Kirk-session and heritors, 'called' him—to use the Scots phrase of invitation to an ecclesiastical charge—on the 7th of August; the invitation was accepted, and on the 6th of November, 1700, just two months to a day after the poet's birth, the Rev. Thomas Thomson was admitted minister of Southdean, a pastoral parish of more importance than Ednam, situated on the lower slopes of the Cheviots, among the southern uplands of Roxburgh. Thither the Thomson household was transferred: and here, from the time of his tenderest infancy to his sixteenth year, the youth of the future poet was nursed, and educated, and found a home. The interest which attaches to Ednam as the birthplace of a great British poet, is thus of the slightest—is, in fact, merely nominal. It is to Southdean the admirer of Thomson must go if he would make acquaintance with those natural influences—commonly, but not quite correctly, described as 'the scenery'—which were the first to salute the senses, and awaken the interest and imagination of the young poet. I am indebted to the present incumbent of Southdean, the venerable and learned Dr. John Mair, for the following graphic description of the old manse, and the view from the manse door: 'His father's straw-thatched manse, in rustic simplicity, and clinging with a nestling snugness to the base of Southdean Law, is placed at a point in the vale where the eye can drink "the pure pleasures of the rural life." Around the garden, like a belt of quicksilver, sweeps the "sylvan Jed." Looking out from that vale is seen in the distance, but not so distant as not to be a part of it, the clear-cut sky-line of Carter Fell, whose huge ridge rose as a natural bulwark against English covetousness, and whose high heathland slopes retain the eye of the spectator above surrounding objects, as the storm-drift careers along them, or as the sunbeam reddens their purple beauty.' Much of the scenery and poetical spirit of *The Seasons* were imported from Jed vale ; *Winter* is especially rich in recollections of Thomson's early home. He tells us himself that it was from the manse doorway or parlour-window at Southdean that he heard the winds roar and the big torrent burst, and saw the deep-fermenting tempest brewed in the grim evening sky. The shepherd perishing in the snow-drift, the winter spate, the visit of the redbreast, are evidently all transcripts from the poet's recollection of real life at Southdean. Here it was that once for all, in the words of Burns,—

> 'grim Nature's visage hoar
> Struck [his] young eye.'

When he was about twelve he began his attendance at a Grammar School which was kept in St. Mary's Chapel in Jedburgh Abbey. The distance from his home was some eight miles, down the Jed. Here he read Latin and Greek. He may not have been what is known as a clever pupil, but there is clear proof that he early felt the soft and reposeful charm of Virgil's verse, and sought to reproduce it in metrical essays of his own composition. There was residing at this time, as farmer at Earlshaugh, about four miles from Southdean, a Mr. Robert Riccaltoun, who, being himself college-bred, and fresh from academical studies, volunteered to assist and direct the reading of the young scholar. Riccaltoun was a man of considerable learning and originality of thought, and occasionally tried his hand at versification. He was Thomson's senior by nine years. About a year after the Thomsons had left Southdean he became a clergyman; and in 1725, when James Thomson had already been six months in England, and was now at work upon his poem of *Winter*, Riccaltoun entered upon the duties of an ordained minister at Hobkirk, in the same district of Roxburgh in which he had been a farmer. Years afterwards, when the fame of the author of *The Seasons* was fully established, he modestly acknowledged that he had been among the first to discover the poetical talent of Thomson, and that his influence in encouraging and directing it had been considerable. His influence did not cease with the exercises of the schoolboy; it accompanied Thomson to England, and inspired the idea of *The Seasons*. Thomson's own testimony is express on this point: 'Nature delights me in every form; I am just now painting her in her most lugubrious dress for my own amusement, describing Winter as it presents itself.... Mr. Riccaltoun's poem on Winter, which I still have, first put the design into my head—in it are some masterly strokes which awakened me.' (*Letter to Dr. Cranston, written at Barnet, near London, September* 1725.) Among others who looked favourably upon young Thomson's essays in verse during his school days were Sir William Bennet of Chesters, and Sir Gilbert Elliot of Minto. It was probably through his uncle and cousin, who were gardeners at Minto House, about four miles due west from Jedburgh, that young Thomson made the acquaintance of Sir Gilbert Elliot; but he was a more frequent visitor at Chesters, a couple of miles down the Teviot from Minto, where indeed he used to spend part of his summer vacations, and write a good deal of juvenile poetry. Bennet was of a liberal disposition and frank manners, wrote verses himself, and courted the society of the wits and poets of Edinburgh—Allan Ramsay among the rest. Here is part of a juvenile poem descriptive of Sir William Bennet's house and grounds, which will serve to show Thomson's poetical attainment as a schoolboy :

> 'What is the task that to the muse belongs?
> What—but to deck in her harmonious songs

The beauteous works of nature and of art,
Rural retreats that cheer the heavy heart.
Then Marléfield begin, my muse, and sing;
With Marléfield the hills and vales shall ring.
O what delight and pleasure 'tis to rove
Through all the walks and alleys of this grove,
Where spreading trees a checkered scene display,
Partly admitting and excluding day, . . .
Where little birds employ their narrow throats
To sing its praises in unlaboured notes.
To it adjoined a rising fabric stands,
Which with its state our silent awe commands;
Its endless beauties mock the poet's pen,
So to the garden I'll return again.
Pomona makes the trees with fruit abound,
And blushing Flora paints the enamelled ground.
Here lavish nature does her stores disclose,
Flowers of all hue, their queen the bashful rose.'

In these lines may be detected traces of the influence of Virgil and Milton, and echoes of the fine old Scots ballad of *Leader Haughs and Yarrow*. Little of Thomson's juvenile poetry is in existence, the youthful scribbler having included as part of the festivities of each New Year's Day of his boyhood, regularly as it came round, a holocaust of the verses he had produced during the preceding twelve months. As a boy young Thomson seems to have been natural, healthy, and happy; well and sympathetically acquainted with the rustic life and rural scenery of the whole of his native county; of active and enterprising habits; and animated by a quiet love of fun and good-humoured joking, similar to that which marked the youth-time of Walter Scott.

Towards the end of 1715 he was despatched to Edinburgh University, the design of his parents being, as Johnson expresses it, to breed him a minister. It was a sore trial to the boy to surrender the freedom of country life for the strict discipline and confinement of college and town. It was at first, indeed, beyond his endurance; and he returned to Southdean not many hours after the servant behind whom he had ridden into Edinburgh, declaring that 'he could study as well, or better, on the haughs of Sudan' (Southdean). His father did not see it in that light ; and he returned to college. Here he had not been many months when the news reached him that his father was dead. This event occurred on the 9th of February, 1716. The cause of death seems to have been an apoplectic fit, which seized the minister of South-dean as he was in the act of exorcising what was believed to be an evil spirit, known in the parish as 'the Woolie Ghost.' The tragic event produced a great sensation in the neighbourhood, having been, as was then common in such cases, attributed to super-natural agency. It threw young Thomson into such a state of terror, that for some years afterwards he had more than a child's dread of solitude and darkness. He lived to conquer the terror, but the feeling of the supernatural remained in his mind to the last, and finds expression in various passages of his poetry. Thus in *Summer*, written in 1726, the lines occur—

> 'Shook sudden from the bosom of the sky,
> A thousand shapes or glide athwart the dusk,
> Or stalk majestic on. Deep-roused I feel
> A sacred terror, a severe delight,
> Creep through my mortal frame ; and thus, methinks,
> A voice, than human more, the abstracted ear
> Of Fancy strikes : "Be not of us afraid,
> Poor kindred man ! Thy fellow-creatures, we
> From the same Parent-Power our beings drew,
> The same our Lord, and laws, and great pursuit." '
>
> (ll. 538-47.)

The home of the Thomsons was now transferred to Edinburgh, and the mother made shift to support herself and her children, and keep James at college, by mortgaging her interest in the little property of Widehope, of which she was co-heiress, and by prac-tising a strict economy. The struggles of the family to maintain the gentility of their station are implied in the poem *On the Death of his Mother* :

'No more the widow's lonely state she feels,
The shock severe that modest want conceals,
The oppressor's scourge, the scorn of wealthy pride,
And poverty's unnumbered ills beside.'

Thomson was in attendance upon classes at the University
for eight or nine years in all, and though he did not distinguish
himself as a student—not being of a nature to absorb the
spirit of competition—he took congenially to philosophical speculations on the phenomena of external nature and the human
mind. Natural philosophy was at this time the principal study
in the Faculty of Arts at Edinburgh, constituting along with
Ethics—with which it was taught conjointly—the subject of the
fourth or final year of the curriculum. Scottish latinity had
declined, and the study of English literature had not yet received
academical recognition. Edinburgh had caught the Baconian
and Newtonian impulse more fully than the English Universities,
and the study of mathematical science was beginning to be
actively pursued. There are numerous proofs in Thomson's
poetry of his interest in the general subject. See, for example,
his 'inquiry into the rise of fountains and rivers' in *Autumn*
(ll. 735–834), and his proposed scheme of future poetical study
as sketched in the same poem (ll. 1351–65). There is also a
significant reference bearing directly on the point in the first
letter of his published correspondence, of the 11th December,
1720 : 'There are some come from London here lately that teach
natural philosophy by way of shows, by the beat of drum ; but
more of this afterwards.' At the same time he was by private
study extending his acquaintance with literature—reading
Shakespeare, Milton, and Pope, and sharing in the interest, now
beginning to be felt beyond Edinburgh, in the writings of Allan
Ramsay. He still kept up his practice of versifying, and in
conjunction with Malloch, and probably Hamilton of Bangour,
was contributing a poem now and again to the collections of
verse which were beginning to mark the rise of periodical literature in Edinburgh. These verse exercises of Thomson while he

was still a student include the lines *On a Country Life*, in heroic couplets, in which some see the germ of *The Seasons*; a poem *On Happiness*, interesting as containing several ideas and images which afterwards reappeared in the *Castle of Indolence*; and two shorter pieces, also in the heroic couplet, *Morning in the Country*, and *On Beauty*, the former of which betrays the influence, while the latter makes special mention, of Allan Ramsay. From the *Morning in the Country* I extract the following lines :

'The herd his plaid around his shoulders throws,
Grasps his dear crook, calls on his dog, and goes
Around the fold : he walks with careful pace,
And fallen clods sets in their wonted place ;
Then opes the door, unfolds his fleecy care,
And gladly sees them crop their morning fare ;
Down upon easy moss his limbs he lays,
And sings some charming shepherdess's praise.'

Thomson became a student of divinity in 1719 or 1720, having finished his Arts course—as was then the general custom—without proceeding to graduation. He figures, it is true, as M.A. on the title-page of the first edition of *Winter*; but the mistake was probably not his, and was cancelled in the second and subsequent editions. It is remarkable that, while in 1705 as many as 105 students graduated M.A. at Edinburgh, the number had fallen in 1749 to 3 ! Sir Alexander Grant, in his history of the University, explains that after 1708, when the Arts Faculty was re-modelled on its present basis, it ceased to be the interest of any Professor to promote graduation (except the Professor of Natural Philosophy, who got fees for laureating his class) ; that public laureation was abandoned ; and that, in consequence, the degree fell into disregard. Thomson's career as a student of theology is marked in his continued poetical exercises by several pieces of little merit, mainly a few hymns and paraphrases of portions of Scripture, the most ambitious being a version in heroic couplets of Psalm civ. The only interest of this version is its diction, in which one finds such tumid phrases (*e. g.* 'the bleating kind,' 'the feathered nation,' 'genial moisture,' 'vital juice' &c.) as were afterwards to offend the ear in *The Seasons.* In 1724 Thomson arrived at the turning-point of his life. He had prepared, as an exercise in connection with the class of divinity of which he was a member, a lecture on Psalm cxix, which was severely criticised, if not condemned, by Professor Hamilton for its floridity of style. If he meant to be of any service in the ministry, he was told, he must learn to use a plainer language. The censure which the Professor's criticism implied determined Thomson to a step which he had probably been for some time already meditating. He seems to have been feeling a growing dislike to what he called 'the thorny paths of systems and school divinity;' and he was undoubtedly under the impulse of poetical ambition. Suddenly he resolved to try his fortune in London. What his plans were is not definitely known, and he communicated them to few. He refers to them vaguely in letters to confidential friends as 'the business you know I design.' Some have thought that he went up to London merely as a literary adventurer; others that his intention was to join, and seek preferment in, the Church of England. More probably his expectation was to fill some minor post in the political service of the Government, which would secure him an independency, and afford him an opportunity of cultivating his poetical talents. His resolution was at least a noble one : writing to one of his many friends in Teviotdale—with which county he had kept up a close and constant connection during the whole period of his studentship—he declares, ' I will do all that is in my power, act, hope, and so either make something out, or be buried in obscurity.' He set about preparations for his departure, collected recommendations and letters of introduction, and took farewell of his friends. It is noteworthy that the indolence which certainly overtook Thomson before he was middle-aged, was no characteristic of his youth and early manhood. At this time he was of active habits; an early riser, who had seen the

dawns he was afterwards to describe so gloriously ; a keen and
accurate observer of the whole phenomena of nature within his
range ; no great lover of the town, and by no means averse to
solitude, yet fond of society, and with a strong relish for humour
and fun.   He was healthy and strong; of a fresh complexion,
and frank open countenance which made him friends wherever he
went ; above the middle height, and without that studious stoop
and slovenliness of dress which struck Shenstone some twenty
years later as indicative of vulgarity.   The following extract from
one of his farewell letters will show better than description the
geniality and brave hopefulness of his nature in the spring of
1725 : ' My spirits have gotten such a serious turn by these reflections, that, although I be thinking on Misjohn, I declare
I shall hardly force a laugh before we part—for this I think will
be my last letter from Edinburgh (I expect to sail every day).
Well ! since I am speaking of that merry soul, I hope he is as
bright, as easy, as *dégagé*, as susceptible of an intense laugh
as he used to be.   Tell him when you see him that I laugh
in imagination with him—ha! ha! ha! Mass John, how in
the name of wonder dragged you so much good humour
along with you through the thorny paths of systems and school
divinity ? . . . . . May wit, humour, and everlasting joy surround
you both ! '

He embarked at Leith, and arrived in London before the end
of March, 1725.   Here his first experience was the loss of his
letters of introduction, of which a pickpocket—with little advantage to himself—relieved him, as with bewildered looks he
journeyed along the crowded streets of the great capital.   The
inconvenience was soon got over, and he presented himself to
the influential persons from whom he expected some aid in the
furtherance of the design which had brought him to England.
Among others he saw Duncan Forbes of Culloden, afterward
Lord President of the Court of Session ; Mr. Elliot, a member
of the Minto family; and relatives of Lady Grizel Baillie, a
friend of his mother, and not unknown to himself.   The inter-

views were disappointing, and almost made him confess regret at the bold step he had taken in breaking away from Scotland and the ministry of the Scottish Kirk. Here is part of his own report of one of those interviews : ' I went and delivered it [letter of introduction to Mr. Elliot] ; he received me affably enough, and promised me his assistance, though at the same time he told me—what every one tells me—that it will be prodigiously difficult to succeed in the business you know I design. However, come what will come, I will make an effort and leave the rest to providence. There is, I am persuaded, a necessary fixed chain of things, and I hope my fortune, whatever it be, shall be linked to diligence and honesty. If I should not succeed, in your next advise me what I should do. Succeed or not, I firmly resolve to pursue divinity as the only thing now I am fit for. Now if I cannot accomplish the design on which I came up, I think I had best make interest and pass my trials here, so that if I be obliged soon to return to Scotland again, I may not return no better than I came away. And, to be deeply serious with you, the more I see of the vanity and wickedness of the world, the more I am inclined to that sacred office. I was going to bid you suppress that rising laugh, but I check myself severely again for suffering such an unbecoming thought of you to enter into my mind.' (*Letter to Dr. Cranston, Ancrum, in Roxburghshire, of date 3rd April,* 1725.) Thomson waited on in London for the promised assistance, which did not come, and meanwhile fell in with his former college companion David Malloch, who had come up to London to act as tutor to the two sons of the Duke of Montrose. Malloch proved a kind friend, and Thomson was grateful. More than a year afterwards, taking a retrospect of his experiences since his arrival in England, Thomson wrote to Malloch, in friendly criticism of some MS. verses of the latter, that 'the comprehensive compound-epithet *All-shunned* was a beauty he had had too good reason to relish.' 'Thank heaven,' he added, 'there was one exception'—meaning that Malloch had stood by him when all

others neglected him. He had been only six weeks in London
when the sad news reached him that his mother was dead. It
was probably on receipt of the news that he penned the
affectionate lines *On the Death of his Mother.* They have the
ring of genuine sorrow. They suggest so irresistibly another
and more famous poem on a similar subject, that one is tempted
to think that Thomson's tribute was in the mind of Cowper
when he wrote those ineffably pathetic lines *On the Receipt of
my Mother's Picture.* The loss of a home seems to have
determined Thomson to pursue his fortune in London. Partly
through the influence of Lady Grizel Baillie, and partly through
the services of Malloch, he received a tutorship in the family of
Lord Binning some time in July. The family were resident at
Barnet, about ten miles from London, and here Thomson
utilised his leisure by composing his poem of *Winter.* It was
here he first felt, as a personal thing, the pressure of poverty.
He was by no means, at any time of his life, in absolute want,
but he was improvident enough on several occasions to incur
debts which he could not always meet just when payment was
demanded. About this time the share of the little property at
Widehope which had belonged to his mother was realised, and
the balance that remained, after the claim of the mortgagee was
satisfied, was divided among the family. Thomson was now
dependent upon his own efforts for his maintenance. *Winter*
was published in March, 1726, and may fairly be said to have
been successful from the first. Its publication brought him
many friends and patrons—among others the Countess of
Hertford, Mr. Bubb Dodington, Mrs. Stanley, and Dr. Thomas
Rundle, afterwards Bishop of Derry; besides the approval
and active services of such influential critics of the time as
Aaron Hill, the Rev. Joseph Spence, and the Rev. Robert
Whatley. A second edition was in preparation within about a
year, and before the end of 1728 the fifth edition was out.
Thomson took full advantage of the tide that was rising in his
favour. He gave up his tutorship at East Barnet; and, coming

into London—where he was still obliged to devote part of his
time to teaching—he set about the composition of *Summer* with
the utmost enthusiasm. By this time he had planned the series
of *The Seasons*, a work which he had not thought of when
writing *Winter*, and was in haste to accomplish his task. He
was cheered with the friendship and encouragement of Malloch
and Hill. Hill was fond of flattery, and Thomson—submitting
his better judgment probably to the dictation of Malloch—did
not stint or spare. In any case, the young friendless Scotsman,
'all-shunned' where he had looked for aid, and feeling with keen
delight the first sunshine of fame, was, as Johnson charitably
allows, naturally glad of Hill's kindness, and may be excused
for some phrases of unusual warmth, the blame of which,
indeed, rests as much upon Hill as upon Thomson. Thomson
was to be far more famous, was to number among his friends
men of higher standing than Hill, and was to approve himself
in his relation to them, at all points a gentleman. *Summer*,
preceded by a poem *To the Memory of Sir Isaac Newton*, was
published in 1727. In the same year he wrote *Britannia*, in the
interest of English commerce against the action of Spain, but
the poem was not published till early in 1729. *Spring*, which
fully maintained the credit of the new poet, followed in 1728 ;
and in 1730 the publication of the collected *Seasons*, including
Autumn and the *Hymn* for the first time, brought the task
which he had set himself, and in which the interest of so many
admirers was enlisted, gloriously to a close. Meanwhile his
poetical energy was finding a new channel. From the first
week of his arrival in London he had been attracted to the
theatre, and his interest in the drama at last took the form of
a tragedy of his own composition, *Sophonisba*, which was produced at Drury Lane in February, 1730. This was a department
of poetry in which Thomson was to work for some time
assiduously, but in which the peculiar nature of his genius
forbade him to excel. Voltaire's temperate opinion of Thomson's
eloquent but frigid tragedies is now—whatever temporary suc-

cess they achieved—generally endorsed, even by his most enthusiastic admirers: 'Mr. Thomson's tragedies seem to me wisely intricated, and elegantly writ; they want perhaps some fire, and it may be that his heroes are neither moving nor busy enough.'

In 1730, through the friendship of Dr. Rundle, Thomson was appointed tutor to Mr. Charles Richard Talbot, eldest son of the Solicitor-General, and future Lord Chancellor, and travelled with his pupil on the Continent for nearly two years. They visited France and Italy, staying at Paris and at Rome for considerable periods. During his absence Thomson kept up a correspondence with Dodington, which shows that he enjoyed a complete holiday from literary work of every kind, but that, while apparently idle, he was receiving many new and important impressions. He writes: 'Travelling has long been my fondest wish. . . The storing one's imagination with ideas of all-beautiful, all-great, and all-perfect nature—these are the true *materia poetica*, the light and colours with which fancy kindles up her whole creation, paints a sentiment, and even embodies an abstracted thought. I long to see the fields where Virgil gathered his immortal honey, and tread the same ground where men have thought and acted so greatly.' In the same letter occurs the significant remark: 'I resolve not to neglect the more prosaic advantages [of travel], for it is no less my ambition to be capable of serving my country in an active than in a contemplative way.' This remark should be read along with the Dedication of *Autumn* (ll. 18–22). It seems to show that Thomson had still in his mind the original design for an independent settlement in life which brought him up to London in 1725. In a later letter to his big patron he makes a charming confession: 'Now I mention poetry, should you inquire after my muse, all that I can answer is, that I believe she did not cross the channel with me.'

In the end of 1731 Thomson was back again in England, and immediately set about the composition of an epic poem, in five parts, on the subject of *Liberty*. The first part was published in 1734 ; the next two parts in 1735 ; and in 1736 the concluding parts made their appearance. It is usual to condemn this poem as blighted, and many critics have done so without having read it—and without having confessed the neglect. It is, notwithstanding, a great poem, full of learning, eloquence, imagination, and occasionally rising to altitudes of rare poetical vision ; but the subject, and more especially the length at which it is treated, was a mistake. Liberty is a lyrical theme ; to treat it didactically the proper form to use is prose. This, however, may be said, that, given the subject and the method of treatment, no poet of his century could have done better than Thomson.

In September, 1733, while Thomson was busy with the first part of *Liberty*, Charles Talbot the younger died, and a graceful tribute to his memory was paid in the opening lines of the poem. Two months later Sir Charles Talbot became Lord Chancellor, and appointed Thomson to the office of Secretary of Briefs in the Court of Chancery. This office he occupied till the death of the Chancellor in the spring of 1737, and might still have held it but for his own neglect in making application : the new Chancellor conferred it upon another. Meanwhile Thomson had settled in a garden-house in Kew-foot Lane at Richmond, where he spent the remainder of his life in comparative luxury, and a retirement that was far from unsocial. Here he entertained Pope, Hammond, Collins, and Quin ; Lyttelton was no infrequent visitor ; and he made many friends in the neighbourhood. In the first flush of prosperity he did not forget his Scottish friends and relatives. He invited one of his brothers to stay with him, allowed his sisters a small annuity, and by and by two of his kinsmen, gardeners by occupation, were pensioners upon his bounty at Richmond. His brother, after acting for some time as his amanuensis, fell into ill health, and returned to Scotland, where he died. The news of his death called forth the following reflections from Thomson, in a

letter to his old Roxburgh friend Cranston : 'The living are to
be lamented, not the dead. . . Death is a limit which human
passions ought not, but with great caution and reverence, to
pass. . . This I think we may be sure of, that a future state
must be better than this ; and so on through the never-ceasing
succession of future states—every one rising upon the last, an
everlasting new display of infinite goodness. But hereby hangs
a system, not calculated perhaps for the meridian in which you
live.' After the loss of the Secretaryship, Thomson was for a
little in somewhat embarrassed circumstances, in the midst of
which he was arrested for a debt, which Quin the actor most
generously insisted on paying ; his fortunes, however, to use his
own phrase, blossomed again, and a pension of £100 a year
from the Prince of Wales, to whom he had been introduced by
Lyttelton, secured him against want. He again turned his
attention to dramatic writing, and in April 1738, *Agamemnon*
was brought out in the presence of a large and distinguished
house at Drury Lane. The same year he published a new
edition of *The Seasons.* Next year he was ready with another
play, *Edward and Eleanora,* but the Lord Chamberlain suppressed it on account of its political allusions. In 1740 he wrote
a Preface for Milton's *Areopagitica*; and, conjointly with Malloch,
composed *The Masque of Alfred*—the gem of the production, the well-known national lyric 'Rule, Britannia,' being his.
In 1743 he paid his first visit to his best friends, the Lytteltons, at
Hagley in Worcestershire; and in the following year, Lyttelton
being then a Lord of the Treasury, he was appointed to the
sinecure office of Surveyor-General of the Leeward Islands.
After paying a deputy to discharge the active duties of the post,
he found himself benefited to the extent of about £300 a year.
This year a new edition of *The Seasons* was published. About
this time Thomson, who all his life was very susceptible of the
charms of female beauty, had serious thoughts of marrying.
The object of his affections was a Miss Young, sister of the first
wife of his friend Robertson, a surgeon at Kew, and identified

with the *Amanda* of his later poetry. 'It was Mrs. Young,' wrote John Ramsay of Ochtertyre (*Scotland and Scotsmen in the Eighteenth Century*, edited by Alex. Allardyce), 'a coarse, vulgar woman, who constantly opposed the poet's pretensions to her daughter; saying to her one day, "What! would you marry Thomson? He will make ballads, and you will sing them!"' Thomson seems not to have been ignorant of the maternal dislike to his suit: 'If I am so happy as to have your heart,' he writes on one occasion to Miss Young, 'I know you have spirit to maintain your choice.' The refusal of the lady—she afterwards became the wife of Admiral Campbell—was the great disappointment of Thomson's life. His humour remained with him to the last, but all his gaiety left him; he slipt into profoundly indolent habits, became careless of his appearance and of fortune, and seemed utterly indifferent to life.

In 1745 his best drama, *Tancred and Sigismunda*, was enacted at Drury Lane, with Garrick as Tancred. Part of the summer or autumn of this and the next two years he spent at Hagley. Lyttelton was affectionately concerned at his listlessness, and strove by various means to divert his attention and rouse his energies. In 1746 the poet made way for his old friend, and deputy, Paterson, in the office of Surveyor-General. The same year was published the last edition of *The Seasons* that had the benefit of the author's revision. 1748 was marked by three occurrences—the discontinuance of his pension, owing to a quarrel between the Prince of Wales and Lyttelton; the appearance of *The Castle of Indolence*, which had been long on the way; and his lamented death from a neglected cold, on the 27th of August. About four months before his death we find him expressing himself, in a letter to Paterson, in the following melancholy strain on the disappointments and vexations of life: 'Let us have a little more patience, Paterson; nay, let us be cheerful. At last all will be well, at least all will be over; here, I mean—God forbid it should be so hereafter. But, as sure as there is a God, that will not be so.' It is to be

C

regretted that he did not carry out the intention, which he had half formed the year before his death, of visiting Scotland. The change would have done him good, and the visit might have originated a personal regard for him among his country-men, the only thing wanting to make his poetical reputation almost as dear to the national memory as that of Burns or of Scott.

CHRONOLOGY TO ELUCIDATE THE LIFE OF THOMSON.

1692. *In July*, Mr. Thomas Thomson, son of a gardener in the employ-ment of Mr. Edmonston of Ednam, is appointed—being then about twenty-five years of age—minister of the parish of Ednam, in the north-east of Roxburghshire.

1693. *In October*, marries Beatrix, one of the daughters of Mr. Alexander Trotter of Widehope, in the parish of Morebattle, Roxburgh-shire.

1700. Their fourth child, who was also their third son, JAMES, born (it is believed) on the 7th, baptized on the 15th *September*. In the *November* following, the Rev. Thomas Thomson inducted into the parish of Southdean, in the south of Roxburghshire, his son James being then just two months old. [This year Dryden died.]

1712. Young Thomson in attendance at a Grammar School kept in the aisle of Jedburgh Abbey, some eight miles or so distant from his home at Southdean. His acquaintance with Mr. Robert Riccaltoun, farmer at Earlshaugh, begins about this time. First attempts at poetizing a year or two later.

1715. *Towards the end of the year* Thomson becomes a student at Edinburgh University. Still writing verse—blank, and heroic couplets, on the model of Dryden.

1716. Unexpected death of his father, on 9th *February*. Home transferred to Edinburgh some time after.

1720. Now a student of Divinity. Continues to write verse, chiefly on rural subjects contributed to *The Edinburgh Miscellany*.

1724. Still at college. Adverse criticism, by the Professor of Divinity, of one of his college exercises. The turning-point and middle of his life. [This year Allan Ramsay published his *Evergreen*, and his *Tea-Table Miscellany*.]

C 2

1725. *In March* Thomson embarks at Leith for London, not again to see Scotland. *In May*, death of his mother. *In July*, tutor to Lord Binning's son, at Barnet, near London. Composition of *Winter*. [The *Gentle Shepherd* in complete form was published this year.]

1726. *In March*, publication of *Winter*. Thomson acting as tutor in an academy in London. Acquaintance with Aaron Hill.

1727. Poem *To the Memory of Sir Isaac Newton*. *Summer* published. Wrote *Britannia, A Poem*. Relying on literature for his support.

1728. Publication of *Spring*. [Goldsmith born.]

1729. *In January, Britannia* published. A poem *To the Memory of Congreve* also published, anonymously, but undoubtedly Thomson's.

1730. *In February, Sophonisba* produced at Drury Lane. Publication of *The Seasons* (including *Autumn* and *The Hymn* for the first time). Appointed travelling tutor to Charles Richard Talbot, eldest son of the Solicitor-General, with whom he visits France and Italy.

1731. Correspondence with Dodington. Collecting material for his projected poem on *Liberty*. Returns from the Continent at the close of the year. [Birth of Cowper.]

1733. *In September*, death of Mr. C. R. Talbot. *In November*, Thomson appointed Secretary of Briefs in the Court of Chancery.

1734. *In December*, publication of *Liberty*, Part First.

1735. *Liberty*, Parts Second and Third. Death of a brother in *September*.

1736. *Liberty*, Parts Fourth and Fifth. *In May*, Thomson settles in a garden-house in Kew-foot Lane, Richmond. Sends assistance to his sisters in Edinburgh.

1737. *In June*, poem to *The Memory of Lord Chancellor Talbot*. Loss of Secretaryship. Acquaintance with George (afterwards Lord) Lyttelton. Pension of £100 a year from the Prince of Wales, about this time. [Shenstone's *The Schoolmistress* appeared this year; in its complete form in 1742.]

1738. *Agamemnon* at Drury Lane, *in April*. A new edition of *The Seasons* published.

1739. Tragedy of *Edward and Eleanora* suppressed on account of its political allusions.

1740. Preface to Milton's *Areopagitica.* Conjointly with Malloch, *The Masque of Alfred*—performed 1st August, in Clifden gardens, before the Prince of Wales—containing the lyric, 'Rule, Britannia,' by Thomson.

1743. *In August,* visits the Lytteltons at Hagley, in Worcestershire.

1744. Appointed to the sinecure office of Surveyor-General of the Leeward Islands, through Lyttelton's influence. A new edition of *The Seasons.* [Armstrong's *Art of Preserving Health* published in this year. Death of Pope.]

1745. *Tancred and Sigismunda* at Drury Lane, with Garrick as Tancred. Spends part of the summer at Hagley.

1746. Thomson makes way for his friend and deputy, Paterson, in the office of Surveyor-General. Part of the autumn at Hagley. Publication of the last of the author's editions of *The Seasons.*

1747. Thomson at Hagley in the autumn. Visits Shenstone at the Leasowes, probably not for the first time.

1748. Pension of £100 discontinued, *early in this year. The Castle of Indolence,* in May. Death, in his house at Richmond, on the 27th of August. Buried at Richmond. [Collins's *Ode on Thomson's Death.*]

1749. *Coriolanus* produced—the prologue by Lyttelton.

1762. Monument in Westminster Abbey, between those of Shakespeare and Rowe.

1791. *In the autumn of this year* Burns wrote his *Address to the Shade of Thomson.*

GENERAL INTRODUCTION TO
'THE SEASONS.'

WHEN Thomson came up to London from Scotland in March 1725, he brought with him no MS. poetry of his own composition—at least none that was of sufficient value for publication. All his published poems of any merit, including of course *The Seasons*, from beginning to end, were planned and produced in England. What he did bring with him was a consciousness of poetical power, a strong ambition to manifest it, and a predilection for some great and serious subject which should involve a description of the works of nature. He had not been many months in England when he found such a subject in Winter. His management of this stormy theme was his warrant for the opinion he had formed of his poetical genius, and justified the ambition which had brought him to London. He encountered Winter in the course of an exercise in blank verse, and—in the words of Cowden Clarke—'rose instantly as if on the wings of the blast' to his full altitude. It looked at first, indeed, as if the subject was to have no better fate at his hands than its predecessors[1], which had only served him for the exercise of rhyming. In September, when he had already made some progress in the work, he could still only speak of it as a study in blank verse, which was amusing him, but which he might drop at any moment. Erelong, as he was drawn into living touch with his subject, he perceived its magnitude and capabilities; the memories of Scottish winters rose up in dread magnificence before him; he

---

[1] Such as the verses *On a Country Life*, written before he was twenty, and of no great interest in respect of matter or style. The subject, however, was significant.

applied himself enthusiastically to his task, and, before his first winter in England was well over, he had dashed off a succession of descriptions and reflections which, when pieced together, made up the poem of *Winter*. It is to be noted that the subject was defined and clearly before him so early as September, 1725, and that the title was no afterthought, and no suggestion of his friend Malloch's. The very first draught of the poem opened with the explicit boldness of the old epic style :

> 'I sing of Winter and his gelid reign ;
> Nor let a rhyming insect of the Spring
> Deem it a barren theme : to me 'tis full
> Of manly charms,—to me who court the shade,
> Whom the gay Season suits not, and who shun
> The glare of Summer. Welcome, kindred glooms !
> Drear, awful Wintry horrors, welcome all !'

Winter was published in March, 1726. It was so far immediately successful, that a second edition was printed off by the end of June. *The Seasons*, which had not been contemplated in the production of *Winter*, grew out of its success. In a significant preface which was prefixed to the second edition of *Winter*, and which may be regarded as Thomson's Defence of Poesy, he first unfolded his scheme by announcing to the public his purpose of describing the various appearances of nature in the other seasons as well. When he made this announcement he had already begun *Summer*, which he had selected as being the antithesis of *Winter*, and by the month of August he was so far advanced as to have three-fourths of it written. It was published in 1727. *Spring* followed in 1728 ; and in 1730 *Autumn* appeared in its regular place in the first edition of *The Seasons*, where it formed, with the final *Hymn*, the new feature of the completed and collected work.

The Seasons, singly and collectively, passed through many editions in their author's lifetime ; and the changes he made in the text, especially in the later editions, were very numerous. Here he introduced, there he struck out ; this he condensed, that he expanded ; he was never done substituting a new word or phrase for an old one, and he carried his passion for correcting,

or rather for altering, so far as to shift whole passages from one
Season to another. In short, he practised upon the original text
all the methods of arithmetic—adding, subtracting, multiplying,
and distributing to an extent unknown in the practice of any
other author. Shortly before his death, he even delegated a
continuance of this kind of work to his literary executor, Lord
Lyttelton. These textual changes in *The Seasons* are comparatively few and slight down to the edition of 1738. Some idea
of the changes afterwards made in the text may be gathered
from an arithmetical comparison of the impression of that year
with the edition of 1746, the last to be issued in the author's
lifetime. In the earlier of these editions *Spring* consisted of
1089 numbered lines; *Summer*, of 1205; *Autumn*, of 1274;
Winter, of 787; and *The Hymn*, of 121—4476 verses in all. If
now we turn to the edition of 1746, we find the numbers to be
—for *Spring*, 1176; for *Summer*, 1805; for *Autumn*, 1372;
for *Winter*, 1069; and for *The Hymn*, 118—5540 in all. The
numerical increase in the later edition is thus shown to be considerably over a thousand lines. These thousand and odd lines
do not, of course, represent the total amount of new matter
incorporated with the earlier text, but the surplus of the new
matter over and above what was required to balance the matter
withdrawn. The withdrawn matter was not only of very considerable amount, but was largely made up of innumerable
isolated words and phrases abstracted from every quarter of the
text. A variorum edition of *The Seasons* would doubtless be
a boon to students of the art of Thomson, but it would demand
a Hercules to accomplish it. It would probably reveal that kind
of development of the poetic art in which refinement and repose
are gained, not without some expense of vigour and vitality.
There is sound criticism in the judgment of Johnson, who
thought that *The Seasons* were improved in general by the poet's
alterations, but suspected that in the process they had lost part
of their original race or flavour. The suspicion was a shrewd
one. The keenness, for example, of Thomson's colour-sense,
was a more pronounced feature of the original *Seasons* than of
the later editions. It was in deference to English taste that he

economized his reds and yellows, and toned down those glowing
tints, a love for which he had inherited from the Scottish school
of poetry. His scotticisms too were expressive. But the loss
of raciness is chiefly seen in the substitution, for example, of so
comparatively tame a line as—

> 'Then scale the mountains to their woody tops,'

for

> 'Then snatch the mountains by their woody tops,'

in the description of the fox-hunt in the third Season ; or in the
exchange of 'shook from the corn' for 'scared from the corn' in
the hare-hunt ; or by the clean withdrawal from *Winter* of
so characteristic a passage as the following :—

> 'Tempted, vigorous, o'er the marble waste,
> On sleds reclined, the furry Russian sits ;
> And, by his reindeer drawn, behind him throws
> A shining kingdom in a winter's day.'

In his choice of subject Thomson made a new departure in
English poetry of great historical importance. He introduced,
or more properly re-introduced into literature, from which they
had been banished for at least two generations, the wild pagan
graces and savage grandeur of external nature. And this he did
with such imaginative pomp, such romantic charm, as to secure
the permanence of a sympathetic study of nature, and the
vitality of naturalism in our literature to the present day. He
had even the honour of being followed by a school of French
writers : ' Ce poëme [Des Saisons] a été imité chez nous par
Saint Lambert, et ne fut pas sans influence sur l'école descriptive
de Delille.'—*Nouv. Biog. Gen.* (1877). His choice of subject
was deliberate, and made with full consciousness of the prevailing
taste, so successfully developed by Dryden and Pope, for artificial
poetry. With that taste he had little sympathy. In his preface
to the second edition of *Winter* he cries out for the restoration of
poetry to her ancient purity and truth : ' Let her be inspired
from heaven,' he exclaims ; 'let her exchange her low, venal,
trifling subjects for such as are fair, useful, and magnificent.'
He further characterizes the popular subjects as 'the reigning

fopperies of a tasteless age'; and he goes on to declare that 'nothing can have a better influence towards the revival of poetry than the choosing of great and serious subjects, such as at once amuse the fancy, enlighten the head, and warm the heart.' 'What,' he asks, 'are we commonly entertained with, save forced unaffecting fancies, little glittering prettinesses, mixed terms of wit and expression, which are as widely different from native poetry as buffoonery is from the perfection of human thinking?' His practical suggestions for the much desiderated restoration and revival of poetry are valuable for their significance : 'I know no subject more elevating, more amusing, more ready to awake the poetical enthusiasm, the philosophical reflection, and the moral sentiment, than the works of Nature. Where can we meet with such variety, such beauty, such magnificence—all that enlarges and transports the soul? What more inspiring than a calm wide survey of them? In every dress Nature is greatly charming, whether she puts on the crimson robes of the morning, the strong effulgence of noon, the sober suit of the evening, or the deep sables of blackness and tempest. How gay looks the Spring! how glorious the Summer! how pleasing the Autumn! and how venerable the Winter! But there is no thinking of these things without breaking out into poetry.' Thomson's mind was directed to the study of nature from the very first. Rural life and the varied scenery of the open country as affected by the changing seasons, were the themes even of his boyish verse. Nature was his first love, and remained a passion with him to the end. It was a passion entirely Scottish in its origin, born of the scenery of his native Teviotdale, and fostered by the ballad poetry of the Border. But the influence of Virgil's Georgics helped to confirm it; and it found encouragement in the poetry of Milton and the later Elizabethans, and even drew some sustenance from the arid pastorals of Pope. If he did not invent, Thomson was the first in England to invest with national interest that class of poetry which Dryden, referring to Denham's *Cooper's Hill*, regarded as a variety of the epic, and for which Johnson proposed the name of local poetry. Local poems, that is, poems directly devoted to the description of some particular region of country, and better defined as topographical poems, had already, before the publication of the first section of the *Seasons*, been written and received with more or less favour in England. They were, however, both few and comparatively short, and none of them —not even the best known—can be said to have been really popular. Of these, beginning with *Cooper's Hill*, published in 1642—'the first of the new species of composition,' according to Johnson—we have next, in 1645, following the order of publication, *L'Allegro* and *Il Penseroso*, which may be regarded as an idealized description, with sunlight and moonlight effects, of the landscape around Horton; then *Windsor Forest*, published in 1713; and then Garth's *Claremont*, published in 1715, said to have been directly suggested by Denham's poem. Dyer's *Grongar Hill* appeared in 1726, the year of Thomson's *Winter*. But *Winter* and the other *Seasons* are something more than a series of topographical poems. They include an imaginative survey of almost every variety of landscape, under almost every conceivable variety of weather, ranging all round the globe in circles that widen gradually and grandly to the horizon of a hemisphere, and again contract and close to the narrow dimensions of a Scottish dale. They are geographical rather than topographical. Their range and scope are wide enough to warrant the larger connotative term.

The blank verse of *The Seasons* is Thomson's own. It is distinct from Milton's, with which it is most likely to be compared, yet there is now and again in its flowing and sonorous lines a suggestion of the statelier and more sustained music of the great master. The highest praise of Thomson's style is that it suits the general subject. He moves through a vast variety of scenes with a lofty sedateness, a serene moral dignity, which sometimes, but rarely, verges on pomposity. With such a style it is really remarkable how varied his verse can be, and with what sedate ease he can make his transitions from homeliness to sublimity, from humour to tenderness. He is never at a loss for suggestive words, and is often indeed copious to redundancy. This copiousness of language is the result of an

enthusiastic love for his subject, and will be pardoned by those who
have caught from it the enthusiasm it conveys. Campbell finely
compares it to 'the flowing vesture of the Druid.' His diction
is not free from the conventional phrases which were the
common stock-in-trade of the Augustan poets : upon these he is
constantly falling back when he is in a reflective, or speculative,
or preaching mood ; but in his descriptions, especially when the
theme is more than usually familiar and congenial to him, he
readily finds a language which is at once natural and original,
and either picturesque or melodious, often both. Before the
publication of *Winter* the heroic couplet had for over half a
century been the fashionable verse, and had come to be regarded
as the indispensable vehicle of all serious poetry. It had been
brought to such a pitch of perfection by Pope, that at last the
younger poets, in despair at his excellence, ceased to practise it.
Of these Thomson was one, and indeed the chief. In his youth
he had exercised himself in the composition of the heroic
measure, but with extremely indifferent success. He had also
made a few trivial efforts in blank verse, with no better result.
He adopted blank verse in the composition of *Winter* as the
measure which best suited the nature of his subject, and which,
besides leaving his natural genius free from the restraints of
rhyme, protected him from comparison with Pope. It was with
just a touch of contempt in his tone that he took almost
complete farewell of the heroic couplet in 1725, and ventured
daringly upon a form of verse which had only once before been
used in a great way for other than dramatic purposes, and which
was probably beginning to be considered as sacred to the
epical genius of Milton :

> 'I sing of Winter and his gelid reign;
> Nor let a rhyming insect of the Spring
> Deem it a barren theme !'

Thomson was a great innovator : his introduction of blank
verse as a form of popular poetry in the year 1726 was no
inconsiderable part of his innovations. Almost equally with his
choice of subject, his blank verse was a blow to the artificial

school. He was speedily followed in his use of it by many imitators, some of whom—notably Savage[1], Somerville, and Dyer, and such minor poets among his own countrymen as Malloch, Armstrong, and Michael Bruce—copied his style with remarkable but mostly unmeritorious fidelity. His use of blank verse for non-heroic natural subjects was approved not only by the popular voice, but by the influential practice of Cowper and Wordsworth. One feature of the blank verse of *The Seasons* remains to be noted, its wonderful homogeneity. Thomson seems to have attained his peculiar mastery of the measure at a bound.

[1] In *The Wanderer* (1729), an anticipation of Goldsmith's *Traveller*.

THE SEASONS.

—◆—

SPRING.

COME, gentle Spring, ethereal mildness, come;
And from the bosom of yon dropping cloud,
While music wakes around, veiled in a shower
Of shadowing roses, on our plains descend.

  O Hertford, fitted or to shine in courts   5
With unaffected grace, or walk the plain
With innocence and meditation joined
In soft assemblage, listen to my song,
Which thy own Season paints, when Nature all
Is blooming and benevolent—like thee.   10

  And see where surly Winter passes off
Far to the north, and calls his ruffian blasts:
His blasts obey, and quit the howling hill,
The shattered forest, and the ravished vale;
While softer gales succeed, at whose kind touch,   15
Dissolving snows in livid torrents lost,
The mountains lift their green heads to the sky.
  As yet the trembling year is unconfirmed,
And Winter oft at eve resumes the breeze,
Chills the pale morn, and bids his driving sleets   20
Deform the day delightless,—so that scarce
The bittern knows his time with bill ingulfed
To shake the sounding marsh, or from the shore
The plovers when to scatter o'er the heath,
And sing their wild notes to the listening waste.   25

At last from Aries rolls the bounteous sun,
And the bright Bull receives him. Then no more
The expansive atmosphere is cramped with cold,
But, full of life and vivifying soul,
Lifts the light clouds sublime, and spreads them thin,   30
Fleecy, and white o'er all surrounding heaven.
    Forth fly the tepid airs; and unconfined,
Unbinding earth, the moving softness strays.
Joyous the impatient husbandman perceives
Relenting nature, and his lusty steers   35
Drives from their stalls to where the well-used plough
Lies in the furrow loosened from the frost.
There, unrefusing, to the harnessed yoke
They lend their shoulder, and begin their toil,
Cheered by the simple song and soaring lark.   40
Meanwhile incumbent o'er the shining share
The master leans, removes the obstructing clay,
Winds the whole work, and sidelong lays the glebe.
    White through the neighbouring fields the sower stalks,
With measured step, and liberal throws the grain   45
Into the faithful bosom of the ground.
The harrow follows harsh, and shuts the scene.
    Be gracious, Heaven, for now laborious man
Has done his part. Ye fostering breezes, blow;
Ye softening dews, ye tender showers, descend;   50
And temper all, thou world-reviving sun,
Into the perfect year. Nor, ye who live
In luxury and ease, in pomp and pride,
Think these lost themes unworthy of your ear.
Such themes as these the rural Maro sung   55
To wide-imperial Rome, in the full height
Of elegance and taste, by Greece refined.
In ancient times the sacred plough employed
The kings and awful fathers of mankind;
And some, with whom compared your insect tribes   60
Are but the beings of a summer's day,
Have held the scale of empire, ruled the storm

Of mighty war, then with victorious hand,
Disdaining little delicacies, seized
The plough, and greatly independent lived.   65
   Ye generous Britons, venerate the plough;
And o'er your hills and long withdrawing vales
Let Autumn spread his treasures to the sun,
Luxuriant and unbounded. As the sea,
Far through his azure turbulent domain,   70
Your empire owns, and from a thousand shores
Wafts all the pomp of life into your ports,
So with superior boon may your rich soil,
Exuberant, Nature's better blessings pour
O'er every land, the naked nations clothe,   75
And be the exhaustless granary of a world!
   Nor only through the lenient air this change
Delicious breathes: the penetrative sun,
His force deep-darting to the dark retreat
Of vegetation, sets the steaming power   80
At large, to wander o'er the vernant earth,
In various hues,—but chiefly thee, gay green,
Thou smiling Nature's universal robe,
United light and shade, where the sight dwells
With growing strength and ever-new delight.   85
   From the moist meadow to the withered hill,
Led by the breeze, the vivid verdure runs,
And swells, and deepens to the cherished eye.
The hawthorn whitens; and the juicy groves
Put forth their buds, unfolding by degrees,   90
Till the whole leafy forest stands displayed
In full luxuriance to the sighing gales;
Where the deer rustle through the twining brake,
And the birds sing concealed. At once, arrayed
In all the colours of the flushing year   95
By Nature's swift and secret-working hand,
The garden glows, and fills the liberal air
With lavish fragrance; while the promised fruit
Lies yet a little embryo, unperceived,

D

Within its crimson folds. Now from the town   100
Buried in smoke, and sleep, and noisome damps,
Oft let me wander o'er the dewy fields
Where freshness breathes, and dash the trembling drops
From the bent bush, as through the verdant maze
Of sweet-briar hedges I pursue my walk;   105
Or taste the smell of dairy; or ascend
Some eminence, Augusta, in thy plains,
And see the country far diffused around
One boundless blush, one white-empurpled shower
Of mingled blossoms, where the raptured eye   110
Hurries from joy to joy, and, hid beneath
The fair profusion, yellow Autumn spies—
If, brushed from Russian wilds, a cutting gale
Rise not, and scatter from his humid wings
The clammy mildew; or, dry-blowing, breathe   115
Untimely frost, before whose baleful blast
The full-blown Spring through all her foliage shrinks,
Joyless and dead, a wide-dejected waste.
For oft, engendered by the hazy north,
Myriads on myriads, insect armies warp   120
Keen in the poisoned breeze; and wasteful eat
Through buds and bark into the blackened core
Their eager way. A feeble race, yet oft
The sacred sons of vengeance; on whose course
Corrosive famine waits, and kills the year.   125
To check this plague, the skilful farmer chaff
And blazing straw before his orchard burns,
Till, all involved in smoke, the latent foe
From every cranny suffocated falls;
Or scatters o'er the blooms the pungent dust   130
Of pepper, fatal to the frosty tribe;
Or, when the envenomed leaf begins to curl,
With sprinkled water drowns them in their nest;
Nor, while they pick them up with busy bill,
The little trooping birds unwisely scares.   135
   Be patient, swains; these cruel-seeming winds

Blow not in vain. Far hence they keep repressed
Those deepening clouds on clouds, surcharged with rain,
That, o'er the vast Atlantic hither borne
In endless train, would quench the summer blaze, 140
And cheerless drown the crude unripened year.
 The north-east spends his rage, and now shut up
Within his iron cave, the effusive south
Warms the wide air, and o'er the void of heaven
Breathes the big clouds with vernal showers distent. 145
At first a dusky wreath they seem to rise,
Scarce staining ether; but by fast degrees,
In heaps on heaps, the doubling vapour sails
Along the loaded sky, and mingling deep
Sits on the horizon round, a settled gloom,— 150
Not such as wintry storms on mortals shed,
Oppressing life, but lovely, gentle, kind,
And full of every hope and every joy,
The wish of Nature. Gradual sinks the breeze
Into a perfect calm, that not a breath 155
Is heard to quiver through the closing woods, .
Or rustling turn the many-twinkling leaves
Of aspen tall. The uncurling floods, diffused
In glassy breadth, seem through delusive lapse
Forgetful of their course. 'Tis silence all, 160
And pleasing expectation. Herds and flocks
Drop the dry sprig, and mute-imploring eye
The falling verdure. Hushed in short suspense,
The plumy people streak their wings with oil,
To throw the lucid moisture trickling off, 165
And wait the approaching sign to strike at once
Into the general choir. Even mountains, vales,
And forests seem impatient to demand
The promised sweetness. Man superior walks
Amid the glad creation, musing praise, 170
And looking lively gratitude. At last
The clouds consign their treasures to the fields,
And, softly shaking on the dimpled pool

Prelusive drops, let all their moisture flow
In large effusion o'er the freshened world.   175
The stealing shower is scarce to patter heard
By such as wander through the forest walks
Beneath the umbrageous multitude of leaves.
But who can hold the shade while heaven descends
In universal bounty, shedding herbs   180
And fruits and flowers on Nature's ample lap?
Swift fancy fired anticipates their growth,
And, while the milky nutriment distils,
Beholds the kindling country colour round.
   Thus all day long the full-distended clouds   185
Indulge their genial stores, and well-showered earth
Is deep enriched with vegetable life;
Till, in the western sky, the downward sun
Looks out effulgent from amid the flush
Of broken clouds gay-shifting to his beam.   190
The rapid radiance instantaneous strikes
The illumined mountain; through the forest streams;
Shakes on the floods; and in a yellow mist,
Far smoking o'er the interminable plain,
In twinkling myriads lights the dewy gems.   195
Moist, bright, and green, the landscape laughs around.
Full swell the woods; their every music wakes,
Mixed in wild concert with the warbling brooks
Increased, the distant bleatings of the hills,
And hollow lows responsive from the vales,   200
Whence blending all the sweetened zephyr springs.
Meantime, refracted from yon eastern cloud,
Bestriding earth, the grand ethereal bow
Shoots up immense, and every hue unfolds,
In fair proportion running from the red   205
To where the violet fades into the sky.
Here, awful Newton, the dissolving clouds
Form, fronting on the sun, thy showery prism;
And to the sage-instructed eye unfold
The various twine of light, by thee disclosed   210

From the white mingling maze. Not so the swain:
He wondering views the bright enchantment bend
Delightful o'er the radiant fields, and runs
To catch the falling glory; but amazed
Beholds the amusive arch before him fly,   215
Then vanish quite away. Still night succeeds,
A softened shade; and saturated earth
Awaits the morning beam, to give to light,
Raised through ten thousand different plastic tubes,
The balmy treasures of the former day.   220
   Then spring the living herbs, profusely wild,
O'er all the deep-green earth, beyond the power
Of botanist to number up their tribes,—
Whether he steals along the lonely dale
In silent search; or through the forest, rank   225
With what the dull incurious weeds account,
Bursts his blind way; or climbs the mountain-rock,
Fired by the nodding verdure of its brow:
With such a liberal hand has Nature flung
Their seeds abroad, blown them about in winds,   230
Innumerous mixed them with the nursing mould,
The moistening current, and prolific rain.
   But who their virtues can declare? who pierce
With vision pure into these secret stores
Of life, and health, and joy? the food of man   235
While yet he lived in innocence, and told
A length of golden years, unfleshed in blood,
A stranger to the savage arts of life,
Death, rapine, carnage, surfeit, and disease,
The lord, and not the tyrant, of the world.   240
   The first fresh dawn then waked the gladdened race
Of uncorrupted man, nor blushed to see
The sluggard sleep beneath its sacred beam;
For their light slumbers gently fumed away,
And up they rose as vigorous as the sun,   245
Or to the culture of the willing glebe,
Or to the cheerful tendance of the flock.

Meantime the song went round; and dance and sport,
Wisdom and friendly talk, successive stole
Their hours away; while in the rosy vale   250
Love breathed his infant sighs, from anguish free,
And full replete with bliss,—save the sweet pain,
That, inly thrilling, but exalts it more.
Nor yet injurious act, nor surly deed,
Was known among those happy sons of heaven;   255
For reason and benevolence were law.
Harmonious Nature too looked smiling on.
Clear shone the skies, cooled with eternal gales,
And balmy spirit all. The youthful sun
Shot his best rays, and still the gracious clouds   , 260
Dropped fatness down, as o'er the swelling mead
The herds and flocks commixing played secure.
This when, emergent from the gloomy wood,
The glaring lion saw, his horrid heart
Was meekened, and he joined his sullen joy,   265
For music held the whole in perfect peace :
Soft sighed the flute; the tender voice was heard,
Warbling the varied heart; the woodlands round
Applied their quire; and winds and waters flowed
In consonance. Such were those prime of days.   270
  But now those white unblemished minutes, whence
The fabling poets took their golden age,
Are found no more amid these iron times,
These dregs of life! Now the distempered mind
Has lost that concord of harmonious powers,   275
Which forms the soul of happiness; and all
Is off the poise within : the passions all
Have burst their bounds; and reason half extinct,
Or impotent, or else approving, sees
The foul disorder. Senseless and deformed,   280
Convulsive anger storms at large; or, pale
And silent, settles into fell revenge.
Base envy withers at another's joy,
And hates that excellence it cannot reach.

Desponding fear, of feeble fancies full, 285
Weak and unmanly, loosens every power.
Even love itself is bitterness of soul,
A pensive anguish pining at the heart ;
Or, sunk to sordid interest, feels no more
That noble wish, that never-cloyed desire, 290
Which, selfish joy disdaining, seeks alone
To bless the dearer object of its flame.
Hope sickens with extravagance ; and grief,
Of life impatient, into madness swells,
Or in dead silence wastes the weeping hours. 295
These, and a thousand mixed emotions more,
From ever-changing views of good and ill
Formed infinitely various, vex the mind
With endless storm ; whence, deeply rankling, grows
The partial thought, a listless unconcern 300
Cold, and averting from our neighbour's good,
Then dark disgust, and hatred, winding wiles,
Coward deceit, and ruffian violence.
At last, extinct each social feeling, fell
And joyless inhumanity pervades 305
And petrifies the heart. Nature disturbed
Is deemed vindictive to have changed her course.
  Hence, in old dusky time, a deluge came ;
When the deep-cleft disparting orb, that arched
The central waters round, impetuous rushed 310
With universal burst into the gulf,
And o'er the high-piled hills of fractured earth
Wide dashed the waves in undulation vast,
Till from the centre to the streaming clouds
A shoreless ocean tumbled round the globe. 315
  The Seasons since have with severer sway
Oppressed a broken world ; the Winter keen
Shook forth his waste of snows, and Summer shot
His pestilential heats. Great Spring before
Greened all the year ; and fruits and blossoms blushed 320
In social sweetness on the self-same bough.

Pure was the temperate air; an even calm
Perpetual reigned, save what the zephyrs bland
Breathed o'er the blue expanse; for then nor storms
Were taught to blow nor hurricanes to rage;   325
Sound slept the waters; no sulphureous glooms
Swelled in the sky, and sent the lightning forth;
While sickly damps and cold autumnal fogs
Hung not, relaxing, on the springs of life.
But now, of turbid elements the sport,   330
From clear to cloudy tossed, from hot to cold,
And dry to moist, with inward-eating change,
Our drooping days are dwindled down to nought,
Their period finished ere 'tis well begun.
   And yet the wholesome herb neglected dies;   335
Though with the pure exhilarating soul
Of nutriment, and health, and vital powers,
Beyond the search of art, 'tis copious blest.
For, with hot ravin fired, ensanguined man
Is now become the lion of the plain,   340
And worse. The wolf, who from the nightly fold
Fierce drags the bleating prey, ne'er drunk her milk,
Nor wore her warming fleece; nor has the steer,
At whose strong chest the deadly tiger hangs,
E'er ploughed for him. They too are tempered high, 345
With hunger stung and wild necessity;
Nor lodges pity in their shaggy breast.
But man, whom Nature formed of milder clay,
With every kind emotion in his heart,
And taught alone to weep—while from her lap   350
She pours ten thousand delicacies, herbs
And fruits, as numerous as the drops of rain
Or beams that gave them birth—shall he, fair form!
Who wears sweet smiles, and looks erect on heaven,
E'er stoop to mingle with the prowling herd,   355
And dip his tongue in gore? The beast of prey,
Blood-stained, deserves to bleed; but you, ye flocks,
What have ye done? ye peaceful people, what,

To merit death? you, who have given us milk
In luscious streams, and lent us your own coat   360
Against the Winter's cold? And the plain ox,
That harmless, honest, guileless animal,
In what has he offended? he, whose toil,
Patient and ever-ready, clothes the land
With all the pomp of harvest—shall he bleed,   365
And struggling groan beneath the cruel hands
Even of the clowns he feeds? and that, perhaps,
To swell the riot of the autumnal feast
Won by his labour. Thus the feeling heart
Would tenderly suggest; but 'tis enough   370
In this late age adventurous to have touched
Light on the numbers of the Samian sage.
High Heaven forbids the bold presumptuous strain,
Whose wisest will has fixed us in a state
That must not yet to pure perfection rise: 375
Besides, who knows how, raised to higher life,
From stage to stage the vital scale ascends?

Now when the first foul torrent of the brooks,
Swelled with the vernal rains, is ebbed away,
And whitening down their mossy-tinctured stream   380
Descends the billowy foam—now is the time,
While yet the dark-brown water aids the guile,
To tempt the trout. The well-dissembled fly,
The rod fine-tapering with elastic spring,
Snatched from the hoary steed the floating line,   385
And all thy slender watery stores prepare.
But let not on thy hook the tortured worm
Convulsive twist in agonizing folds;
Which, by rapacious hunger swallowed deep,
Gives, as you tear it from the bleeding breast   390
Of the weak, helpless, uncomplaining wretch,
Harsh pain and horror to the tender hand.
When with his lively ray the potent sun
Has pierced the streams, and roused the finny race,

Then, issuing cheerful, to thy sport repair;   395
Chief should the western breezes curling play,
And light o'er ether bear the shadowy clouds.
High to their fount, this day, amid the hills
And woodlands warbling round, trace up the brooks;
The next, pursue their rocky-channelled maze   400
Down to the river, in whose ample wave
Their little naiads love to sport at large.
Just in the dubious point where with the pool
Is mixed the trembling stream, or where it boils
Around the stone, or from the hollowed bank   405
Reverted plays in undulating flow,
There throw, nice-judging, the delusive fly;
And, as you lead it round in artful curve,
With eye attentive mark the springing game.
Straight as above the surface of the flood   410
They wanton rise, or urged by hunger leap,
Then fix, with gentle twitch, the barbed hook,—
Some lightly tossing to the grassy bank,
And to the shelving shore slow-dragging some,
With various hand proportioned to their force.   415
If yet too young, and easily deceived,
A worthless prey scarce bends your pliant rod,
Him, piteous of his youth and the short space
He has enjoyed the vital light of heaven,
Soft disengage, and back into the stream   420
The speckled infant throw. But should you lure
From his dark haunt beneath the tangled roots
Of pendent trees the monarch of the brook,
Behoves you then to ply your finest art.
Long time he, following cautious, scans the fly;   425
And oft attempts to seize it, but as oft
The dimpled water speaks his jealous fear.
At last, while haply o'er the shaded sun
Passes a cloud, he desperate takes the death
With sullen plunge. At once he darts along,   430
Deep-struck, and runs out all the lengthened line;

Then seeks the farthest ooze, the sheltering weed,
The caverned bank, his old secure abode;
And flies aloft, and flounces round the pool,
Indignant of the guile. With yielding hand, 435
That feels him still, yet to his furious course
Gives way, you, now retiring, following now
Across the stream, exhaust his idle rage;
Till, floating broad upon his breathless side,
And to his fate abandoned, to the shore 440
You gaily drag your unresisting prize.
   Thus pass the temperate hours; but when the sun
Shakes from his noon-day throne the scattering clouds,
Even shooting listless languor through the deeps,
Then seek the bank where flowering elders crowd, 445
Where scattered wild the lily of the vale
Its balmy essence breathes, where cowslips hang
The dewy head, where purple violets lurk
With all the lowly children of the shade;
Or lie reclined beneath yon spreading ash 450
Hung o'er the steep, whence borne on liquid wing
The sounding culver shoots; or where the hawk
High in the beetling cliff his eyry builds.
There let the classic page thy fancy lead
Through rural scenes, such as the Mantuan swain 455
Paints in the matchless harmony of song;
Or catch thyself the landscape, gliding swift
Athwart imagination's vivid eye;
Or, by the vocal woods and waters lulled,
And lost in lonely musing, in a dream 460
Confused of careless solitude, where mix
Ten thousand wandering images of things,
Soothe every gust of passion into peace—
All but the swellings of the softened heart,
That waken, not disturb, the tranquil mind. 465

Behold, yon breathing prospect bids the muse

Throw all her beauty forth. But who can paint
Like Nature? Can imagination boast,
Amid its gay creation, hues like hers?
Or can it mix them with that matchless skill,   470
And lose them in each other, as appears
In every bud that blows? If fancy then,
Unequal, fails beneath the pleasing task,
Ah what shall language do? ah, where find words
Tinged with so many colours, and whose power,   475
To life approaching, may perfume my lays
With that fine oil, those aromatic gales,
That inexhaustive flow continual round?
   Yet, though successless, will the toil delight.
Come then, ye virgins and ye youths whose hearts   480
Have felt the raptures of refining love!
And thou, Amanda, come, pride of my song!
Formed by the Graces, loveliness itself!
Come with those downcast eyes, sedate and sweet,
Those looks demure, that deeply pierce the soul,   485
Where, with the light of thoughtful reason mixed,
Shines lively fancy, and the feeling heart—
O come! and while the rosy-footed May
Steals blushing on, together let us tread
The morning dews, and gather in their prime   490
Fresh-blooming flowers to grace thy braided hair,
And thy loved bosom that improves their sweets.
   See where the winding vale its lavish stores,
Irriguous, spreads. See how the lily drinks
The latent rill, scarce oozing through the grass   495
Of growth luxuriant; or the humid bank,
In fair profusion, decks. Long let us walk
Where the breeze blows from yon extended field
Of blossomed beans. Arabia cannot boast
A fuller gale of joy than liberal thence   500
Breathes through the sense, and takes the ravished soul.
Nor is the mead unworthy of thy foot,
Full of fresh verdure, and unnumbered flowers,

The negligence of Nature, wide and wild;
Where, undisguised by mimic Art, she spreads   505
Unbounded beauty to the roving eye.
Here their delicious task the fervent bees
In swarming millions tend; around, athwart,
Through the soft air the busy nations fly,
Cling to the bud, and with inserted tube   510
Suck its pure essence, its ethereal soul;
And oft with bolder wing they soaring dare
The purple heath, or where the wild-thyme grows,
And yellow load them with the luscious spoil.
At length the finished garden to the view   515
Its vistas opens, and its alleys green.
Snatched through the verdant maze, the hurried eye
Distracted wanders; now the bowery walk
Of covert close, where scarce a speck of day
Falls on the lengthened gloom, protracted sweeps;   520
Now meets the bending sky; the river now,
Dimpling along, the breezy-ruffled lake,
The forest darkening round, the glittering spire,
The ethereal mountain, and the distant main.
But why so far excursive? when at hand,   525
Along these blushing borders bright with dew,
And in yon mingled wilderness of flowers,
Fair-handed Spring unbosoms every grace;
Throws out the snowdrop and the crocus first,
The daisy, primrose, violet darkly blue,   530
And polyanthus of unnumbered dyes,
The yellow wallflower, stained with iron brown,
And lavish stock that scents the garden round;
From the soft wing of vernal breezes shed,
Anemones; auriculas, enriched   535
With shining meal o'er all their velvet leaves;
And full ranunculus of glowing red.
Then comes the tulip race, where beauty plays
Her idle freaks: from family diffused
To family, as flies the father-dust,   540

The varied colours run ; and, while they break
On the charmed eye, the exulting florist marks
With secret pride the wonders of his hand.
No gradual bloom is wanting, from the bud
First-born of Spring to Summer's musky tribes;   545
Nor hyacinths, of purest virgin white,
Low-bent, and blushing inward ; nor jonquils,
Of potent fragrance ; nor narcissus fair,
As o'er the fabled fountain hanging still ;
Nor broad carnations ; nor gay-spotted pinks;   550
Nor, showered from every bush, the damask-rose :
Infinite numbers, delicacies, smells,
With hues on hues expression cannot paint,
The breath of Nature, and her endless bloom !
  Hail, Source of Being! Universal Soul   555
Of heaven and earth, Essential Presence, hail!
To Thee I bend the knee ; to Thee my thoughts
Continual climb; who, with a master-hand,
Hast the great whole into perfection touched.
By Thee the various vegetative tribes,   560
Wrapt in a filmy net, and clad with leaves,
Draw the live ether, and imbibe the dew.
By Thee disposed into congenial soils
Stands each attractive plant, and sucks and swells
The juicy tide—a twining mass of tubes.   565
At Thy command the vernal sun awakes
The torpid sap, detruded to the root
By wintry winds, that now in fluent dance
And lively fermentation, mounting, spreads
All this innumerous-coloured scene of things.   570

  As rising from the vegetable world
My theme ascends, with equal wing ascend,
My panting muse ; and hark, how loud the woods
Invite you forth in all your gayest trim.
Lend me your song, ye nightingales ; oh pour   575

The mazy-running soul of melody
Into my varied verse; while I deduce,
From the first note the hollow cuckoo sings,
The symphony of Spring, and touch a theme
Unknown to fame—the passion of the groves.   580
   When first the soul of love is sent abroad
Warm through the vital air, and on the heart
Harmonious seizes, the gay troops begin
In gallant thought to plume the painted wing;
And try again the long-forgotten strain,   585
At first faint-warbled. But no sooner grows
The soft infusion prevalent and wide,
Than, all alive, at once their joy o'erflows
In music unconfined. Up springs the lark,
Shrill-voiced and loud, the messenger of morn: 590
Ere yet the shadows fly, he mounted sings
Amid the dawning clouds, and from their haunts
Calls up the tuneful nations. Every copse
Deep-tangled, tree irregular, and bush
Bending with dewy moisture, o'er the heads   595
Of the coy quiristers that lodge within,
Are prodigal of harmony. The thrush
And woodlark, o'er the kind-contending throng
Superior heard, run through the sweetest length
Of notes; when listening Philomela deigns   600
To let them joy, and purposes, in thought
Elate, to make her night excel their day.
The blackbird whistles from the thorny brake;
The mellow bullfinch answers from the grove;
Nor are the linnets, o'er the flowering furze   605
Poured out profusely, silent. Joined to these,
Innumerous songsters, in the freshening shade
Of new-sprung leaves, their modulations mix
Mellifluous. The jay, the rook, the daw,
And each harsh pipe, discordant heard alone,   610
Aid the full concert; while the stockdove breathes
A melancholy murmur through the whole.

'Tis love creates their melody, and all
This waste of music is the voice of love;
That even to birds and beasts the tender arts   615
Of pleasing teaches. Hence the glossy kind
Try every winning way inventive love
Can dictate, and in courtship to their mates
Pour forth their little souls. First, wide around,
With distant awe, in airy rings they rove,   620
Endeavouring by a thousand tricks to catch
The cunning, conscious, half-averted glance
Of their regardless charmer. Should she seem,
Softening, the least approvance to bestow,
Their colours burnish, and, by hope inspired,   625
They brisk advance; then, on a sudden struck,
Retire disordered; then again approach;
In fond rotation spread the spotted wing,
And shiver every feather with desire.
      Connubial leagues agreed, to the deep woods   630
They haste away, all as their fancy leads,
Pleasure, or food, or secret safety prompts;
That Nature's great command may be obeyed,
Nor all the sweet sensations they perceive
Indulged in vain. Some to the holly-hedge   635
Nestling repair, and to the thicket some;
Some to the rude protection of the thorn
Commit their feeble offspring. The cleft tree
Offers its kind concealment to a few,
Their food its insects, and its moss their nests.   640
Others, apart, far in the grassy dale
Or roughening waste, their humble texture weave.
But most in woodland solitudes delight,
In unfrequented glooms, or shaggy banks,
Steep, and divided by a babbling brook,   645
Whose murmurs soothe them all the live-long day,
When by kind duty fixed. Among the roots
Of hazel, pendent o'er the plaintive stream,
They frame the first foundation of their domes,—

Dry sprigs of trees, in artful fabric laid,   650
And bound with clay together. Now 'tis nought
But restless hurry through the busy air,
Beat by unnumbered wings. The swallow sweeps
The slimy pool, to build his hanging house
Intent. And often, from the careless back   655
Of herds and flocks, a thousand tugging bills
Pluck hair and wool ; and oft, when unobserved,
Steal from the barn a straw; till soft and warm,
Clean and complete their habitation grows.
As thus the patient dam assiduous sits,   660
Not to be tempted from her tender task
Or by sharp hunger or by smooth delight,
Though the whole loosened Spring around her blows,
Her sympathizing lover takes his stand
High on the opponent bank, and ceaseless sings   665
The tedious time away ; or else supplies
Her place a moment, while she sudden flits
To pick the scanty meal. The appointed time
With pious toil fulfilled, the callow young,
Warmed and expanded into perfect life,   670
Their brittle bondage break, and come to light,—
A helpless family, demanding food
With constant clamour. O what passions then,
What melting sentiments of kindly care,
On the new parents seize! Away they fly,   675
Affectionate, and undesiring bear
The most delicious morsel to their young;
Which equally distributed, again
The search begins. Even so a gentle pair,
By fortune sunk, but formed of generous mould,   680
And charmed with cares beyond the vulgar breast,
In some lone cot amid the distant woods,
Sustained alone by providential Heaven,
Oft, as they weeping eye their infant train,
Check their own appetites and give them all.   685
Nor toil alone they scorn : exalting love,

E

By the great Father of the Spring inspired,
Gives instant courage to the fearful race,
And to the simple art. With stealthy wing,
Should some rude foot their woody haunts molest,   690
Amid a neighbouring bush they silent drop,
And whirring thence, as if alarmed, deceive
The unfeeling school-boy. Hence, around the head
Of wandering swain, the white-winged plover wheels
Her sounding flight, and then directly on   695
In long excursion skims the level lawn
To tempt him from her nest. The wild-duck, hence,
O'er the rough moss, and o'er the trackless waste
The heath-hen flutters, pious fraud! to lead
The hot pursuing spaniel far astray.   700
      Be not the muse ashamed, here to bemoan
Her brothers of the grove, by tyrant man
Inhuman caught, and in the narrow cage
From liberty confined and boundless air.
Dull are the pretty slaves, their plumage dull,   705
Ragged, and all its brightening lustre lost;
Nor is that sprightly wildness in their notes,
Which, clear and vigorous, warbles from the beech.
Oh then, ye friends of love and love-taught song,
Spare the soft tribes, this barbarous act forbear!   710
If on your bosom innocence can win,
Music engage, or piety persuade.
      But let not chief the nightingale lament
Her ruined care, too delicately framed
To brook the harsh confinement of the cage.   715
Oft when, returning with her loaded bill,
The astonished mother finds a vacant nest,
By the hard hand of unrelenting clowns
Robbed, to the ground the vain provision falls;
Her pinions ruffle, and, low-drooping, scarce   720
Can bear the mourner to the poplar shade,—
Where, all abandoned to despair, she sings
Her sorrows through the night, and, on the bough

Sole-sitting, still at every dying fall
Takes up again her lamentable strain   725
Of winding woe, till wide around the woods
Sigh to her song and with her wail resound.
  But now the feathered youth their former bounds,
Ardent, disdain; and, weighing oft their wings,
Demand the free possession of the sky.   •   730
This one glad office more, and then dissolves
Parental love at once, now needless grown:
Unlavish Wisdom never works in vain.
'Tis on some evening, sunny, grateful, mild,
When nought but balm is breathing through the woods, 735
With yellow lustre bright, that the new tribes
Visit the spacious heavens, and look abroad
On nature's common,—far as they can see
Or wing, their range and pasture. O'er the boughs
Dancing about, still at the giddy verge   740
Their resolution fails; their pinions still,
In loose libration stretched, to trust the void
Trembling refuse; till down before them fly
The parent-guides, and chide, exhort, command,
Or push them off. The surging air receives   745
The plumy burden; and their self-taught wings
Winnow the waving element. On ground
Alighted, bolder up again they lead,
Farther and farther on, the lengthening flight;
Till, vanished every fear, and every power   750
Roused into life and action, light in air
The acquitted parents see their soaring race,
And, once rejoicing, never know them more.
  High from the summit of a craggy cliff
Hung o'er the deep, such as amazing frowns   755
On utmost Kilda's shore, whose lonely race
Resign the setting sun to Indian worlds,
The royal eagle draws his vigorous young,
Strong-pounced, and ardent with paternal fire.
Now fit to raise a kingdom of their own,   760

He drives them from his fort, the towering seat
For ages of his empire; which, in peace,
Unstained he holds, while many a league to sea
He wings his course, and preys in distant isles.
   Should I my steps turn to the rural seat   765
Whose lofty elms and venerable oaks
Invite the rook, who high amid the boughs,
In early Spring, his airy city builds,
And ceaseless caws amusive; there, well-pleased,
I might the various polity survey   770
Of the mixed household kind. The careful hen
Calls all her chirping family around,
Fed and defended by the fearless cock;
Whose breast with ardour flames, as on he walks
Graceful, and crows defiance. In the pond   775
The finely-checkered duck before her train
Rows garrulous. The stately-sailing swan
Gives out his snowy plumage to the gale;
And, arching proud his neck, with oary feet
Bears forward fierce, and guards his osier-isle,   780
Protective of his young. The turkey nigh,
Loud-threatening, reddens; while the peacock spreads
His every-coloured glory to the sun,
And swims in radiant majesty along.
O'er the whole homely scene, the cooing dove   785
Flies thick in amorous chase, and wanton rolls
The glancing eye, and turns the changeful neck.
   While thus the gentle tenants of the shade
Indulge their purer loves, the rougher world
Of brutes, below, rush furious into flame   790
And fierce desire. Through all his lusty veins
The bull, deep-scorched, the raging passion feels.
Of pasture sick, and negligent of food,
Scarce seen he wades among the yellow broom,
While o'er his ample sides the rambling sprays   795
Luxuriant shoot; or through the mazy wood
Dejected wanders, nor the enticing bud

Crops, though it presses on his careless sense.
And oft, with jealous maddening fancy rapt,
He seeks the fight ; and, idly-butting, feigns   800
His rival gored in every knotty trunk.
Him should he meet, the bellowing war begins :
Their eyes flash fury; to the hollowed earth,
Whence the sand flies, they mutter bloody deeds,
And groaning deep the impetuous battle mix;   805
While the fair heifer, balmy-breathing near,
Stands kindling up their rage. The trembling steed,
With this hot impulse seized in every nerve,
Nor heeds the rein, nor hears the sounding thong;
Blows are not felt; but, tossing high his head,   810
And by the well-known joy to distant plains
Attracted strong, all wild he bursts away;
O'er rocks, and woods, and craggy mountains flies;
And neighing, on the aërial summit takes
The exciting gale ; then, deep-descending, cleaves   815
The headlong torrents foaming down the hills,
Even where the madness of the straitened stream
Turns in black eddies round : such is the force
With which his frantic heart and sinews swell.
   Nor undelighted by the boundless Spring   820
Are the broad monsters of the foaming deep :
From the deep ooze and gelid cavern roused,
They flounce and tumble in unwieldy joy.
Dire were the strain and dissonant, to sing
The cruel raptures of the savage kind;   825
How, by this flame their native wrath sublimed,
They roam, amid the fury of their heart,
The far-resounding waste in fiercer bands,
And growl their horrid loves. But this the theme
I sing, enraptured, to the British fair   830
Forbids; and leads me to the mountain-brow,
Where sits the shepherd on the grassy turf,
Inhaling healthful the descending sun.
Around him feeds his many-bleating flock,

Of various cadence; and his sportive lambs,   835
This way and that convolved, in friskful glee
Their frolics play. And now the sprightly race
Invites them forth; when swift, the signal given,
They start away, and sweep the massy mound
That runs around the hill—the rampart once   840
Of iron war, in ancient barbarous times,
When disunited Britain ever bled,
Lost in eternal broil; ere yet she grew
To this deep-laid indissoluble state,
Where wealth and commerce lift their golden heads,   845
And o'er our labours liberty and law
Impartial watch—the wonder of a world!
   What is this mighty breath, ye curious, say,
That in a powerful language, felt not heard,
Instructs the fowls of heaven, and through their breast
These arts of love diffuses? What but God?   851
Inspiring God! who, boundless spirit all,
And unremitting energy, pervades,
Adjusts, sustains, and agitates the whole.
He ceaseless works alone, and yet alone   855
Seems not to work; with such perfection framed
Is this complex stupendous scheme of things.
But, though concealed, to every purer eye
The informing Author in his works appears:
Chief, lovely Spring, in thee and thy soft scenes   860
The smiling God is seen; while water, earth,
And air attest his bounty—which exalts
The brute creation to this finer thought,
And annual melts their undesigning hearts
Profusely thus in tenderness and joy.   865

   Still let my song a nobler note assume,
And sing the infusive force of Spring on man;
When heaven and earth, as if contending, vie
To raise his being, and serene his soul.
Can he forbear to join the general smile   870

Of Nature? Can fierce passions vex his breast,
While every gale is peace, and every grove
Is melody? Hence! from the bounteous walks
Of flowing Spring, ye sordid sons of earth,
Hard, and unfeeling of another's woe,   875
Or only lavish to yourselves ; away!
But come, ye generous minds, in whose wide thought,
Of all his works, creative Bounty burns
With warmest beam, and, on your open front
And liberal eye, sits, from his dark retreat   880
Inviting modest want. Nor till invoked
Can restless goodness wait : your active search
Leaves no cold wintry corner unexplored ;
Like silent-working heaven, surprising oft
The lonely heart with unexpected good.   885
For you the roving spirit of the wind
Blows Spring abroad ; for you the teeming clouds
Descend in gladsome plenty o'er the world ;
And the sun sheds his kindest rays for you,
Ye flower of human race! In these green days   890
Reviving sickness lifts her languid head ;
Life flows afresh ; and young-eyed health exalts
The whole creation round. Contentment walks
The sunny glade, and feels an inward bliss
Spring o'er his mind, beyond the power of kings   895
To purchase. Pure serenity apace
Induces thought and contemplation still.
By swift degrees the love of nature works,
And warms the bosom ; till at last, sublimed
To rapture and enthusiastic heat,   900
We feel the present Deity, and taste
The joy of God to see a happy world.
   These are the sacred feelings of thy heart,
Thy heart informed by reason's purer ray,
O Lyttelton, the friend! thy passions thus   905
And meditations vary, as at large,
Courting the muse, through Hagley-park you stray—

Thy British Tempè! There along the dale
With woods o'er-hung, and shagged with mossy rocks,
Whence on each hand the gushing waters play,   910
And down the rough cascade white-dashing fall,
Or gleam in lengthened vista through the trees,
You silent steal; or sit beneath the shade
Of solemn oaks, that tuft the swelling mounts
Thrown graceful round by Nature's careless hand,   915
And pensive listen to the various voice
Of rural peace—the herds, the flocks, the birds,
The hollow-whispering breeze, the plaint of rills
That, purling down amid the twisted roots
Which creep around, their dewy murmurs shake   920
On the soothed ear. From these abstracted oft
You wander through the philosophic world,
Where in bright train continual wonders rise
Or to the curious or the pious eye.
And oft, conducted by historic truth,   925
You tread the long extent of backward time,
Planning with warm benevolence of mind
And honest zeal, unwarped by party-rage,
Britannia's weal,—how from the venal gulf
To raise her virtue, and her arts revive.   930
Or, turning thence thy view, these graver thoughts
The muses charm, while with sure taste refined
You draw the inspiring breath of ancient song,
Till nobly rises emulous thy own.
Perhaps thy loved Lucinda shares thy walk,   935
With soul to thine attuned. Then Nature all
Wears to the lover's eye a look of love;
And all the tumult of a guilty world,
Tossed by ungenerous passions, sinks away.
The tender heart is animated peace,   940
And, as it pours its copious treasures forth
In varied converse, softening every theme,
You frequent-pausing turn, and from her eyes,
Where meekened sense and amiable grace

And lively sweetness dwell, enraptured drink   945
That nameless spirit of ethereal joy,
Inimitable happiness! which love
Alone bestows, and on a favoured few.
Meantime you gain the height, from whose fair brow
The bursting prospect spreads immense around;   950
And, snatched o'er hill and dale, and wood and lawn,
And verdant field, and darkening heath between,
And villages embosomed soft in trees,
And spiry towns by surging columns marked
Of household smoke, your eye excursive roams,——   955
Wide-stretching from the hall, in whose kind haunt
The hospitable genius lingers still,.
To where the broken landscape, by degrees
Ascending, roughens into rigid hills
O'er which the Cambrian mountains, like far clouds   960
That skirt the blue horizon, dusky rise.
    Flushed by the spirit of the genial year,
Now from the virgin's cheek a fresher bloom
Shoots less and less the live carnation round;
Her lips blush deeper sweets; she breathes of youth; 965
The shining moisture swells into her eyes
In brighter flow; her wishing bosom heaves
With palpitations wild; kind tumults seize
Her veins, and all her yielding soul is love.
From the keen gaze her lover turns away,   970
Full of the dear ecstatic power, and sick
With sighing languishment. Ah then, ye fair!
Be greatly cautious of your sliding hearts;
Dare not the infectious sigh, the pleading look
Downcast and low, in meek submission dressed,   975
But full of guile. Let not the fervent tongue,
Prompt to deceive, with adulation smooth,
Gain on your purposed will. Nor in the bower,
Where woodbines flaunt and roses shed a couch,
While evening draws her crimson curtains round,   980
Trust your soft minutes with betraying man.

And let the aspiring youth beware of love,
Of the smooth glance beware; for 'tis too late
When on his heart the torrent softness pours.
Then wisdom prostrate lies, and fading fame   985
Dissolves in air away; while the fond soul,
Wrapt in gay visions of unreal bliss,
Still paints the illusive form, the kindling grace,
The enticing smile, the modest-seeming eye.
Beneath whose beauteous beams, belying heaven,   990
Lurk searchless cunning, cruelty, and death :
And still, false-warbling in his cheated ear,
Her syren voice, enchanting, draws him on
To guileful shores, and meads of fatal joy.
Even present, in the very lap of love   995
Inglorious laid, while music flows around,
Perfumes, and oils, and wines, and wanton hours,
Amid the roses fierce repentance rears
Her snaky crest; a quick-returning pang
Shoots through the conscious heart, where honour still 1000
And great design against the oppressive load
Of luxury by fits impatient heave.
But absent, what fantastic woes aroused
Rage in each thought, by restless musing fed,
Chill the warm cheek, and blast the bloom of life! 1005
Neglected fortune flies; and, sliding swift,
Prone into ruin fall his scorned affairs.
'Tis nought but gloom around. The darkened sun
Loses his light. The rosy-bosomed Spring
To weeping fancy pines; and yon bright arch   1010
Contracted bends into a dusky vault.
All nature fades extinct; and she alone
Heard, felt, and seen, possesses every thought,
Fills every sense, and pants in every vein.
Books are but formal dulness, tedious friends;   1015
And sad amid the social band he sits
Lonely and inattentive. From the tongue
The unfinished period falls; while, borne away

On swelling thought, his wafted spirit flies
To the vain bosom of his distant fair,   1020
And leaves the semblance of a lover, fixed
In melancholy site, with head declined
And love-dejected eyes. Sudden he starts,
Shook from his tender trance, and restless runs
To glimmering shades and sympathetic glooms,   1025
Where the dun umbrage o'er the falling stream
Romantic hangs; there through the pensive dusk
Strays, in heart-thrilling meditation lost,
Indulging all to love; or on the bank
Thrown, amid drooping lilies, swells the breeze   1030
With sighs unceasing, and the brook with tears.
Thus in soft anguish he consumes the day;
Nor quits his deep retirement, till the moon
Peeps through the chambers of the fleecy east,
Enlightened by degrees, and in her train   1035
Leads on the gentle hours; then forth he walks,
Beneath the trembling languish of her beam,
With softened soul, and woos the bird of eve
To mingle woes with his; or, while the world
And all the sons of care lie hushed in sleep,   1040
Associates with the midnight shadows drear,
And, sighing to the lonely taper, pours
His idly-tortured heart into the page
Meant for the moving messenger of love—
Where rapture burns on rapture, every line   1045
With rising frenzy fired. But if on bed
Delirious flung, sleep from his pillow flies.
All night he tosses, nor the balmy power
In any posture finds; till the grey morn
Lifts her pale lustre on the paler wretch,   1050
Exanimate by love; and then perhaps
Exhausted nature sinks a while to rest,
Still interrupted by distracted dreams,
That o'er the sick imagination rise,
And in black colours paint the mimic scene.   1055

Oft with the enchantress of his soul he talks;
Sometimes in crowds distressed; or, if retired
To secret-winding flower-enwoven bowers
Far from the dull impertinence of man,
Just as he, credulous, his endless cares   1060
Begins to lose in blind oblivious love,
Snatched from her yielded hand, he knows not how,
Through forest huge, and long untravelled heaths
With desolation brown, he wanders waste,
In night and tempest wrapt; or shrinks aghast   1065
Back from the bending precipice; or wades
The turbid stream below, and strives to reach
The farther shore, where succourless and sad
She with extended arms his aid implores,
But strives in vain: borne by the outrageous flood   1070
To distance down, he rides the ridgy wave,
Or whelmed beneath the boiling eddy sinks.
  These are the charming agonies of love,
Whose misery delights. But through the heart
Should jealousy its venom once diffuse,   1075
'Tis then delightful misery no more,
But agony unmixed, incessant gall,
Corroding every thought, and blasting all
Love's paradise. Ye fairy prospects, then,
Ye beds of roses, and ye bowers of joy,   1080
Farewell! Ye gleamings of departed peace,
Shine out your last! The yellow-tingeing plague
Internal vision taints, and in a night
Of livid gloom imagination wraps.
Ah! then, instead of love-enlivened cheeks,   1085
Of sunny features, and of ardent eyes
With flowing rapture bright, dark looks succeed,
Suffused and glaring with untender fire,
A clouded aspect, and a burning cheek,
Where the whole poisoned soul malignant sits   1090
And frightens love away. Ten thousand fears
Invented wild, ten thousand frantic views

Of horrid rivals, hanging on the charms
For which he melts in fondness, eat him up
With fervent anguish, and consuming rage.   1095
In vain reproaches lend their idle aid,
Deceitful pride, and resolution frail,
Giving false peace a moment. Fancy pours
Afresh her beauties on his busy thought,—
Her first endearments twining round the soul   1100
With all the witchcraft of ensnaring love.
Straight the fierce storm involves his mind anew,
Flames through the nerves, and boils along the veins;
While anxious doubt distracts the tortured heart,—
For even the sad assurance of his fears   1105
Were peace to what he feels. Thus the warm youth,
Whom love deludes into his thorny wilds
Through flowery-tempting paths, or leads a life
Of fevered rapture or of cruel care,
His brightest flames extinguished all, and all   1110
His lively moments running down to waste.
  But happy they, the happiest of their kind !
Whom gentler stars unite, and in one fate
Their hearts, their fortunes, and their beings blend.
'Tis not the coarser tie of human laws,   1115
Unnatural oft, and foreign to the mind,
That binds their peace, but harmony itself,
Attuning all their passions into love ;
Where friendship full-exerts her softest power,
Perfect esteem enlivened by desire   1120
Ineffable, and sympathy of soul ;
Thought meeting thought, and will preventing will,
With boundless confidence,—for nought but love
Can answer love, and render bliss secure.
Let him, ungenerous, who, alone intent   1125
To bless himself, from sordid parents buys
The loathing virgin, in eternal care,
Well-merited, consume his nights and days ;
Let barbarous nations, whose inhuman love

Is wild desire, fierce as the suns they feel;   1130
Let eastern tyrants from the light of heaven
Seclude their bosom slaves, meanly possessed
Of a mere lifeless violated form :
While those, whom love cements in holy faith
And equal transport, free as Nature live,   1135
Disdaining fear. What is the world to them,
Its pomp, its pleasure, and its nonsense all,
Who in each other clasp whatever fair
High fancy forms, and lavish hearts can wish;
Something than beauty dearer, should they look   1140
Or on the mind, or mind-illumined face—
Truth, goodness, honour, harmony, and love,
The richest bounty of indulgent Heaven.
Meantime a smiling offspring rises round,
And mingles both their graces. By degrees   1145
The human blossom blows, and every day,
Soft as it rolls along, shows some new charm,
The father's lustre and the mother's bloom.
Then infant reason grows apace, and calls
For the kind hand of an assiduous care.   1150
Delightful task! to rear the tender thought,
To teach the young idea how to shoot,
To pour the fresh instruction o'er the mind,
To breathe the enlivening spirit, and to fix
The generous purpose in the glowing breast.   1155
Oh speak the joy! ye whom the sudden tear
Surprises often while you look around
And nothing strikes your eye but sights of bliss,
All various Nature pressing on the heart ;
An elegant sufficiency, content,   1160
Retirement, rural quiet, friendship, books,
Ease and alternate labour, useful life,
Progressive virtue, and approving Heaven.
These are the matchless joys of virtuous love,
And thus their moments fly. The Seasons thus,   1165
As ceaseless round a jarring world they roll,

Still find them happy; and consenting Spring
Sheds her own rosy garland on their heads:
Till evening comes at last, serene and mild;
When after the long vernal day of life,   1170
Enamoured more, as more remembrance swells
With many a proof of recollected love,
Together down they sink in social sleep;
Together freed, their gentle spirits fly
To scenes where love and bliss immortal reign.   1175

END OF SPRING.

SUMMER.

FROM brightening fields of ether fair disclosed,
Child of the Sun, refulgent Summer comes
In pride of youth, and felt through Nature's depth!
He comes, attended by the sultry hours
And ever-fanning breezes on his way;   5
While from his ardent look the turning Spring
Averts her blushful face, and earth and skies
All-smiling to his hot dominion leaves.
  Hence let me haste into the mid-wood shade
Where scarce a sunbeam wanders through the gloom,   10
And on the dark green grass, beside the brink
Of haunted stream that by the roots of oak
Rolls o'er the rocky channel, lie at large,
And sing the glories of the circling year.

  Come, Inspiration! from thy hermit seat,   15
By mortal seldom found: may Fancy dare,
From thy fixed serious eye, and raptured glance
Shot on surrounding Heaven, to steal one look
Creative of the poet, every power
Exalting to an ecstasy of soul!   20
  And thou, my youthful muse's early friend,
In whom the human graces all unite—
Pure light of mind, and tenderness of heart,
Genius and wisdom, the gay social sense
By decency chastised, goodness and wit   25
In seldom-meeting harmony combined,

F

Unblemished honour, and an active zeal
For Britain's glory, liberty, and man—
O Dodington! attend my rural song,
Stoop to my theme, inspirit every line,   30
And teach me to deserve thy just applause.

  With what an awful world-revolving power
Were first the unwieldy planets launched along
The illimitable void! thus to remain—
Amid the flux of many thousand years,   35
That oft has swept the toiling race of men
And all their laboured monuments away—
Firm, unremitting, matchless in their course;
To the kind-tempered change of night and day
And of the Seasons ever stealing round   40
Minutely faithful: such the all-perfect Hand
That poised, impels, and rules the steady whole.

  When now no more the alternate Twins are fired,
And Cancer reddens with the solar blaze,
Short is the doubtful empire of the night;   45
And soon, observant of approaching day,
The meek-eyed morn appears, mother of dews,
At first faint-gleaming in the dappled east;
Till far o'er ether spreads the widening glow,
And from before the lustre of her face   50
White break the clouds away. With quickened step
Brown night retires. Young day pours in apace,
And opens all the lawny prospect wide.
The dripping rock, the mountain's misty top
Swell on the sight, and brighten with the dawn.   55
Blue through the dusk the smoking currents shine;
And from the bladed field the fearful hare
Limps awkward; while along the forest glade
The wild deer trip, and often turning gaze
At early passenger. Music awakes,   60

The native voice of undissembled joy;
And thick around the woodland hymns arise.
Roused by the cock, the soon-clad shepherd leaves
His mossy cottage, where with peace he dwells ;
And from the crowded fold in order drives   65
His flock to taste the verdure of the morn.
　　Falsely luxurious, will not man awake,
And, springing from the bed of sloth, enjoy
The cool, the fragrant, and the silent hour,
To meditation due and sacred song?   70
For is there aught in sleep can charm the wise?
To lie in dead oblivion, losing half
The fleeting moments of too short a life,—
Total extinction of the enlightened soul!
Or else to feverish vanity alive,   75
Wildered, and tossing through distempered dreams!
Who would in such a gloomy state remain
Longer than Nature craves, when every muse
And every blooming pleasure wait without
To bless the wildly-devious morning-walk?   80
　　But yonder comes the powerful king of day
Rejoicing in the east. The lessening cloud,
The kindling azure, and the mountain's brow
Illumed with fluid gold, his near approach
Betoken glad. Lo! now, apparent all,   85
Aslant the dew-bright earth and coloured air
He looks in boundless majesty abroad,
And sheds the shining day, that burnished plays
On rocks, and hills, and towers, and wandering streams,
High-gleaming from afar. Prime cheerer, Light!   90
Of all material beings first and best ;
Efflux divine ; nature's resplendent robe,
Without whose vesting beauty all were wrapt
In unessential gloom! and thou, O Sun!
Soul of surrounding worlds, in whom best seen   95
Shines out thy Maker, may I sing of thee!
　　'Tis by thy secret strong attractive force,

As with a chain indissoluble bound,
Thy system rolls entire,—from the far bourn
Of utmost Saturn, wheeling wide his round   100
Of thirty years, to Mercury, whose disk
Can scarce be caught by philosophic eye,
Lost in the near effulgence of thy blaze.
　　Informer of the planetary train,
Without whose quickening glance their cumbrous orbs 105
Were brute unlovely mass, inert and dead,
And not as now the green abodes of life—
How many forms of being wait on thee
Inhaling spirit, from the unfettered mind,
By thee sublimed, down to the daily race,   110
The mixing myriads of thy setting beam.
　　The vegetable world is also thine,
Parent of Seasons! who the pomp precede
That waits thy throne, as through thy vast domain,
Annual, along the bright ecliptic-road,   115
In world-rejoicing state it moves sublime.
Meantime the expecting nations, circled gay
With all the various tribes of foodful earth,
Implore thy bounty, or send grateful up
A common hymn; while round thy beaming car   120
High-seen the Seasons lead, in sprightly dance
Harmonious knit, the rosy-fingered hours,
The zephyrs floating loose, the timely rains,
Of bloom ethereal the light-footed dews,
And, softened into joy, the surly storms.   125
These in successive turn with lavish hand
Shower every beauty, every fragrance shower,
Herbs, flowers, and fruits; till, kindling at thy touch,
From land to land is flushed the vernal year.
　　Nor to the surface of enlivened earth,   130
Graceful with hills and dales, and leafy woods—
Her liberal tresses—is thy force confined;
But, to the bowelled cavern darting deep,
The mineral kinds confess thy mighty power.

Effulgent hence the veiny marble shines;   135
Hence labour draws his tools; hence burnished war
Gleams on the day; the nobler works of peace
Hence bless mankind; and generous commerce binds
The round of nations in a golden chain.

    The unfruitful rock itself, impregned by thee,   140
In dark retirement forms the lucid stone.
The lively diamond drinks thy purest rays,
Collected light compact! that, polished bright,
And all its native lustre let abroad,
Dares, as it sparkles on the fair one's breast,   145
With vain ambition emulate her eyes.
At thee the ruby lights its deepening glow,
And with a waving radiance inward flames.
From thee the sapphire, solid ether, takes
Its hue cerulean; and, of evening tinct,   150
The purple-streaming amethyst is thine.
With thy own smile the yellow topaz burns;
Nor deeper verdure dyes the robe of Spring
When first she gives it to the southern gale
Than the green emerald shows. But, all combined, 155
Thick through the whitening opal play thy beams;
Or, flying several from its surface, form
A trembling variance of revolving hues
As the site varies in the gazer's hand.

    The very dead creation from thy touch   160
Assumes a mimic life. By thee refined,
In brighter mazes the reluctent stream
Plays o'er the mead. The precipice abrupt,
Projecting horror on the blackened flood,
Softens at thy return. The desert joys   165
Wildly through all his melancholy bounds.
Rude ruins glitter; and the briny deep,
Seen from some pointed promontory's top,
Far to the blue horizon's utmost verge
Restless reflects a floating gleam. But this,   170
And all the much-transported muse can sing,

Are to thy beauty, dignity, and use,
Unequal far, great delegated source
Of light, and life, and grace, and joy below!
   How shall I then attempt to sing of Him,   175
Who, Light Himself, in uncreated light
Invested deep, dwells awfully retired
From mortal eye or angels' purer ken?
Whose single smile has, from the first of time,
Filled overflowing all those lamps of heaven,   180
That beam for ever through the boundless sky:
But, should He hide His face, the astonished sun,
And all the extinguished stars, would loosening reel
Wide from their spheres, and chaos come again.
   And yet was every faltering tongue of man,   185
Almighty Father! silent in Thy praise,
Thy works themselves would raise a general voice;
Even in the depth of solitary woods,
By human foot untrod, proclaim Thy power;
And, to the quire celestial, Thee resound,   190
The eternal cause, support, and end of all!
   To me be Nature's volume broad-displayed;
And to peruse its all-instructing page,
Or, haply catching inspiration thence,
Some easy passage raptured to translate,   195
My sole delight,—as through the falling glooms
Pensive I stray, or with the rising dawn
On fancy's eagle-wing excursive soar.

   Now flaming up the heavens, the potent sun
Melts into limpid air the high-raised clouds   200
And morning fogs that hovered round the hills
In party-coloured bands, till wide unveiled
The face of Nature shines, from where earth seems,
Far-stretched around, to meet the bending sphere.
   Half in a blush of clustering roses lost,   205
Dew-dropping Coolness to the shade retires,
There, on the verdant turf or flowery bed,

By gelid founts and careless rills to muse;
While tyrant Heat, dispreading through the sky
With rapid sway, his burning influence darts   210
On man, and beast, and herb, and tepid stream.
　Who can unpitying see the flowery race,
Shed by the morn, their new-flushed bloom resign
Before the parching beam? So fade the fair
When fevers revel through their azure veins.   215
But one, the lofty follower of the sun,
Sad when he sets, shuts up her yellow leaves,
Drooping all night; and, when he warm returns,
Points her enamoured bosom to his ray.
　Home from his morning task the swain retreats,   220
His flock before him stepping to the fold;
While the full-uddered mother lows around
The cheerful cottage, then expecting food,
The food of innocence and health. The daw,
The rook, and magpie, to the grey-grown oaks   225
That the calm village in their verdant arms
Sheltering embrace, direct their lazy flight;
Where on the mingling boughs they sit embowered
All the hot noon, till cooler hours arise.
Faint underneath the household fowls convene;   230
And in a corner of the buzzing shade
The housedog, with the vacant greyhound, lies
Out-stretched and sleepy. In his slumbers one
Attacks the nightly thief, and one exults
O'er hill and dale; till, wakened by the wasp,   235
They starting snap. Nor shall the muse disdain
To let the little noisy summer-race
Live in her lay and flutter through her song;
Not mean though simple,—to the sun allied,
From him they draw their animating fire.   240
　Waked by his warmer ray, the reptile young
Come winged abroad; by the light air upborne,
Lighter, and full of soul. From every chink
And secret corner, where they slept away

The wintry storms, or rising from their tombs   245
To higher life, [by myriads forth at once
Swarming they pour, of all the varied hues
Their beauty-beaming parent can disclose.]
Ten thousand forms, ten thousand different tribes
People the blaze. To sunny waters some   250
By fatal instinct fly; where on the pool
They sportive wheel, or sailing down the stream
Are snatched immediate by the quick-eyed trout
Or darting salmon. Through the greenwood glade
Some love to stray,—there lodged, amused, and fed   255
In the fresh leaf. Luxurious, others make
The meads their choice, and visit every flower
And every latent herb; for the sweet task
To propagate their kinds, and where to wrap
In what soft beds their young, yet undisclosed,   260
Employs their tender care. Some to the house,
The fold, the dairy, hungry bend their flight,
Sip round the pail, or taste the curdling cheese:
Oft, inadvertent, from the milky stream
They meet their fate; or, weltering in the bowl,   265
With powerless wings around them wrapt, expire.
   But chief to heedless flies the window proves
A constant death; where gloomily retired
The villain spider lives, cunning and fierce,
Mixture abhorred! Amid a mangled heap   270
Of carcases in eager watch he sits,
O'erlooking all his waving snares around.
Near the dire cell the dreadless wanderer oft
Passes: as oft the ruffian shows his front.
The prey at last ensnared, he dreadful darts   275
With rapid glide along the leaning line,
And, fixing in the wretch his cruel fangs,
Strikes backward, grimly pleased: the fluttering wing
And shriller sound declare extreme distress,
And ask the helping hospitable hand.   280
   Resounds the living surface of the ground.

Nor undelightful is the ceaseless hum
To him who muses through the woods at noon;
Or drowsy shepherd, as he lies reclined
With half-shut eyes beneath the floating shade   285
Of willows grey, close-crowding o'er the brook.
   Gradual from these what numerous kinds descend,
Evading even the microscopic eye!
Full nature swarms with life; one wondrous mass
Of animals, or atoms organised,   290
Waiting the vital breath, when Parent-Heaven
Shall bid his spirit blow. The hoary fen
In putrid streams emits the living cloud
Of pestilence. Through subterranean cells,
Where searching sunbeams scarce can find a way,   295
Earth animated heaves. The flowery leaf
Wants not its soft inhabitants. Secure
Within its winding citadel the stone
Holds multitudes. But chief the forest-boughs,
That dance unnumbered to the playful breeze,   300
The downy orchard, and the melting pulp
Of mellow fruit the nameless nations feed
Of evanescent insects. Where the pool
Stands mantled o'er with green, invisible
Amid the floating verdure, millions stray.   305
Each liquid too, whether it pierces, soothes,
Inflames, refreshes, or exalts the taste,
With various forms abounds. Nor is the stream
Of purest crystal, nor the lucid air,
Though one transparent vacancy it seems,   310
Void of their unseen people. These, concealed
By the kind art of forming Heaven, escape
The grosser eye of man; for, if the worlds
In worlds enclosed should on his senses burst,
From cates ambrosial and the nectared bowl   315
He would abhorrent turn, and in dead night,
When silence sleeps o'er all, be stunned with noise.
   Let no presuming impious railer tax

Creative Wisdom, as if aught was formed
In vain, or not for admirable ends.   320
Shall little haughty Ignorance pronounce
His works unwise, of-which the smallest part
Exceeds the narrow vision of her mind?
As if, upon a full proportioned dome
On swelling columns heaved—the pride of art,   325
A critic-fly, whose feeble ray scarce spreads
An inch around, with blind presumption bold
Should dare to tax the structure of the whole.
And lives the man whose universal eye
Has swept at once the unbounded scheme of things,   330
Marked their dependence so, and firm accord,
As with unfaltering accent to conclude
That this availeth nought? Has any seen
The mighty chain of beings, lessening down
From infinite perfection to the brink   335
Of dreary nothing, desolate abyss!
From which astonished thought recoiling turns?
Till then, alone let zealous praise ascend
And hymns of holy wonder to that Power
Whose wisdom shines as lovely on our minds   340
As on our smiling eyes his servant-sun.
    Thick in yon stream of light, a thousand ways
Upward and downward thwarting and convolved,
The quivering nations sport; till, tempest-winged,
Fierce Winter sweeps them from the face of day.   345
Even so luxurious men unheeding pass
An idle summer life in fortune's shine,
A season's glitter! Thus they flutter on
From toy to toy, from vanity to vice;
Till, blown away by death, oblivion comes   350
Behind, and strikes them from the book of life.

    Now swarms the village o'er the jovial mead,—
The rustic youth, brown with meridian toil,
Healthful and strong; full as the summer rose

Blown by prevailing suns, the ruddy maid,   355
Half naked, swelling on the sight, and all
Her kindling graces burning o'er her cheek.
Even stooping age is here; and infant hands
Trail the long rake, or, with the fragrant load
O'ercharged, amid the kind oppression roll.   360
Wide flies the tedded grain; all in a row
Advancing broad, or wheeling round the field,
They spread their breathing harvest to the sun,
That throws refreshful round a rural smell;
Or, as they rake the green-appearing ground,   365
And drive the dusky wave along the mead,
The russet haycock rises thick behind,
In order gay; while, heard from dale to dale,
Waking the breeze, resounds the blended voice
Of happy labour, love, and social glee.   370
  Or, rushing thence in one diffusive band,
They drive the troubled flocks, by many a dog
Compelled, to where the mazy-running brook
Forms a deep pool, this bank abrupt and high,
And that fair-spreading in a pebbled shore.   375
Urged to the giddy brink, much is the toil,
The clamour much, of men, and boys, and dogs,
Ere the soft fearful people to the flood
Commit their woolly sides; and oft the swain,
On some impatient seizing, hurls them in.   380
Emboldened then, nor hesitating more,
Fast, fast they plunge amid the flashing wave,
And panting labour to the farthest shore.
Repeated this, till deep the well-washed fleece
Has drunk the flood, and from his lively haunt   385
The trout is banished by the sordid stream,
Heavy and dripping to the breezy brow
Slow move the harmless race; where, as they spread
Their swelling treasures to the sunny ray,
Inly disturbed, and wondering what this wild   390
Outrageous tumult means, their loud complaints

The country fill, and, tossed from rock to rock,
Incessant bleatings run around the hills.
At last of snowy white, the gathered flocks
Are in the wattled pen innumerous pressed,   395
Head above head; and, ranged in lusty rows,
The shepherds sit, and whet the sounding shears.
The housewife waits to roll her fleecy stores,
With all her gay-drest maids attending round.
One, chief, in gracious dignity enthroned,   400
Shines o'er the rest the pastoral queen, and rays
Her smiles sweet-beaming on her shepherd-king;
While the glad circle round them yield their souls
To festive mirth, and wit that knows no gall.
Meantime their joyous task goes on apace.   405
Some mingling stir the melted tar, and some
Deep on the new-shorn vagrant's heaving side
To stamp his master's cipher ready stand;
Others the unwilling wether drag along;
And, glorying in his might, the sturdy boy   410
Holds by the twisted horns the indignant ram.
Behold where bound, and of its robe bereft
By needy man, that all-depending lord,
How meek, how patient the mild creature lies!
What softness in its melancholy face,   415
What dumb-complaining innocence appears!
Fear not, ye gentle tribes, 'tis not the knife
Of horrid slaughter that is o'er you waved;
No, 'tis the tender swain's well-guided shears,
Who having now, to pay his annual care,   420
Borrowed your fleece, to you a cumbrous load,
Will send you bounding to your hills again.
  A simple scene! Yet hence Britannia sees
Her solid grandeur rise: hence she commands
The exalted stores of every brighter clime,   425
The treasures of the sun without his rage:
Hence, fervent all with culture, toil, and arts,
Wide glows her land; her dreadful thunder hence

Rides o'er the waves sublime, and now, even now,
Impending hangs o'er Gallia's humbled coast ;   430
Hence rules the circling deep, and awes the world.

'Tis raging noon ; and, vertical, the sun
Darts on the head direct his forceful rays.
O'er heaven and earth, far as the ranging eye
Can sweep, a dazzling deluge reigns ; and all   435
From pole to pole is undistinguished blaze.
In vain the sight, dejected to the ground,
Stoops for relief ; thence hot-ascending steams
And keen reflection pain. Deep to the root
Of vegetation parched, the cleaving fields   440
And slippery lawn an arid hue disclose,
Blast fancy's bloom, and wither even the soul.
Echo no more returns the cheerful sound
Of sharpening scythe ; the mower, sinking, heaps
O'er him the humid hay, with flowers perfumed ;   445
And scarce a chirping grasshopper is heard
Through the dumb mead. Distressful nature pants.
The very streams look languid from afar ;
Or, through the unsheltered glade, impatient, seem
To hurl into the covert of the grove.   450
   All-conquering heat ! oh intermit thy wrath,
And on my throbbing temples potent thus
Beam not so fierce. Incessant still you flow,
And still another fervent flood succeeds,
Poured on the head profuse. In vain I sigh,   455
And restless turn, and look around for night.
Night is far off ; and hotter hours approach.
Thrice happy he, who on the sunless side
Of a romantic mountain, forest-crowned,
Beneath the whole collected shade reclines ;   460
Or in the gelid caverns, woodbine-wrought,
And fresh bedewed with ever-spouting streams,
Sits coolly calm, while all the world without,
Unsatisfied and sick, tosses in noon,—

Emblem instructive of the virtuous man,   465
Who keeps his tempered mind serene and pure
And every passion aptly harmonized
Amid a jarring world with vice inflamed.
    Welcome, ye shades! ye bowery thickets, hail!
Ye lofty pines! ye venerable oaks!   470
Ye ashes wild, resounding o'er the steep!
Delicious is your shelter to the soul,
As to the hunted hart the sallying spring
Or stream full-flowing, that his swelling sides
Laves as he floats along the herbaged brink.   475
Cool through the nerves your pleasing comfort glides;
The heart beats glad; the fresh expanded eye
And ear resume their watch; the sinews knit;
And life shoots swift through all the lightened limbs.
    Around the adjoining brook that purls along   480
The vocal grove, now fretting o'er a rock,
Now scarcely moving through a reedy pool,
Now starting to a sudden stream, and now
Gently diffused into a limpid plain,
A various group the herds and flocks compose.   485
Rural confusion! On the grassy bank
Some ruminating lie; while others stand
Half in the flood, and often bending sip
The circling surface. In the middle droops
The strong laborious ox, of honest front,   490
Which incomposed he shakes; and from his sides
The troublous insects lashes with his tail,
Returning still. Amid his subjects safe
Slumbers the monarch-swain, his careless arm
Thrown round his head on downy moss sustained,   495
Here laid his scrip with wholesome viands filled,
And there his sceptre-crook and watchful dog.
    Light fly his slumbers, if perchance a flight
Of angry gadflies fasten on the herd,
That startling scatters from the shallow brook   500
In search of lavish stream. Tossing the foam,

They scorn the keeper's voice, and scour the plain
Through all the bright severity of noon,
While from their labouring breasts a hollow moan
Proceeding runs low-bellowing round the hills.   505
  Oft in this season too the horse provoked,
While his big sinews full of spirits swell,
Trembling with vigour, in the heat of blood
Springs the high fence; and, o'er the field effused,
Darts on the gloomy flood with stedfast eye   510
And heart estranged to fear: his nervous chest,
Luxuriant and erect, the seat of strength,
Bears down the opposing stream; quenchless his thirst,
He takes the river at redoubled draughts;
And with wide nostrils snorting skims the wave.   515
  Still let me pierce into the midnight depth
Of yonder grove of wildest largest growth,
That, forming high in air a woodland quire,
Nods o'er the mount beneath. At every step
Solemn and slow the shadows blacker fall,   520
And all is awful listening gloom around.
  These are the haunts of meditation, these
The scenes where ancient bards the inspiring breath
Ecstatic felt, and, from this world retired,
Conversed with angels and immortal forms   525
On gracious errands bent,—to save the fall
Of virtue struggling on the brink of vice;
In waking whispers and repeated dreams
To hint pure thought and warn the favoured soul
For future trials fated to prepare;   530
To prompt the poet, who devoted gives
His muse to better themes; to soothe the pangs
Of dying worth, and from the patriot's breast
(Backward to mingle in detested war,
But foremost when engaged) to turn the death;   535
And numberless such offices of love,
Daily and nightly, zealous to perform.
  Shook sudden from the bosom of the sky

A thousand shapes or glide athwart the dusk
Or stalk majestic on. Deep-roused I feel   540
A sacred terror, a severe delight,
Creep through my mortal frame; and thus, methinks,
A voice, than human more, the abstracted ear
Of fancy strikes : ' Be not of us afraid,
Poor kindred man! thy fellow-creatures we   545
From the same Parent-Power our beings drew;
The same our Lord, and laws, and great pursuit.
Once some of us, like thee, through stormy life
Toiled tempest-beaten ere we could attain
This holy calm, this harmony of mind,   550
Where purity and peace immingle charms.
Then fear not us; but with responsive song,
Amid these dim recesses, undisturbed
By noisy folly and discordant vice,
Of Nature sing with us, and Nature's God.   555
Here frequent, at the visionary hour
When musing midnight reigns or silent noon,
Angelic harps are in full concert heard,
And voices chanting from the wood-crowned hill,
The deepening dale, or inmost sylvan glade,—   560
A privilege bestowed by us alone
On contemplation, or the hallowed ear
Of poet swelling to seraphic strain.'
     And art thou, Stanley, of that sacred band?
Alas, for us too soon! Though raised above   565
The reach of human pain, above the flight
Of human joy, yet with a mingled ray
Of sadly pleased remembrance must thou feel
A mother's love, a mother's tender woe,
Who seeks thee still in many a former scene,   570
Seeks thy fair form, thy lovely beaming eyes,
Thy pleasing converse, by gay lively sense
Inspired, where moral wisdom mildly shone
Without the toil of art, and virtue glowed
In all her smiles without forbidding pride.   575

But, O thou best of parents, wipe thy tears;
Or rather to parental Nature pay
The tears of grateful joy, who for a while
Lent thee this younger self, this opening bloom
Of thy enlightened mind and gentle worth. 580
Believe the muse, the wintry blast of death
Kills not the buds of virtue; no, they spread
Beneath the heavenly beam of brighter suns
Through endless ages into higher powers.

Thus up the mount, in airy vision rapt, 585
I stray, regardless whither, till the sound
Of a near fall of water every sense
Wakes from the charm of thought: swift-shrinking back,
I check my steps, and view the broken scene.

Smooth to the shelving brink a copious flood 590
Rolls fair and placid; where, collected all,
In one impetuous torrent down the steep
It thundering shoots, and shakes the country round.
At first an azure sheet it rushes broad;
Then whitening by degrees as prone it falls, 595
And from the loud-resounding rocks below
Dashed in a cloud of foam, it sends aloft
A hoary mist, and forms a ceaseless shower.
Nor can the tortured wave here find repose,
But, raging still amid the shaggy rocks, 600
Now flashes o'er the scattered fragments, now
Aslant the hollowed channel rapid darts,
And, falling fast from gradual slope to slope
With wild infracted course and lessened roar,
It gains a safer bed, and steals at last 605
Along the mazes of the quiet vale.

Invited from the cliff, to whose dark brow
He clings, the steep-ascending eagle soars
With upward pinions through the flood of day,
And, giving full his bosom to the blaze, 610
Gains on the sun; while all the tuneful race,
Smote with afflictive noon, disordered droop

G

Deep in the thicket, or, from bower to bower
Responsive, force an interrupted strain.
The stockdove only through the forest coos,   615
Mournfully hoarse ; oft ceasing from his plaint
(Short interval of weary woe !) again
The sad idea of his murdered mate,
Struck from his side by savage fowler's guile,
Across his fancy comes, and then resounds   620
A louder song of sorrow through the grove.
   Beside the dewy border let me sit,
All in the freshness of the humid air,
There, in that hollowed rock grotesque and wild,—
An ample chair, moss-lined and overhead,   625
By flowering umbrage shaded, where the bee
Strays diligent, and with the extracted balm
Of fragrant woodbine loads his little thigh.
   Now, while I taste the sweetness of the shade,
While Nature lies around deep lulled in noon,   630
Now come, bold Fancy! spread a daring flight,
And view the wonders of the torrid zone—
Climes unrelenting ! with whose rage compared
Yon blaze is feeble and yon skies are cool.

   See how at once the bright-effulgent sun,   635
Rising direct, swift chases from the sky
The short-lived twilight; and with ardent blaze
Looks gaily fierce through all the dazzling air.
He mounts his throne ; but kind before him sends,
Issuing from out the portals of the morn,   640
The general breeze to mitigate his fire
And breathe refreshment on a fainting world.
Great are the scenes, with dreadful beauty crowned
And barbarous wealth, that see, each circling year,
Returning suns and double seasons pass,—   645
Rocks rich in gems; and mountains big with mines,
That on the high equator ridgy rise,
Whence many a bursting stream auriferous plays;

Majestic woods of every vigorous green,
Stage above stage high waving o'er the hills,   650
Or to the far horizon wide diffused,
A boundless deep immensity of shade.
Here lofty trees, to ancient song unknown,
The noble sons of potent heat and floods
Prone-rushing from the clouds, rear high to heaven   655
Their thorny stems, and broad around them throw
Meridian gloom. Here in eternal prime
Unnumbered fruits, of keen delicious taste
And vital spirit, drink amid the cliffs
And burning sands that bank the shrubby vales   660
Redoubled day; yet in their rugged coats
A friendly juice to cool its rage contain.
   Bear me, Pomona, to thy citron groves,
To where the lemon and the piercing lime
With the deep orange glowing through the green   665
Their lighter glories blend. Lay me reclined
Beneath the spreading tamarind, that shakes,
Fanned by the breeze, its fever-cooling fruit.
Deep in the night the massy locust sheds
Quench my hot limbs; or lead me through the maze, 670
Embowering endless, of the Indian fig;
Or, thrown at gayer ease on some fair brow,
Let me behold, by breezy murmurs cooled,
Broad o'er my head the verdant cedar wave,
And high palmettos lift their graceful shade.   675
Oh, stretched amid these orchards of the sun,
Give me to drain the cocoa's milky bowl,
And from the palm to draw its freshening wine,
More bounteous far than all the frantic juice
Which Bacchus pours. Nor, on its slender twigs   680
Low-bending, be the full pomegranate scorned;
Nor, creeping through the woods, the gelid race   ✓
Of berries. Oft in humble station dwells
Unboastful worth, above fastidious pomp.
Witness, thou best anana, thou the pride   685

Of vegetable life, beyond whate'er
The poets imaged in the golden age!
Quick let me strip thee of thy tufty coat,
Spread thy ambrosial stores, and feast with Jove!
    From these the prospect varies. Plains immense   690
Lie stretched below, interminable meads
And vast savannahs, where the wandering eye,
Unfixed, is in a verdant ocean lost.
Another Flora there, of bolder hues
And richer sweets beyond our garden's pride,   695
Plays o'er the fields, and showers with sudden hand
Exuberant Spring; for oft these valleys shift
Their green-embroidered robe to fiery brown,
And swift to green again, as scorching suns
Or streaming dews and torrent rains prevail.   700
    Along these lonely regions where, retired
From little scenes of art, great Nature dwells
In awful solitude, and nought is seen
But the wild herds that own no master's stall,
Prodigious rivers roll their fattening seas;   705
On whose luxuriant herbage, half-concealed,
Like a fallen cedar, far diffused his train,
Cased in green scales, the crocodile extends.
The flood disparts—behold! in plaited mail
Behemoth rears his head. Glanced from his side,   710
The darted steel in idle shivers flies.
He fearless walks the plain, or seeks the hills,
Where, as he crops his varied fare, the herds
In widening circle round forget their food,
And at the harmless stranger wondering gaze.   715
    Peaceful beneath primeval trees that cast
Their ample shade o'er Niger's yellow stream,
And where the Ganges rolls his sacred wave,
Or 'mid the central depth of blackening woods
High-raised in solemn theatre around,   720
Leans the huge elephant, wisest of brutes!
O truly wise! with gentle might endowed,

Though powerful not destructive. Here he sees
Revolving ages sweep the changeful earth,
And empires rise and fall,—regardless he   725
Of what the never-resting race of men
Project ; thrice happy, could he 'scape their guile
Who mine from cruel avarice his steps;
Or with his towery grandeur swell their state,
The pride of kings; or else his strength pervert, 730
And bid him rage amid the mortal fray,
Astonished at the madness of mankind.
  Wide o'er the winding umbrage of the floods,
Like vivid blossoms glowing from afar,
Thick-swarm the brighter birds; for Nature's hand, 735
That with a sportive vanity has decked
The plumy nations, there her gayest hues
Profusely pours. But if she bids them shine
Arrayed in all the beauteous beams of day,
Yet, frugal still, she humbles them in song.   740
Nor envy we the gaudy robes they lent
Proud Montezuma's realm, whose legions cast
A boundless radiance waving on the sun,
While Philomel is ours,—while in our shades
Through the soft silence of the listening night   745
The sober-suited songstress trills her lay.
  But come, my muse! the desert-barrier burst,
A wild expanse of lifeless sand and sky,
And, swifter than the toiling caravan,
Shoot o'er the vale of Sennar, ardent climb   750
The Nubian mountains, and the secret bounds
Of jealous Abyssinia boldly pierce.
Thou art no ruffian who beneath the mask
Of social commerce com'st to rob their wealth;
No holy fury thou, blaspheming heaven,   755
With consecrated steel to stab their peace,
And through the land, yet red from civil wounds,
To spread the purple tyranny of Rome.
Thou, like the harmless bee, mayst freely range

From mead to mead bright with exalted flowers,   760
From jasmine grove to grove ; mayst wander gay
Through palmy shades and aromatic woods
That grace the plains, invest the peopled hills,
And up the more than Alpine mountains wave.
There, on the breezy summit spreading fair   765
For many a league, or on stupendous rocks
That from the sun-redoubling valley lift
Cool to the middle air their lawny tops,
Where palaces and fanes and villas rise,
And gardens smile around and cultured fields,   770
And fountains gush, and careless herds and flocks
Securely stray, a world within itself
Disdaining all assault—there let me draw
Ethereal soul ; there drink reviving gales
Profusely breathing from the spicy groves   775
And vales of fragrance ; there at distance hear
The roaring floods and cataracts that sweep
From disembowelled earth the virgin gold,
And o'er the varied landscape restless rove,
Fervent with life of every fairer kind.   780
A land of wonders ! which the sun still eyes
With ray direct, as of the lovely realm
Enamoured, and delighting there to dwell.
  How changed the scene ! In blazing height of noon,
The sun, oppressed, is plunged in thickest gloom.   785
Still horror reigns, a dreary twilight round
Of struggling night and day malignant mixed ;
For to the hot equator crowding fast,
Where highly rarefied the yielding air
Admits their stream, incessant vapours roll,   790
Amazing clouds on clouds continual heaped,—
Or whirled tempestuous by the gusty wind,
Or silent borne along, heavy and slow,
With the big stores of steaming oceans charged.
Meantime, amid these upper seas, condensed   795
Around the cold aërial mountain's brow,

And by conflicting winds together dashed,
The thunder holds his black tremendous throne.
From cloud to cloud the rending lightnings rage;
Till, in the furious elemental war   800
Dissolved, the whole precipitated mass
Unbroken floods and solid torrents pours.
   The treasures these, hid from the bounded search
Of ancient knowledge; whence with annual pomp,
Rich king of floods, o'erflows the swelling Nile.   805
From his two springs, in Gojam's sunny realm,
Pure-welling out, he through the lucid lake
Of fair Dambea rolls his infant stream.
There, by the Naiads nursed, he sports away
His playful youth amid the fragrant isles   810
That with unfading verdure smile around.
Ambitious thence the manly river breaks,
And gathering many a flood, and copious fed
With all the mellowed treasures of the sky,
Winds in progressive majesty along.   815
Through splendid kingdoms now devolves his maze;
Now wanders wild o'er solitary tracts
Of life-deserted sand; till, glad to quit
The joyless desert, down the Nubian rocks
From thundering steep to steep he pours his urn,   820
And Egypt joys beneath the spreading wave.
   His brother Niger too, and all the floods
In which the full-formed maids of Afric lave
Their jetty limbs, and all that from the tract
Of woody mountains stretched through gorgeous Ind   825
Fall on Cormandel's coast or Malabar,
From Menam's orient stream, that nightly shines
With insect-lamps, to where Aurora sheds
On Indus' smiling banks the rosy shower—
All at this bounteous season ope their urns,   830
And pour untoiling harvest o'er the land.
   Nor less thy world, Columbus, drinks refreshed
The lavish moisture of the melting year.

Wide o'er his isles the branching Oronoque
Rolls a brown deluge, and the native drives   835
To dwell aloft on life-sufficing trees,
At once his dome, his robe, his food, and arms.
Swelled by a thousand streams impetuous hurled
From all the roaring Andes, huge descends
The mighty Orellana. Scarce the Muse   840
Dares stretch her wing o'er this enormous mass
Of rushing water; scarce she dares attempt
The sea-like Plata,—to whose dread expanse,
Continuous depth, and wondrous length of course,
Our floods are rills. With unabated force   845
In silent dignity they sweep along,
And traverse realms unknown and blooming wilds
And fruitful deserts, worlds of solitude,
Where the sun smiles and seasons teem in vain,
Unseen and unenjoyed. Forsaking these,   850
O'er peopled plains they fair-diffusive flow,
And many a nation feed, and circle safe
In their soft bosom many a happy isle,
The seat of blameless Pan, yet undisturbed
By Christian crimes and Europe's cruel sons.   855
Thus pouring on they proudly seek the deep,
Whose vanquished tide, recoiling from the shock,
Yields to the liquid weight of half the globe;
And ocean trembles for his green domain.
   But what avails this wondrous waste of wealth,   860
This gay profusion of luxurious bliss,
This pomp of Nature? what their balmy meads,
Their powerful herbs, and Ceres void of pain?
By vagrant birds dispersed, and wafting winds,
What their unplanted fruits? what the cool draughts, 865
The ambrosial food, rich gums, and spicy health,
Their forests yield? their toiling insects what,
Their silky pride, and vegetable robes?
Ah! what avail their fatal treasures, hid
Deep in the bowels of the pitying earth,   870

Golconda's gems, and sad Potosi's mines
Where dwelt the gentlest children of the sun?
What all that Afric's golden rivers roll,
Her odorous woods, and shining ivory stores?
Ill-fated race! the softening arts of peace, 875
Whate'er the humanizing muses teach;
The godlike wisdom of the tempered breast;
Progressive truth, the patient force of thought;
Investigation calm, whose silent powers
Command the world; the light that leads to heaven; 880
Kind equal rule, the government of laws,
And all-protecting freedom, which alone
Sustains the name and dignity of man—
These are not theirs. The parent-sun himself
Seems o'er this world of slaves to tyrannize; 885
And, with oppressive ray, the roseate bloom
Of beauty blasting, gives the gloomy hue
And feature gross; or worse, to ruthless deeds,
Mad jealousy, blind rage, and fell revenge,
Their fervid spirit fires. Love dwells not there; 890
The soft regards, the tenderness of life,
The heart-shed tear, the ineffable delight
Of sweet humanity—these court the beam
Of milder climes; in selfish fierce desire
And the wild fury of voluptuous sense 895
There lost. The very brute creation there
This rage partakes, and burns with horrid fire.
  Lo! the green serpent, from his dark abode,
Which even imagination fears to tread,
At noon forth-issuing, gathers up his train 900
In orbs immense, then, darting out anew,
Seeks the refreshing fount, by which diffused
He throws his folds; and while, with threatening tongue
And deathful jaws erect, the monster curls
His flaming crest, all other thirst appalled 905
Or shivering flies, or checked at distance stands,
Nor dares approach. But still more direful he,

The small close-lurking minister of fate,
Whose high-concocted venom through the veins
A rapid lightning darts, arresting swift   910
The vital current. Formed to humble man,
This child of vengeful Nature! There, sublimed
To fearless lust of blood, the savage race
Roam, licensed by the shading hour of guilt
And foul misdeed, when the pure day has shut   915
His sacred eye. The tiger darting fierce
Impetuous on the prey his glance has doomed;
The lively-shining leopard, speckled o'er
With many a spot, the beauty of the waste;
And, scorning all the taming arts of man,   920
The keen hyæna, fellest of the fell—
These, rushing from the inhospitable woods
Of Mauritania, or the tufted isles
That verdant rise amid the Libyan wild,
Innumerous glare around their shaggy king,   925
Majestic stalking o'er the printed sand;
And with imperious and repeated roars
Demand their fated food. The fearful flocks
Crowd near the guardian swain; the nobler herds,
Where round their lordly bull in rural ease   930
They ruminating lie, with horror hear
The coming rage. The awakened village starts;
And to her fluttering breast the mother strains
Her thoughtless infant. From the pirate's den
Or stern Morocco's tyrant fang escaped,   935
The wretch half-wishes for his bonds again;
While, uproar all, the wilderness resounds,
From Atlas eastward to the frighted Nile.
    Unhappy he, who from the first of joys,
Society, cut off, is left alone   940
Amid this world of death. Day after day,
Sad on the jutting eminence he sits,
And views the main that ever toils below,—
Still fondly forming in the farthest verge,

Where the round ether mixes with the wave,   945
Ships, dim-discovered, dropping from the clouds.
At evening to the setting sun he turns
A mournful eye, and down his dying heart
Sinks helpless, while the wonted roar is up
And hiss continual through the tedious night.   950
Yet here, even here, into these black abodes
Of monsters unappalled, from stooping Rome
And guilty Cæsar Liberty retired,
Her Cato following through Numidian wilds,
Disdainful of Campania's gentle plains   955
And all the green delights Ausonia pours
When for them she must bend the servile knee,
And fawning take the splendid robber's boon.
  Nor stop the terrors of these regions here.
Commissioned demons oft, angels of wrath,   960
Let loose the raging elements. Breathed hot
From all the boundless furnace of the sky
And the wide glittering waste of burning sand,
A suffocating wind the pilgrim smites
With instant death. Patient of thirst and toil,   965
Son of the desert, even the camel feels,
Shot through his withered heart, the fiery blast.
Or, from the black-red ether bursting broad,
Sallies the sudden whirlwind. Straight the sands,
Commoved around, in gathering eddies play;   970
Nearer and nearer still they darkening come;
Till, with the general all-involving storm
Swept up, the whole continuous wilds arise;
And, by their noonday fount dejected thrown,
Or sunk at night in sad disastrous sleep,   975
Beneath descending hills the caravan
Is buried deep. In Cairo's crowded streets
The impatient merchant, wondering, waits in vain,
And Mecca saddens at the long delay.
  But chief at sea, whose every flexile wave   980
Obeys the blast, the aërial tumult swells.

In the dread ocean, undulating wide
Beneath the radiant line that girts the globe,
The circling Typhon, whirled from point to point,
Exhausting all the rage of all the sky,   985
And dire Ecnephia reign. Amid the heavens,
Falsely serene, deep in a cloudy speck
Compressed, the mighty tempest brooding dwells.
Of no regard save to the skilful eye,
Fiery and foul the small prognostic hangs   990
Aloft, or on the promontory's brow
Musters its force. A faint deceitful calm,
A fluttering gale, the demon sends before
To tempt the spreading sail. Then down at once
Precipitant descends a mingled mass   995
Of roaring winds and flame and rushing floods.
In wild amazement fixed the sailor stands.
Art is too slow ; by rapid fate oppressed,
His broad-winged vessel drinks the whelming tide,
Hid in the bosom of the black abyss.   1000
With such mad seas the daring Gama fought
For many a day and many a dreadful night
Incessant, labouring round the stormy Cape,
By bold ambition led and bolder thirst
Of gold. For then from ancient gloom emerged   1005
The rising world of trade : the genius, then,
Of navigation, that in hopeless sloth
Had slumbered on the vast Atlantic deep
For idle ages, starting, heard at last
The Lusitanian Prince,—who, heaven-inspired,   1010
To love of useful glory roused mankind,
And in unbounded commerce mixed the world.
   Increasing still the terrors of these storms,
His jaws horrific armed with threefold fate,
Here dwells the direful shark. Lured by the scent   1015
Of steaming crowds, of rank disease, and death,
Behold he rushing cuts the briny flood
Swift as the gale can bear the ship along,

And from the partners of that cruel trade
Which spoils unhappy Guinea of her sons   1020
Demands his share of prey, demands themselves.
The stormy fates descend: one death involves
Tyrants and slaves; when straight, their mangled limbs
Crashing at once, he dyes the purple seas
With gore, and riots in the vengeful meal.   1025
  When o'er this world, by equinoctial rains
Flooded immense, looks out the joyless sun,
And draws the copious steam from swampy fens
Where putrefaction into life ferments
And breathes destructive myriads, or from woods,   1030
Impenetrable shades, recesses foul,
In vapours rank and blue corruption wrapt,
Whose gloomy horrors yet no desperate foot
Has ever dared to pierce—then wasteful forth
Walks the dire power of pestilent disease.   1035
A thousand hideous fiends her course attend,
Sick nature blasting, and to heartless woe
And feeble desolation casting down
The towering hopes and all the pride of man;
Such as of late at Carthagena quenched   1040
The British fire. You, gallant Vernon, saw
The miserable scene; you pitying saw
To infant weakness sunk the warrior's arm;
Saw the deep-racking pang, the ghastly form,
The lip pale-quivering, and the beamless eye   1045
No more with ardour bright; you heard the groans
Of agonizing ships from shore to shore;
Heard, nightly plunged amid the sullen waves,
The frequent corse,—while, on each other fixed,
In sad presage the blank assistants seemed   1050
Silent to ask whom Fate would next demand.
  What need I mention those inclement skies
Where frequent o'er the sickening city Plague,
The fiercest child of Nemesis divine,
Descends? From Ethiopia's poisoned woods,   1055

From stifled Cairo's filth, and fetid fields
With locust-armies putrefying heaped,
This great destroyer sprung. Her awful rage
The brutes escape: man is her destined prey,
Intemperate man, and o'er his guilty domes   1060
She draws a close incumbent cloud of death,
Uninterrupted by the living winds,
Forbid to blow a wholesome breeze, and stained
With many a mixture by the sun, suffused,
Of angry aspect. Princely wisdom then   1065
Dejects his watchful eye ; and from the hand
Of feeble justice ineffectual drop
The sword and balance. Mute the voice of joy,
And hushed the clamour of the busy world.
Empty the streets, with uncouth verdure clad ;   1070
Into the worst of deserts sudden turned
The cheerful haunt of men,—unless, escaped
From the doomed house where matchless horror reigns,
Shut up by barbarous fear, the smitten wretch
With frenzy wild breaks loose, and, loud to heaven 1075
Screaming, the dreadful policy arraigns
Inhuman and unwise. The sullen door,
Yet uninfected, on its cautious hinge
Fearing to turn, abhors society.
Dependants, friends, relations, love himself,   1080
Savaged by woe, forget the tender tie,
The sweet engagement of the feeling heart.
But vain their selfish care : the circling sky,
The wide enlivening air is full of fate ;
And, struck by turns, in solitary pangs   1085
They fall unblest, untended, and unmourned.
Thus o'er the prostrate city black despair
Extends her raven wing ; while, to complete
The scene of desolation, stretched around
The grim guards stand, denying all retreat,   1090
And give the flying wretch a better death.
    Much yet remains unsung,—the rage intense

Of brazen-vaulted skies, of iron fields
Where drought and famine starve the blasted year;
Fired by the torch of noon to tenfold rage,   1095
The infuriate hill that shoots the pillared flame;
And, roused within the subterranean world,
The expanding earthquake, that resistless shakes
Aspiring cities from their solid base,
And buries mountains in the flaming gulf.   1100
But 'tis enough; return, my vagrant muse,—
A nearer scene of horror calls thee home.

Behold, slow-settling o'er the lurid grove,
Unusual darkness broods, and growing gains
The full possession of the sky, surcharged   1105
With wrathful vapour, from the secret beds
Where sleep the mineral generations drawn.
Thence nitre, sulphur, and the fiery spume
Of fat bitumen, steaming on the day,
With various-tinctured trains of latent flame,   1110
Pollute the sky, and in yon baleful cloud
A reddening gloom, a magazine of fate,
Ferment; till, by the touch ethereal roused,
The dash of clouds, or irritating war
Of fighting winds, while all is calm below,   1115
They furious spring. A boding silence reigns
Dread through the dun expanse, save the dull sound
That from the mountain, previous to the storm,
Rolls o'er the muttering earth, disturbs the flood,
And stirs the forest-leaf without a breath.   1120
Prone to the lowest vale the aërial tribes
Descend; the tempest-loving raven scarce
Dares wing the dubious dusk. In rueful gaze
The cattle stand, and on the scowling heavens
Cast a deploring eye, by man forsook—   1125
Who to the crowded cottage hies him fast,
Or seeks the shelter of the downward cave.
  'Tis listening fear and dumb amazement all,

When to the startled eye the sudden glance
Appears far south eruptive through the cloud,   1130
And following slower in explosion vast
The thunder raises his tremendous voice.
At first, heard solemn o'er the verge of heaven,
The tempest growls; but, as it nearer comes
And rolls its awful burden on the wind,   1135
The lightnings flash a larger curve, and more
The noise astounds, till over head a sheet
Of livid flame discloses wide, then shuts
And opens wider, shuts and opens still
Expansive, wrapping ether in a blaze.   1140
Follows the loosened aggravated roar,
Enlarging, deepening, mingling, peal on peal
Crushed horrible, convulsing heaven and earth.
   Down comes a deluge of sonorous hail,
Or prone-descending rain. Wide-rent, the clouds   1145
Pour a whole flood; and yet, its flame unquenched,
The inconquerable lightning struggles through,
Ragged and fierce or in red whirling balls,
And fires the mountains with redoubled rage.
Black from the stroke, above, the smouldering pine   1150
Stands a sad shattered trunk; and, stretched below,
A lifeless group the blasted cattle lie,
Here the soft flocks, with that same harmless look
They wore alive, and ruminating still
In fancy's eye, and there the frowning bull,   1155
And ox half-raised. Struck on the castled cliff,
The venerable tower and spiry fane
Resign their aged pride. The gloomy woods
Start at the flash, and from their deep recess,
Wide-flaming out, their trembling inmates shake.   1160
Amid Carnarvon's mountains rages loud
The repercussive roar; with mighty crush,
Into the flashing deep, from the rude rocks
Of Penmanmaur heaped hideous to the sky,
Tumble the smitten cliffs; and Snowdon's peak,   1165

Dissolving, instant yields his wintry load.
Far seen the heights of heathy Cheviot blaze,
And Thule bellows through her utmost isles.
    Guilt hears appalled, with deeply troubled thought.
And yet not always on the guilty head   1170
Descends the fated flash. Young Celadon
And his Amelia were a matchless pair,
With equal virtue formed and equal grace—
The same, distinguished by their sex alone :
Hers the mild lustre of the blooming morn,   1175
And his the radiance of the risen day.
    They loved ; but such their guileless passion was
As in the dawn of time informed the heart
Of innocence and undissembling truth.
'Twas friendship heightened by the mutual wish,   1180
The enchanting hope, and sympathetic glow
Beamed from the mutual eye. Devoting all
To love, each was to each a dearer self,
Supremely happy in the awakened power
Of giving joy. Alone amid the shades   1185
Still in harmonious intercourse they lived
The rural day, and talked the flowing heart,
Or sighed and looked unutterable things.
    So passed their life, a clear united stream,
By care unruffled ; till, in evil hour,   1190
The tempest caught them on the tender walk,
Heedless how far and where its mazes strayed,
While, with each other blest, creative love
Still bade eternal Eden smile around.
Presaging instant fate, her bosom heaved   1195
Unwonted sighs, and stealing oft a look
Of the big gloom, on Celadon her eye
Fell tearful, wetting her disordered cheek.
In vain assuring love and confidence
In Heaven repressed her fear ; it grew, and shook 1200
Her frame near dissolution. He perceived
The unequal conflict, and, as angels look

H

On dying saints, his eyes compassion shed,
With love illumined high. 'Fear not,' he said,
'Sweet innocence! thou stranger to offence,   1205
And inward storm! He who yon skies involves
In frowns of darkness ever smiles on thee
With kind regard. O'er thee the secret shaft,
That wastes at midnight or the undreaded hour
Of noon, flies harmless; and that very voice   1210
Which thunders terror through the guilty heart,
With tongues of seraphs whispers peace to thine.
'Tis safety to be near thee, sure, and thus
To clasp perfection!' From his void embrace
(Mysterious Heaven!) that moment to the ground,   1215
A blackened corse, was struck the beauteous maid.
But who can paint the lover, as he stood,
Pierced by severe amazement, hating life,
Speechless, and fixed in all the death of woe?
So (faint resemblance) on the marble tomb   1220
The well-dissembled mourner stooping stands,
For ever silent and for ever sad.

    As from the face of heaven the shattered clouds
Tumultuous rove, the interminable sky
Sublimer swells, and o'er the world expands   1225
A purer azure. Nature from the storm
Shines out afresh; and through the lightened air
A higher lustre and a clearer calm
Diffusive tremble; while, as if in sign
Of danger past, a glittering robe of joy,   1230
Set off abundant by the yellow ray,
Invests the fields, and nature smiles revived.
    'Tis beauty all, and grateful song around,
Joined to the low of kine and numerous bleat
Of flocks thick-nibbling through the clovered vale.   1235
And shall the hymn be marred by thankless man,
Most-favoured, who with voice articulate
Should lead the chorus of this lower world?

Shall he, so soon forgetful of the hand
That hushed the thunder, and serenes the sky,　　　1240
Extinguished feel that spark the tempest waked,
That sense of powers exceeding far his own,
Ere yet his feeble heart has lost its fears?
　　Cheered by the milder beam, the sprightly youth
Speeds to the well-known pool whose crystal depth　　1245
A sandy bottom shows.　Awhile he stands
Gazing the inverted landscape, half afraid
To meditate the blue profound below;
Then plunges headlong down the circling flood.
His ebon tresses and his rosy cheek　　　1250
Instant emerge; and through the obedient wave,
At each short breathing by his lip repelled,
With arms and legs according well, he makes,
As humour leads, an easy winding path;
While from his polished sides a dewy light　　　1255
Effuses on the pleased spectators round.
　　This is the purest exercise of health,
The kind refresher of the summer heats;
Nor, when cold Winter keens the brightening flood,
Would I weak-shivering linger on the brink.　　　1260
Thus life redoubles; and is oft preserved
By the bold swimmer in the swift illapse
Of accident disastrous.　Hence the limbs
Knit into force; and the same Roman arm
That rose victorious o'er the conquered earth　　　1265
First learned while tender to subdue the wave.
Even from the body's purity the mind
Receives a secret sympathetic aid.

　　Close in the covert of a hazel copse,
Where winded into pleasing solitudes　　　1270
Runs out the rambling dale, young Damon sat,
Pensive, and pierced with love's delightful pangs.
There to the stream that down the distant rocks
Hoarse-murmuring fell, and plaintive breeze that played

H 2

Among the bending willows, falsely he   1275
Of Musidora's cruelty complained.
She felt his flame; but deep within her breast,
In bashful coyness or in maiden pride,
The soft return concealed,—save when it stole
In sidelong glances from her downcast eye,   1280
Or from her swelling soul in stifled sighs.
Touched by the scene, no stranger to his vows,
He framed a melting lay to try her heart,
And, if an infant passion struggled there,
To call that passion forth. Thrice happy swain!   1285
A lucky chance, that oft decides the fate
Of mighty monarchs, then decided thine.
For lo! conducted by the laughing loves,
This cool retreat his Musidora sought.
Warm in her cheek the sultry season glowed: 1290
And, robed in loose array, she came to bathe
Her fervent limbs in the refreshing stream.
What shall he do? In sweet confusion lost,
And dubious flutterings, he awhile remained.
A pure ingenuous elegance of soul,   1295
A delicate refinement, known to few,
Perplexed his breast and urged him to retire:
But love forbade. Ye prudes in virtue, say,
Say, ye severest, what would you have done?
Meantime, this fairer nymph than ever blest   1300
Arcadian stream, with timid eye around
The banks surveying, stripped her beauteous limbs
To taste the lucid coolness of the flood.
Ah! then, not Paris on the piny top
Of Ida panted stronger, when aside   1305
The rival goddesses the veil divine
Cast unconfined, and gave him all their charms,
Than, Damon, thou, as from the snowy leg
And slender foot the inverted silk she drew;
As the soft touch dissolved the virgin zone,   1310
And through the parting robe the alternate breast,

With youth wild-throbbing, on thy lawless gaze
In full luxuriance rose. But, desperate youth!
How durst thou risk the soul-distracting view,
As from her naked limbs of glowing white,   1315
Harmonious swelled by Nature's finest hand,
In folds loose—floating fell the fainter lawn,
And fair-exposed she stood, shrunk from herself,
With fancy blushing, at the doubtful breeze
Alarmed, and starting like the fearful fawn?   1320
Then to the flood she rushed; the parted flood
Its lovely guest with closing waves received;
And every beauty softening, every grace
Flushing anew a mellow lustre shed,
As shines the lily through the crystal mild,   1325
Or as the rose amid the morning dew,
Fresh from Aurora's hand, more sweetly glows.
While thus she wantoned, now beneath the wave
But ill-concealed, and now with streaming locks,
That half-embraced her in a humid veil,   1330
Rising again, the latent Damon drew
Such maddening draughts of beauty to the soul,
As for awhile o'erwhelmed his raptured thought
With luxury too daring. Checked at last
By love's respectful modesty, he deemed   1335
The theft profane, if aught profane to love
Can e'er be deemed, and struggling from the shade
With headlong fury fled; but first these lines,
Traced by his ready pencil, on the bank
With trembling hand he threw: 'Bathe on, my fair, 1340
Yet unbeheld—save by the sacred eye
Of faithful love; I go to guard thy haunt,
To keep from thy recess each vagrant foot
And each licentious eye.' With wild surprise,
As if to marble struck, devoid of sense,   1345
A stupid moment motionless she stood:
So stands the statue that enchants the world,
So bending tries to veil the matchless boast,

The mingled beauties of exulting Greece.
Recovering, swift she flew to find those robes   1350
Which blissful Eden knew not; and, arrayed
In careless haste, the alarming paper snatched.
But, when her Damon's well-known hand she saw,
Her terrors vanished, and a softer train
Of mixed emotions, hard to be described,   1355
Her sudden bosom seized,—shame void of guilt,
The charming blush of innocence, esteem
And admiration of her lover's flame,
By modesty exalted; even a sense
Of self-approving beauty stole across   1360
Her busy thought. At length a tender calm
Hushed by degrees the tumult of her soul;
And on the spreading beech, that o'er the stream
Incumbent hung, she with the sylvan pen
Of rural lovers this confession carved,   1365
Which soon her Damon kissed with weeping joy:
'Dear youth! sole judge of what these verses mean,
By fortune too much favoured, but by love
Alas! not favoured less, be still as now,
Discreet; the time may come you need not fly.'   1370

   The sun has lost his rage: his downward orb
Shoots nothing now but animating warmth
And vital lustre, that with various ray
Lights up the clouds, those beauteous robes of heaven,
Incessant rolled into romantic shapes,   1375
The dream of waking fancy. Broad below,
Covered with ripening fruits, and swelling fast
Into the perfect year, the pregnant earth
And all her tribes rejoice. Now the soft hour
Of walking comes, for him who lonely loves   1380
To seek the distant hills, and there converse
With Nature—there to harmonize his heart,
And in pathetic song to breathe around
The harmony to others. Social friends,

Attuned to happy unison of soul,   1385
To whose exalting eye a fairer world,
Of which the vulgar never had a glimpse,
Displays its charms, whose minds are richly fraught
With philosophic stores, superior light,
And in whose breast enthusiastic burns   1390
Virtue the sons of interest deem romance,
Now called abroad enjoy the falling day;
Now to the verdant portico of woods,
To Nature's vast Lyceum, forth they walk,—
By that kind School where no proud master reigns,   1395
The full free converse of the friendly heart
Improving and improved. Now from the world,
Sacred to sweet retirement, lovers steal,
And pour their souls in transport, which the sire
Of love approving hears, and calls it good.   1400
Which way, Amanda, shall we bend our course?
The choice perplexes. Wherefore should we choose?
All is the same with thee. Say, shall we wind
Along the streams? or walk the smiling mead?
Or court the forest-glades? or wander wild   1405
Among the waving harvests? or ascend,
While radiant Summer opens all its pride,
Thy hill, delightful Shene? Here let us sweep
The boundless landscape,—now the raptured eye,
Exulting swift, to huge Augusta send,   1410
Now to the sister-hills that skirt her plain,
To lofty Harrow now, and now to where
Majestic Windsor lifts his princely brow.
In lovely contrast to this glorious view
Calmly magnificent, then will we turn   1415
To where the silver Thames first rural grows.
There let the feasted eye unwearied stray;
Luxurious there rove through the pendent woods
That nodding hang o'er Harrington's retreat;
And, stooping thence to Ham's embowering walks,   1420
Beneath whose shades, in spotless peace retired,

With her, the pleasing partner of his heart,
The worthy Queensberry yet laments his Gay,
And polished Cornbury woos the willing muse,
Slow let us trace the matchless vale of Thames   1425
Fair-winding up to where the muses haunt
In Twickenham's bowers, and for their Pope implore
The healing god, to royal Hampton's pile,
To Clermont's terraced height, and Esher's groves,
Where in the sweetest solitude, embraced   1430
By the soft windings of the silent Mole,
From courts and senates Pelham finds repose.
Enchanting vale! beyond whate'er the muse
Has of Achaia or Hesperia sung.
O vale of bliss! O softly swelling hills!   1435
On which the power of cultivation lies,
And joys to see the wonders of his toil.
    Heavens! what a goodly prospect spreads around,
Of hills and dales and woods and lawns and spires
And glittering towns and gilded streams, till all   1440
The stretching landscape into smoke decays!
Happy Britannia! where the Queen of Arts,
Inspiring vigour, LIBERTY, abroad
Walks unconfined even to thy farthest cots,
And scatters plenty with unsparing hand.   1445
    Rich is thy soil, and merciful thy clime;
Thy streams unfailing in the Summer's drought;
Unmatched thy guardian-oaks; thy valleys float
With golden waves; and on thy mountains flocks
Bleat numberless, while, roving round their sides,   1450
Bellow the blackening herds in lusty droves.
Beneath, thy meadows glow, and rise unquelled
Against the mower's scythe. On every hand
Thy villas shine. Thy country teems with wealth;
And Property assures it to the swain,   1455
Pleased, and unwearied in his guarded toil.
    Full are thy cities with the sons of art,
And trade and joy in every busy street

Mingling are heard ; even Drudgery himself,
As at the car he sweats, or dusty hews   1460
The palace-stone, looks gay. Thy crowded ports,
Where rising masts an endless prospect yield,
With labour burn, and echo to the shouts
Of hurried sailor, as he hearty waves
His last adieu, and, loosening every sheet,   1465
Resigns the spreading vessel to the wind.
   Bold, firm, and graceful, are thy generous youth,
By hardship sinewed, and by danger fired,
Scattering the nations where they go, and first
Or on the listed plain or stormy seas.   1470
Mild are thy glories too, as o'er the plans
Of thriving peace thy thoughtful sires preside ;
In genius and substantial learning high ;
For every virtue, every worth, renowned ;
Sincere, plain-hearted, hospitable, kind ;   1475
Yet like the mustering thunder when provoked,
The dread of tyrants, and the sole resource
Of those that under grim impression groan.
   Thy sons of glory many ! Alfred thine,
In whom the splendour of heroic war   1480
And more heroic peace, when governed well,
Combine ; whose hallowed name the virtues saint,
And his own muses love ; the best of kings.
With him thy Edwards and thy Henrys shine,
Names dear to fame ; the first who deep impressed   1485
On haughty Gaul the terror of thy arms,
That awes her genius still. In statesmen thou,
And patriots, fertile. Thine a steady More,
Who with a generous though mistaken zeal
Withstood a brutal tyrant's useful rage ;   1490
Like Cato firm, like Aristides just,
Like rigid Cincinnatus nobly poor ;
A dauntless soul erect, who smiled on death.
Frugal and wise, a Walsingham is thine ;
A Drake, who made thee mistress of the deep   1495

And bore thy name in thunder round the world.
Then flamed thy spirit high ; but who can speak
The numerous worthies of the maiden-reign?
In Raleigh mark their every glory mixed,
Raleigh, the scourge of Spain ! whose breast with all   1500
The sage, the patriot, and the hero burned.
Nor sunk his vigour when a coward reign
The warrior fettered, and at last resigned
To glut the vengeance of a vanquished foe.
Then, active still and unrestrained, his mind   1505
Explored the vast extent of ages past,
And with his prison-hours enriched the world ;
Yet found no times in all the long research
So glorious or so base as those he proved,
In which he conquered, and in which he bled.   1510
Nor can the muse the gallant Sidney pass,
The plume of war ! with early laurels crowned,
The lover's myrtle, and the poet's bay.
A Hampden too is thine, illustrious land !
Wise, strenuous, firm, of unsubmitting soul,   1515
Who stemmed the torrent of a downward age
To slavery prone, and bade thee rise again
In all thy native pomp of freedom bold.
Bright at his call thy age of men effulged,—   ∨
Of men on whom late time a kindling eye   1520
Shall turn, and tyrants tremble while they read.
Bring every sweetest flower, and let me strew
The grave where Russell lies ; whose tempered blood,
With calmest cheerfulness for thee resigned,
Stained the sad annals of a giddy reign   1525
Aiming at lawless power, though meanly sunk
In loose inglorious luxury. With him
His friend, the British Cassius, fearless bled ;
Of high determined spirit, roughly brave,
By ancient learning to the enlightened love   1530
Of ancient freedom warmed. Fair thy renown
In awful sages and in noble bards,

Soon as the light of dawning science spread
Her orient ray, and waked the muses' song.
Thine is a Bacon, hapless in his choice,   1535
Unfit to stand the civil storm of state,
And through the smooth barbarity of courts
With firm but pliant virtue forward still
To urge his course. Him for the studious shade
Kind Nature formed, deep, comprehensive, clear,   1540
Exact, and elegant; in one rich soul
Plato, the Stagyrite, and Tully joined.
The great deliverer he, who from the gloom
Of cloistered monks and jargon-teaching schools
Led forth the true philosophy, there long   1545
Held in the magic chain of words and forms
And definitions void : he led her forth,
Daughter of heaven, who slow-ascending still,
Investigating sure the chain of things,
With radiant finger points to heaven again.   1550
The generous Ashley thine, the friend of man,
Who scanned his nature with a brother's eye,
His weakness prompt to shade, to raise his aim,
To touch the finer movements of the mind,
And with the moral beauty charm the heart.   1555
Why need I name thy Boyle, whose pious search
Amid the dark recesses of His works
The great Creator sought? And why thy Locke,
Who made the whole internal world his own?
Let Newton, pure intelligence, whom God   1560
To mortals lent to trace his boundless works
From laws sublimely simple, speak thy fame
In all philosophy. For lofty sense,
Creative fancy, and inspection keen
Through the deep windings of the human heart,   1565
Is not wild Shakespeare thine and Nature's boast ?
Is not each great, each amiable muse
Of classic ages in thy Milton met?
A genius universal as his theme,

Astonishing as chaos, as the bloom   1570
Of blowing Eden fair, as Heaven sublime.
Nor shall my verse that elder bard forget,
The gentle Spenser, fancy's pleasing son,
Who, like a copious river, poured his song
O'er all the mazes of enchanted ground ;   1575
Nor thee, his ancient master, laughing sage,
Chaucer, whose native manners-painting verse,
Well moralized, shines through the Gothic cloud
Of time and language o'er thy genius thrown.
    May my song soften, as thy daughters I,   1580
Britannia, hail ; for beauty is their own,
The feeling heart, simplicity of life,
And elegance, and taste; the faultless form,
Shaped by the hand of harmony ; the cheek,
Where the live crimson, through the native white 1585
Soft-shooting, o'er the face diffuses bloom
And every nameless grace ; the parted lip,
Like the red rosebud moist with morning dew,
Breathing delight; and, under flowing jet,
Or sunny ringlets, or of circling brown,   1590
The neck slight-shaded, and the swelling breast;
The look resistless, piercing to the soul,
And by the soul informed, when dressed in love
She sits high-smiling in the conscious eye.
    Island of bliss ! amid the subject seas,   1595
That thunder round thy rocky coast, set up
At once the wonder, terror, and delight
Of distant nations, whose remotest shore
Can soon be shaken by thy naval arm—
Not to be shook thyself, but all assaults   1600
Baffling, as thy hoar cliffs the loud sea-wave.
  O Thou by whose almighty nod the scale
Of empire rises or alternate falls,
Send forth the saving virtues round the land
In bright patrol,—white peace, and social love ; 1605
The tender-looking charity, intent

On gentle deeds, and shedding tears through smiles;
Undaunted truth, and dignity of mind;
Courage, composed and keen; sound temperance,
Healthful in heart and look; clear chastity,   1610
With blushes reddening as she moves along,
Disordered at the deep regard she draws;
Rough industry; activity untired,
With copious life informed, and all awake;
While in the radiant front superior shines   1615
That first paternal virtue, public zeal,
That throws o'er all an equal wide survey,
And, ever musing on the common weal,
Still labours glorious with some great design.

Low walks the sun, and broadens by degrees   1620
Just o'er the verge of day. The shifting clouds
Assembled gay, a richly gorgeous train,
In all their pomp attend his setting throne.
Air, earth, and ocean smile immense. And now,
As if his weary chariot sought the bowers   1625
Of Amphitrite and her tending nymphs.
(So Grecian fable sung) he dips his orb;
Now half immersed; and now, a golden curve,
Gives one bright glance, then total disappears.
  For ever running an enchanted round,   1630
Passes the day, deceitful, vain, and void;
As fleets the vision o'er the formful brain,
This moment hurrying wild the impassioned soul,
The next in nothing lost: 'tis so to him,
The dreamer of this earth, an idle blank.   1635
A sight of horror to the cruel wretch
Who, all day long in sordid pleasure rolled,
Himself a useless load, has squandered vile
Upon his scoundrel train what might have cheered
A drooping family of modest worth.   1640
But to the generous still-improving mind,
That gives the hopeless heart to sing for joy,

Diffusing kind beneficence around
Boastless, as now descends the silent dew,
To him the long review of ordered life   1645
Is inward rapture, only to be felt.
   Confessed from yonder slow-extinguished clouds,
All ether softening, sober evening takes
Her wonted station in the middle air,
A thousand shadows at her beck. First this   1650
She sends on earth; then that of deeper dye
Steals soft behind; and then a deeper still,
In circle following circle, gathers round
To close the face of things. A fresher gale
Begins to wave the wood and stir the stream,   1655
Sweeping with shadowy gust the fields of corn,
While the quail clamours for his running mate.
Wide o'er the thistly lawn, as swells the breeze,
A whitening shower of vegetable down
Amusive floats. The kind impartial care   1660
Of nature nought disdains; thoughtful to feed
Her lowest sons, and clothe the coming year,
From field to field the feathered seeds she wings.
   His folded flock secure, the shepherd home
Hies merry-hearted; and by turns relieves   1665
The ruddy milkmaid of her brimming pail,—
The beauty whom perhaps his witless heart,
Unknowing what the joy-mixed anguish means,
Sincerely loves, by that best language shown
Of cordial glances and obliging deeds.   1670
Onward they pass o'er many a panting height
And valley sunk and unfrequented, where
At fall of eve the fairy people throng,
In various game and revelry to pass
The summer-night, as village-stories tell.   1675
But far about they wander from the grave
Of him whom his ungentle fortune urged
Against his own sad breast to lift the hand
Of impious violence. The lonely tower

Is also shunned, whose mournful chambers hold   1680
(So night-struck fancy dreams) the yelling ghost.
   Among the crooked lanes, on every hedge,
The glow-worm lights his lamp, and through the dark
Twinkles a moving gem. On Evening's heel
Night follows fast; not in her winter robe   1685
Of massy Stygian woof, but loose arrayed
In mantle dun. A faint erroneous ray,
Glanced from the imperfect surfaces of things,
Flings half an image on the straining eye,
While wavering woods and villages and streams   1690
And rocks and mountain-tops, that long retained
The ascending gleam, are all one swimming scene,
Uncertain if beheld. Sudden to heaven
Thence weary vision turns; where, leading soft
The silent hours of love, with purest ray   1695
Sweet Venus shines, and from her genial rise,
When daylight sickens, till it springs afresh,
Unrivalled reigns the fairest lamp of night.
As thus the effulgence tremulous I drink
With cherished gaze, the lambent lightnings shoot   1700
Across the sky, or horizontal dart
In wondrous shapes, by fearful murmuring crowds
Portentous deemed. Amid the radiant orbs
That more than deck, that animate the sky,
The life-infusing suns of other worlds,   1705
Lo! from the dread immensity of space
Returning, with accelerated course
The rushing comet to the sun descends;
And, as he sinks below the shading earth,
With awful train projected o'er the heavens,   1710
The guilty nations tremble. But, above
Those superstitious horrors that enslave
The fond sequacious herd, to mystic faith
And blind amazement prone, the enlightened few,
Whose godlike minds philosophy exalts,   1715
The glorious stranger hail. They feel a joy

Divinely great; they in their power exult,—
That wondrous force of thought which mounting spurns
This dusky spot and measures all the sky,
While from his far excursion through the wilds   1720
Of barren ether, faithful to his time,
They see the blazing wonder rise anew,
In seeming terror clad, but kindly bent
To work the will of all-sustaining Love,—
From his huge vapoury train perhaps to shake   1725
Reviving moisture on the numerous orbs
Through which his long ellipsis winds, perhaps
To lend new fuel to declining suns,
To light up worlds, and feed the eternal fire.

   With thee, serene Philosophy! with thee   1730
And thy bright garland let me crown my song.
Effusive source of evidence and truth!
A lustre shedding o'er the ennobled mind
Stronger than summer noon, and pure as that
Whose mild vibrations soothe the parted soul   1735
New to the dawning of celestial day.
Hence through her nourished powers, enlarged by thee,
She springs aloft with elevated pride
Above the tangling mass of low desires
That bind the fluttering crowd, and, angel-winged,   1740
The heights of science and of virtue gains
Where all is calm and clear, with nature round,
Or in the starry regions or the abyss,
To reason's and to fancy's eye displayed,—
The first up-tracing from the dreary void   1745
The chain of causes and effects to Him,
The world-producing Essence, who alone
Possesses being; while the last receives
The whole magnificence of heaven and earth,
And every beauty, delicate or bold,   1750
Obvious or more remote, with livelier sense,
Diffusive painted on the rapid mind.

   Tutored by thee, hence poetry exalts

Her voice to ages, and informs the page
With music, image, sentiment, and thought,   1755
Never to die,—the treasure of mankind,
Their highest honour, and their truest joy!
　Without thee what were unenlightened man?
A savage roaming through the woods and wilds
In quest of prey; and with the unfashioned fur   1760
Rough-clad; devoid of every finer art
And elegance of life. Nor happiness
Domestic, mixed of tenderness and care,
Nor moral excellence, nor social bliss,
Nor guardian law were his; nor various skill   1765
To turn the furrow, or to guide the tool
Mechanic; nor the heaven-conducted prow
Of navigation bold, that fearless braves
The burning line or dares the wintry pole,—
Mother severe of infinite delights!   1770
Nothing save rapine, indolence, and guile,
And woes on woes, a still-revolving train,
Whose horrid circle had made human life
Than non-existence worse; but, taught by thee,
Ours are the plans of policy and peace   1775
To live like brothers, and conjunctive all
Embellish life. While thus laborious crowds
Ply the tough oar, philosophy directs
The ruling helm; or, like the liberal breath
Of potent heaven, invisible, the sail   1780
Swells out, and bears the inferior world along.
　Nor to this evanescent speck of earth
Poorly confined, the radiant tracts on high
Are her exalted range; intent to gaze
Creation through, and, from that full complex   1785
Of never-ending wonders, to conceive
Of the Sole Being right, who spoke the word,
And Nature moved complete. With inward view,
Thence on the ideal kingdom swift she turns
Her eye, and instant at her powerful glance   1790

I

The obedient phantoms vanish or appear,
Compound, divide, and into order shift,
Each to his rank, from plain perception up
To the fair forms of fancy's fleeting train ;
To reason then, deducing truth from truth,   1795
And notion quite abstract; where first begins
The world of spirits, action all, and life
Unfettered and unmixed. But here the cloud
(So wills Eternal Providence) sits deep.
Enough for us to know that this dark state,   1800
In wayward passions lost and vain pursuits,
This infancy of being, cannot prove
The final issue of the works of God,
By boundless love and perfect wisdom formed,
And ever rising with the rising mind.   1805

END OF SUMMER.

AUTUMN.

CROWNED with the sickle and the wheaten sheaf,
While Autumn, nodding o'er the yellow plain,
Comes jovial on, the Doric reed once more,
Well pleased, I tune. Whate'er the wintry frost
Nitrous prepared, the various-blossomed Spring   5
Put in white promise forth, and Summer suns
Concocted strong rush boundless now to view,
Full, perfect all, and swell my glorious theme.

Onslow ! the muse, ambitious of thy name
To grace, inspire, and dignify her song,   10
Would from the public voice thy gentle ear
Awhile engage. Thy noble cares she knows,
The patriot virtues that distend thy thought,
Spread on thy front, and in thy bosom glow,
While listening senates hang upon thy tongue   15
Devolving through the maze of eloquence
A roll of periods sweeter than her song.
But she too pants for public virtue; she,
Though weak of power yet strong in ardent will,
Whene'er her country rushes on her heart,   20
Assumes a bolder note, and fondly tries
To mix the patriot's with the poet's flame.

When the bright Virgin gives the beauteous days,
And Libra weighs in equal scales the year,
From heaven's high cope the fierce effulgence shook   25
Of parting Summer, a serener blue,
With golden light enlivened, wide invests

The happy world. Attempered suns arise,
Sweet-beamed, and shedding oft through lucid clouds
A pleasing calm ; while broad and brown below   30
Extensive harvests hang the heavy head.
Rich, silent, deep they stand ; for not a gale
Rolls its light billows o'er the bending plain.
A calm of plenty ! till the ruffled air
Falls from its poise, and gives the breeze to blow.   35
Rent is the fleecy mantle of the sky ;
The clouds fly different ; and the sudden sun
By fits effulgent gilds the illumined field,
And black by fits the shadows sweep along.
A gaily-chequered heart-expanding view,   40
Far as the circling eye can shoot around
Unbounded tossing in a flood of corn.
   These are thy blessings, Industry ! rough power
Whom labour still attends and sweat and pain,
Yet the kind source of every gentle art   45
And all the soft civility of life,
Raiser of human kind, by Nature cast
Naked and helpless out amid the woods
And wilds to rude inclement elements,
With various seeds of art deep in the mind   50
Implanted, and profusely poured around
Materials infinite, but idle all.
Still unexerted, in the unconscious breast
Slept the lethargic powers ; corruption still
Voracious swallowed what the liberal hand   55
Of bounty scattered o'er the savage year ;
And still the sad barbarian roving mixed
With beasts of prey, or for his acorn meal
Fought the fierce tusky boar. A shivering wretch !
Aghast and comfortless when the bleak north,   60
With Winter charged, let the mixed tempest fly,
Hail, rain, and snow, and bitter-breathing frost.
Then to the shelter of the hut he fled,
And the wild season, sordid, pined away ;

For home he had not : home is the resort   65
Of love, of joy, of peace and plenty, where,
Supporting and supported, polished friends
And dear relations mingle into bliss.
But this the rugged savage never felt,
Even desolate in crowds ; and thus his days   70
Rolled heavy, dark, and unenjoyed along,
A waste of time ! till Industry approached
And roused him from his miserable sloth,
His faculties unfolded, pointed out
Where lavish Nature the directing hand   75
Of art demanded, showed him how to raise
His feeble force by the mechanic powers,
To dig the mineral from the vaulted earth,
On what to turn the piercing rage of fire,
On what the torrent and the gathered blast ;   80
Gave the tall ancient forest to his axe,
Taught him to chip the wood and hew the stone
Till by degrees the finished fabric rose ;
Tore from his limbs the blood-polluted fur
And wrapt them in the woolly vestment warm,   85
Or bright in glossy silk and flowing lawn ;
With wholesome viands filled his table, poured
The generous glass around—inspired to wake
The life-refining soul of decent wit ;
Nor stopped at barren bare necessity,   90
But, still advancing bolder, led him on
To pomp, to pleasure, elegance and grace ;
And, breathing high ambition through his soul,
Set science, wisdom, glory, in his view,
And bade him be the lord of all below.   95
   Then gathering men their natural powers combined
And formed a public, to the general good
Submitting, aiming, and conducting all.
For this the patriot-council met, the full,
The free, and fairly represented whole ;   100
For this they planned the holy guardian laws,

Distinguished orders, animated arts,
And, with joint force oppression chaining, set
Imperial justice at the helm, yet still
To them accountable ; nor slavish dreamed   105
That toiling millions must resign their weal
And all the honey of their search to such
As for themselves alone themselves have raised.
  Hence every form of cultivated life,
In order set, protected, and inspired,   110
Into perfection wrought. Uniting all,
Society grew numerous, high, polite,
And happy. Nurse of art, the city reared
In beauteous pride her tower-encircled head ;
And, stretching street on street, by thousands drew,   115
From twining woody haunts, or the tough yew
To bows strong-straining, her aspiring sons.
  Then commerce brought into the public walk
The busy merchant ; the big warehouse built ;
Raised the strong crane ; choked up the loaded street   120
With foreign plenty ; and thy stream, O Thames,
Large, gentle, deep, majestic, king of floods !
Chose for his grand resort. On either hand,
Like a long wintry forest, groves of masts
Shot up their spires ; the bellying sheet between   125
Possessed the breezy void ; the sooty hulk
Steered sluggish on ; the splendid barge along
Rowed regular to harmony ; around,
The boat light-skimming stretched its oary wings ;
While deep the various voice of fervent toil   130
From bank to bank increased,—whence, ribbed with oak
To bear the British thunder, black and bold
The roaring vessel rushed into the main.
  Then too the pillared dome magnific heaved
Its ample roof, and luxury within   135
Poured out her glittering stores : the canvas smooth,
With glowing life protuberant, to the view
Embodied rose ; the statue seemed to breathe

And soften into flesh beneath the touch
Of forming art, imagination-flushed.   140
  All is the gift of Industry,—whate'er
Exalts, embellishes, and renders life
Delightful. Pensive Winter, cheered by him,
Sits at the social fire, and happy hears
The excluded tempest idly rave along;   145
His hardened fingers deck the gaudy Spring;
Without him Summer were an arid waste;
Nor to the Autumnal months could thus transmit
Those full, mature, immeasurable stores
That, waving round, recal my wandering song.   150

  Soon as the morning trembles o'er the sky
And unperceived unfolds the spreading day,
Before the ripened field the reapers stand
In fair array, each by the lass he loves—
To bear the rougher part and mitigate   155
By nameless gentle offices her toil.
At once they stoop and swell the lusty sheaves:
While through their cheerful band the rural talk,
The rural scandal, and the rural jest,
Fly harmless, to deceive the tedious time   160
And steal unfelt the sultry hours away.
Behind the master walks, builds up the shocks,
And conscious, glancing oft on every side
His stated eye, feels his heart heave with joy.
The gleaners spread around, and here and there,   165
Spike after spike, their scanty harvest pick.
Be not too narrow, husbandmen! but fling
From the full sheaf with charitable stealth
The liberal handful. Think, oh! grateful think
How good the God of harvest is to you,   170
Who pours abundance o'er your flowing fields
While these unhappy partners of your kind
Wide-hover round you like the fowls of heaven,
And ask their humble dole. The various turns

Of fortune ponder,—how your sons may want   175
What now with hard reluctance faint ye give.

  The lovely young Lavinia once had friends :
And fortune smiled deceitful on her birth ;
For, in her helpless years deprived of all,
Of every stay save innocence and heaven,   180
She with her widowed mother—feeble, old,
And poor—lived in a cottage far retired
Among the windings of a woody vale,
By solitude and deep surrounding shades
But more by bashful modesty concealed.   185
Together thus they shunned the cruel scorn
Which virtue, sunk to poverty, would meet
From giddy fashion and low-minded pride ;
Almost on nature's common bounty fed ;
Like the gay birds that sung them to repose,   190
Content and careless of to-morrow's fare.
Her form was fresher than the morning rose
When the dew wets its leaves, unstained and pure
As is the lily or the mountain snow.
The modest virtues mingled in her eyes,   195
Still on the ground dejected, darting all
Their humid beams into the blooming flowers ;
Or, when the mournful tale her mother told
Of what her faithless fortune promised once
Thrilled in her thought, they, like the dewy star   200
Of evening, shone in tears. A native grace
Sat fair-proportioned on her polished limbs,
Veiled in a simple robe, their best attire,
Beyond the pomp of dress ; for loveliness
Needs not the foreign aid of ornament,   205
But is when unadorned adorned the most.
Thoughtless of beauty, she was beauty's self,
Recluse amid the close-embowering woods.
As in the hollow breast of Apennine,
Beneath the shelter of encircling hills,   210

A myrtle rises far from human eye
And breathes its balmy fragrance o'er the wild,
So flourished blooming and unseen by all
The sweet Lavinia ; till, at length, compelled
By strong necessity's supreme command,   215
With smiling patience in her looks she went
To glean Palemon's fields. The pride of swains
Palemon was, the generous and the rich,
Who led the rural life in all its joy
And elegance, such as Arcadian song   220
Transmits from ancient uncorrupted times
When tyrant custom had not shackled man
But free to follow nature was the mode.
He then, his fancy with autumnal scenes
Amusing, chanced beside his reaper-train   225
To walk, when poor Lavinia drew his eye,
Unconscious of her power, and turning quick
With unaffected blushes from his gaze.
He saw her charming, but he saw not half
The charms her downcast modesty concealed.   230
That very moment love and chaste desire
Sprung in his bosom, to himself unknown ;
For still the world prevailed and its dread laugh,
Which scarce the firm philosopher can scorn,
Should his heart own a gleaner in the field ;   235
And thus in secret to his soul he sighed :
  'What pity that so delicate a form,
By beauty kindled, where enlivening sense
And more than vulgar goodness seem to dwell,
Should be devoted to the rude embrace   240
Of some indecent clown ! She looks, methinks,
Of old Acasto's line ; and to my mind
Recals that patron of my happy life
From whom my liberal fortune took its rise,
Now to the dust gone down,—his houses, lands,   245
And once fair-spreading family dissolved.
'Tis said that in some lone obscure retreat,

Urged by remembrance sad, and decent pride,
Far from those scenes which knew their better days,
His aged widow and his daughter live,   250
Whom yet my fruitless search could never find.
Romantic wish, would this the daughter were!'
  When, strict inquiring, from herself he found
She was the same, the daughter of his friend,
Of bountiful Acasto, who can speak   255
The mingled passions that surprised his heart
And through his nerves in shivering transport ran?
Then blazed his smothered flame, avowed and bold ;
And, as he viewed her ardent o'er and o'er,
Love, gratitude, and pity wept at once.   .   260
Confused, and frightened at his sudden tears,
Her rising beauties flushed a higher bloom,
As thus Palemon, passionate and just,
Poured out the pious rapture of his soul :
  'And art thou then Acasto's dear remains?   265
She whom my restless gratitude has sought
So long in vain? O heavens! the very same,
The softened image of my noble friend,
Alive his every look, his every feature
More elegantly touched. Sweeter than Spring !   270
Thou sole-surviving blossom from the root
That nourished up my fortune, say, ah where,
In what sequestered desert, hast thou drawn
The kindest aspect of delighted Heaven,
Into such beauty spread, and blown so fair,   275
Though poverty's cold wind and crushing rain
Beat keen and heavy on thy tender years?
Oh! let me now into a richer soil
Transplant thee safe, where vernal suns and showers
Diffuse their warmest, largest influence ;   280
And of my garden be the pride and joy!
It ill befits thee, oh! it ill befits
Acasto's daughter, his whose open stores,
Though vast, were little to his ample heart,

The father of a country, thus to pick   285
The very refuse of those harvest-fields
Which from his bounteous friendship I enjoy.
Then throw that shameful pittance from thy hand,
But ill applied to such a rugged task ;
The fields, the master, all, my fair, are thine,—   290
If to the various blessings which thy house
Has on me lavished thou wilt add that bliss,
That dearest bliss, the power of blessing thee.'
  Here ceased the youth ; yet still his speaking eye
Expressed the sacred triumph of his soul,   295
With conscious virtue, gratitude, and love
Above the vulgar joy divinely raised.
Nor waited he reply. Won by the charm
Of goodness irresistible, and all
In sweet disorder lost, she blushed consent.   300
The news immediate to her mother brought,
While, pierced with anxious thought, she pined away
The lonely moments for Lavinia's fate,
Amazed, and scarce believing what she heard,
Joy seized her withered veins, and one bright gleam 305
Of setting life shone on her evening-hours,
Not less enraptured than the happy pair ;
Who flourished long in tender bliss, and reared
A numerous offspring, lovely like themselves,
And good, the grace of all the country round.   310

  Defeating oft the labours of the year,
The sultry south collects a potent blast.
At first, the groves are scarcely seen to stir
Their trembling tops, and a still murmur runs
Along the soft-inclining fields of corn ;   315
But, as the aërial tempest fuller swells,
And in one mighty stream, invisible,
Immense, the whole excited atmosphere
Impetuous rushes o'er the sounding world,
Strained to the root, the stooping forest pours   320

A rustling shower of yet untimely leaves.
High-beat, the circling mountains eddy in
From the bare wild the dissipated storm,
And send it in a torrent down the vale.
Exposed and naked to its utmost rage,   325
Through all the sea of harvest rolling round
The billowy plain floats wide ; nor can evade,
Though pliant to the blast, its seizing force,—
Or whirled in air, or into vacant chaff
Shook waste. And sometimes too a burst of rain,   330
Swept from the black horizon, broad descends
In one continuous flood. Still overhead
The mingling tempest weaves its gloom, and still
The deluge deepens, till the fields around
Lie sunk and flatted in the sordid wave.   335
Sudden the ditches swell ; the meadows swim.
Red from the hills innumerable streams
Tumultuous roar, and high above its bank
The river lift,—before whose rushing tide,
Herds, flocks, and harvests, cottages, and swains,   340
Roll mingled down, all that the winds had spared
In one wild moment ruined, the big hopes
And well-earned treasures of the painful year.
Fled to some eminence, the husbandman
Helpless beholds the miserable wreck   345
Driving along ; his drowning ox at once
Descending with his labours scattered round
He sees ; and instant o'er his shivering thought
Comes Winter unprovided, and a train
Of clamant children dear. Ye masters, then,   350
Be mindful of the rough laborious hand
That sinks you soft in elegance and ease ;
Be mindful of those limbs, in russet clad,
Whose toil to yours is warmth and graceful pride ;
And oh ! be mindful of that sparing board   355
Which covers yours with luxury profuse,
Makes your glass sparkle, and your sense rejoice ;

Nor cruelly demand what the deep rains
And all-involving winds have swept away.

Here the rude clamour of the sportsman's joy,   360
The gun fast-thundering and the winded horn,
Would tempt the muse to sing the rural game,—
How, in his mid-career, the spaniel, struck
Stiff by the tainted gale, with open nose
Outstretched and finely sensible, draws full,   365
Fearful and cautious, on the latent prey;
As in the sun the circling covey bask
Their varied plumes, and, watchful every way,
Through the rough stubble turn the secret eye.
Caught in the meshy snare, in vain they beat   370
Their idle wings, entangled more and more:
Nor on the surges of the boundless air,
Though borne triumphant, are they safe; the gun,
Glanced just and sudden from the fowler's eye,
O'ertakes their sounding pinions, and again   375
Immediate brings them from the towering wing
Dead to the ground, or drives them wide-dispersed,
Wounded, and wheeling various, down the wind.
These are not subjects for the peaceful muse,
Nor will she stain with such her spotless song,   380
Then most delighted when she social sees
The whole mixed animal-creation round
Alive and happy. 'Tis not joy to her,
This falsely-cheerful barbarous game of death,
This rage of pleasure, which the restless youth   385
Awakes impatient with the gleaming morn,
When beasts of prey retire, that all night long,
Urged by necessity, had ranged the dark,
As if their conscious ravage shunned the light
Ashamed. Not so the steady tyrant man,   390
Who with the thoughtless insolence of power
Inflamed, beyond the most infuriate wrath
Of the worst monster that e'er roamed the waste,

For sport alone pursues the cruel chase,
Amid the beamings of the gentle days.   395
Upbraid, ye ravening tribes, our wanton rage,
For hunger kindles you, and lawless want;
But, lavish fed, in Nature's bounty rolled,
To joy at anguish and delight in blood
Is what your horrid bosoms never knew.   400
   Poor is the triumph o'er the timid hare,
Scared from the corn, and now to some lone seat
Retired—the rushy fen, the ragged furze
Stretched o'er the stony heath, the stubble chapt,
The thistly lawn, the thick entangled broom,   405
Of the same friendly hue the withered fern,
The fallow ground laid open to the sun
Concoctive, and the nodding sandy bank
Hung o'er the mazes of the mountain brook.
Vain is her best precaution, though she sits   410
Concealed with folded ears, unsleeping eyes
By Nature raised to take the horizon in,
And head couched close betwixt her hairy feet,
In act to spring away. The scented dew
Betrays her early labyrinth; and deep,   415
In scattered sullen openings, far behind,
With every breeze she hears the coming storm.
But, nearer and more frequent as it loads
The sighing gale, she springs amazed, and all
The savage soul of game is up at once—   420
The pack full-opening various, the shrill horn
Resounded from the hills, the neighing steed
Wild for the chase, and the loud hunter's shout,—
O'er a weak harmless flying creature, all
Mixed in mad tumult and discordant joy.   425
   The stag too, singled from the herd, where long
He ranged the branching monarch of the shades,
Before the tempest drives. At first in speed
He, sprightly, puts his faith, and, roused by fear,
Gives all his swift aërial soul to flight.   430

Against the breeze he darts, that way the more
To leave the lessening murderous cry behind.
Deception short! though, fleeter than the winds
Blown o'er the keen-aired mountain by the north,
He bursts the thickets, glances through the glades,   435
And plunges deep into the wildest wood;
If slow, yet sure, adhesive to the track
Hot-steaming, up behind him come again
The inhuman rout, and from the shady depth
Expel him, circling through his every shift.   440
He sweeps the forest oft, and sobbing sees
The glades mild-opening to the golden day,
Where in kind contest with his butting friends
He wont to struggle, or his loves enjoy.
Oft in the full-descending flood he tries   445
To lose the scent, and lave his burning sides;
Oft seeks the herd: the watchful herd, alarmed,
With selfish care avoid a brother's woe.
What shall he do? His once so vivid nerves,
So full of buoyant spirit, now no more   450
Inspire the course; but fainting breathless toil,
Sick, seizes on his heart: he stands at bay,
And puts his last weak refuge in despair.
The big round tears run down his dappled face;
He groans in anguish; while the growling pack,   455
Blood-happy, hang at his fair jutting chest,
And mark his beauteous chequered sides with gore.
  Of this enough. But if the sylvan youth
Whose fervent blood boils into violence
Must have the chase, behold! despising flight,   460
The roused-up lion, resolute and slow,
Advancing full on the protended spear
And coward-band that circling wheel aloof.
Slunk from the cavern and the troubled wood,
See the grim wolf: on him his shaggy foe   465
Vindictive fix, and let the ruffian die;
Or, growling horrid, as the brindled boar

Grins fell destruction, to the monster's heart
Let the dart lighten from the nervous arm.
   These Britain knows not. Give, ye Britons, then   470
Your sportive fury, pitiless, to pour
Loose on the nightly robber of the fold.
Him, from his craggy winding haunts unearthed,
Let all the thunder of the chase pursue.
Throw the broad ditch behind you; o'er the hedge   475
High bound resistless; nor the deep morass
Refuse, but through the shaking wilderness
Pick your nice way; into the perilous flood
Bear fearless, of the raging instinct full;
And, as you ride the torrent, to the banks   480
Your triumph sound sonorous, running round
From rock to rock, in circling echoes tossed;
Then snatch the mountains by their woody tops;
Rush down the dangerous steep; and o'er the lawn,
In fancy swallowing up the space between, ·   485
Pour all your speed into the rapid game.
For happy he who tops the wheeling chase;
Has every maze evolved, and every guile
Disclosed; who knows the merits of the pack;
Who saw the villain seized and dying hard,   490
Without complaint though by a hundred mouths
Relentless torn. Oh! glorious he beyond
His daring peers, when the retreating horn
Calls them to ghostly halls of grey renown
— -With woodland honours graced,—the fox's fur, ' ~   495
Depending decent from the roof, and, spread
Round the drear walls, with antic figures fierce,
The stag's large front: he then is loudest heard,
When the night staggers with severer toils,
With feats Thessalian Centaurs never knew,   500
And their repeated wonders shake the dome.
   But first the fuelled chimney blazes wide;
The tankards foam; and the strong table groans
Beneath the smoking sirloin stretched immense

From side to side, in which with desperate knife   505
They deep incision make, talking the while
Of England's glory ne'er to be defaced
While hence they borrow vigour, or, amain
Into the pasty plunged, at intervals—
If stomach keen can intervals allow—   510
Relating all the glories of the chase.
Then sated Hunger bids his brother Thirst
Produce the mighty bowl; the mighty bowl,
Swelled high with fiery juice, steams liberal round
A potent gale, delicious as the breath   515
Of Maia to the love-sick shepherdess,
On violets diffused, while soft she hears
Her panting shepherd stealing to her arms.
Nor wanting is the brown October, drawn
Mature and perfect from his dark retreat   520
Of thirty years; and now his honest front
Flames in the light refulgent, not afraid
Even with the vineyard's best produce to vie.
To cheat the thirsty moments, Whist a while
Walks his dull round, beneath a cloud of smoke   525
Wreathed fragrant from the pipe; or the quick dice,
In thunder leaping from the box, awake
The sounding gammon; while romp-loving miss
Is hauled about in gallantry robust.
  At last, these puling idlenesses laid   530
Aside, frequent and full the dry divan
Close in firm circle, and set ardent in
For serious drinking. Nor evasion sly
Nor sober shift is to the puking wretch
Indulged apart; but earnest brimming bowls   535
Lave every soul, the table floating round,
And pavement, faithless to the fuddled foot.
Thus as they swim in mutual swill, the talk,
Vociferous at once from twenty tongues,
Reels fast from theme to theme—from horses, hounds,
To church or mistress, politics or ghost—   541

K

In endless mazes intricate, perplexed.
Meantime, with sudden interruption loud,
The impatient catch bursts from the joyous heart.
That moment touched is every kindred soul;   545
And, opening in a full-mouthed cry of joy,
The laugh, the slap, the jocund curse go round,—
While, from their slumbers shook, the kennelled hounds
Mix in the music of the day again.
As when the tempest, that has vexed the deep   550
The dark night long, with fainter murmurs falls,
So gradual sinks their mirth. Their feeble tongues,
Unable to take up the cumbrous word,
Lie quite dissolved. Before their maudlin eyes,
Seen dim and blue the double tapers dance,   555
Like the sun wading through the misty sky.
Then, sliding soft, they drop. Confused above,
Glasses and bottles, pipes and gazetteers,
As if the table even itself was drunk,
Lie a wet broken scene; and wide below   560
Is heaped the social slaughter, where, astride,
The lubber power in filthy triumph sits
Slumbrous, inclining still from side to side,
And steeps them drenched in potent sleep till morn.
Perhaps some doctor of tremendous paunch   565
Awful and deep, a black abyss of drink,
Outlives them all; and from his buried flock
Retiring, full of rumination sad,
Laments the weakness of these latter times.
   But if the rougher sex by this fierce sport   570
Is hurried wild, let not such horrid joy
E'er stain the bosom of the British fair.
Far be the spirit of the chase from them,
Uncomely courage, unbeseeming skill—
To spring the fence, to rein the prancing steed—   575
The cap, the whip, the masculine attire,
In which they roughen to the sense, and all
The winning softness of their sex is lost!

In them 'tis graceful to dissolve at woe;
With every motion, every word, to wave   580
Quick o'er the kindling cheek the ready blush;
And from the smallest violence to shrink
Unequal, then the loveliest in their fears;
And by this silent adulation soft
To their protection more engaging man.   585
Oh! may their eyes no miserable sight,
Save weeping lovers, see—a nobler game,
Through love's enchanting wiles pursued, yet fled,
In chase ambiguous. May their tender limbs
Float in the loose simplicity of dress;   590
And, fashioned all to harmony, alone
Know they to seize the captivated soul,
In rapture warbled from love-breathing lips;
To teach the lute to languish; with smooth step,
Disclosing motion in its every charm,   595
To swim along and swell the mazy dance;
To train the foliage o'er the snowy lawn;
To guide the pencil, turn the tuneful page;
To lend new flavour to the fruitful year
And heighten Nature's dainties; in their race   600
To rear their graces into second life;
To give society its highest taste;
Well-ordered home, man's best delight, to make;
And by submissive wisdom, modest skill,
With every gentle care-eluding art,   605
To raise the virtues, animate the bliss,
Even charm the pains to something more than joy,
And sweeten all the toils of human life:
This be the female dignity, and praise.

Ye swains, now hasten to the hazel bank,   610
Where, down yon dale, the wildly-winding brook
Falls hoarse from steep to steep. In close array,
Fit for the thickets and the tangling shrub,
Ye virgins, come. For you their latest song

The woodlands raise; the clustering nuts for you   615
The lover finds amid the secret shade,
And, where they burnish on the topmost bough,
With active vigour crushes down the tree,
Or shakes them ripe from the resigning husk,
A glossy shower, and of an ardent brown,   620
As are the ringlets of Melinda's hair—
Melinda, formed with every grace complete,
Yet these neglecting, above beauty wise,
And far transcending such a vulgar praise.
    Hence from the busy joy-resounding fields,   625
In cheerful error let us tread the maze
Of Autumn unconfined, and taste revived
The breath of orchard big with bending fruit.
Obedient to the breeze and beating ray,
From the deep-loaded bough a mellow shower   630
Incessant melts away. The juicy pear
Lies in a soft profusion scattered round.
A various sweetness swells the gentle race,
By Nature's all-refining hand prepared,
Of tempered sun, and water, earth, and air,   635
In ever-changing composition mixed.
Such, falling frequent through the chiller night,
The fragrant stores, the wide-projected heaps
Of apples,—which the lusty-handed year
Innumerous o'er the blushing orchard shakes.   640
A various spirit, fresh, delicious, keen,
Dwells in their gelid pores, and active points
The piercing cider for the thirsty tongue—
Thy native theme, and boon inspirer too,
Phillips, Pomona's bard! The second thou   -   645
Who nobly durst, in rhyme-unfettered verse,
With British freedom sing the British song,—
How from Silurian vats high-sparkling wines
Foam in transparent floods, some strong to cheer
The wintry revels of the labouring hind,   650
And tasteful some to cool the summer hours.

In this glad season, while his sweetest beams
The sun sheds equal o'er the meekened day,
Oh! lose me in the green delightful walks
Of, Dodington, thy seat, serene and plain,   655
Where simple Nature reigns, and every view
Diffusive spreads the pure Dorsetian downs
In boundless prospect—yonder shagged with wood,
Here rich with harvest, and there white with flocks.
Meantime the grandeur of thy lofty dome   660
Far-splendid seizes on the ravished eye.
New beauties rise with each revolving day;
New columns swell; and still the fresh Spring finds
New plants to quicken, and new groves to green.
Full of thy genius all! the muses' seat,   665
Where, in the secret bower and winding walk,
For virtuous Young and thee they twine the bay.
Here wandering oft, fired with the restless thirst
Of thy applause, I solitary court
The inspiring breeze, and meditate the book   670
Of Nature ever open, aiming thence
Warm from the heart to learn the moral song.
Here, as I steal along the sunny wall,
Where Autumn basks, with fruit empurpled deep,
My pleasing theme continual prompts my thought—   675
Presents the downy peach, the shining plum
With a fine bluish mist of animals
Clouded, the ruddy nectarine, and dark
Beneath his ample leaf the luscious fig.
The vine too here her curling tendrils shoots,   680
Hangs out her clusters glowing to the south,
And scarcely wishes for a warmer sky.

Turn we a moment fancy's rapid flight
To vigorous soils and climes of fair extent,
Where, by the potent sun elated high,   685
The vineyard swells refulgent on the day,
Spreads o'er the vale, or up the mountain climbs

Profuse, and drinks amid the sunny rocks,
From cliff to cliff increased, the heightened blaze.
Low bend the gravid boughs. The clusters clear,   690
Half through the foliage seen, or ardent flame
Or shine transparent ; while perfection breathes
White o'er the turgent film the living dew.
As thus they brighten with exalted juice,
Touched into flavour by the mingling ray,   695
The rural youth and virgins o'er the field—
Each fond for each to cull the autumnal prime—
Exulting rove, and speak the vintage nigh.
Then comes the crushing swain : the country floats
And foams unbounded with the mashy flood,   700
That, by degrees fermented and refined,
Round the raised nations pours the cup of joy—
The claret smooth, red as the lip we press
In sparkling fancy while we drain the bowl ;
The mellow-tasted burgundy ; and, quick   705
As is the wit it gives, the gay champagne.

Now, by the cool declining year condensed,
Descend the copious exhalations, checked
As up the middle sky unseen they stole,
And roll the doubling fogs around the hill.   710
No more the mountain, horrid, vast, sublime,
Who pours a sweep of rivers from his sides,
And high between contending kingdoms rears
The rocky long division, fills the view
With great variety ; but, in a night   715
Of gathering vapour, from the baffled sense
Sinks dark and dreary. Thence expanding far,
The huge dusk gradual swallows up the plain.
Vanish the woods. The dim-seen river seems
Sullen and slow to roll the misty wave.   720
Even in the height of noon oppressed, the sun
Sheds weak and blunt his wide-refracted ray ;

Whence glaring oft, with many a broadened orb,
He frights the nations. Indistinct on earth,
Seen through the turbid air, beyond the life   725
Objects appear; and wildered o'er the waste
The shepherd stalks gigantic; till at last,
Wreathed dun around, in deeper circles still
Successive closing, sits the general fog
Unbounded o'er the world; and, mingling thick,   730
A formless grey confusion covers all:
As when of old (so sung the Hebrew bard)
Light, uncollected, through the chaos urged
Its infant way; nor order yet had drawn
His lovely train from out the dubious gloom.   735
   These roving mists, that constant now begin
To smoke along the hilly country, these,
With weighty rains and melted Alpine snows,
The mountain-cisterns fill,—those ample stores
Of water, scooped among the hollow rocks,   740
Whence gush the streams, the ceaseless fountains play,
And their unfailing wealth the rivers draw.
Some sages say that, where the numerous wave
For ever lashes the resounding shore,
Sucked through the sandy stratum every way,   745
The waters with the sandy stratum rise;
Amid whose angles infinitely strained
They joyful leave their jaggy salts behind,
And clear and sweeten as they soak along.
Nor stops the restless fluid, mounting still,   750
Though oft amidst the irriguous vale it springs;
But to the mountain courted by the sand,
That leads it darkling on in faithful maze,
Far from the parent main it boils again
Fresh into day, and all the glittering hill   755
Is bright with spouting rills. But hence! this vain
Amusive dream. Why should the waters love
To take so far a journey to the hills,
When the sweet valleys offer to their toil

Inviting quiet and a nearer bed?					760
Or if, by blind ambition led astray,
They must aspire, why should they sudden stop
Among the broken mountain's rushy dells,
And, ere they gain its highest peak, desert
The attractive sand that charmed their course so long?
Besides, the hard agglomerating salts,					766
The spoil of ages, would impervious choke
Their secret channels, or by slow degrees
High as the hills protrude the swelling vales.
Old ocean too, sucked through the porous globe,		770
Had long ere now forsook his horrid bed,
And brought Deucalion's watery times again.
    Say then where lurk the vast eternal springs
That, like creating Nature, lie concealed
From mortal eye, yet with their lavish stores			775
Refresh the globe and all its joyous tribes?
O thou pervading genius, given to man,
To trace the secrets of the dark abyss,
Oh! lay the mountains bare, and wide display
Their hidden structure to the astonished view.			780
Strip from the branching Alps their piny load;
The huge incumbrance of horrific woods
From Asian Taurus,—from Imaüs stretched
Athwart the roving Tartar's sullen bounds;
Give opening Hemus to my searching eye,				785
And high Olympus pouring many a stream.
Oh! from the sounding summits of the north,
The Dofrine Hills, through Scandinavia rolled
To farthest Lapland and the frozen main;
From lofty Caucasus, far-seen by those					790
Who in the Caspian and black Euxine toil;
From cold Riphean rocks, which the wild Russ
Believes the stony girdle of the world;
And all the dreadful mountains, wrapt in storm,
Whence wide Siberia draws her lonely floods—			795
Oh! sweep the eternal snows. Hung o'er the deep,

That ever works beneath his sounding base,
Bid Atlas, propping heaven, as poets feign,
His subterranean wonders spread.   Unveil
The miny caverns, blazing on the day,   800
Of Abyssinia's cloud-compelling cliffs,
And of the bending Mountains of the Moon.
O'ertopping all these giant sons of earth,
Let the dire Andes, from the radiant line
Stretched to the stormy seas that thunder round   805
The southern pole, their hideous deeps unfold.
Amazing scene! behold, the glooms disclose!
I see the rivers in their infant beds;
Deep, deep I hear them, labouring to get free.
I see the leaning strata, artful ranged,   810
The gaping fissures to receive the rains,
The melting snows, and ever-dripping fogs.
Strowed bibulous above, I see the sands,
The pebbly gravel next, the layers then
Of mingled moulds, of more retentive earths,   815
The guttered rocks and mazy-running clefts,
That, while the stealing moisture they transmit,
Retard its motion, and forbid its waste.
Beneath the incessant weeping of these drains,
I see the rocky siphons stretched immense,   820
The mighty reservoirs, of hardened chalk
Or stiff compacted clay capacious formed.
O'erflowing thence, the congregated stores,
The crystal treasures of the liquid world,
Through the stirred sands a bubbling passage burst, 825
And, welling out, around the middle steep,
Or from the bottoms of the bosomed hills,
In pure effusion flow.   United thus
The exhaling sun, the vapour-burdened air,
The gelid mountains that, to rain condensed,   830
These vapours in continual current draw,
And send them o'er the fair-divided earth
In bounteous rivers to the deep again,

A social commerce hold, and firm support
The full-adjusted harmony of things.   835

When Autumn scatters his departing gleams,
Warned of approaching Winter, gathered play
The swallow-people, and, tossed wide around,
O'er the calm sky in convolution swift
The feathered eddy floats, rejoicing once,   840
Ere to their wintry slumbers they retire,
In clusters clung, beneath the mouldering bank,
And where unpierced by frost the cavern sweats;
Or rather into warmer climes conveyed,
With other kindred birds of season : there   845
They twitter cheerful till the vernal months
Invite them welcome back. For, thronging, now
Innumerous wings are in commotion all.
    Where the Rhine loses his majestic force
In Belgian plains, won from the raging deep   850
By diligence amazing and the strong
Unconquerable hand of liberty,
The stork-assembly meets,—for many a day
Consulting deep and various ere they take
Their arduous voyage through the liquid sky.   855
And now, their route designed, their leaders chose,
Their tribes adjusted, cleaned their vigorous wings,
And many a circle, many a short essay,
Wheeled round and round, in congregation full
The figured flight ascends, and, riding high   860
The aërial billows, mixes with the clouds.
    Or, where the Northern Ocean in vast whirls
Boils round the naked melancholy isles
Of farthest Thule, and the Atlantic surge
Pours in among the stormy Hebrides—   865
Who can recount what transmigrations there
Are annual made? what nations come and go?
And how the living clouds on clouds arise?
Infinite wings! till all the plume-dark air

And rude resounding shore are one wild cry. 870
Here the plain harmless native his small flock
And herd diminutive of many hues
Tends on the little island's verdant swell,
The shepherd's seagirt reign; or, to the rocks
Dire-clinging, gathers his ovarious food; 875
Or sweeps the fishy shore; or treasures up
The plumage, rising full, to form the bed
Of luxury. And here awhile the muse,
High-hovering o'er the broad cerulean scene,
Sees Caledonia in romantic view— 880
Her airy mountains, from the waving main
Invested with a keen diffusive sky
Breathing the soul acute; her forests huge,
Incult, robust, and tall, by Nature's hand
Planted of old; her azure lakes between, 885
Poured out extensive, and of watery wealth
Full; winding deep and green, her fertile vales,
With many a cool translucent brimming flood
Washed lovely, from the Tweed (pure parent stream
Whose pastoral banks first heard my Doric reed, 890
With, sylvan Jed, thy tributary brook)
To where the north-inflated tempest foams
O'er Orca's or Berubium's highest peak—
Nurse of a people, in misfortune's school
Trained up to hardy deeds, soon visited 895
By learning, when before the Gothic rage
She took her western flight,—a manly race,
Of unsubmitting spirit, wise and brave,
Who still through bleeding ages struggled hard
(As well unhappy Wallace can attest, 900
Great patriot hero! ill-requited chief!)
To hold a generous undiminished state,
Too much in vain! Hence, of unequal bounds
Impatient, and by tempting glory borne
O'er every land, for every land their life 905
Has flowed profuse, their piercing genius planned,

And swelled the pomp of peace their faithful toil:
As from their own clear north in radiant streams
Bright over Europe bursts the Boreal morn.

Oh! is there not some patriot, in whose power   910
That best, that godlike luxury is placed,
Of blessing thousands, thousands yet unborn,
Through late posterity? some, large of soul,
To cheer dejected industry? to give
A double harvest to the pining swain,   915
And teach the labouring hand the sweets of toil?
How by the finest art the native robe
To weave; how, white as hyperborean snow,
To form the lucid lawn; with venturous oar
How to dash wide the billow, nor look on   920
Shamefully passive while Batavian fleets
Defraud us of the glittering finny swarms
That heave our friths and crowd upon our shores;
How all-enlivening trade to rouse, and wing
The prosperous sail from every growing port   925
Uninjured round the sea-encircled globe;
And thus, in soul united as in name,
Bid Britain reign the mistress of the deep?

Yes, there are such. And full on thee, Argyle,
Her hope, her stay, her darling, and her boast,   930
From her first patriots and her heroes sprung,
Thy fond-imploring country turns her eye;
In thee with all a mother's triumph sees
Her every virtue, every grace combined,
Her genius, wisdom, her engaging turn,   935
Her pride of honour, and her courage tried,
Calm, and intrepid, in the very throat
Of sulphurous war, on Tenier's dreadful field.
Nor less the palm of peace inwreathes thy brow;
For, powerful as thy sword, from thy rich tongue   940
Persuasion flows, and wins the high debate;
While, mixed in thee, combine the charm of youth,
The force of manhood, and the depth of age.

Thee, Forbes, too, whom every worth attends,
As truth sincere, as weeping friendship kind,   945
Thee truly generous, and in silence great,
Thy country feels through her reviving arts,
Planned by thy wisdom, by thy soul informed;
And seldom has she known a friend like thee.

But see, the fading many-coloured woods,   950
Shade deepening over shade, the country round
Imbrown,—a crowded umbrage, dusk, and dun,
Of every hue from wan declining green
To sooty dark. These now the lonesome muse,
Low-whispering, lead into their leaf-strown walks;   955
And give the season in its latest view.
  Meantime, light-shadowing all, a sober calm
Fleeces unbounded ether, whose least wave
Stands tremulous, uncertain where to turn
The gentle current: while, illumined wide,   960
The dewy-skirted clouds imbibe the sun,
And through their lucid veil his softened force
Shed o'er the peaceful world. Then is the time
For those whom wisdom and whom nature charm
To steal themselves from the degenerate crowd,   965
And soar above this little scene of things;
To tread low-thoughted vice beneath their feet,
To soothe the throbbing passions into peace,
And woo lone quiet in her silent walks.
  Thus solitary and in pensive guise   970
Oft let me wander o'er the russet mead
And through the saddened grove, where scarce is heard
One dying strain to cheer the woodman's toil.
Haply some widowed songster pours his plaint
Far in faint warblings through the tawny copse;   975
While congregated thrushes, linnets, larks,
And each wild throat whose artless strains so late
Swelled all the music of the swarming shades,
Robbed of their tuneful souls, now shivering sit

On the dead tree, a dull despondent flock,   980
With not a brightness waving o'er their plumes,
And nought save chattering discord in their note.
Oh! let not, aimed from some inhuman eye,
The gun the music of the coming year
Destroy, and harmless, unsuspecting harm,   985
Lay the weak tribes, a miserable prey,
In mingled murder fluttering on the ground.
    The pale descending year, yet pleasing still,
A gentler mood inspires ; for now the leaf
Incessant rustles from the mournful grove,   990
Oft startling such as studious walk below,
And slowly circles through the waving air.
But, should a quicker breeze amid the boughs
Sob, o'er the sky the leafy ruin streams,
Till, choked and matted with the dreary shower,   995
The forest-walks at every rising gale
Roll wide the withered waste, and whistle bleak.
Fled is the blasted verdure of the fields,
And, shrunk into their beds, the flowery race
Their sunny robes resign. Even what remained   1000
Of stronger fruits falls from the naked tree;
And woods, fields, gardens, orchards, all around
A desolated prospect thrills the soul.
    He comes ! he comes ! in every breeze the power
Of philosophic Melancholy comes !   1005
His near approach the sudden-starting tear,
The glowing cheek, the mild dejected air,
The softened feature, and the beating heart
Pierced deep with many a virtuous pang declare.
O'er all the soul his sacred influence breathes,—   1010
Inflames imagination, through the breast
Infuses every tenderness, and far
Beyond dim earth exalts the swelling thought.
Ten thousand thousand fleet ideas, such
As never mingled with the vulgar dream,   1015
Crowd fast into the mind's creative eye.

As fast the correspondent passions rise,
As varied, and as high,—devotion raised
To rapture and divine astonishment ;
The love of Nature unconfined, and chief   1020
Of human race ; the large ambitious wish
To make them blest ; the sigh for suffering worth
Lost in obscurity ; the noble scorn
Of tyrant pride ; the fearless great resolve ;
The wonder which the dying patriot draws,   1025
Inspiring glory through remotest time ;
The awakened throb for virtue and for fame ;
The sympathies of love and friendship dear,
With all the social offspring of the heart.

    Oh ! bear me then to vast embowering shades,   1030
To twilight groves and visionary vales,
To weeping grottos and prophetic glooms,
Where angel-forms athwart the solemn dúsk
Tremendous sweep, or seem to sweep, along,
And voices more than human, through the void   1035
Deep-sounding, seize the enthusiastic ear.

    Or is this gloom too much ? Then lead, ye powers
That o'er the garden and the rural seat
Preside, which shining through the cheerful land
In countless numbers blest Britannia sees—   1040
Oh ! lead me to the wide-extended walks,
The fair majestic paradise of Stowe.
Not Persian Cyrus on Ionia's shore
E'er saw such sylvan scenes, such various art
By genius fired, such ardent genius tamed   1045
By cool judicious art, that in the strife
All-beauteous Nature fears to be outdone.
And there, O Pitt, thy country's early boast,
There let me sit beneath the sheltered slopes,
Or in that temple where in future times   1050
Thou well shalt merit a distinguished name,
And, with thy converse blest, catch the last smiles
Of Autumn beaming o'er the yellow woods.

While there with thee the enchanted round I walk,
The regulated wild, gay fancy then   1055
Will tread in thought the groves of Attic land,
Will from thy standard taste refine her own,
Correct her pencil to the purest truth
Of Nature, or, the unimpassioned shades
Forsaking, raise it to the human mind.   1060
Or if hereafter she with juster hand
Shall draw the tragic scene, instruct her thou
To mark the varied movements of the heart,
What every decent character requires,
And every passion speaks. Oh! through her strain 1065
Breathe thy pathetic eloquence, that moulds
The attentive senate, charms, persuades, exalts,
Of honest zeal the indignant lightning throws,
And shakes corruption on her venal throne.
While thus we talk, and through Elysian vales   1070
Delighted rove, perhaps a sigh escapes—
What pity, Cobham, thou thy verdant files
Of ordered trees shouldst here inglorious range,
Instead of squadrons flaming o'er the field,
And long embattled hosts! when the proud foe,   1075
The faithless vain disturber of mankind,
Insulting Gaul, has roused the world to war;
When keen once more within their bounds to press
Those polished robbers, those ambitious slaves,
The British youth would hail thy wise command,   1080
Thy tempered ardour, and thy veteran skill.

    The western sun withdraws the shortened day;
And humid evening, gliding o'er the sky,
In her chill progress to the ground condensed
The vapours throws. Where creeping waters ooze,   1685
Where marshes stagnate, and where rivers wind,
Cluster the rolling fogs, and swim along
The dusky-mantled lawn. Meanwhile the moon,
Full-orbed, and breaking through the scattered clouds,

Shows her broad visage in the crimsoned east. 1090
Turned to the sun direct, her spotted disk—
Where mountains rise, umbrageous dales descend,
And caverns deep, as optic tube descries—
A smaller earth, gives us his blaze again
Void of its flame, and sheds a softer day. 1095
Now through the passing cloud she seems to stoop,
Now up the pure cerulean rides sublime.
Wide the pale deluge floats, and, streaming mild
O'er the skied mountain to the shadowy vale,
While rocks and floods reflect the quivering gleam, 1100
The whole air whitens with a boundless tide
Of silver radiance trembling round the world.
  But when, half-blotted from the sky, her light
Fainting permits the starry fires to burn
With keener lustre through the depth of heaven, 1105
Or near extinct her deadened orb appears,
And scarce appears, of sickly beamless white,
Oft in this season, silent from the north
A blaze of meteors shoots : ensweeping first
The lower skies, they all at once converge 1110
High to the crown of heaven, and, all at once
Relapsing quick, as quickly reascend,
And mix, and thwart, extinguish, and renew,
All ether coursing in a maze of light.
From look to look, contagious through the crowd, 1115
The panic runs, and into wondrous shapes
The appearance throws—armies in meet array,
Thronged with aërial spears, and steeds of fire,
Till, the long lines of full-extended war
In bleeding fight commixed, the sanguine flood 1120
Rolls a broad slaughter o'er the plains of heaven.
As thus they scan the visionary scene,
On all sides swells the superstitious din
Incontinent, and busy frenzy talks
Of blood and battle ; cities overturned, 1125
And late at night in swallowing earthquake sunk,

L

Or hideous wrapt in fierce ascending flame;
Of sallow famine, inundation, storm;
Of pestilence, and every great distress;
Empires subversed, when ruling fate has struck   1130
The unalterable hour : even Nature's self
Is deemed to totter on the brink of time.
Not so the man of philosophic eye
And inspect sage; the waving brightness he
Curious surveys, inquisitive to know   1135
The causes and materials, yet unfixed,
Of this appearance beautiful and new.

    Now black and deep the night begins to fall,
A shade immense. Sunk in the quenching gloom,
Magnificent and vast, are heaven and earth.   1140
Order confounded lies ; all beauty void ;
Distinction lost; and gay variety
One universal blot : such the fair power
Of light to kindle and create the whole.
Drear is the state of the benighted - wretch   1145
Who then bewildered wanders through the dark,
Full of pale fancies and chimeras huge,
Nor visited by one directive ray
From cottage streaming or from airy hall.
Perhaps, impatient as he stumbles on,   1150
Struck from the root of slimy rushes, blue
The wild-fire scatters round, or gathered trails
A length of flame deceitful o'er the moss ;
Whither decoyed by the fantastic blaze,
Now lost and now renewed, he sinks absorpt,   1155
Rider and horse, amid the miry gulf ;
While still, from day to day, his pining wife
And plaintive children his return await,
In wild conjecture lost. At other times,
Sent by the better genius of the night,   1160
Innoxious gleaming on the horse's mane
The meteor sits, and shows the narrow path

That winding leads through pits of death, or else
Instructs him how to take the dangerous ford.
  The lengthened night elapsed, the morning shines   1165
Serene, in all her dewy beauty bright,
Unfolding fair the last autumnal day.
And now the mountain sun dispels the fog;
The rigid hoar-frost melts before his beam;
And, hung on every spray, on every blade   1170
Of grass, the myriad dewdrops twinkle round.

  Ah! see where, robbed and murdered, in that pit
Lies the still-heaving hive,—at evening snatched
Beneath the cloud of guilt-concealing night,
And fixed o'er sulphur; while, not dreaming ill,   1175
The happy people in their waxen cells
Sat tending public cares, and planning schemes
Of temperance for Winter poor, rejoiced
To mark, full-flowing round, their copious stores.
Sudden the dark oppressive steam ascends;   1180
And, used to milder scents, the tender race
By thousands tumble from their honeyed domes,
Convolved, and agonizing in the dust.
And was it then for this ye roamed the Spring,
Intent from flower to flower? for this ye toiled   1185
Ceaseless the burning Summer-heats away?
For this in Autumn searched the blooming waste,
Nor lost one sunny gleam? for this sad fate?
O man! tyrannic lord! how long, how long
Shall prostrate Nature groan beneath your rage   1190
Awaiting renovation? When obliged,
Must you destroy? Of their ambrosial food
Can you not borrow, and in just return
Afford them shelter from the wintry winds;
Or, as the sharp year pinches, with their own   1195
Again regale them on some smiling day?
See where the stony bottom of their town

Looks desolate and wild, with here and there
A helpless number, who the ruined state
Survive, lamenting weak, cast out to death.   1200
Thus a proud city populous and rich,
Full of the works of peace and high in joy
At theatre or feast, or sunk in sleep
(As late, Palermo, was thy fate) is seized
By some dread earthquake, and convulsive hurled   1205
Sheer from the black foundation, stench-involved,
Into a gulf of blue sulphureous flame.

Hence every harsher sight! for now the day,
O'er heaven and earth diffused, grows warm and high,
Infinite splendour! wide investing all.   1210
How still the breeze! save what the filmy threads
Of dew evaporate brushes from the plain.
How clear the cloudless sky! how deeply tinged
With a peculiar blue! the ethereal arch
How swelled immense! amid whose azure throned   1215
The radiant sun how gay! how calm below
The gilded earth! the harvest-treasures all
Now gathered in beyond the rage of storms
Sure to the swain, the circling fence shut up,
And instant Winter's utmost rage defied;   1220
While, loose to festive joy, the country round
Laughs with the loud sincerity of mirth,
Shook to the wind their cares. The toil-strung youth,
By the quick sense of music taught alone,
Leaps wildly graceful in the lively dance.   1225
Her every charm abroad, the village toast,
Young, buxom, warm, in native beauty rich,
Darts not unmeaning looks; and, where her eye
Points an approving smile, with double force
The cudgel rattles, and the wrestler twines.   1230
Age too shines out, and garrulous recounts
The feats of youth. Thus they rejoice; nor think

That with to-morrow's sun their annual toil
Begins again the never-ceasing round.

 Oh! knew he but his happiness, of men   1235
The happiest he who far from public rage,
Deep in the vale, with a choice few retired,
Drinks the pure pleasures of the rural life.
What though the dome be wanting, whose proud gate
Each morning vomits out the sneaking crowd   1240
Of flatterers false, and in their turn abused?
Vile intercourse! What though the glittering robe,
Of every hue reflected light can give,
Or floating loose or stiff with mazy gold,
The pride and gaze of fools, oppress him not?   1245
What though, from utmost land and sea purveyed,
For him each rarer tributary life
Bleeds not, and his insatiate table heaps
With luxury and death? What though his bowl
Flames not with costly juice; nor sunk in beds,   1250
Oft of gay care, he tosses out the night,
Or melts the thoughtless hours in idle state?
What though he knows not those fantastic joys
That still amuse the wanton, still deceive—
A face of pleasure, but a heart of pain—   1255
Their hollow moments undelighted all?
Sure peace is his; a solid life, estranged
To disappointment and fallacious hope;
Rich in content, in Nature's bounty rich,
In herbs and fruits; whatever greens the Spring   1260
When heaven descends in showers, or bends the bough
When Summer reddens and when Autumn beams,
Or in the wintry glebe whatever lies
Concealed, and fattens with the richest sap—
These are not wanting; nor the milky drove,   1265
Luxuriant spread o'er all the lowing vale;
Nor bleating mountains; nor the chide of streams
And hum of bees, inviting sleep sincere

Into the guiltless breast, beneath the shade,
Or thrown at large amid the fragrant hay;　　　1270
Nor aught besides of prospect, grove, or song,
Dim grottos, gleaming lakes, and fountain clear.
Here too dwells simple truth; plain innocence;
Unsullied beauty; sound unbroken youth,
Patient of labour, with a little pleased;　　　1275
Health ever blooming; unambitious toil;
Calm contemplation, and poetic ease.
　Let others brave the flood in quest of gain,
And beat for joyless months the gloomy wave.
Let such as deem it glory to destroy　　　1280
Rush into blood, the sack of cities seek,—
Unpierced exulting in the widow's wail,
The virgin's shriek, and infant's trembling cry.
Let some, far distant from their native soil,
Urged or by want or hardened avarice,　　　1285
Find other lands beneath another sun.
Let this through cities work his eager way
By legal outrage and established guile,
The social sense extinct; and that ferment
Mad into tumult the seditious herd,　　　1290
Or melt them down to slavery. Let these
Insnare the wretched in the toils of law,
Fomenting discord and perplexing right,
An iron race! and those, of fairer front
But equal inhumanity, in courts,　　　1295
Delusive pomp, and dark cabals delight,
Wreathe the deep bow, diffuse the lying smile,
And tread the weary labyrinth of state;
While he, from all the stormy passions free
That restless men involve, hears, and but hears,　　　1300
At distance safe, the human tempest roar,
Wrapped close in conscious peace. The fall of kings,
The rage of nations, and the crush of states
Move not the man who, from the world escaped,
In still retreats and flowery solitudes　　　1305

To Nature's voice attends from month to month
And day to day through the revolving year,
Admiring sees her in her every shape,
Feels all her sweet emotions at his heart,
Takes what she liberal gives, nor thinks of more.   1310
He, when young Spring protrudes the bursting gems,
Marks the first bud, and sucks the healthful gale
Into his freshened soul; her genial hours
He full enjoys; and not a beauty blows,
And not an opening blossom breathes in vain.   1315
In Summer he, beneath the living shade,
Such as o'er frigid Tempe wont to wave,
Or Hemus cool, reads what the muse, of these
Perhaps, has in immortal numbers sung;
Or what she dictates writes; and, oft an eye   1320
Shot round, rejoices in the vigorous year.
When Autumn's yellow lustre gilds the world
And tempts the sickled swain into the field,
Seized by the general joy, his heart distends
With gentle throes, and, through the tepid gleams   1325
Deep musing, then he best exerts his song.
Even Winter wild to him is full of bliss.
The mighty tempest, and the hoary waste
Abrupt and deep, stretched o'er the buried earth,
Awake to solemn thought. At night the skies,   1330
Disclosed and kindled by refining frost,
Pour every lustre on the exalted eye.
A friend, a book, the stealing hours secure,
And mark them down for wisdom. With swift wing,
O'er land and sea imagination roams;   1335
Or truth, divinely breaking on his mind,
Elates his being and unfolds his powers;
Or in his breast heroic virtue burns.
The touch of kindred too and love he feels,—
The modest eye whose beams on his alone   1340
Ecstatic shine, the little strong embrace
Of prattling children twined around his neck

And emulous to please him, calling forth
The fond parental soul. Nor purpose gay,
Amusement, dance, or song he sternly scorns;   1345
For happiness and true philosophy
Are of the social still and smiling kind.
This is the life which those who fret in guilt
And guilty cities never knew, the life
Led by primeval ages uncorrupt,   1350
When angels dwelt, and God himself, with man.
    O Nature all-sufficient! over all!
Enrich me with the knowledge of thy works.
Snatch me to heaven,—thy rolling wonders there,
World beyond world, in infinite extent   1355
Profusely scattered o'er the blue immense,
Shew me; their motions, periods, and their laws
Give me to scan. Through the disclosing deep
Light my blind way,—the mineral strata there,
Thrust blooming thence the vegetable world,   1360
O'er that the rising system, more complex,
Of animals, and, higher still, the mind,
The varied scene of quick-compounded thought
And where the mixing passions endless shift,
These ever open to my ravished eye—   1365
A search the flight of time can ne'er exhaust.
But if to that unequal, if the blood,
In sluggish streams about my heart, forbid
That best ambition, under closing shades
Inglorious lay me by the lowly brook,   1370
And whisper to my dreams. From thee begin,
Dwell all on thee, with thee conclude my song;
And let me never, never stray from thee!

                    END OF AUTUMN.

WINTER.

SEE, Winter comes to rule the varied year,
Sullen and sad, with all his rising train—
Vapours, and clouds, and storms. Be these my theme,
These, that exalt the soul to solemn thought
And heavenly musing. Welcome, kindred glooms!   5
Congenial horrors, hail! With frequent foot,
Pleased have I in my cheerful morn of life,
When nursed by careless solitude I lived
And sung of Nature with unceasing joy,
Pleased have I wandered through your rough domain;   10
Trod the pure virgin-snows, myself as pure;
Heard the winds roar, and the big torrent burst;
Or seen the deep-fermenting tempest brewed
In the grim evening sky. Thus passed the time,
Till through the lucid chambers of the south   15
Looked out the joyous Spring—looked out and smiled.

To thee, the patron of this first essay,
The muse, O Wilmington! renews her song.
Since has she rounded the revolving year:
Skimmed the gay Spring; on eagle-pinions borne,   20
Attempted through the Summer blaze to rise;
Then swept o'er Autumn with the shadowy gale;
And now among the wintry clouds again,
Rolled in the doubling storm, she tries to soar,
To swell her note with all the rushing winds,   25
To suit her sounding cadence to the floods,—
As is her theme, her numbers wildly great.
Thrice happy, could she fill thy judging ear

With bold description and with manly thought!
Nor art thou skilled in awful schemes alone,   30
And how to make a mighty people thrive;
But equal goodness, sound integrity,   .
A firm unshaken uncorrupted soul
Amid a sliding age, and burning strong,
Not vainly blazing, for thy country's weal,   35
A steady spirit, regularly free—
These, each exalting each, the statesman light
Into the patriot; these, the public hope
And eye to thee converting, bid the muse
Record what envy dares not flattery call.   40

Now when the cheerless empire of the sky
To Capricorn the Centaur Archer yields,
And fierce Aquarius stains the inverted year—
Hung o'er the farthest verge of heaven, the sun
Scarce spreads o'er ether the dejected day.   45
Faint are his gleams, and ineffectual shoot
His struggling rays in horizontal lines
Through the thick air, as, clothed in cloudy storm,
Weak, wan, and broad, he skirts the southern sky,
And, soon-descending, to the long dark night,   50
Wide-shading all, the prostrate world resigns.
Nor is the night unwished, while vital heat,
Light, life, and joy, the dubious day forsake.
Meantime in sable cincture shadows vast,
Deep-tinged, and damp, and congregated clouds   55
And all the vapoury turbulence of heaven
Involve the face of things. Thus Winter falls
A heavy gloom oppressive o'er the world,
Through Nature shedding influence malign,
And rouses up the seeds of dark disease.   60
The soul of man dies in him, loathing life,
And black with more than melancholy views.
The cattle droop; and o'er the furrowed land,
Fresh from the plough, the dun-discoloured flocks,

Untended spreading, crop the wholesome root.　65
Along the woods, along the moorish fens,
Sighs the sad genius of the coming storm ;
And up among the loose disjointed cliffs
And fractured mountains wild, the brawling brook
And cave presageful send a hollow moan,　70
Resounding long in listening fancy's ear.
　Then comes the father of the tempest forth,
Wrapt in black glooms.　First, joyless rains obscure
Drive through the mingling skies with vapour foul,
Dash on the mountain's brow, and shake the woods　75
That grumbling wave below.　The unsightly plain
Lies a brown deluge,—as the low-bent clouds
Pour flood on flood, yet unexhausted still
Combine, and deepening into night shut up
The day's fair face.　The wanderers of heaven,　80
Each to his home, retire,—save those that love
To take their pastime in the troubled air,
Or skimming flutter round the dimply pool.
The cattle from the untasted fields return,
And ask with meaning low their wonted stalls,　85
Or ruminate in the contiguous shade.
Thither the household feathery people crowd—
The crested cock with all his female train,
Pensive and dripping : while the cottage hind
Hangs o'er the enlivening blaze, and taleful there　90
Recounts his simple frolic ; much he talks,
And much he laughs, nor recks the storm that blows
Without, and rattles on his humble roof.
　Wide o'er the brim, with many a torrent swelled,
And the mixed ruin of its banks o'erspread,　95
At last the roused-up river pours along
Resistless, roaring ; dreadful down it comes
From the rude mountain and the mossy wild,
Tumbling through rocks abrupt, and sounding far ;
Then o'er the sanded valley floating spreads,　100
Calm, sluggish, silent ; till, again constrained,

Between two meeting hills it bursts away,
Where rocks and woods o'erhang the turbid stream :
There gathering triple force, rapid and deep,
It boils, and wheels, and foams, and thunders through. 105
  Nature, great parent ! whose unceasing hand
Rolls round the seasons of the changeful year,
How mighty, how majestic are thy works !
With what a pleasing dread they swell the soul,
That sees astonished, and astonished sings !   110

  Ye too, ye winds ! that now begin to blow
With boisterous sweep, I raise my voice to you.
Where are your stores, ye powerful beings ! say,
Where your aërial magazines, reserved
To swell the brooding terrors of the storm ?   115
In what far-distant region of the sky,
Hushed in deep silence, sleep ye when 'tis calm ?
  When from the pallid sky the sun descends,
With many a spot, that o'er his glaring orb
Uncertain wanders, stained—red fiery streaks   120
Begin to flush around. The reeling clouds
Stagger with dizzy poise, as doubting yet
Which master to obey ; while rising slow,
Blank in the leaden-coloured east, the moon
Wears a wan circle round her blunted horns.   125
Seen through the turbid fluctuating air,
The stars obtuse emit a shivering ray ;
Or frequent seem to shoot athwart the gloom,
And long behind them trail the whitening blaze.
Snatched in short eddies, plays the withered leaf ;   130
And on the flood the dancing feather floats.
With broadened nostrils to the sky upturned,
The conscious heifer snuffs the stormy gale.
Even, as the matron at her nightly task
With pensive labour draws the flaxen thread,   135
The wasted taper and the crackling flame
Foretell the blast. But chief the plumy race,

The tenants of the sky, its changes speak.
Retiring from the downs, where all day long
They picked their scanty fare, a blackening train   140
Of clamorous rooks thick-urge their weary flight,
And seek the closing shelter of the grove.
Assiduous in his bower the wailing owl
Plies his sad song. The cormorant on high
Wheels from the deep and screams along the land.   145
Loud shrieks the soaring hern; and with wild wing
The circling sea-fowl cleave the flaky clouds.
Ocean, unequal pressed, with broken tide
And blind commotion heaves; while from the shore,
Eat into caverns by the restless wave,   150
And forest-rustling mountain, comes a voice
That solemn-sounding bids the world prepare.
Then issues forth the storm with sudden burst,
And hurls the whole precipitated air
Down in a torrent. On the passive main   155
Descends the ethereal force, and with strong gust
Turns from its bottom the discoloured deep.
Through the black night that sits immense around,
Lashed into foam, the fierce conflicting brine
Seems o'er a thousand raging waves to burn.   160
Meantime the mountain-billows, to the clouds
In dreadful tumult swelled, surge above surge,
Burst into chaos with tremendous roar,
And anchored navies from their stations drive
Wild as the winds across the howling waste   165
Of mighty waters : now the inflated wave
Straining they scale, and now impetuous shoot
Into the secret chambers of the deep,
The wintry Baltic thundering o'er their head;
Emerging thence again, before the breath   170
Of full-exerted heaven they wing their course,
And dart on distant coasts,—if some sharp rock
Or shoal insidious break not their career,
And in loose fragments fling them floating round.

Nor less at land the loosened tempest reigns.   175
The mountain thunders; and its sturdy sons
Stoop to the bottom of the rocks they shade.
Lone on the midnight steep, and all aghast,
The dark wayfaring stranger breathless toils,
And, often falling, climbs against the blast.   180
Low waves the rooted forest, vexed, and sheds
What of its tarnished honours yet remain,—
Dashed down and scattered by the tearing wind's
Assiduous fury its gigantic limbs.
Thus struggling through the dissipated grove,   185
The whirling tempest raves along the plain;
And, on the cottage thatched or lordly roof
Keen-fastening, shakes them to the solid base.
Sleep frighted flies; and round the rocking dome
For entrance eager howls the savage blast.   190
Then too, they say, through all the burdened air
Long groans are heard, shrill sounds, and distant sighs,
That, uttered by the demon of the night,
Warn the devoted wretch of woe and death.
Huge uproar lords it wide. The clouds, commixed   195
With stars swift-gliding, sweep along the sky.
All nature reels : till Nature's King, who oft
Amid tempestuous darkness dwells alone,
And on the wings of the careering wind
Walks dreadfully serene, commands a calm;   200
Then straight air, sea, and earth are hushed at once.
As yet 'tis midnight deep. The weary clouds,
Slow-meeting, mingle into solid gloom.
Now, while the drowsy world lies lost in sleep,
Let me associate with the serious night,   205
And contemplation, her sedate compeer ;
Let me shake off the intrusive cares of day,
And lay the meddling senses all aside.
Where now, ye lying vanities of life !
Ye ever-tempting, ever-cheating train !   210
Where are you now ? and what is your amount ?

Vexation, disappointment, and remorse.
Sad, sickening thought! and yet deluded man,
A scene of crude disjointed visions past,
And broken slumbers, rises still resolved 215
With new-flushed hopes to run the giddy round.

Father of light and life! thou Good Supreme!
O teach me what is good; teach me Thyself!
Save me from folly, vanity, and vice,
From every low pursuit; and feed my soul 220
With knowledge, conscious peace, and virtue pure—
Sacred, substantial, never-fading bliss!

The keener tempests come; and fuming dun
From all the livid east or piercing north
Thick clouds ascend, in whose capacious womb 225
A vapoury deluge lies, to snow congealed.
Heavy they roll their fleecy world along;
And the sky saddens with the gathered storm.
Through the hushed air the whitening shower descends,
At first thin-wavering; till at last the flakes 230
Fall broad and wide and fast, dimming the day
With a continual flow. The cherished fields
Put on their winter-robe of purest white.
'Tis brightness all,—save where the new snow melts
Along the mazy current. Low the woods 235
Bow their hoar heads; and, ere the languid sun
Faint from the west emits his evening ray,
Earth's universal face, deep-hid and chill,
Is one wild dazzling waste, that buries wide
The works of man. Drooping, the labourer-ox 240
Stands covered o'er with snow, and then demands
The fruit of all his toil. The fowls of heaven,
Tamed by the cruel season, crowd around
The winnowing store, and claim the little boon
Which Providence assigns them. One alone, 245

The redbreast, sacred to the household gods,
Wisely regardful of the embroiling sky,
In joyless fields and thorny thickets leaves
His shivering mates, and pays to trusted man
His annual visit. Half-afraid, he first   250
Against the window beats; then, brisk, alights
On the warm hearth; then, hopping o'er the floor,
Eyes all the smiling family askance,
And pecks, and starts, and wonders where he is;
Till, more familiar grown, the table-crumbs   255
Attract his slender feet. The foodless wilds
Pour forth their brown inhabitants. The hare,
Though timorous of heart, and hard beset
By death in various forms—dark snares, and dogs,
And more unpitying men—the garden seeks,   260
Urged on by fearless want. The bleating kind
Eye the bleak heaven, and next the glistening earth,
With looks of dumb despair; then, sad dispersed,
Dig for the withered herb through heaps of snow.
   Now, shepherds, to your helpless charge be kind;   265
Baffle the raging year, and fill their pens
With food at will; lodge them below the storm,
And watch them strict: for from the bellowing east,
In this dire season, oft the whirlwind's wing
Sweeps up the burden of whole wintry plains   270
In one wide waft, and o'er the hapless flocks,
Hid in the hollow of two neighbouring hills,
The billowy tempest whelms; till, upward urged,
The valley to a shining mountain swells,
Tipt with a wreath high-curling in the sky.   275
   As thus the snows arise, and foul and fierce
All Winter drives along the darkened air,
In his own loose-revolving fields the swain
Disastered stands; sees other hills ascend,
Of unknown joyless brow; and other scenes,   280
Of horrid prospect, shag the trackless plain;
Nor finds the river nor the forest, hid

Beneath the formless wild ; but wanders on
From hill to dale still more and more astray,
Impatient flouncing through the drifted heaps,   285
Stung with the thoughts of home. The thoughts of home
Rush on his nerves, and call their vigour forth
In many a vain attempt. How sinks his soul!
What black despair, what horror fills his heart
When, for the dusky spot which fancy feigned   290
His tufted cottage rising through the snow,
He meets the roughness of the middle waste,
Far from the track and blest abode of man,—
While round him night resistless closes fast,
And every tempest, howling o'er his head,   295
Renders the savage wilderness more wild !
Then throng the busy shapes into his mind
Of covered pits unfathomably deep,
A dire descent ! beyond the power of frost ;
Of faithless bogs; of precipices huge,   300
Smoothed up with snow; and—what is land unknown,
What water--of the still unfrozen spring,
In the loose marsh or solitary lake,
Where the fresh fountain from the bottom boils.
These check his fearful steps ; and down he sinks   305
Beneath the shelter of the shapeless drift,
Thinking o'er all the bitterness of death,
Mixed with the tender anguish Nature shoots
Through the wrung bosom of the dying man—
His wife, his children, and his friends unseen.   310
In vain for him the officious wife prepares
The fire fair-blazing and the vestment warm ;
In vain his little children, peeping out
Into the mingling storm, demand their sire
With tears of artless innocence. Alas !   315
Nor wife nor children more shall he behold,
Nor friends nor sacred home. On every nerve
The deadly Winter seizes, shuts up sense,
And, o'er his inmost vitals creeping cold,

M

Lays him along the snows a stiffened corse,   320
Stretched out, and bleaching in the northern blast.

Ah! little think the gay licentious proud,
Whom pleasure, power, and affluence, surround,—
They, who their thoughtless hours in giddy mirth,
And wanton, often cruel, riot waste,—   325
Ah! little think they, while they dance along,
How many feel this very moment death,
And all the sad variety of pain:
How many sink in the devouring flood
Or more devouring flame; how many bleed   330
By shameful variance betwixt man and man;
How many pine in want and dungeon-glooms,
Shut from the common air, and common use
Of their own limbs; how many drink the cup
Of baleful grief, or eat the bitter bread   335
Of misery; sore pierced by wintry winds,
How many shrink into the sordid hut
Of cheerless poverty; how many shake
With all the fiercer tortures of the mind,
Unbounded passion, madness, guilt, remorse,—   340
Whence tumbled headlong from the height of life
They furnish matter for the tragic muse;
Even in the vale, where wisdom loves to dwell
With friendship, peace, and contemplation joined,
How many, racked with honest passions, droop   345
In deep retired distress; how many stand
Around the deathbed of their dearest friends,
And point the parting anguish. Thought fond man
Of these and all the thousand nameless ills
That one incessant struggle render life,—   350
One scene of toil, of suffering, and of fate,—
Vice in his high career would stand appalled,
And heedless rambling impulse learn to think;
The conscious heart of charity would warm,
And her wide wish benevolence dilate;   355

The social tear would rise, the social sigh;
And into clear perfection, gradual bliss,
Refining still, the social passions work.
   And here can I forget the generous band,
Who, touched with human woe, redressive searched   360
Into the horrors of the gloomy jail,—
Unpitied and unheard where misery moans,
Where sickness pines, where thirst and hunger burn,
And poor misfortune feels the lash of vice?
While in the land of liberty, the land   365
Whose every street and public meeting glows
With open freedom, little tyrants raged,—
Snatched the lean morsel from the starving mouth,
Tore from cold wintry limbs the tattered weed,
Even robbed them of the last of comforts—sleep,   370
The free-born Briton to the dungeon chained,
Or, as the lust of cruelty prevailed,
At pleasure marked him with inglorious stripes ;
And crushed out lives by secret barbarous ways
That for their country would have toiled or bled.   375
O great design! if executed well,
With patient care and wisdom-tempered zeal.
Ye sons of mercy! yet resume the search ;
Drag forth the legal monsters into light,
Wrench from their hands oppression's iron rod,   380
And bid the cruel feel the pains they give.
Much still untouched remains; in this rank age,
Much is the patriot's weeding hand required.
The toils of law (what dark insidious men
Have cumbrous added to perplex the truth   385
And lengthen simple justice into trade)—
How glorious were the day that saw these broke,
And every man within the reach of right!

   By wintry famine roused, from all the tract
Of horrid mountains which the shining Alps,   390

And wavy Apennines and Pyrenees
Branch out stupendous into distant lands—
Cruel as death, and hungry as the grave,
Burning for blood, bony, and gaunt, and grim,
Assembling wolves in raging troops descend ;   395
And, pouring o'er the country, bear along,
Keen as the north-wind sweeps the glossy snow.
All is their prize. They fasten on the steed,
Press him to earth, and pierce his mighty heart.
Nor can the bull his awful front defend,   400
Or shake the murdering savages away.
Rapacious at the mother's throat they fly,
And tear the screaming infant from her breast.
The godlike face of man avails him nought.
Even beauty, force divine! at whose bright glance   405
The generous lion stands in softened gaze,
Here bleeds, a hapless undistinguished prey.
But if, apprized of the severe attack,
The country be shut up—lured by the scent,
On churchyards drear (inhuman to relate !)   410
The disappointed prowlers fall, and dig
The shrouded body from the grave ; o'er which,
Mixed with foul shades and frighted ghosts, they howl.

    Among those hilly regions, where embraced
In peaceful vales the happy Grisons dwell,   415
Oft, rushing sudden from the loaded cliffs,
Mountains of snow their gathering terrors roll.
From steep to steep, loud-thundering, down they come,
A wintry waste in dire commotion all ;
And herds, and flocks, and travellers, and swains,   420
And sometimes whole brigades of marching troops,
Or hamlets sleeping in the dead of night,
Are deep beneath the smothering ruin whelmed.

    Now, all amid the rigours of the year,
In the wild depth of Winter, while without   425

The ceaseless winds blow ice, be my retreat
Between the groaning forest and the shore
Beat by a boundless multitude of waves,—
A rural, sheltered, solitary scene,
Where ruddy fire and beaming tapers join   430
To cheer the gloom. There studious let me sit,
And hold high converse with the mighty dead,—
Sages of ancient time, as gods revered,
As gods beneficent, who blessed mankind
With arts and arms, and humanized a world.   435
Roused at the inspiring thought, I throw aside
The long-lived volume ; and deep-musing hail
The sacred shades, that slowly-rising pass
Before my wondering eyes. First Socrates,
Who, firmly good in a corrupted state,   440
Against the rage of tyrants single stood,
Invincible,—calm reason's holy law,
That voice of God within the attentive mind,
Obeying fearless or in life or death :
Great moral teacher ! wisest of mankind !   445
Solon the next, who built his commonweal
On equity's wide base,—by tender laws
A lively people curbing, yet undamped
Preserving still that quick peculiar fire
Whence, in the laurelled field of finer arts   450
And of bold freedom, they unequalled shone
The pride of smiling Greece and human-kind.
Lycurgus then, who bowed beneath the force
Of strictest discipline, severely wise,
All human passions. Following him, I see,   455
As at Thermopylæ he glorious fell,
The firm devoted chief, who proved by deeds
The hardest lesson which the other taught.
Then Aristides lifts his honest front,—
Spotless of heart, to whom the unflattering voice   460
Of freedom gave the noblest name of Just,
In pure majestic poverty revered ;

Who, even his glory to his country's weal
Submitting, swelled a haughty rival's fame.
Reared by his care, of softer ray appears   465
Cimon sweet-souled,—whose genius, rising strong,
Shook off the load of young debauch; abroad
The scourge of Persian pride, at home the friend
Of every worth and every splendid art;
Modest and simple in the pomp of wealth.   470
Then the last worthies of declining Greece,
Late-called to glory in unequal times,
Pensive appear. The fair Corinthian boast,
Timoleon,—tempered happy, mild and firm,
Who wept the brother while the tyrant bled.   475
And, equal to the best, the Theban pair,—
Whose virtues, in heroic concord joined,
Their country raised to freedom, empire, fame.
He too, with whom Athenian honour sunk,
And left a mass of sordid lees behind,   480
Phocion the Good,—in public life severe,
To virtue still inexorably firm;
But when, beneath his low illustrious roof,
Sweet peace and happy wisdom smoothed his brow,
Not friendship softer was, nor love more kind.   485
And he, the last of old Lycurgus' sons,
The generous victim to that vain attempt
To save a rotten state, Agis,—who saw
Even Sparta's self to servile avarice sunk.
The two Achæan heroes close the train,—   490
Aratus, who awhile relumed the soul
Of fondly lingering liberty in Greece;
And he, her darling as her latest hope,
The gallant Philopœmen, who to arms
Turned the luxurious pomp he could not cure,   495
Or toiling in his farm a simple swain,
Or bold and skilful thundering in the field.
   Of rougher front, a mighty people come!
A race of heroes! in those virtuous times

Which knew no stain, save that with partial flame   500
Their dearest country they too fondly loved.
Her better founder first, the light of Rome,
Numa,—who softened her rapacious sons.
Servius,—the king who laid the solid base
On which o'er earth the vast republic spread.   505
Then the great consuls venerable rise,—
The public father who the private quelled,
As on the dread tribunal sternly sad;
He whom his thankless country could not lose,
Camillus, only vengeful to her foes;   510
Fabricius, scorner of all-conquering gold;
And Cincinnatus, awful from the plough;
Thy willing victim, Carthage, bursting loose
From all that pleading Nature could oppose,
From a whole city's tears, by rigid faith   515
Imperious called, and honour's dire command;
Scipio, the gentle chief, humanely brave,
Who soon the race of spotless glory ran,
And warm in youth to the poetic shade
With friendship and philosophy retired;   520
Tully, whose powerful eloquence awhile
Restrained the rapid fate of rushing Rome;
Unconquered Cato, virtuous in extreme;
And thou, unhappy Brutus, kind of heart,
Whose steady arm, by awful virtue urged,   525
Lifted the Roman steel against thy friend.
Thousands besides the tribute of a verse
Demand; but who can count the stars of heaven?
Who sing their influence on this lower world?

   Behold who yonder comes in sober state,   530
Fair, mild, and strong, as is a vernal sun—
'Tis Phœbus' self, or else the Mantuan swain!
Great Homer too appears, of daring wing,
Parent of song! and equal by his side
The British muse; joined hand in hand they walk   535
Darkling full up the middle steep to fame.
Nor absent are those shades whose skilful touch

Pathetic drew the impassioned heart, and charmed
Transported Athens with the moral scene;
Nor those who tuneful waked the enchanting lyre.   540
　First of your kind! society divine!
Still visit thus my nights, for you reserved,
And mount my soaring soul to thoughts like yours.
Silence, thou lonely power! the door be thine;
See on the hallowed hour that none intrude   545
Save a few chosen friends, who sometimes deign
To bless my humble roof, with sense refined,
Learning digested well, exalted faith,
Unstudied wit, and humour ever gay.
Or from the muses' hill will Pope descend,   550
To raise the sacred hour, to bid it smile,
And with the social spirit warm the heart,—
For though not sweeter his own Homer sings
Yet is his life the more endearing song.
　Where art thou, Hammond? thou the darling pride, 555
The friend and lover of the tuneful throng!
Ah! why, dear youth, in all the blooming prime
Of vernal genius, where disclosing fast
Each active worth, each manly virtue lay,
Why wert thou ravished from our hope so soon?   560
What now avails that noble thirst of fame
Which stung thy fervent breast? that treasured store
Of knowledge early gained? that eager zeal
To serve thy country, glowing in the band
Of youthful patriots who sustain her name?   565
What now, alas! that life-diffusing charm
Of sprightly wit? that rapture for the muse,
That heart of friendship, and that soul of joy,
Which bade with softest light thy virtue smile?
Ah! only showed to check our fond pursuits,   570
And teach our humbled hopes that life is vain!
　Thus in some deep retirement would I pass
The winter-glooms with friends of pliant soul,
Or blithe or solemn as the theme inspired;

With them would search if Nature's boundless frame   575
Was called late-rising from the void of night,
Or sprung eternal from the Eternal Mind,
Its life, its laws, its progress, and its end.
Hence larger prospects of the beauteous whole
Would gradual open on our opening minds,   580
And each diffusive harmony unite
In full perfection to the astonished eye.
Then would we try to scan the moral world,—
Which, though to us it seems embroiled, moves on
In higher order, fitted and impelled   585
By wisdom's finest hand, and issuing all
In general good. The sage historic muse
Should next conduct us through the deeps of time—
Show us how empire grew, declined, and fell
In scattered states; what makes the nations smile,   590
Improves their soil, and gives them double suns;
And why they pine beneath the brightest skies
In Nature's richest lap. As thus we talked
Our hearts would burn within us—would inhale
That portion of divinity, that ray   595
Of purest heaven, which lights the public soul
Of patriots and of heroes. But if doomed
In powerless humble fortune to repress
These ardent risings of the kindling soul,
Then, even superior to ambition, we   600
Would learn the private virtues—how to glide
Through shades and plains along the smoothest stream
Of rural life; or, snatched away by hope
Through the dim spaces of futurity,
With earnest eye anticipate those scenes   605
Of happiness and wonder,—where the mind'
In endless growth and infinite ascent
Rises from state to state and world to world.
But, when with these the serious thought is foiled,
We, shifting for relief, would play the shapes   610
Of frolic fancy, and incessant form

Those rapid pictures, that assembled train
Of fleet ideas never joined before,
Whence lively wit excites to gay surprise,
Or folly-painting humour, grave himself,   615
Calls laughter forth deep-shaking every nerve.

Meantime the village rouses up the fire ;
While, well attested and as well believed,
Heard solemn, goes the goblin story round,
Till superstitious horror creeps o'er all ;   620
Or frequent in the sounding hall they wake
The rural gambol : rustic mirth goes round,—
The simple joke that takes the shepherd's heart,
Easily pleased ; the long loud laugh sincere ;
The kiss, snatched hasty from the sidelong maid   625
On purpose guardless, or pretending sleep ;
The leap, the slap, the haul ; and, shook to notes
Of native music, the respondent dance.
Thus jocund fleets with them the winter night.

The city swarms intense. The public haunt,   630
Full of each theme and warm with mixed discourse,
Hums indistinct. The sons of riot flow
Down the loose stream of false enchanted joy
To swift destruction. On the rankled soul
The gaming fury falls ; and in one gulf   635
Of total ruin honour, virtue, peace,
Friends, families, and fortune headlong sink.
Up springs the dance along the lighted dome,
Mixed and evolved a thousand sprightly ways.
The glittering court effuses every pomp ;   640
The circle deepens ; beamed from gaudy robes,
Tapers, and sparkling gems, and radiant eyes,
A soft effulgence o'er the palace waves,
While, a gay insect in his summer shine,
The fop light-fluttering spreads his mealy wings.   645
    Dread o'er the scene the ghost of Hamlet stalks ;

Othello rages ; poor Monimia mourns ;
And Belvidera pours her soul in love :
Terror alarms the breast ; the comely tear
Steals o'er the cheek. Or else the comic muse   650
Holds to the world a picture of itself,
And raises sly the fair impartial laugh.
Sometimes she lifts her strain, and paints the scenes
Of beauteous life,—whate'er can deck mankind,
Or charm the heart, in generous Bevil showed.   655

   O thou whose wisdom, solid yet refined,
Whose patriot virtues, and consummate skill
To touch the finer springs that move the world,
Joined to whate'er the Graces can bestow
And all Apollo's animating fire,   660
Give thee with pleasing dignity to shine
At once the guardian, ornament, and joy
Of polished life—permit the rural muse,
O Chesterfield, to grace with thee her song!
Ere to the shades again she humbly flies,   665
Indulge her fond ambition,—in thy train
(For every muse has in thy train a place)
To mark thy various full-accomplished mind ;
To mark that spirit, which with British scorn
Rejects the allurements of corrupted power ;   670
That elegant politeness, which excels
Even in the judgment of presumptuous France
The boasted manners of her shining court ;
That wit, the vivid energy of sense,
The truth of nature, which with Attic point   675
And kind well-tempered satire, smoothly keen,
Steals through the soul, and without pain corrects.
Or, rising thence with yet a brighter flame,
O let me hail thee on some glorious day
When to the listening senate ardent crowd   680
Britannia's sons to hear her pleaded cause.
Then dressed by thee, more amiably fair,

Truth the soft robe of mild persuasion wears;
Thou to assenting reason giv'st again
Her own enlightened thoughts; called from the heart, 685
The obedient passions on thy voice attend;
And even reluctant party feels awhile
Thy gracious power—as through the varied maze
Of eloquence, now smooth, now quick, now strong,
Profound and clear, you roll the copious flood.   690

    To thy loved haunt return, my happy muse;
For now, behold, the joyous winter-days
Frosty succeed, and through the blue serene,
For sight too fine, the ethereal nitre flies,
Killing infectious damps, and the spent air   695
Storing afresh with elemental life.
Close crowds the shining atmosphere, and binds
Our strengthened bodies in its cold embrace
Constringent; feeds and animates our blood;
Refines our spirits, through the new-strung nerves   700
In swifter sallies darting to the brain,—
Where sits the soul, intense, collected, cool,
Bright as the skies, and as the season keen.
All Nature feels the renovating force
Of Winter,—only to the thoughtless eye   705
In ruin seen. The frost-concocted glebe
Draws in abundant vegetable soul,
And gathers vigour for the coming year.
A stronger glow sits on the lively cheek
Of ruddy fire; and luculent along   710
The purer rivers flow. Their sullen deeps
Transparent open to the shepherd's gaze,
And murmur hoarser at the fixing frost.
    What art thou, frost? and whence are thy keen stores
Derived, thou secret all-invading power,   715
Whom even the illusive fluid cannot fly?
Is not thy potent energy, unseen,

Myriads of little salts, or hooked, or shaped
Like double wedges, and diffused immense
Through water, earth, and ether? Hence at eve,   720
Steamed eager from the red horizon round,
With the fierce rage of Winter deep suffused,
An icy gale, oft shifting, o'er the pool
Breathes a blue film, and in its mid career
Arrests the bickering stream. The loosened ice,   725
Let down the flood and half dissolved by day,
Rustles no more, but to the sedgy bank
Fast grows, or gathers round the pointed stone—
A crystal pavement by the breath of heaven
Cemented firm; till, seized from shore to shore,   730
The whole imprisoned river growls below.
Loud rings the frozen earth and hard reflects
A double noise, while at his evening watch
The village dog deters the nightly thief,
The heifer lows, the distant waterfall   735
Swells in the breeze, and with the hasty tread
Of traveller the hollow-sounding plain
Shakes from afar. The full ethereal round,
Infinite worlds disclosing to the view,
Shines out intensely keen and—all one cope   740
Of starry glitter—glows from pole to pole.
From pole to pole the rigid influence falls
Through the still night incessant, heavy, strong,
And seizes Nature fast. It freezes on,
Till morn late rising o'er the drooping world   745
Lifts her pale eye unjoyous. Then appears
The various labour of the silent night—
Prone from the dripping eave and dumb cascade,
Whose idle torrents only seem to roar,
The pendent icicle; the frost-work fair,   750
Where transient hues and fancied figures rise;
Wide-spouted o'er the hill the frozen brook,
A livid tract cold-gleaming on the morn;
The forest bent beneath the plumy wave;

And by the frost refined the whiter snow,   755
Incrusted hard, and sounding to the tread
Of early shepherd as he pensive seeks
His pining flock, or from the mountain top,
Pleased with the slippery surface, swift descends.
 On blithesome frolics bent, the youthful swains,   760
While every work of man is laid at rest,
Fond o'er the river crowd, in various sport
And revelry dissolved ; where mixing glad,
Happiest of all the train, the raptured boy
Lashes the whirling top. Or, where the Rhine   765
Branched out in many a long canal extends,
From every province swarming, void of care
Batavia rushes forth ; and, as they sweep
On sounding skates a thousand different ways
In circling poise swift as the winds along,   770
The then gay land is maddened all to joy.
Nor less the northern courts wide o'er the snow
Pour a new pomp. Eager on rapid sleds
Their vigorous youth in bold contention wheel
The long-resounding course. Meantime, to raise   775
The manly strife, with highly blooming charms
Flushed by the season, Scandinavia's dames
Or Russia's buxom daughters glow around.
 Pure, quick, and sportful is the wholesome day ;
But soon elapsed. The horizontal sun   780
Broad o'er the south hangs at his utmost noon,
And ineffectual strikes the gelid cliff.
His azure gloss the mountain still maintains,
Nor feels the feeble touch. Perhaps the vale
Relents awhile to the reflected ray ;   785
Or from the forest falls the clustered snow—
Myriads of gems, that in the waving gleam
Gay-twinkle as they scatter. Thick around
Thunders the sport of those who with the gun,
And dog impatient bounding at the shot,   790
Worse than the season, desolate the fields,

And, adding to the ruins of the year,
Distress the footed or the feathered game.

But what is this? Our infant Winter sinks
Divested of his grandeur, should our eye   795
Astonished shoot into the frigid zone,—
Where for relentless months continual night
Holds o'er the glittering waste her starry reign.
  There through the prison of unbounded wilds,
Barred by the hand of Nature from escape,   800
Wide roams the Russian exile. Nought around
Strikes his sad eye but deserts lost in snow,
And heavy loaded groves, and solid floods
That stretch athwart the solitary vast
Their icy horrors to the frozen main,   805
And cheerless towns far-distant—never blessed,
Save when its annual course the caravan
Bends to the golden coast of rich Cathay,
With news of human-kind. Yet there life glows;
Yet cherished there beneath the shining waste   810
The furry nations harbour—tipped with jet,
Fair ermines, spotless as the snows they press;
Sables, of glossy black; and dark-embrowned,
Or beauteous freaked with many a mingled hue,
Thousands besides, the costly pride of courts.   815
There, warm together pressed, the trooping deer
Sleep on the new-fallen snows; and, scarce his head
Raised o'er the heapy wreath, the branching elk
Lies slumbering sullen in the white abyss.
The ruthless hunter wants nor dogs nor toils,   820
Nor with the dread of sounding bows he drives
The fearful flying race: with ponderous clubs,
As weak against the mountain-heaps they push
Their beating breast in vain, and piteous bray,
He lays them quivering on the ensanguined snows,   825
And with loud shouts rejoicing bears them home.
There through the piny forest half-absorpt,

Rough tenant of these shades, the shapeless bear,
With dangling ice all horrid, stalks forlorn :
Slow-paced, and sourer as the storms increase,   830
He makes his bed beneath the inclement drift,
And with stern patience, scorning weak complaint,
Hardens his heart against assailing want.

    Wide o'er the spacious regions of the north
That see Bootes urge his tardy wain,   835
A boisterous race, by frosty Caurus pierced,
Who little pleasure know and fear no pain,
Prolific swarm. They once relumed the flame
Of lost mankind in polished slavery sunk,
Drove martial horde on horde, with dreadful sweep   840
Resistless rushing o'er the enfeebled south,
And gave the vanquished world another form.
Not such the sons of Lapland : wisely they
Despise the insensate barbarous trade of war ;
They ask no more than simple Nature gives ;   845
They love their mountains and enjoy their storms.
No false desires, no pride-created wants,
Disturb the peaceful current of their time,
And, through the restless ever-tortured maze
Of pleasure or ambition, bid it rage.   850
Their reindeer form their riches. These their tents,
Their robes, their beds, and all their homely wealth
Supply, their wholesome fare, and cheerful cups.
Obsequious at their call, the docile tribe
Yield to the sled their necks, and whirl them swift   855
O'er hill and dale, heaped into one expanse
Of marbled snow, as far as eye can sweep
With a blue crust of ice unbounded glazed.
By dancing meteors then, that ceaseless shake
A waving blaze refracted o'er the heavens,   860
And vivid moons, and stars that keener play
With doubled lustre from the radiant waste,
Even in the depth of polar night they find

A wondrous day—enough to light the chase,
Or guide their daring steps to Finland fairs.   865
Wished Spring returns; and from the hazy south,
While dim Aurora slowly moves before,
The welcome sun, just verging up at first,
By small degrees extends the swelling curve;
Till, seen at last for gay rejoicing months,   870
Still round and round his spiral course he winds,
And, as he nearly dips his flaming orb,
Wheels up again and reascends the sky.
In that glad season, from the lakes and floods
Where pure Niemi's fairy mountains rise,   875
And fringed with roses Tenglio rolls his stream,
They draw the copious fry. With these at eve
They cheerful loaded to their tents repair;
Where, all day long in useful cares employed,
Their kind unblemished wives the fire prepare.   880
Thrice happy race ! by poverty secured
From legal plunder and rapacious power;
In whom fell interest never yet has sown
The seeds of vice; whose spotless swains ne'er knew
Injurious deed; nor, blasted by the breath   885
Of faithless love, their blooming daughters woe.
    Still pressing on, beyond Tornea's lake,
And Hecla flaming through a waste of snow,
And farthest Greenland, to the pole itself,
Where, failing gradual, life at length goes out,   890
The muse expands her solitary flight;
And, hovering o'er the wild stupendous scene,
Beholds new seas beneath another sky.
Throned in his palace of cerulean ice,
Here Winter holds his unrejoicing court;   895
And through his airy hall the loud misrule
Of driving tempest is for ever heard.
Here the grim tyrant meditates his wrath;
Here arms his winds with all-subduing frost;
Moulds his fierce hail, and treasures up his snows,   900

N

With which he now oppresses half the globe.
   Thence winding eastward to the Tartar's coast,
She sweeps the howling margin of the main,—
Where undissolving from the first of time
Snows swell on snows amazing to the sky,   905
And icy mountains high on mountains piled
Seem to the shivering sailor from afar,
Shapeless and white, an atmosphere of clouds.
Projected huge and horrid o'er the surge
Alps frown on Alps; or rushing hideous down,   910
As if old chaos was again returned,
Wide rend the deep, and shake the solid pole.
Ocean itself no longer can resist
The binding fury; but, in all its rage
Of tempest taken by the boundless frost,   915
Is many a fathom to the bottom chained,
And bid to roar no more,—a bleak expanse
Shagged o'er with wavy rocks, cheerless and void
Of every life, that from the dreary months
Flies conscious southward. Miserable they,   920
Who, here entangled in the gathering ice,
Take their last look of the descending sun;
While, full of death, and fierce with tenfold frost,
The long long night, incumbent o'er their heads,
Falls horrible. Such was the Briton's fate,   925
As with first prow (what have not Britons dared?)
He for the passage sought, attempted since
So much in vain, and seeming to be shut
By jealous Nature with eternal bars.
In these fell regions, in Arzina caught,   930
And to the stony deep his idle ship
Immediate sealed, he with his hapless crew,
Each full exerted at his several task,
Froze into statues,—to the cordage glued
The sailor, and the pilot to the helm.   935
   Hard by these shores, where scarce his freezing stream
Rolls the wild Oby, live the last of men;

And, half enlivened by the distant sun
(That rears and ripens man as well as plants),
Here human nature wears its rudest form. 940
Deep from the piercing season sunk in caves,
Here by dull fires and with unjoyous cheer
They waste the tedious gloom ; immersed in furs
Doze the gross race ; nor sprightly jest, nor song,
Nor tenderness they know, nor aught of life 945
Beyond the kindred bears that stalk without ;
Till morn at length, her roses drooping all,
Sheds a long twilight brightening o'er the fields,
And calls the quivered savage to the chase.
What cannot active government perform, 950
New-moulding man ? Wide-stretching from these shores,
A people savage from remotest time,
A huge neglected empire—one vast mind,
By Heaven inspired, from Gothic darkness called.
Immortal Peter, first of monarchs !—he 955
His stubborn country tamed, her rocks, her fens,
Her floods, her seas, her ill-submitting sons ;
And, while the fierce barbarian he subdued,
To more exalted soul he raised the man.
Ye shades of ancient heroes, ye who toiled 960
Through long successive ages to build up
A labouring plan of state, behold at once
The wonder done ! Behold the matchless prince
Who left his native throne, where reigned till then
A mighty shadow of unreal power ; 965
Who greatly spurned the slothful pomp of courts ;
And, roaming every land—in every port
(His sceptre laid aside) with glorious hand
Unwearied plying the mechanic tool—
Gathered the seeds of trade, of useful arts, 970
Of civil wisdom, and of martial skill.
Charged with the stores of Europe, home he goes ;
Then cities rise amid the illumined waste ;
O'er joyless deserts smiles the rural reign ;

Far-distant flood to flood is social joined;   975
The astonished Euxine hears the Baltic roar;
Proud navies ride on seas that never foamed
With daring keel before; and armies stretch
Each way their dazzling files, repressing here
The frantic Alexander of the north,   980
And awing there stern Othman's shrinking sons.
Sloth flies the land, and ignorance, and vice,
Of old dishonour proud: it glows around,
Taught by the royal hand that roused the whole,
One scene of arts, of arms, of rising trade;   985
For what his wisdom planned and power enforced
More potent still his great example showed.

    Muttering, the winds at eve with blunted point
Blow hollow-blustering from the south. Subdued,
The frost resolves into a trickling thaw.   990
Spotted, the mountains shine; loose sleet descends,
And floods the country round. The rivers swell,
Of bonds impatient. Sudden from the hills,
O'er rocks and woods, in broad brown cataracts,
A thousand snow-fed torrents shoot at once;   995
And, where they rush, the wide-resounding plain
Is left one slimy waste. Those sullen seas,
That wash the ungenial pole, will rest no more
Beneath the shackles of the mighty north;
But, rousing all their waves, resistless heave—   1000
And hark! the lengthening roar continuous runs
Athwart the rifted deep: at once it bursts,
And piles a thousand mountains to the clouds.
Ill fares the bark with trembling wretches charged,
That, tossed amid the floating fragments, moors   1005
Beneath the shelter of an icy isle,
While night o'erwhelms the sea, and horror looks
More horrible. Can human force endure
The assembled mischiefs that besiege them round,—

Heart-gnawing hunger, fainting weariness, 1010
The roar of winds and waves, the crush of ice,
Now ceasing, now renewed with louder rage,
And in dire echoes bellowing round the main?
More to embroil the deep, Leviathan
And his unwieldy train in dreadful sport 1015
Tempest the loosened brine; while through the gloom,
Far from the bleak inhospitable shore,
Loading the winds, is heard the hungry howl
Of famished monsters, there awaiting wrecks.
Yet Providence, that ever-waking eye, 1020
Looks down with pity on the feeble toil
Of mortals lost to hope, and lights them safe
Through all this dreary labyrinth of fate.

'Tis done! dread Winter spreads his latest glooms,
And reigns tremendous o'er the conquered year. 1025
How dead the vegetable kingdom lies!
How dumb the tuneful! Horror wide extends
His desolate domain. Behold, fond man!
See here thy pictured life: pass some few years,
Thy flowering Spring, thy Summer's ardent strength, 1030
Thy sober Autumn fading into age,—
And pale concluding Winter comes at last
And shuts the scene. Ah! whither now are fled
Those dreams of greatness, those unsolid hopes
Of happiness, those longings after fame, 1035
Those restless cares, those busy bustling days,
Those gay-spent festive nights, those veering thoughts,
Lost between good and ill, that shared thy life?
All now are vanished! Virtue sole survives,
Immortal, never-failing friend of man, 1040
His guide to happiness on high.—And see!
'Tis come, the glorious morn! the second birth
Of heaven and earth! Awakening Nature hears
The new-creating word, and starts to life

In every heightened form, from pain and death   1045
For ever free. The great eternal scheme
Involving all, and in a perfect whole
Uniting, as the prospect wider spreads,
To reason's eye refined clears up apace.
Ye vainly wise! ye blind presumptuous! now,   1050
Confounded in the dust, adore that Power
And Wisdom oft arraigned : see now the cause
Why unassuming worth in secret lived,
And died neglected ; why the good man's share
In life was gall and bitterness of soul ;   1055
Why the lone widow and her orphans pined
In starving solitude, while luxury
In palaces lay straining her low thought
To form unreal wants ; why heaven-born truth
And moderation fair wore the red marks   1060
Of superstition's scourge ; why licensed pain,
That cruel spoiler, that embosomed foe,
Embittered all our bliss. Ye good distressed!
Ye noble few! who here unbending stand
Beneath life's pressure, yet bear up awhile ;   1065
And, what your bounded view—which only saw
A little part—deemed evil, is no more :
The storms of wintry time will quickly pass,
And one unbounded Spring encircle all.

END OF WINTER.

A HYMN.

—**+**—

THESE, as they change, Almighty Father! these
Are but the varied God. The rolling year
Is full of Thee. Forth in the pleasing Spring
Thy beauty walks, Thy tenderness and love.
Wide flush the fields; the softening air is balm; 5
Echo the mountains round; the forest smiles;
And every sense, and every heart, is joy.
Then comes Thy glory in the summer months,
With light and heat refulgent. Then Thy sun
Shoots full perfection through the swelling year; 10
And oft Thy voice in dreadful thunder speaks,
And oft at dawn, deep noon, or falling eve,
By brooks and groves, in hollow-whispering gales.
Thy bounty shines in Autumn unconfined,
And spreads a common feast for all that lives. 15
In Winter, awful Thou! with clouds and storms
Around Thee thrown, tempest o'er tempest rolled,
Majestic darkness! On the whirlwind's wing
Riding sublime, Thou bidd'st the world adore,
And humblest Nature with thy northern blast. 20
 Mysterious round! what skill, what force divine,
Deep felt, in these appear!—a simple train,
Yet so delightful mixed, with such kind art,
Such beauty and beneficence combined,
Shade unperceived so softening into shade, 25
And all so forming an harmonious whole
That, as they still succeed, they ravish still.
But wondering oft with brute unconscious gaze
Man marks Thee not,—marks not the mighty hand

That ever-busy wheels the silent spheres,   30
Works in the secret deep, shoots steaming thence
The fair profusion that o'erspreads the Spring,
Flings from the sun direct the flaming day,
Feeds every creature, hurls the tempest forth,
And, as on earth this grateful change revolves,   35
With transport touches all the springs of life.
   Nature, attend! join, every living soul
Beneath the spacious temple of the sky,
In adoration join, and ardent raise
One general song. To Him, ye vocal gales,   40
Breathe soft, whose Spirit in your freshness breathes;
Oh talk of Him in solitary glooms
Where, o'er the rock, the scarcely waving pine
Fills the brown shade with a religious awe.
And ye, whose bolder note is heard afar,   45
Who shake the astonished world, lift high to heaven
The impetuous song, and say from whom you rage.
His praise, ye brooks, attune, ye trembling rills,
And let me catch it as I muse along.
Ye headlong torrents, rapid and profound;   50
Ye softer floods, that lead the humid maze
Along the vale; and thou, majestic main,
A secret world of wonders in thyself,
Sound His stupendous praise whose greater voice
Or bids you roar, or bids your roarings fall.   55
Soft roll your incense, herbs, and fruits, and flowers,
In mingled clouds to Him whose sun exalts,
Whose breath perfumes you, and whose pencil paints.
Ye forests bend, ye harvests wave, to Him;
Breathe your still song into the reaper's heart,   60
As home he goes beneath the joyous moon.
Ye that keep watch in heaven, as earth asleep
Unconscious lies, effuse your mildest beams,
Ye constellations, while your angels strike
Amid the spangled sky the silver lyre.   65
Great source of day, best image here below

Of thy Creator, ever pouring wide,
From world to world, the vital ocean round,—
On Nature write with every beam His praise.
The thunder rolls: be hushed the prostrate world; 70
While cloud to cloud returns the solemn hymn.
Bleat out afresh, ye hills; ye mossy rocks,
Retain the sound; the broad responsive low,
Ye valleys, raise; for the Great Shepherd reigns,
And his unsuffering kingdom yet will come. 75
Ye woodlands all, awake: a boundless song
Burst from the groves; and when the restless day,
Expiring, lays the warbling world asleep,
Sweetest of birds, sweet Philomela, charm
The listening shades, and teach the night His praise. 80
Ye chief, for whom the whole creation smiles,
At once the head, the heart, and tongue of all,
Crown the great hymn; in swarming cities vast,
Assembled men, to the deep organ join
The long-resounding voice, oft-breaking clear 85
At solemn pauses through the swelling bass;
And, as each mingling flame increases each,
In one united ardour rise to heaven.
Or, if you rather choose the rural shade,
And find a fane in every sacred grove— 90
There let the shepherd's flute, the virgin's lay,
The prompting seraph, and the poet's lyre
Still sing the God of Seasons, as they roll.
For me, when I forget the darling theme,
Whether the blossom blows, the Summer ray 95
Russets the plain, inspiring Autumn gleams,
Or Winter rises in the blackening east,
Be my tongue mute, my fancy paint no more,
And, dead to joy, forget my heart to beat!
  Should fate command me to the farthest verge 100
Of the green earth, to distant barbarous climes,
Rivers unknown to song, where first the sun
Gilds Indian mountains, or his setting beam

Flames on the Atlantic isles—'tis nought to me;
Since God is ever present, ever felt,   105
In the void waste as in the city full;
And where He vital breathes there must be joy.
When even at last the solemn hour shall come,
And wing my mystic flight to future worlds,
I cheerful will obey; there, with new powers,   110
Will rising wonders sing. I cannot go
Where Universal Love not smiles around,
Sustaining all yon orbs, and all their sons;
From seeming evil still educing good,
And better thence again, and better still,   115
In infinite progression.—But I lose
Myself in Him, in light ineffable!
Come then, expressive silence, muse His praise.

END OF HYMN.

.

THE CASTLE OF INDOLENCE.

CANTO I.

The Castle hight of Indolence,
And its false luxury ;
Where for a little time, alas !
We lived right jollily.

I.

O MORTAL man, who livest here by toil,
Do not complain of this thy hard estate ;
That like an emmet thou must ever moil
Is a sad sentence of an ancient date :
And, certes, there is for it reason great ;   5
For, though sometimes it makes thee weep and wail,
And curse thy stars, and early drudge and late,
Withouten that would come an heavier bale,
Loose life, unruly passions, and diseases pale.

II.

In lowly dale, fast by a river's side,   10
With woody hill o'er hill encompassed round,
A most enchanting wizard did abide,
Than whom a fiend more fell is nowhere found.
It was, I ween, a lovely spot of ground ;
And there a season atween June and May,   15
Half prankt with spring, with summer half imbrowned,
A listless climate made, where, sooth to say,
No living wight could work, ne carèd ev'n for play.

III.

Was nought around but images of rest:
Sleep-soothing groves, and quiet lawns between ;   20
And flowery beds that slumbrous influence kest,
From poppies breathed ; and beds of pleasant green,
Where never yet was creeping creature seen.
Meantime, unnumbered glittering streamlets played,
And hurlèd everywhere their waters sheen ;   25
That, as they bickered through the sunny glade,
Though restless still themselves, a lulling murmur made.

IV.

Joined to the prattle of the purling rills
Were heard the lowing herds along the vale,
And flocks loud bleating from the distant hills,   30
And vacant shepherds piping in the dale ;
And now and then sweet Philomel would wail,
Or stockdoves 'plain amid the forest deep,
That drowsy rustled to the sighing gale ;
And still a coil the grasshopper did keep :   35
Yet all these sounds yblent inclinèd all to sleep.

V.

Full in the passage of the vale, above,
A sable, silent, solemn forest stood ;
Where nought but shadowy forms were seen to move,
As Idless fancied in her dreaming mood.   40
And up the hills, on either side, a wood
Of blackening pines, aye waving to and fro,
Sent forth a sleepy horror through the blood ;
And where this valley winded out, below,
The murmuring main was heard, and scarcely heard, to flow.

VI.

A pleasing land of drowsyhed it was :   46
Of dreams that wave before the half-shut eye ;
And of gay castles in the clouds that pass,
Forever flushing round a summer sky :
There eke the soft delights, that witchingly   50
Instil a wanton sweetness through the breast,
And the calm pleasures always hovered nigh ;
But whate'er smacked of 'noyance, or unrest,
Was far far off expelled from this delicious nest.

VII.

The landskip such, inspiring perfect ease,   55
Where INDOLENCE (for so the wizard hight)
Close hid his castle 'mid embowering trees,
That half shut out the beams of Phoebus bright,
And made a kind of checkered day and night.
Meanwhile, unceasing at the massy gate,   60
Beneath a spacious palm, the wicked wight
Was placed ; and, to his lute, of cruel fate
And labour harsh complained, lamenting man's estate.

VIII.

Thither continual pilgrims crowded still,
From all the roads of earth that pass there by :   65
For, as they chaunced to breathe on neighbouring hill,
The freshness of this valley smote their eye,
And drew them ever and anon more nigh,
Till clustering round th' enchanter false they hung,
Ymolten with his syren melody ;   70
While o'er th' enfeebling lute his hand he flung,
And to the trembling chord these tempting verses sung :

IX.

'Behold! ye pilgrims of this earth, behold!
See all but man with unearned pleasure gay.
See her bright robes the butterfly unfold,   75
Broke from her wintry tomb in prime of May.
What youthful bride can equal her array?
Who can with her for easy pleasure vie?
From mead to mead with gentle wing to stray,
From flower to flower on balmy gales to fly,   80
Is all she has to do beneath the radiant sky.

X.

'Behold the merry minstrels of the morn,
The swarming songsters of the careless grove,
Ten thousand throats! that, from the flowering thorn,
Hymn their good God, and carol sweet of love,   85
Such grateful kindly raptures them emove:
They neither plough, nor sow; ne, fit for flail,
E'er to the barn the nodding sheaves they drove;
Yet theirs each harvest dancing in the gale,
Whatever crowns the hill, or smiles along the vale.   90

XI.

'Outcast of nature, man! the wretched thrall
Of bitter-dropping sweat, of sweltry pain,
Of cares that eat away thy heart with gall,
And of the vices, an inhuman train,
That all proceed from savage thirst of gain: 95
For when hard-hearted Interest first began
To poison earth, Astræa left the plain;
Guile, Violence, and Murder seized on man;
And, for soft milky streams, with blood the rivers ran.

XII.

'Come, ye, who still the cumbrous load of life   100
Push hard up hill; but, as the farthest steep
You trust to gain, and put an end to strife,
Down thunders back the stone with mighty sweep,
And hurls your labours to the valley deep,
Forever vain : come, and withouten fee   105
I in oblivion will your sorrows steep,
Your cares, your toils; will steep you in a sea
Of full delight : O come, ye weary wights, to me!

XIII.

'With me, you need not rise at early dawn,
To pass the joyless day in various stounds;   110
Or, louting low, on upstart fortune fawn,
And sell fair honour for some paltry pounds;
Or through the city take your dirty rounds,
To cheat, and dun, and lie, and visit pay,
Now flattering base, now giving secret wounds;   115
Or prowl in courts of law for human prey,
In venal senate thieve, or rob on broad highway.

XIV.

'No cocks, with me, to rustic labour call,
From village on to village sounding clear;
To tardy swain no shrill-voiced matrons squall;   120
No dogs, no babes, no wives, to stun your ear;
No hammers thump; no horrid blacksmith sear,
Ne noisy tradesman your sweet slumbers start
With sounds that are a misery to hear:
But all is calm as would delight the heart   125
Of Sybarite of old, all nature, and all art.

XV.

'Here nought but candour reigns, indulgent ease,
Good-natured lounging, sauntering up and down :
They who are pleased themselves must always please ;
On others' ways they never squint a frown,   130
Nor heed what haps in hamlet or in town.
Thus, from the source of tender indolence,
With milky blood the heart is overflown,
Is soothed and sweetened by the social sense ;
For interest, envy, pride, and strife are banished hence.

XVI.

'What, what is virtue, but repose of mind ?   136
A pure ethereal calm that knows no storm,
Above the reach of wild ambition's wind,
Above those passions that this world deform,
And torture man, a proud malignant worm!   140
But here, instead, soft gales of passion play,
And gently stir the heart, thereby to form
A quicker sense of joy; as breezes stray
Across th' enlivened skies, and make them still more gay.

XVII.

'The best of men have ever loved repose :   145
They hate to mingle in the filthy fray,
Where the soul sours, and gradual rancour grows,
Imbittered more from peevish day to day.
Even those whom fame has lent her fairest ray,
The most renowned of worthy wights of yore,   150
From a base world at last have stolen away :
So Scipio, to the soft Cumæan shore
Retiring, tasted joy he never knew before.

XVIII.

'But if a little exercise you choose,
Some zest for ease, 'tis not forbidden here.   155
Amid the groves you may indulge the muse,
Or tend the blooms, and deck the vernal year;
Or softly stealing, with your watery gear,
Along the brooks, the crimson-spotted fry
You may delude: the whilst, amused, you hear   160
Now the hoarse stream, and now the zephyr's sigh,
Attuned to the birds, and woodland melody.

XIX.

'O grievous folly! to heap up estate,
Losing the days you see beneath the sun;
When, sudden, comes blind unrelenting fate,   165
And gives th' untasted portion you have won
With ruthless toil, and many a wretch undone,
To those who mock you gone to Pluto's reign,
There with sad ghosts to pine, and shadows dun:
But sure it is of vanities most vain,   170
To toil for what you here untoiling may obtain.'

XX.

He ceased. But still their trembling ears retained
The deep vibrations of his 'witching song;
That, by a kind of magic power, constrained
To enter in, pell-mell, the listening throng.   175
Heaps poured on heaps, and yet they slipt along
In silent ease: as when, beneath the beam
Of summer moons, the distant woods among,
Or by some flood all silvered with the gleam,
The soft-embodied fays through airy portal stream.   180

O

XXI.

By the smooth demon so it ordered was,
And here his baneful bounty first began;
Though some there were who would not further pass,
And his alluring baits suspected han.
The wise distrust the too fair-spoken man.   185
Yet through the gate they cast a wishful eye:
Not to move on, perdie, is all they can;
For do their very best they cannot fly,
But often each way look, and often sorely sigh.

XXII.

When this the watchful wicked wizard saw,   190
With sudden spring he leaped upon them straight;
And, soon as touched by his unhallowed paw,
They found themselves within the cursed gate;
Full hard to be repassed, like that of fate.
Not stronger were of old the giant crew,   195
Who sought to pull high Jove from regal state;
Though feeble wretch he seemed, of sallow hue:
Certes, who bides his grasp will that encounter rue.

XXIII.

For, whomsoe'er the villain takes in hand,
Their joints unknit, their sinews melt apace;   200
As lithe they grow as any willow-wand,
And of their vanished force remains no trace.

  * * * * *
  * * * * *
  * * * * *
  * * * * *
  * * * * *

XXIV.

Waked by the crowd, slow from his bench arose
A comely full-spread porter, swoln with sleep:
His calm, broad, thoughtless aspect breathed repose;   210
And in sweet torpor he was plungèd deep,
Ne could himself from ceaseless yawning keep;
While o'er his eyes the drowsy liquor ran,
Through which his half-waked soul would faintly peep.
Then, taking his black staff, he called his man,   215
And roused himself as much as rouse himself he can.

XXV.

The lad leapt lightly at his master's call.
He was, to weet, a little roguish page,
Save sleep and play who minded nought at all,
Like most the untaught striplings of his age.   220
This boy he kept each band to disengage,
Garters and buckles, task for him unfit,
But ill becoming his grave personage,
And which his portly paunch would not permit.
So this same limber page to all performèd it.   225

XXVI.

Meantime the master-porter wide displayed
Great store of caps, of slippers, and of gowns,
Wherewith he those who entered in arrayed,
Loose as the breeze that plays along the downs,
And waves the summer woods when evening frowns.   230
O fair undress, best dress! it checks no vein,
But every flowing limb in pleasure drowns,
And heightens ease with grace. This done, right fain,
Sir Porter sat him down, and turned to sleep again.

O 2

XXVII.

Thus easy-robed, they to the fountain sped   235
That in the middle of the court up-threw
A stream, high spouting from its liquid bed,
And falling back again in drizzly dew:
There each deep draughts, as deep he thirsted, drew.
It was a fountain of nepenthe rare;   240
Whence, as Dan Homer sings, huge pleasaunce grew,
And sweet oblivion of vile earthly care,—
Fair gladsome waking thoughts, and joyous dreams more fair.

XXVIII.

This rite performed, all inly pleased and still,
Withouten trump, was proclamation made: 245
'Ye sons of Indolence, do what you will,
And wander where you list, through hall or glade:
Be no man's pleasure for another's stayed;
Let each as likes him best his hours employ,
And cursed be he who minds his neighbour's trade!   250
Here dwells kind ease, and unreproving joy:
He little merits bliss who others can annoy.'

XXIX.

Straight of these endless numbers, swarming round,
As thick as idle motes in sunny ray,
Not one eftsoons in view was to be found,   255
But every man strolled off his own glad way.
Wide o'er this ample court's blank area,
With all the lodges that thereto pertained,
No living creature could be seen to stray;
While solitude and perfect silence reigned: 260
So that to think you dreamt, you almost was constrained.

XXX.

As when a shepherd of the Hebrid Isles,
Placed far amid the melancholy main,
(Whether it be lone fancy him beguiles,
Or that aerial beings sometimes deign 265
To stand, embodied, to our senses plain)
Sees on the naked hill, or valley low,
The whilst in ocean Phœbus dips his wain,
A vast assembly moving to and fro;
Then all at once in air dissolves the wondrous show. 270

XXXI.

Ye gods of quiet, and of sleep profound,
Whose soft dominion o'er this castle sways,
And all the widely silent places round,—
Forgive me, if my trembling pen displays
What never yet was sung in mortal lays. 275
But how shall I attempt such arduous string?
I, who have spent my nights and nightly days,
In this soul-deadening place loose-loitering:
Ah! how shall I for this uprear my moulted wing?

XXXII.

Come on, my muse, nor stoop to low despair, 280
Thou imp of Jove, touched by celestial fire!
Thou yet shalt sing of war, and actions fair,
Which the bold sons of Britain will inspire;
Of ancient bards thou yet shalt sweep the lyre;
Thou yet shalt tread in tragic pall the stage, 285
Paint love's enchanting woes, the hero's ire,
The sage's calm, the patriot's noble rage,
Dashing corruption down through every worthless age.

XXXIII.

The doors, that knew no shrill alarming bell,
Ne cursèd knocker plied by villain's hand,　　　290
Self-opened into halls, where, who can tell
What elegance and grandeur wide expand
The pride of Turkey and of Persia land?
Soft quilts on quilts, on carpets carpets spread,
And couches stretch around in seemly band,　　　295
And endless pillows rise to prop the head,
So that each spacious room was one full-swelling bed.

XXXIV.

And everywhere huge covered tables stood,
With wines high-flavoured and rich viands crowned;
Whatever sprightly juice or tasteful food　　　300
On the green bosom of this earth are found,
And all old ocean genders in his round:
Some hand unseen these silently displayed,
Even undemanded by a sign or sound;
You need but wish, and, instantly obeyed,　　　305
Fair-ranged the dishes rose, and thick the glasses played.

XXXV.

Here freedom reigned, without the least alloy;
Nor gossip's tale, nor ancient maiden's gall,
Nor saintly spleen durst murmur at our joy,
And with envenomed tongue our pleasures pall.　　　310
For why? There was but one great rule for all;
To wit, that each should work his own desire,
And eat, drink, study, sleep, as it may fall,
Or melt the time in love, or wake the lyre,
And carol what, unbid, the muses might inspire.　　　315

XXXVI.

The rooms with costly tapestry were hung,
Where was inwoven many a gentle tale,
Such as of old the rural poets sung
Or of Arcadian or Sicilian vale:
Reclining lovers, in the lonely dale,   320
Poured forth at large the sweetly tortured heart;
Or, looking tender passion, swelled the gale,
And taught charmed echo to resound their smart;
While flocks, woods, streams around, repose and peace
    impart.

XXXVII.

Those pleased the most, where, by a cunning hand,   325
Depeinten was the patriarchal age;
What time Dan Abraham left the Chaldee land,
And pastured on from verdant stage to stage,
Where fields and fountains fresh could best engage.
Toil was not then. Of nothing took they heed,   330
But with wild beasts the silvan war to wage,
And o'er vast plains their herds and flocks to feed:
Blessed sons of nature they! true golden age indeed!

XXXVIII.

Sometimes the pencil, in cool airy halls,
Bade the gay bloom of vernal landskips rise,   335
Or Autumn's varied shades imbrown the walls:
Now the black tempest strikes the astonished eyes;
Now down the steep the flashing torrent flies;
The trembling sun now plays o'er ocean blue,
And now rude mountains frown amid the skies;   340
Whate'er Lorrain light-touched with softening hue,
Or savage Rosa dashed, or learned Poussin drew.

XXXIX.

Each sound, too, here to languishment inclined,
Lulled the weak bosom, and inducèd ease.
Aerial music in the warbling wind,   345
At distance rising oft, by small degrees,
Nearer and nearer came, till o'er the trees
It hung, and breathed such soul-dissolving airs,
As did, alas! with soft perdition please:
Entangled deep in its enchanting snares,   350
The listening heart forgot all duties and all cares.

XL.

A certain music, never known before,
Here soothed the pensive, melancholy mind;
Full easily obtained. Behoves no more,
But sidelong, to the gently waving wind,   355
To lay the well-tuned instrument reclined;
From which, the airy flying fingers light,
Beyond each mortal touch the most refined,
The god of winds drew sounds of deep delight:
Whence, with just cause, *The Harp of Æolus* it hight.   360.

XLI.

Ah me! what hand can touch the string so fine?
Who up the lofty diapason roll
Such sweet, such sad, such solemn airs divine,
Then let them down again into the soul?
Now rising love they fanned; now pleasing dole   365
They breathed, in tender musings, thro' the heart;
And now a graver sacred strain they stole,
As when seraphic hands an hymn impart:
Wild warbling nature all, above the reach of art.

XLII.

Such the gay splendour, the luxurious state,   370
Of Caliphs old, who on the Tygris' shore,
In mighty Bagdat, populous and great,
Held their bright court, where was of ladies store;
And verse, love, music still the garland wore:
When sleep was coy, the bard, in waiting there,   375
Cheered the lone midnight with the muse's lore;
Composing music bade his dreams be fair,
And music lent new gladness to the morning air.

XLIII.

Near the pavilions where we slept, still ran
Soft-tinkling streams, and dashing waters fell,   380
And sobbing breezes sighed, and oft began
(So worked the wizard) wintry storms to swell,
As heaven and earth they would together mell:
At doors and windows, threatening, seemed to call
The demons of the tempest, growling fell;   385
Yet the least entrance found they none at all;
Whence sweeter grew our sleep, secure in massy hall.

XLIV.

And hither Morpheus sent his kindest dreams,
Raising a world of gayer tinct and grace;
O'er which were shadowy cast Elysian gleams,   390
That played, in waving lights, from place to place,
And shed a roseate smile on nature's face.
Not Titian's pencil e'er could so array,
So fleece with clouds the pure ethereal space;
Ne could it e'er such melting forms display,   395
As loose on flowery beds all languishingly lay.

XLV.

No, fair illusions! artful phantoms, no!
My muse will not attempt your fairy-land :
She has no colours that like you can glow ;
To catch your vivid scenes too gross her hand.   400
But sure it is, was ne'er a subtler band
Than these same guileful angel-seeming sprights,
Who thus in dreams voluptuous, soft, and bland,
Poured all th' Arabian heaven upon our nights,
And blessed them oft besides with more refined delights. 405

XLVI.

They were, in sooth, a most enchanting train,
Even feigning virtue ; skilful to unite
With evil good, and strew with pleasure pain.
But for those fiends, whom blood and broils delight,
Who hurl the wretch, as if to hell outright,   410
Down, down black gulfs, where sullen waters sleep,
Or hold him clambering all the fearful night
On beetling cliffs, or pent in ruins deep, —
They, till due time should serve, were bid far hence to keep.

XLVII.

Ye guardian spirits, to whom man is dear,   415
From these foul demons shield the midnight gloom!
Angels of fancy and of love, be near,
And o'er the wilds of sleep diffuse a bloom ;
Evoke the sacred shades of Greece and Rome,
And let them virtue with a look impart!   420
But chief, a while, oh lend us from the tomb
Those long lost friends for whom in love we smart,
And fill with pious awe and joy-mixed woe the heart!

XLVIII.

Or are you sportive ?—bid the morn of youth
Rise to new light, and beam afresh the days   425
Of innocence, simplicity, and truth,
To cares estranged, and manhood's thorny ways!
What transport to retrace our boyish plays,
Our easy bliss, when each thing joy supplied,—
The woods, the mountains, and the warbling maze   430
Of the wild brooks !—But, fondly wandering wide,
My muse, resume the task that yet doth thee abide.

XLIX.

One great amusement of our household was—
In a huge crystal magic globe to spy,
Still as you turned it, all things that do pass   435
Upon this ant-hill earth ; where constantly
Of idly busy men the restless fry
Run bustling to and fro with foolish haste
In search of pleasures vain, that from them fly,
Or which, obtained, the caitiffs dare not taste :   440
When nothing is enjoyed, can there be greater waste?

L.

Of Vanity the Mirror this was called.
Here you a muckworm of the town might see
At his dull desk, amid his ledgers stalled,
Eat up with carking care and penurie,—   445
Most like to carcase parched on gallow-tree.
'A penny savèd is a penny got'—
Firm to this scoundrel maxim keepeth he,
Ne of its rigour will he bate a jot,
Till it has quenched his fire, and banishèd his pot.   450

LI.

Straight from the filth of this low grub, behold,
Comes fluttering forth a gaudy spendthrift heir,
All glossy gay, enamelled all with gold,
The silly tenant of the summer air !
In folly lost, of nothing takes he care ;   455
Pimps, lawyers, stewards, harlots, flatterers vile,
And thieving tradesmen him among them share :
His father's ghost from limbo lake, the while,
Sees this, which more damnation does upon him pile.

LII.

This globe pourtrayed the race of learnèd men,   460
Still at their books, and turning o'er the page
Backwards and forwards : oft they snatch the pen
As if inspired and in a Thespian rage,
Then write and blot as would your ruth engage.
Why, authors, all this scrawl and scribbling sore ?   465
To lose the present, gain the future age,
Praisèd to be when you can hear no more,
And much enriched with fame when useless worldly store.

LIII.

Then would a splendid city rise to view,
With carts, and cars, and coaches roaring all :   470
Wide-poured abroad behold the prowling crew !
See how they dash along from wall to wall!
At every door hark how they thundering call!
Good lord ! what can this giddy rout excite ?
Why,—each on each to prey by guile or gall,   475
With flattery these, with slander those to blight,
And make new tiresome parties for the coming night.

LIV.

The puzzling sons of party next appeared,
In dark cabals and nightly juntos met;
And now they whispered close, now shrugging reared 480
The important shoulder; then, as if to get
New light, their twinkling eyes were inward set.
No sooner Lucifer recalls affairs,
Than forth they various rush in mighty fret;
When lo ! pushed up to power, and crowned their cares, 485
In cómes another set, and kicketh them down stairs.

LV.

But what most showed the vanity of life,
Was to behold the nations all on fire,
In cruel broils engaged, and deadly strife :
Most Christian kings, inflamed by black desire,   490
With honourable ruffians in their hire,
Cause war to rage, and blood around to pour.
Of this sad work when each begins to tire,
They sit them down just where they were before,
Till for new scenes of woe peace shall their force restore. 495

LVI.

To number up the thousands dwelling here,
An useless were, and eke an endless task,—
From kings, and those who at the helm appear,
To gipsies brown in summer-glades who bask.
Yea, many a man, perdie, I could unmask,   500
Whose desk and table make a solemn show,
With tape-tied trash, and suits of fools that ask
For place or pension, laid in decent row;
But these I passen by, with nameless numbers moe.

LVII.

Of all the gentle tenants of the place,   505
There was a man of special grave remark:
A certain tender gloom o'erspread his face,
Pensive, not sad; in thought involved, not dark.
As soot this man could sing as morning lark,
And teach the noblest morals of the heart;   510
But these his talents were yburied stark;
Of the fine stores he nothing would impart,
Which or boon nature gave, or nature-painting art.

LVIII.

To noontide shades incontinent he ran,
Where purls the brook with sleep-inviting sound;   515
Or, when Dan Sol to slope his wheels began,
Amid the broom he basked him on the ground,
Where the wild thyme and camomil are found:
There would he linger, till the latest ray
Of light sat quivering on the welkin's bound;   520
Then homeward through the twilight shadows stray,
Sauntering and slow. So had he passèd many a day.

LIX.

Yet not in thoughtless slumber were they past;
For oft the heavenly fire, that lay concealed
Emongst the sleeping embers, mounted fast,   525
And all its native light anew revealed.
Oft as he traversed the cerulean field,
And marked the clouds that drove before the wind,
Ten thousand glorious systems would he build,
Ten thousand great ideas filled his mind;   530
But with the clouds they fled, and left no trace behind.

LX.

With him was sometimes joined, in silent walk,
(Profoundly silent, for they never spoke)
One shyer still, who quite detested talk:
Oft, stung by spleen, at once away he broke   535
To groves of pine and broad o'ershadowing oak;
There, inly thrilled, he wandered all alone,
And on himself his pensive fury wroke,
Ne ever uttered word, save when first shone
The glittering star of eve—'Thank heaven! the day is done.'

LXI.

Here lurked a wretch, who had not crept abroad   541
For forty years, ne face of mortal seen,—
In chamber brooding like a loathly toad;
And sure his linen was not very clean.
Through secret loophole, that had practised been   545
Near to his bed, his dinner vile he took;
Unkempt, and rough, of squalid face and mien,
Our castle's shame! whence, from his filthy nook,
We drove the villain out for fitter lair to look.

LXII.

One day there chanced into these halls to rove   550
A joyous youth, who took you at first sight;
Him the wild wave of pleasure hither drove,
Before the sprightly tempest tossing light:
Certes, he was a most engaging wight,
Of social glee, and wit humane though keen,   555
Turning the night to day and day to night:
For him the merry bells had rung, I ween,
If, in this nook of quiet, bells had ever been.

LXIII.

But not even pleasure to excess is good:
What most elates, then sinks the soul as low ;   560
When springtide joy pours in with copious flood,
The higher still the exulting billows flow,
The farther back again they flagging go,
And leave us groveling on the dreary shore:
Taught by this son of joy, we found it so ;   565
Who, whilst he staid, kept in a gay uproar
Our maddened castle all, the abode of sleep no more.

LXIV.

As when in prime of June a burnished fly,
Sprung from the meads, o'er which he sweeps along,
Cheered by the breathing bloom and vital sky,   570
Tunes up amid these airy halls his song,
Soothing at first the gay reposing throng ;
And oft he sips their bowl ; or, nearly drowned,
He, thence recovering, drives their beds among,
And scares their tender sleep, with trump profound ;   575
Then out again he flies, to wing his mazy round.

LXV.

Another guest there was, of sense refined,
Who felt each worth, for every worth he had ;
Serene yet warm, humane yet firm his mind,
As little touched as any man's with bad.   580
Him through their inmost walks the Muses lad,
To him the sacred love of nature lent ;
And sometimes would he make our valley glad.
Whenas we found he would not here be pent,
To him the better sort this friendly message sent :   585

LXVI.

'Come, dwell with us! true son of virtue, come!
But if, alas! we cannot thee persuade
To lie content beneath our peaceful dome,
Ne ever more to quit our quiet glade;
Yet when at last thy toils, but ill apaid,   590
Shall dead thy fire, and damp its heavenly spark,
Thou wilt be glad to seek the rural shade,
There to indulge the muse, and nature mark:
We then a lodge for thee will rear in Hagley Park.'

LXVII.

Here whilom ligged th' Esopus of the age;   595
But, called by fame, in soul yprickèd deep,
A noble pride restored him to the stage,
And roused him like a giant from his sleep.
Even from his slumbers we advantage reap:
With double force the astonished scene he wakes,   600
Yet quits not nature's bounds. He knows to keep
Each due decorum : now the heart he shakes,
And now with well-urged sense the enlightened judgment takes.

LXVIII.

A bard here dwelt, more fat than bard beseems;
Who, void of envy, guile, and lust of gain,   605
On virtue still, and nature's pleasing themes,
Poured forth his unpremeditated strain,
The world forsaking with a calm disdain:
Here laughed he careless in his easy seat;
Here quaffed, encircled with the joyous train;   610
Oft moralizing sage; his ditty sweet
He loathed much to write, ne carèd to repeat.

P

LXIX.

Full oft by holy feet our ground was trod;
Of clerks good plenty here you mote espy.
A little, round, fat, oily man of God,   615
Was one I chiefly marked among the fry:
He had a roguish twinkle in his eye,
And shone all glittering with ungodly dew,
If a tight damsel chanced to trippen by;
Which when observed, he shrunk into his mew,   620
And straight would recollect his piety anew.

LXX.

Nor be forgot a tribe, who minded nought
(Old inmates of the place) but state-affairs:
They looked, perdie, as if they deeply thought;
And on their brow sat every nation's cares.   625
The world by them is parcelled out in shares,
When in the Hall of Smoke they congress hold,
And the sage berry sun-burnt Mocha bears
Has cleared their inward eye: then, smoke-enrolled,
Their oracles break forth, mysterious as of old.   630

LXXI.

Here languid Beauty kept her pale-faced court:
Bevies of dainty dames, of high degree,
From every quarter hither made resort;
Where, from gross mortal care and business free,
They lay, poured out in ease and luxury.   635
Or should they a vain shew of work assume,
Alas and well-a-day! what can it be?
To knot, to twist, to 'range the vernal bloom;
But far is cast the distaff, spinning-wheel, and loom.

LXXII.

Their only labour was to kill the time;   640
And labour dire it is, and weary woe.
They sit, they loll, turn o'er some idle rhyme;
Then, rising sudden, to the glass they go,
Or saunter forth, with tottering step and slow:
This soon too rude an exercise they find;   645
Straight on the couch their limbs again they throw,
Where hours on hours they sighing lie reclined,
And court the vapoury god soft-breathing in the wind.

LXXIII.

Now must I mark the villany we found,
But ah! too late, as shall eftsoons be shewn.   650
A place here was, deep, dreary, under ground;
Where still our inmates, when unpleasing grown,
Diseased, and loathsome, privily were thrown.
Far from the light of heaven, they languished there,
Unpitied uttering many a bitter groan;   655
For of these wretches taken was no care:
Fierce fiends and hags of hell their only nurses were.

LXXIV.

Alas the change! from scenes of joy and rest
To this dark den, where sickness tossed alway.
Here Lethargy, with deadly sleep opprest,   660
Stretched on his back a mighty lubbard lay,
Heaving his sides, and snorèd night and day:
To stir him from his traunce it was not eath,
And his half-opened eyne he shut straightway;
He led, I wot, the softest way to death,   665
And taught withouten pain and strife to yield the breath.

LXXV.

Of limbs enormous, but withal unsound,
Soft-swoln and pale, here lay the Hydropsy:
Unwieldy man! with belly monstrous round,
For ever fed with watery supply;   670
For still he drank, and yet he still was dry.
And moping here did Hypochondria sit,
Mother of spleen, in robes of various dye,
Who vexèd was full oft with ugly fit;
And some her frantic deemed, and some her deemed a wit.

LXXVI.

A lady proud she was, of ancient blood,   676
Yet oft her fear her pride made crouchen low:
She felt, or fancied in her fluttering mood,
All the diseases which the spittles know,
And sought all physic which the shops bestow,   680
And still new leeches and new drugs would try,
Her humour ever wavering to and fro:
For sometimes she would laugh, and sometimes cry,
Then sudden waxèd wroth, and all she knew not why.

LXXVII.

Fast by her side a listless maiden pined,   685
With aching head, and squeamish heart-burnings;
Pale, bloated, cold, she seemed to hate mankind,
Yet loved in secret all forbidden things.
And here the Tertian shakes his chilling wings;
The sleepless Gout here counts the crowing cocks,   690
A wolf now gnaws him, now a serpent stings;
Whilst Apoplexy crammed Intemperance knocks
Down to the ground at once, as butcher felleth ox.

CANTO II.

The Knight of Art and Industry,
And his achievements fair;
That, by this Castle's overthrow,
Secured, and crownèd were.

I.

ESCAPED the castle of the sire of sin,
Ah! where shall I so sweet a dwelling find?
For all around without, and all within,
Nothing save what delightful was and kind,
Of goodness savouring and a tender mind,   5
E'er rose to view. But now another strain,
Of doleful note, alas! remains behind :
I now must sing of pleasure turned to pain,
And of the false enchanter INDOLENCE complain.

II.

Is there no patron to protect the Muse,   10
And fence for her Parnassus' barren soil?
To every labour its reward accrues,
And they are sure of bread who swink and moil;
But a fell tribe the Aonian hive despoil,
As ruthless wasps oft rob the painful bee :   15
Thus while the laws not guard that noblest toil,
Ne for the Muses other meed decree,
They praisèd are alone, and starve right merrily.

III.

I care not, Fortune, what you me deny:
You cannot rob me of free nature's grace ;   20
You cannot shut the windows of the sky,
Through which Aurora shows her brightening face ;
You cannot bar my constant feet to trace
The woods and lawns by living stream at eve:
Let health my nerves and finer fibres brace,   25
And I their toys to the great children leave:
Of fancy, reason, virtue, nought can me bereave.

IV.

Come then, my Muse, and raise a bolder song ;
Come, lig no more upon the bed of sloth,
Dragging the lazy languid line along,   30
Fond to begin, but still to finish loth,
Thy half-writ scrolls all eaten by the moth:
Arise, and sing that generous imp of fame,
Who, with the sons of softness nobly wroth,
To sweep away this human lumber came,   35
Or in a chosen few to rouse the slumbering flame.

V.

In Fairyland there lived a knight of old,
Of feature stern, Selvaggio well ycleped,
A rough unpolished man, robust and bold,
But wondrous poor: he neither sowed nor reaped,   40
Ne stores in summer for cold winter heaped ;
In hunting all his days away he wore ;
Now scorched by June, now in November steeped,
Now pinched by biting January sore,
He still in woods pursued the libbard and the boar.   45

VI.

As he one morning, long before the dawn,
Pricked through the forest to dislodge his prey,
Deep in the winding bosom of a lawn,
With wood wild fringed, he marked a taper's ray,
That from the beating rain and wintry fray   50
Did to a lonely cot his steps decoy :
There, up to earn the needments of the day,
He found dame Poverty, nor fair nor coy ;
And she became his wife, the mother of his boy.

VII.

Amid the greenwood shade this boy was bred,   55
And grew at last a knight of muchel fame,
Of active mind and vigorous lustyhed,
THE KNIGHT OF ARTS AND INDUSTRY by name.
Earth was his bed, the boughs his roof did frame ;
He knew no beverage but the flowing stream ;   6c
His tasteful well earned food the sylvan game,
Or the brown fruit with which the woodlands teem :
The same to him glad summer or the winter breme.

VIII.

So passed his youthly morning, void of care,
Wild as the colts that through the commons run :   65
For him no tender parents troubled were ;
He of the forest seemed to be the son,
And certes had been utterly undone
But that Minerva pity of him took,
With all the gods that love the rural wonne,   70
That teach to tame the soil and rule the crook ;
Ne did the sacred Nine disdain a gentle look.

IX.

Of fertile genius him they nurtured well
In every science and in every art
By which mankind the thoughtless brutes excel,   75
That can or use, or joy, or grace impart,
Disclosing all the powers of head and heart.
Ne were the goodly exercises spared
That brace the nerves or make the limbs alert,
And mix elastic force with firmness hard :   80
Was never knight on ground mote be with him compared.

X.

Sometimes with early morn he mounted gay
The hunter-steed, exulting o'er the dale,
And drew the roseate breath of orient day ;
Sometimes, retiring to the secret vale,   85
Yclad in steel, and bright with burnished mail,
He strained the bow, or tossed the sounding spear,
Or darting on the goal outstript the gale,
Or wheeled the chariot in its mid career,
Or strenuous wrestled hard with many a tough compeer.   90

XI.

At other times he pried through nature's store,
Whate'er she in the ethereal round contains,
Whate'er she hides beneath her verdant floor—
The vegetable and the mineral reigns ;
Or else he scanned the globe—those small domains   95
Where restless mortals such a turmoil keep,
Its seas, its floods, its mountains, and its plains ;
But more he searched the mind, and roused from sleep
Those moral seeds whence we heroic actions reap.

XII.

Nor would he scorn to stoop from high pursuits   100
Of heavenly truth, and practise what she taught.
Vain is the tree of knowledge without fruits.
Sometimes in hand the spade or plough he caught,
Forth calling all with which boon earth is fraught;
Sometimes he plied the strong mechanic tool,   105
Or reared the fabric from the finest draught;
And oft he put himself to Neptune's school,
Fighting with winds and waves on the vexed ocean pool.

XIII.

To solace then these rougher toils he tried
To touch the kindling canvas into life;   110
With nature his creating pencil vied,—
With nature joyous at the mimic strife:
Or to such shapes as graced Pygmalion's wife
He hewed the marble; or with varied fire
He roused the trumpet and the martial fife,   115
Or bade the lute sweet tenderness inspire,
Or verses framed that well might wake Apollo's lyre.

XIV.

Accomplished thus he from the woods issued,
Full of great aims and bent on bold emprise;
The work which long he in his breast had brewed   120
Now to perform he ardent did devise,
To wit, a barbarous world to civilize.
Earth was till then a boundless forest wild—
Nought to be seen but savage wood and skies;
No cities nourished arts, no culture smiled,   125
No government, no laws, no gentle manners mild.

XV.

A rugged wight, the worst of brutes, was man;
On his own wretched kind he ruthless preyed:
The strongest still the weakest over-ran;
In every country mighty robbers swayed,   130
And guile and ruffian force were all their trade.
Life was not life, but rapine, want, and woe;
Which this brave knight, in noble anger, made
To swear he would the rascal rout o'erthrow;
For, by the powers divine, it should no more be so!   135

XVI.

It would exceed the purport of my song
To say how this best sun, from orient climes,
Came beaming life and beauty all along,
Before him chasing indolence and crimes.
Still as he passed, the nations he sublimes,   140
And calls forth arts and virtue with his ray:
Then Egypt, Greece, and Rome their golden times
Successive had; but now in ruins grey
They lie, to slavish sloth and tyranny a prey.

XVII.

To crown his toils, Sir INDUSTRY then spread   145
The swelling sail, and made for Britain's coast.
A silvan life till then the natives led,
In the brown shades and green-wood forest lost,
All careless rambling where it liked them most:
Their wealth the wild deer bouncing through the glade, 150
They lodged at large, and lived at nature's cost,
Save spear and bow, withouten other aid;
Yet not the Roman steel their naked breast dismayed.

XVIII.

He liked the soil, he liked the clement skies,
He liked the verdant hills and flowery plains :   155
'Be this my great, my chosen isle ! (he cries)
This—whilst my labours liberty sustains—
This queen of ocean all assault disdains.'
Nor liked he less the genius of the land,
To freedom apt and persevering pains,   160
Mild to obey, and generous to command,
Tempered by forming Heaven with kindest firmest hand.

XIX.

Here by degrees his master-work arose,
Whatever arts and industry can frame,
Whatever finished agriculture knows,   165
Fair Queen of Arts ! from heaven itself who came,
When Eden flourished in unspotted fame ;
And still with her sweet innocence we find,
And tender peace, and joys without a name,
That, while they rapture, tranquillize the mind ;   170
Nature and art at once, delight and use combined.

XX.

Then towns he quickened by mechanic arts,
And bade the fervent city glow with toil ;
Bade social commerce raise renownèd marts,
Join land to land, and marry soil to soil,   175
Unite the poles, and without bloody spoil
Bring home of either Ind the gorgeous stores ;
Or, should despotic rage the world embroil,
Bade tyrants tremble on remotest shores,
While o'er the encircling deep Britannia's thunder roars. 180

XXI.

The drooping muses then he westward called,
From the famed city by Propontis sea,
What time the Turk th' enfeebled Grecian thralled;
Thence from their cloistered walks he set them free,
And brought them to another Castalie,—   185
Where Isis many a famous nursling breeds,
Or where old Cam soft-paces o'er the lea
In pensive mood, and tunes his doric reeds,
The whilst his flocks at large the lonely shepherd feeds.

XXII.

Yet the fine arts were what he finished least.   19
For why? They are the quintessence of all,
The growth of labouring time, and slow increased;
Unless, as seldom chances, it should fall
That mighty patrons the coy sisters call
Up to the sunshine of uncumbered ease,   195
Where no rude care the mounting thought may thrall,
And where they nothing have to do but please—
Ah, gracious God! thou know'st they ask no other fees.

XXIII.

But now alas! we live too late in time:
Our patrons now even grudge that little claim,   200
Except to such as sleek the soothing rhyme;
And yet, forsooth, they wear Mæcenas' name,
Poor sons of puft-up vanity, not fame.
Unbroken spirits, cheer! still, still remains
The eternal patron, Liberty; whose flame,   205
While she protects, inspires the noblest strains.
The best and sweetest far, are toil-created gains.

XXIV.

Whenas the knight had framed in Britain-land
A matchless form of glorious government,
In which the sovereign laws alone command,   210
Laws stablished by the public free consent,
Whose majesty is to the sceptre lent,—
When this great plan, with each dependent art,
Was settled firm, and to his heart's content,
Then sought he from the toilsome scene to part,   215
And let life's vacant eve breathe quiet through the heart.

XXV.

For this he chose a farm in Deva's vale,
Where his long alleys peeped upon the main.
In this calm seat he drew the healthful gale,
Commixed the chief, the patriot, and the swain,   220
The happy monarch of his silvan train !
Here, sided by the guardians of the fold,
He walked his rounds, and cheered his blest domain;
His days, the days of unstained nature, rolled,
Replete with peace and joy, like patriarch's of old.   225

XXVI.

Witness, ye lowing herds, who lent him milk;
Witness, ye flocks, whose woolly vestments far
Exceed soft India's cotton, or her silk;
Witness, with Autumn charged, the nodding car,
That homeward came beneath sweet evening's star,   230
Or of September moons the radiance mild.
O hide thy head, abominable war !
Of crimes and ruffian idleness the child !
From Heaven this life ysprung, from hell thy glories vild !

XXVII.

Nor from his deep retirement banished was   235
The amusing cares of rural industry.
Still, as with grateful change the seasons pass,
New scenes arise, new landskips strike the eye,
And all the enlivened country beautify :
Gay plains extend where marshes slept before ;   240
O'er recent meads the exulting streamlets fly ;
Dark frowning heaths grow bright with Ceres' store,
And woods imbrown the steep, or wave along the shore.

XXVIII.

As nearer to his farm you made approach,
He polished nature with a finer hand :   245
Yet on her beauties durst not art encroach ;
'Tis art's alone these beauties to expand.
In graceful dance immingled, o'er the land,
Pan, Pales, Flora, and Pomona played :
Even here, sometimes, the rude wild common fand   250
A happy place ; where, free and unafraid,
Amid the flowering brakes each coyer creature strayed.

XXIX.

But in prime vigour what can last for aye ?
That soul-enfeebling wizard, INDOLENCE,
I whilom sung, wrought in his works decay :   255
Spread far and wide was his cursed influence ;
Of public virtue much he dulled the sense,
Even much of private ; eat our spirit out,
And fed our rank luxurious vices : whence
The land was overlaid with many a lout ;   260
Not, as old fame reports, wise generous, bold, and stout.

XXX.

A rage of pleasure maddened every breast;
Down to the lowest lees the ferment ran:
To his licentious wish each must be blest,
With joy be fevered,—snatch it as he can.　　　265
Thus vice the standard reared; her arrier-ban
Corruption called, and loud she gave the word.
'Mind, mind yourselves! why should the vulgar man,
The lacquey, be more virtuous than his lord?
Enjoy this span of life! 'tis all the gods afford.'　　　270

XXXI.

The tidings reached to where in quiet hall
The good old knight enjoyed well earned repose:
'Come, come, Sir Knight! thy children on thee call;
Come, save us yet, ere ruin round us close!
The demon INDOLENCE thy toils o'erthrows.'　　　275
On this the noble colour stained his cheeks,
Indignant glowing through the whitening snows
Of venerable eld; his eye full-speaks
His ardent soul, and from his couch at once he breaks.

XXXII.

'I will (he cried), so help me God! destroy　　　280
That villain Archimage.'—His page then strait
He to him called,—a fiery-footed boy
Benempt Dispatch. 'My steed be at the gate;
My bard attend; quick, bring the net of fate.'
This net was twisted by the sisters three;　　　285
Which, when once cast o'er hardened wretch, too late
Repentance comes: replevy cannot be
From the strong iron grasp of vengeful destiny.

XXXIII.

He came, the bard, a little Druid wight
Of withered aspect; but his eye was keen,   290
With sweetness mixed. In russet brown bedight,
As is his sister of the copses green,
He crept along, unpromising of mien.
Gross he who judges so. His soul was fair,
Bright as the children of yon azure sheen.   295
True comeliness, which nothing can impair,
Dwells in the mind : all else is vanity and glare.

XXXIV.

'Come! (quoth the Knight) a voice has reached mine ear,
The demon INDOLENCE threats overthrow
To all that to mankind is good and dear :   300
Come, Philomelus! let us instant go,
O'erturn his bowers, and lay his castle low.
Those men, those wretched men, who *will* be slaves,
Must drink a bitter wrathful cup of woe ;
But some there be, thy song, as from their graves,   305
Shall raise. Thrice happy he who without rigour saves!'

XXXV.

Issuing forth, the Knight bestrode his steed
Or ardent bay, and on whose front a star
Shone blazing bright ;—sprung from the generous breed
That whirl of active day the rapid car,   310
He pranced along, disdaining gate or bar.
Meantime, the bard on milk-white palfrey rode,—
An honest sober beast, that did not mar
His meditations, but full softly trode.
And much they moralized as thus yfere they yode.   315

XXXVI.

They talked of virtue, and of human bliss.
What else so fit for man to settle well?
And still their long researches met in this,
This truth of truths, which nothing can refel:
'From virtue's fount the purest joys outwell,   320
Sweet rills of thought that cheer the conscious soul;
While vice pours forth the troubled streams of hell,
The which, howe'er disguised, at last with dole
Will through the tortured breast their fiery torrent roll.'

XXXVII.

At length it dawned, that fatal valley gay,   325
O'er which high wood-crowned hills their summits rear.
On the cool height awhile our palmers stay,
And spite even of themselves their senses cheer;
Then to the wizard's wonne their steps they steer.
Like a green isle it broad beneath them spread,   330
With gardens round, and wandering currents clear,
And tufted groves to shade the meadow-bed,
Sweet airs and song; and without hurry all seemed glad.

XXXVIII.

'As God shall judge me, Knight! we must forgive
(The half-enraptured Philomelus cried)   335
The frail good man deluded here to live,
And in these groves his musing fancy hide.
Ah, nought is pure! It cannot be denied
That virtue still some tincture has of vice,
And vice of virtue. What should then betide,   340
But that our charity be not too nice?
Come, let us those we can to real bliss entice.'

Q

XXXIX.

'Ay, sicker (quoth the Knight), all flesh is frail,
To pleasant sin and joyous dalliance bent;
But let not brutish vice of this avail,   345
And think to 'scape deservèd punishment.
Justice were cruel weakly to relent;
From mercy's self she got her sacred glaive :
Grace be to those who can and will repent;
But penance long and dreary to the slave,   350
Who must in floods of fire his gross foul spirit lave.'

XL.

Thus holding high discourse, they came to where
The cursèd carle was at his wonted trade,—
Still tempting heedless men into his snare
In witching wise, as I before have said.   355
But when he saw, in goodly geer arrayed,
The grave majestic Knight approaching nigh,
And by his side the bard so sage and staid,
His countenance fell; yet oft his anxious eye
Marked them, like wily fox who roosted cock doth spy. 360

XLI.

Nathless with feigned respect he bade give back
The rabble rout, and welcomed them full kind.
Struck with the noble twain, they were not slack
His orders to obey, and fall behind.
Then he resumed his song ; and unconfined   365
Poured all his music, ran through all his strings :
With magic dust their eyne he tries to blind,
And virtue's tender airs o'er weakness flings.
What pity base his song who so divinely sings!

XLII.

Elate in thought, he counted them his own,　　　　370
They listened so intent with fixed delight :
But they instead, as if transmewed to stone,
Marvelled he could with such sweet art unite
The lights and shades of manners, wrong and right.
Meantime the silly crowd the charm devour,　　　375
Wide pressing to the gate.　Swift on the Knight
He darted fierce to drag him to his bower,
Who backening shunned his touch, for well he knew its power.

XLIII.

As in thronged amphitheatre of old
The wary retiarius trapped his foe,　　　　　　380
Even so the Knight, returning on him bold,
At once involved him in the net of woe,
Whereof I mention made not long ago.
Enraged at first, he scorned so weak a jail,
And leaped, and flew, and flouncèd to and fro ;　　385
But when he found that nothing could avail
He sat him felly down, and gnawed his bitter nail.

XLIV.

Alarmed, the inferior demons of the place
Raised rueful shrieks and hideous yells around ;
Black ruptured clouds deformed the welkin's face,　　390
And from beneath was heard a wailing sound,
As of infernal sprights in cavern bound ;
A solemn sadness every creature strook,
And lightnings flashed, and horror rocked the ground :
Huge crowds on crowds outpoured, with blemished look, 395
As if on Time's last verge this frame of things had shook.

XLV.

Soon as the short-lived tempest was yspent—
Steamed from the jaws of vexed Avernus' hole—
And hushed the hubbub of the rabblement,
Sir INDUSTRY the first calm moment stole: 400
'There must (he cried) amid so vast a shoal
Be some who are not tainted at the heart,
Not poisoned quite by this same villain's bowl:
Come then, my bard, thy heavenly fire impart;
Touch soul with soul, till forth the latent spirit start.'   405

XLVI.

The bard obeyed; and taking from his side,
Where it in seemly sort depending hung,
His British harp, its speaking strings he tried,
The which with skilful touch he deftly strung,
Till tinkling in clear symphony they rung.   410
Then, as he felt the Muses come along,
Light o'er the chords his raptured hand he flung,
And played a prelude to his rising song:
The whilst, like midnight mute, ten thousands round him
        throng.

XLVII.

Thus ardent burst his strain: 'Ye hapless race,   415
Dire labouring here to smother reason's ray,
That lights our Maker's image in our face,
And gives us wide o'er earth unquestioned sway,—
What is the adored Supreme Perfection, say?
What but eternal never-resting soul,   420
Almighty power, and all-directing day,
By whom each atom stirs, the planets roll,
Who fills, surrounds, informs, and agitates the whole?

XLVIII.

'Come, to the beaming God your hearts unfold!
Draw from its fountain life! 'Tis thence alone   425
We can excel. Up from unfeeling mould
To seraphs burning round the Almighty's throne,
Life rising still on life in higher tone
Perfection forms, and with perfection bliss.
In universal nature this clear shown   430
Not needeth proof: to prove it were, I wis,
To prove the beauteous world excels the brute abyss.

XLIX.

'Is not the field with lively culture green
A sight more joyous than the dead morass?
Do not the skies with active ether clean,   435
And fanned by sprightly zephyrs, far surpass
The foul November fogs and slumbrous mass
With which sad nature veils her drooping face?
Does not the mountain stream, as clear as glass,
Gay-dancing on, the putrid pool disgrace?   440
The same in all holds true, but chief in human race.

L.

'It was not by vile loitering in ease
That Greece obtained the brighter palm of art;
That soft yet ardent Athens learned to please,
To keen the wit, and to sublime the heart,—   445
In all supreme! complete in every part!
It was not thence majestic Rome arose,
And o'er the nations shook her conquering dart:
For sluggard's brow the laurel never grows;
Renown is not the child of indolent repose.   450

LI.

'Had unambitious mortals minded nought
But in loose joy their time to wear away,
Had they alone the lap of dalliance sought,
Pleased on her pillow their dull heads to lay,
Rude nature's state had been our state to-day;   455
No cities e'er their towery fronts had raised,
No arts had made us opulent and gay,
With brother brutes the human race had grazed,
None e'er had soared to fame, none honoured been, none
        praised.

LII.

'Great Homer's song had never fired the breast   460
To thirst of glory and heroic deeds;
Sweet Maro's muse, sunk in inglorious rest,
Had silent slept amid the Mincian reeds;
The wits of modern time had told their beads,
The monkish legends been their only strains;   465
Our Milton's Eden had lain wrapt in weeds,
Our Shakespeare strolled and laughed with Warwick swains,
Ne had my master Spenser charmed his Mulla's plains.

LIII.

'Dumb too had been the sage historic muse,
And perished all the sons of ancient fame;   470
Those starry lights of virtue, that diffuse
Through the dark depth of time their vivid flame,
Had all been lost with such as have no name.
Who then had scorned his ease for others' good?
Who then had toiled rapacious men to tame?   475
Who in the public breach devoted stood,
And for his country's cause been prodigal of blood?

LIV.

'But should to fame your hearts impervious be,
If right I read, you pleasure all require:
Then hear how best may be obtained this fee,　　480
How best enjoyed this nature's wide desire.
Toil and be glad! let Industry inspire
Into your quickened limbs her buoyant breath!
Who does not act is dead; absorpt entire
In miry sloth, no pride, no joy he hath:　　485
O leaden-hearted men, to be in love with death!

LV.

'Better the toiling swain, oh happier far!
Perhaps the happiest of the sons of men!
Who vigorous plies the plough, the team, or car,
Who houghs the field, or ditches in the glen,　　490
Delves in his garden, or secures his pen:
The tooth of avarice poisons not his peace;
He tosses not in sloth's abhorrèd den;
From vanity he has a full release;
And, rich in nature's wealth, he thinks not of increase.　　495

LVI.

'Good Lord! how keen are his sensations all!
His bread is sweeter than the glutton's cates;
The wines of France upon the palate pall
Compared with what his simple soul elates,
The native cup whose flavour thirst creates;　　500
At one deep draught of sleep he takes the night;
And for that heart-felt joy which nothing mates,
Of the pure nuptial bed the chaste delight,—
The losel is to him a miserable wight.

LVII.

'But what avail the largest gifts of Heaven,   505
When sickening health and spirits go amiss?
How tasteless then whatever can be given!
Health is the vital principle of bliss,
And exercise of health. In proof of this,
Behold the wretch who slugs his life away,   510
Soon swallowed in disease's sad abyss;
While he whom toil has braced, or manly play,
Has light as air each limb, each thought as clear as day.

LVIII.

'O who can speak the vigorous joys of health!
Unclogged the body, unobscured the mind;   515
The morning rises gay, with pleasing stealth
The temperate evening falls serene and kind.
In health the wiser brutes true gladness find.
See how the younglings frisk along the meads,
As May comes on and wakes the balmy wind;   520
Rampant with life, their joy all joy exceeds:
Yet what save high-strung health this dancing pleasaunce
        breeds?

LIX.

'But here instead is fostered every ill
Which or distempered minds or bodies know.
Come then, my kindred spirits! do not spill   525
Your talents here. This place is but a show,
Whose charms delude you to the den of woe.
Come, follow me! I will direct you right
Where pleasure's roses void of serpents grow,
Sincere as sweet; come, follow this good Knight,   530
And you will bless the day that brought him to your sight.

·LX.

'Some he will lead to courts, and some to camps;
To senates some, and public sage debates,
Where, by the solemn gleam of midnight lamps,
The world is poised, and managed mighty states;　　535
To high discovery some, that new creates
The face of earth; some to the thriving mart;
Some to the rural reign, and softer fates;
To the sweet muses some, who raise the heart :
All glory shall be yours, all nature, and all art.　　540

LXI.

'There are, I see, who listen to my lay,
Who wretched sigh for virtue, but despair.
"All may be done (methinks I hear them say),
Even death despised by generous actions fair;
All, but for those who to these bowers repair,　　545
Their every power dissolved in luxury,
To quit of torpid sluggishness the lair,
And from the powerful arms of sloth get free—
'Tis rising from the dead! Alas it cannot be!"

LXII.

'Would you then learn to dissipate the band　　550
Of these huge threatening difficulties dire
That in the weak man's way like lions stand,
His soul appal, and damp his rising fire?
Resolve! resolve! and to be men aspire!
Exert that noblest privilege, alone　　555
Here to mankind indulged; control desire;
Let godlike reason from her sovereign throne
Speak the commanding word *I will!* and it is done.

LXIII.

'Heavens! can you then thus waste in shameful wise
Your few important days of trial here?   560
Heirs of eternity, yborn to rise
Through endless states of being, still more near
To bliss approaching and perfection clear,
Can you renounce a fortune so sublime,
Such glorious hopes, your backward steps to steer,   565
And roll, with vilest brutes, through mud and slime?
No! no!—Your heaven-touched hearts disdain the piteous
      crime!'

LXIV.

'Enough! enough!' they cried. Straight from the crowd
The better sort on wings of transport fly,
As, when amid the lifeless summits proud   570
Of Alpine cliffs, where to the gelid sky
Snows piled on snows in wintry torpor lie,
The rays divine of vernal Phœbus play,
The awakened heaps, in streamlets from on high,
Roused into action, lively leap away,   575
Glad warbling through the vales, in their new being gay.

LXV.

Not less the life, the vivid joy serene,
That lighted up these new-created men
Than that which wings the exulting spirit clean
When, just delivered from this fleshly den,   580
It soaring seeks its native skies agen:
How light its essence! how unclogged its powers,
Beyond the blazon of my mortal pen!
Even so we glad forsook these sinful bowers;
Even such enraptured life, such energy was ours.   585

LXVI.

But far the greater part, with rage inflamed,
Dire muttered curses, and blasphemed high Jove.
'Ye sons of hate! (they bitterly exclaimed)
What brought you to this seat of peace and love?
While with kind nature here amid the grove   590
We passed the harmless sabbath of our time,
What to disturb it could, fell men! emove
Your barbarous hearts? Is happiness a crime?
Then do the fiends of hell rule in yon Heaven sublime.'

LXVII.

'Ye impious wretches, (quoth the Knight in wrath)   595
Your happiness behold!' Then straight a wand
He waved, an anti-magic power that hath
Truth from illusive falsehood to command.
Sudden the landskip sinks on every hand;
The pure quick streams are marshy puddles found;   600
On baleful heaths the groves all blackened stand;
And o'er the weedy foul abhorred ground,
Snakes, adders, toads, each loathly creature crawls around.

LXVIII.

And here and there, on trees by lightning scathed,
Unhappy wights who loathèd life yhung;   605
Or in fresh gore and recent murder bathed
They weltering lay; or else, infuriate flung
Into the gloomy flood, while ravens sung
The funeral dirge, they down the torrent rolled: ·
These, by distempered blood to madness stung,   610
Had doomed themselves; whence oft, when night con-
        trolled
The world, returning hither their sad spirits howled.

LXIX.

Meantime a moving scene was open laid.
That lazar-house I whilom in my lay
Depeinten have its horrors deep displayed,   615
And gave unnumbered wretches to the day,
Who tossing there in squalid misery lay.
Soon as of sacred light the unwonted smile
Poured on these living catacombs its ray,
Through the drear caverns stretching many a mile,   620
The sick upraised their heads, and dropped their woes awhile.

LXX.

' O Heaven! (they cried) and do we once more see
Yon blessèd sun, and this green earth so fair?
Are we from noisome damps of pest-house free?
And drink our souls the sweet ethereal air?   625
O thou or Knight or God! who holdest there
That fiend, oh keep him in eternal chains!
But what for us, the children of despair,
Brought to the brink of hell, what hope remains?
Repentance does itself but aggravate our pains.'   630

LXXI.

The gentle Knight, who saw their rueful case,
Let fall adown his silver beard some tears.
' Certes (quoth he) it is not even in grace
To undo the past, and eke your broken years:
Nathless to nobler worlds repentance rears   635
With humble hope her eye; to her is given
A power the truly contrite heart that cheers;
She quells the brand by which the rocks are riven;
She more than merely softens—she rejoices Heaven.

LXXII.

'Then patient bear the sufferings you have earned, 640
And by these sufferings purify the mind;
Let wisdom be by past misconduct learned:
Or pious die, with penitence resigned;
And to a life more happy and refined
Doubt not you shall new creatures yet arise. 645
Till then, you may expect in me to find
One who will wipe your sorrow from your eyes,
One who will soothe your pangs, and wing you to the skies.'

LXXIII.

They silent heard, and poured their thanks in tears.
' For you (resumed the Knight with sterner tone) 650
Whose hard dry hearts th' obdurate demon sears,—
That villain's gifts will cost you many a groan;
In dolorous mansion long you must bemoan
His fatal charms, and weep your stains away;
Till, soft and pure as infant goodness grown, 655
You feel a perfect change: then, who can say
What grace may yet shine forth in Heaven's eternal day '

LXXIV.

This said, his powerful wand he waved anew:
Instant a glorious angel-train descends,
The charities, to wit, of rosy hue: 660
Sweet love their looks a gentle radiance lends,
And with seraphic flame compassion blends.
At once delighted to their charge they fly:
When lo! a goodly hospital ascends,
In which they bade each human aid be nigh, 665
That could the sick-bed smooth of that unhappy fry.

LXXV.

It was a worthy edifying sight,
And gives to human kind peculiar grace,
To see kind hands attending day and night
With tender ministry from place to place.   670
Some prop the head; some from the pallid face
Wipe off the faint cold dews weak nature sheds;
Some reach the healing draught: the whilst, to chase
The fear supreme, around their softened beds,
Some holy man by prayer all opening Heaven dispreds. 675

LXXVI.

Attended by a glad acclaiming train
Of those he rescued had from gaping hell,
Then turned the Knight; and, to his hall again
Soft-pacing, sought of peace the mossy cell,
Yet down his cheeks the gems of pity fell   680
To see the helpless wretches that remained,
There left through delves and deserts dire to yell;
Amazed, their looks with pale dismay were stained,
And, spreading wide their hands, they meek repentance
        feigned.

LXXVII.

But ah! their scornèd day of grace was past: 685
For (horrible to tell!) a desert wild
Before them stretched, bare, comfortless, and vast,
With gibbets, bones, and carcases defiled.
There nor trim field nor lively culture smiled;
Nor waving shade was seen, nor fountain fair;   690
But sands abrupt on sands lay loosely piled,
Through which they floundering toiled with painful care,
Whilst Phœbus smote them sore, and fired the cloudless
        air.

LXXVIII.

Then, varying to a joyless land of bogs,
The saddened country a gray waste appeared,⠀⠀⠀695
Where nought but putrid streams and noisome fogs
For ever hung on drizzly Auster's beard ;
Or else the ground, by piercing Caurus seared,
Was jagged with frost or heaped with glazed snow :
Through these extremes a ceaseless round they steered, 700
By cruel fiends still hurried to and fro,
Gaunt beggary and scorn, with many hell-hounds moe.

LXXIX.

The first was with base dunghill rags yclad,
Tainting the gale, in which they fluttered light ;
Of morbid hue his features, sunk and sad ;⠀⠀⠀705
His hollow eyne shook forth a sickly light ;
And o'er his lank jawbone, in piteous plight,
His black rough beard was matted rank and vile ;
Direful to see ! a heart-appalling sight !
Meantime foul scurf and blotches him defile ;⠀⠀⠀710
And dogs, where'er he went, still barkèd all the while.

LXXX.

The other was a fell despightful fiend :
Hell holds none worse in baleful bower below ;
By pride, and wit, and rage, and rancour keened ;
Of man, alike if good or bad, the foe :⠀⠀⠀715
With nose upturned, he always made a show
As if he smelt some nauseous scent ; his eye
Was cold and keen, like blast from boreal snow ;
And taunts he casten forth most bitterly.
Such were the twain that off drove this ungodly fry.⠀⠀⠀720

LXXXI.

Even so through Brentford town, a town of mud,
A herd of bristly swine is pricked along;
The filthy beasts, that never chew the cud,
Still grunt, and squeak, and sing their troublous song;
And oft they plunge themselves the mire among: 725
But aye the ruthless driver goads them on,
And aye of barking dogs the bitter throng
Makes them renew their unmelodious moan,
Ne ever find they rest from their unresting fone.

END OF THE CASTLE OF INDOLENCE.

NOTES.

—+—

SPRING.

Introductory Note.

Placed in its natural order in the collected seasons, Spring came third in the order of composition. It was published in 1728, with a dedication in prose to the Countess of Hertford, whom Thomson describes as a lady of 'fine imagination' and having 'intimate acquaintance with rural nature.'   He adds the interesting information that the poem grew up under her encouragement, and had therefore a natural claim to her patronage.   Johnson offers a peculiar view of the nature of this encouragement: it was this lady's practice, he says, 'to invite every summer some poet into the country, to hear her verses and assist her studies.   This honour was one summer conferred on Thomson, who took more delight in carousing with Lord Hertford and his friends than assisting her ladyship's poetical operations, and therefore never received another summons.'   The scene of those carousals was Marlborough Castle, in Wiltshire, where, probably in 1727, notwithstanding the alleged dissipations, time was found to write the larger portion, if not the whole, of Spring. 'Here Mr. Thomson composed one of his Seasons' is the testimony of Stephen Duck, the Wiltshire thresher-poet, a contemporary of Thomson, and only some five years his junior. Lady Hertford's manner of life at Marlborough may be inferred from the following verses of her own composition :—

> 'We sometimes ride, and sometimes walk,
> We play at chess, or laugh, or talk;
> Sometimes beside the crystal stream
> We meditate some serious theme ;
> Or in the grot beside the spring
> We hear the feathered warblers sing.

R

> Shakspeare perhaps an hour diverts,
> Or Scott directs to mend our hearts,
> With Clarke God's attributes explore
> And taught by him admire them more.
> Gay's pastorals sometimes delight us,
> Or Tasso's grisly spectres fright us;
> Sometimes we trace Armida's bowers
> And view Rinaldo chained with flowers.
> Often from thoughts sublime as these
> I sink at once—and make a cheese;
> Or see my various poultry fed
> And treat my swans with scraps of bread.'

Sometimes upon the smooth canal they go boating till sundown;

> ' Then tolls the bell, and all unite
> In prayer that God would bless the night.'

From this—

> ' To cards we go till ten has struck,
> And then, however bad our luck,
> Our stomachs ne'er refuse to eat
> Eggs, cream, fresh-butter, or calves'-feet,
> And cooling fruit, or savoury greens,
> 'Sparagus, peas, or kidney beans.
> Our supper past, an hour we sit
> And talk of history, Spain, or wit.'

One may imagine Thomson joining occasionally in some part of all this.

The prose dedication of Spring was not repeated. In the second edition appeared the greater compliment of those half-dozen lines at the commencement of the poem which rendered it unnecessary. Lady Hertford, if she did not again invite Thomson to her country seat, did not cease to admire and praise his genius. Twenty years after the publication of Spring she promised to a correspondent 'much entertainment in Mr. Thomson's Castle of Indolence,' and recommended 'the many pretty paintings in it.'

The publisher of Spring was one Andrew Miller, who did business at the sign of Buchanan's Head, and who seems to have favoured, or been favoured by, Scottish authors. He paid Thomson fifty guineas for copyright. It was not till 1731 that he brought out the second edition, but in the interval, more particularly in 1730, the first edition of the

collected Seasons had appeared. Spring, The Dunciad, and The
Beggars' Opera were the chief London publications of 1728.

In Spring, Thomson's imagination does not carry him beyond the
British Isles. He found at home all that was needful for a poetical
representation of that delightful season. Nowhere, indeed, is nature
lovelier in springtime. 'My genius spreads her wing,' sang Goldsmith,
in 1764, in the character of the Traveller—

> 'And flies where Britain courts the western spring,
> Where lawns extend that scorn Arcadian pride,
> And brighter streams than famed Hydaspes glide :
> There all around the gentlest breezes play,
> There gentle music melts on every spray ;—
> Creation's mildest charms are there combined.'

And the wish of Browning among Italian scenery was 'O to be in
England now that April's there !'

Spring was augmented in the later editions by about one-tenth. The
lines on angling are a charming addition. It is a question, however,
whether the description of Hagley Park and its people greatly improves
the poem. It is only right to say that the Lytteltons deserved the
tribute of that description.

The Argument of the poem, as given in the edition of 1738, offers the
following summary :—

'The subject proposed. Inscribed to Lady Hertford. This Season
is described as it affects the various parts of nature, ascending from the
lower to the higher, and mixed with digressions arising from the subject.
Its influence on inanimate matter, on vegetables, on brute animals, and
last on man ; concluding with a dissuasive from the wild and irregular
passion of love, opposed to that of a purer and more reasonable kind.'

The finest descriptive passages in Spring include a series of views—
not all original—that almost exhaust the poetical aspects of bird-life.
Of these the fullest and most striking are the bird concert, bird courtship, teaching the young birds to fly, the mother bird's return to her
harried nest, and the St. Kilda eagle. Of equal power and fidelity to
nature are the glimpses of the swan on the river, the dove, and the
parading peacock. One misses, however, the return of the swallows—
a theme on which Thomson should have had something good to say.
The capture of the big trout and the bull in the broom are drawn with
as firm and faithful a touch as Thomson has anywhere shown, even in

Winter; while the description of the deluge, compressed into eight wonderful lines, ending in a climax that awes the imagination, reveals the advance which the poet had made in imaginative force since the publication of Winter. There is a tendency to indulge the *preaching* vein in the panegyric on nuptial love; but the most prolix part of the poem is the description of the woes of the lover, especially the jealous lover. The idea of love enters the poet's mind when he is about half through the poem, and a description of the effects of that passion on bird, beast, and man follows and continues to the end. Before Tennyson, Thomson knew that

' In the Spring a young man's fancy lightly turns to thoughts of love.'

The poem opens with a rapid but graphic account of the transition from Winter to Spring, none of the essential phenomena that mark the change being omitted. We are introduced to a scene of snow-clad hills, livid torrents, and cloud-laden skies, and before the poem closes we find ourselves on the threshold of Summer. The work of the farm occupies but a small portion of the poem. It is not merely, nor even mainly, cultivated nature as transformed by the advancing season that forms the subject of the poem. The range is wider; it is rather over nature unmodified by the arts and influence of man. The presence of man is lost in the all-pervading presence of nature. The poet never once follows Spring into village street or town. Even within the flower-garden he looks beyond, as if impatient of its confining wall, to the ethereal mountain or the distant main. The freshness and freedom of the air of the open wilderness are everywhere about him. It is the musical expression of these qualities, so admirably caught from the poem, that recommends Haydn's setting of Spring to every admirer of Thomson.

Lines 1–4. This invocation is simply the poet's way of announcing his choice of subject. Instead of saying, in a prosaic way, that he means to describe the mild winds and refreshing rains, the song-birds and flowers, and other features of the Spring season, he imagines a goddess descending from heaven in response to his call, garlanded with roses and surrounded with music. The image of the goddess is purposely obscured with the cloud and the veil, to harmonize with the shy graces of early Spring-time. For the same reason there is a blending of figure and feeling in the first line, which, though evasively bewildering to one's imagination, admirably suggests a sense of the presence of Spring. Thomson attempted to alter these lines, but never succeeded to his satisfaction.

3, 4. *veiled in a shower Of shadowing roses*. Cp. Milton's description of Eve in the garden of Eden—

'Veiled in a cloud of fragrance, where she stood
Half-spied, so thick the roses bushing round
About her glowed.'—*Par. Lost*, Bk. IX. ll. 425–7.

5. *O Hertford*, &c. Frances Thynne, granddaughter of Viscount Weymouth, and wife of the Earl of Hertford, afterwards Duke of Somerset. She was a lady of considerable literary taste and many acquirements. Her knowledge of history is said to have been particularly extensive. She was fond of the society of poets[1], and made some figure herself as a verse-writer. A specimen of her talent has already been given in the Introductory Note to this poem. To her, in 1750, Shenstone inscribed his ode on Rural Elegance. Watts also inscribed his Miscellanies to her. She is described by Horace Walpole as affable, yet dignified, affectionately devoted to her husband in his long illness, and careful in training her children in virtue and religion. Johnson speaks rather contemptuously of her 'poetical operations.' Walpole, without characterizing her verses, gives her credit for having 'as much taste for the writings of others, as modesty about her own.' Thomson alludes to her fitness for 'shining in courts'—a fitness which Queen Caroline rewarded by making her one of the ladies of the bed-chamber. She died in 1754, four years after the death of her husband.

21, 22. *scarce The bittern knows his time*. The time here referred to is the breeding season. The bittern, or more correctly the bitour or bittor (from the French *butor*), is a genus, or sub-genus, of the heron family of wading birds. It is somewhat less than the heron, and differs from it in building its nest on the ground. It haunts marshy places on upland moors, lies close by day, and wakens up towards evening to fill the air with that peculiar booming cry from which its name seems to be derived. In some localities in England it is familiarly called, from the same peculiarity, the mire-drum, the bull-of-the-bog, &c. Owing to the modern system of drainage it is not now so common in our country as it was in the time of Thomson. The breeding season of this bird is in February or March. It used to be believed that its peculiar cry was produced by the bird inserting its four-inch long bill into a reed, or into the marsh; but it is now known that its cries are uttered in the air, often while the bird is making its lofty spiral ascent. The bittern is of

[1] It was by her intercession with the Queen that a pardon was procured in 1727 for the unfortunate Savage, who had killed a man in a tavern brawl.

a dull yellow colour irregularly marked with black, has a long bare neck, and when wounded is dangerous to approach, as it fights desperately and strikes at the eye of its assailant.

23, 24. *from the shore The plovers.* Crested lapwings, or peewits, are meant. They are a genus of the plover family of wading birds, and well-known in Britain wherever there are moors or marshy tracts. They live in flocks, in the Winter season, chiefly at the seaside : in the early Spring they fly inland to upland moors and waste lands, where they pair, and build their nests on the ground. Their artifices to prevent people from discovering their eggs are described in lines 693-7 *infra.* Plovers are named from the circumstance of their being especially restless, and therefore most seen, in rainy weather (Lat. *pluvialis*, rainy). In Germany the plover is the rain-piper (*Regenpfeiffer*). It is worth noting that Goldsmith also brings the bittern and the lapwing together in poetry, but with a purpose different from that of Thomson: the later poet's object is to accentuate the desolation of the deserted village—

> ' Along thy glades, a solitary guest,
> The hollow-sounding bittern guards its nest ;
> Amidst thy desert walks the lapwing flies
> And tires their echoes with unvaried cries.'

Tennyson makes—

> ' The tufted plover pipe along the fallow lea.'

26, 27. *At last from Aries rolls the bounteous sun, And the bright Bull receives him.* In plain English—poetry, or pedantry, apart—it is now about the end of April. The sun enters the sign (*not* now the constellation) of Aries at the vernal equinox. The precession of the equinoxes has quite disarranged the Zodiac. Thomson rather affects the old-fashioned poetical way of marking the advance of the year. So in Winter, lines 42, 43—

> ' To Capricorn the Centaur-Archer yields,
> And fierce Aquarius stains th' inverted year.'

These references to the position of the sun in the Zodiac, as indicative of the time of the year, are as old in our literature as the age of Chaucer, the author of the Astrolabe. To take a familiar example—

> 'the yonge sonne
> Hath in the Ram his halfe cours i-ronne.'
>
> *Prologue to Tales,* ll. 7, 8.

This was a mere display of learning, but Chaucer had the humanity to surround it with natural images suggestive of the progress of the season which everybody could understand. It was rather late in the day for Thomson seriously to adopt the old method of marking time. The lines are sonorous enough, but they are nothing more.

34-36. *Joyous, the impatient husbandman*, &c. Compare and
contrast—

  'Ac neque jam stabulis gaudet pecus aut arator igni.'

                                        Hor. *Car*. I. 4.
The ox in this country, even in Scotland, is now all but superseded as
a beast of burden and of draught by the horse. Dunbar has a kindly
notice of the plough-ox in the Thistle and the Rose—

        'And lat no bowgle, with his busteous hornis,
          The meik pluch ox oppress, for all his pryd,
        Bot in the yok go peciable him besyd.'   ll. 110–112.
The bowgle is the bugle, or wild ox. Milton's notice in Comus of 'the
laboured ox' returning in loose traces from the furrow, will occur to
every one. So late as the time of Burns, who lived two generations
after Thomson, the ox was still in common use on Scottish farms as a
beast of draught. The ploughman-poet sings in The Lea-rig of ' owsen
frae the furrow'd field ' returning 'dowf an' weary,' but he writes also of
small horses, or 'pownies,' reeking before the plough or harrows. In
the end of last century an ox and a horse were often to be seen on lowland farms dragging the same plough. Thomson's knowledge of the
work of the farm, it may be noted here, was altogether drawn from the
Scottish lowlands.

  40. *the simple song*. Of the ploughman. It is still happily his
practice to sing at the plough. For the song of Thomson's 'husbandman' one may reasonably consult such a collection of old songs,
Scottish and English, as Allan Ramsay brought together in his Tea-
Table Miscellany in 1724.

  42. *The master*. The ploughman proper. The attendance of a boy
or young man as *gadsman*, or goadsman, to walk at the head or side of
the oxen and keep them going with his goad, appears to be implied.

    removes the obstructing clay. From the mould-board. This is
done with the *pattle* or plough-spade. It is the mould-board that
throws the furrow, and it is essential to good ploughing that this should
be done cleanly.

  43. *Winds the whole work*. Plans the method and order of the cultivation of the field ; or directs the progress of the whole work, first
feering, and then *gathering* the furrows into ridges. Or *cleaving*, a
process the reverse of *gathering*, may be adopted. The modern method
of laying out a field with the plough is *casting*. Cp. ' to wind a watch,'
i.e. to set a-going and keep in continual motion.

  52-54. *Nor ye who live in luxury*, &c. Cp. the lines of Gray in the
well-known Elegy (published 1751)—

        ' Let not ambition mock their useful toil,' &c.

55. *the rural Maro.* Virgil, the author of the Georgics. The first of the four Georgics treats of agriculture. The whole work, undertaken at the instance of Mæcenas, occupied the poet seven years—from his 34th to his 41st year; it was mostly written at Naples and is the best specimen of his verse. His descriptions of life and work at the farm are singularly vivid, and are beautifully illustrated with many poetical episodes. He was born, 70 B.C., on his father's farm or estate near Mantua; lived mainly a country life, uninfluenced by personal experience of Rome, till he was thirty; and died 19 B.C., and was buried near his beloved Naples. The Æneid is, of course, regarded as his greatest poem.

Traces of Thomson's study of the first two Georgics may be found in the foregoing passage commencing 'Forth fly the tepid airs' (l. 32)—more especially in those parts of it which suggest the feeling of Spring in the air, and express sympathy with the hopes and fears of the farmer.

59. *awful fathers of mankind.* Such as Cincinnatus—'awful from the plough' (see Winter, l. 512); and Philopœmen 'toiling in his farm a simple swain' or 'thundering in the field' of battle (Winter, l. 494).

60. *your insect tribes.* Thomson is not often so severe. He is of course addressing those 'who live in luxury and ease' and think agriculture, and external nature generally, unworthy of their attention or of poetical treatment. (See ll. 52-54 *supra.*)

65. *and greatly independent lived.* So in the early editions; expanded and weakened in the later thus—

'and greatly independent *scorned*
All the vile stores corruption can bestow.'

66. *venerate the plough.* In the original version, '*cultivate* the plough.'

69-75. The commerce, agriculture, and manufactures of Britain are briefly noticed in these lines, and the wish is expressed that greater national interest were directed to the production of corn and wool. The use of the comparatives, 'superior' and 'better,' shows that Thomson believed in the establishment of the British power upon rural industry at home rather than upon trade and traffic abroad. In various parts of Liberty, a noble and eloquent historical poem strangely neglected ever since Johnson condemned without having read it, the same preference for an agricultural to a commercial basis as the first foundation of national strength and welfare is expressed or implied. Britannia is thus described—

'Great nurse of fruits, of flocks, of commerce, she!
Great nurse of men!'—Part V. ll. 81-2.

In the same Part occurs the following passage—

> 'She, whitening o'er her downs, diffusive pours
> Unnumber'd flocks; she weaves the fleecy robe
> That wraps the nations; she to lusty droves
> The richest pasture spreads ; and, hers, deep wave
> Autumnal seas of pleasing plenty round,' &c.

ll. 38–42, *et seqq.*

80. *the steaming Power.* The sap which had retreated to the roots, 'the dark retreat of vegetation.' It is now ' set at large,' and ' wanders ' again through stems and stalks all over the spring landscape, giving their ' various hues ' to the purpling buds and green unfolding leaves of trees and bushes, ' its vivid verdure ' to 'the wither'd hill,' its white blossoms to the hawthorn, &c.—all as described in the succeeding lines. See also ll. 566–570 *infra.*

84. *United light and shade.* Neither so brilliant as to dazzle, nor yet sombre, but an intermediate cheerful tint that soothes and strengthens the eye.

86, 87. 'The hounds of Spring are on Winter's traces.' (Swinburne.)

89. But the whitening of the hawthorn comes considerably later than the budding of trees—even of the ash.

100–106. Thomson mentions the town in Spring only to leave it. Compare with this passage Milton's fine simile—

> 'As one who, long in populous city pent,
> Where houses thick and sewers annoy the air,
> Forth issuing on a summer's morn, to breathe
> Among the pleasant villages and farms
> Adjoined, from each thing met conceives delight—
> The smell of grain, or tedded grass, or kine,
> Or dairy,' &c.—*Par. Lost*, Bk. IX. ll. 445–451.

107. *Some eminence, Augusta, in thy plains.* Richmond Hill will answer, and is probably intended. Thomson went to live at Richmond in 1736. The surname of *Augusta* was first given to London in the time of Constantine the Great, in the early part of the fourth century. It was then a large and important town, no longer confined to the south bank of the Thames, but extending along the north bank as well, and on the latter side defended by a wall.

111, 112. *hid beneath The fair profusion yellow Autumn spies.* Anticipates a good crop of fruit from the abundance of blossom. Note the colouring, from l. 109 to the reference to ' yellow autumn.'

113. *If, brushed from Russian wilds,* &c. The east winds which visit us in Spring are part of the polar current which then descends upon Europe through Russia. The clause expresses the condition

upon which the poet's expectation of a 'yellow Autumn' will be realized.

115. *The clammy mildew.* Mildew, as it is commonly understood, is not 'clammy,' and does not appear upon plants till the end of summer. The literal meaning of the word is 'honey-dew,'—not 'meal-dew'; and the vegetable disease known by this name, which chiefly appears in Spring, is probably what Thomson here refers to. The word comes from the Anglo-Saxon *mele* or *mil*, allied to the Latin *mel*, honey; and *deáw*, dew. Honey-dew is a sugary exudation of certain plants and trees caused, it is supposed, either by the punctures of such insects as the aphides, or by the rupture of the vegetable tissues from some such cause as dry weather. The exudation coats the leaves or stalks with a clammy film, which, if not washed off by a squirt, produces fungi, or at least catches whatever the air brings to it, and thus clogs the pores of the plant, and injures its growth. Some, however, believe that honey-dew is an exudation of the aphides themselves. Thomson here attributes it to a 'humid,' or—as he first put it—a 'foggy' east wind. To a dry east wind, or north wind, he attributes the blight of leaf and blossom in springtime through the instrumentality of aphides (l. 119 *et seqq.*).

120. *insect armies warp.* Advance with a wavering motion. Cp. Milton's 'cloud of locusts warping on the eastern wind ' (*Par. Lost*, Bk. I. l. 341). Shakespeare, in As You Like It, uses the word causatively—' Though thou [the winter wind] the waters warp.'

125. *Corrosive famine.* An insatiable hunger. Famine is not used here in its ordinary sense of scarcity of food.

127. *before his orchard.* An orchard is no uncommon appendage of an English farm, but on Scottish farms it is far from common.

130, 131. *Scatters o'er the blooms The pungent dust of pepper.* In the early editions Thomson had instead—' onions, steaming hot, beneath his trees exposes.'

135. Here in the early editions followed a passage of thirty-three lines, afterwards transferred with a few alterations to Summer, ll. 289-317.

141. *drown the crude unripened year.* See, for a description of a wet summer, A Midsummer-Night's Dream, Act II, Sc. i. ll. 89-114—

          ' Therefore the winds . . . .
               . . . . have sucked up from the sea
          Contagious fogs,' &c.

151, 152. *wintry storms . . . Oppressing life.* Cp. Winter—
                    ' Thus Winter falls
     A heavy gloom oppressive o'er the world.'—ll. 57, 58.

156. *the closing woods.* The innumerable leaves of the forest, no longer stirred by the wind, fall into their natural places, and remaining motionless, give the idea of a closed tent or curtained tabernacle.

157. *many-twinkling leaves.* Gray, in The Progress of Poesy, has the same expression, but applied to dancers—'glance their many-twinkling feet' (l. 35).

168. *forests seem, impatient, to demand.* In the early editions 'expansive' had the place of 'impatient.' The change is no improvement.

176. This line at first stood ''Tis scarce to patter heard, the stealing shower,'—a common Scottish inversion.

182. This line explains the bold metaphor of the three preceding lines.

186. *Indulge their genial stores.* Here 'indulge' means 'freely bestow,' or 'set no check or restraint upon.'

191, 192. *strikes the illumined mountains.* Cp. Tennyson's—

> 'wildly dash'd on tower and tree
> The sunbeam strikes along the world.'—*In Memoriam*, XV.

195. *Increased*; i. e. with rain.

207. *Here, awful Newton.* Shortly after Newton's death, at the age of 84, in March 1727, Thomson wrote and published his poem, To the Memory of Sir Isaac Newton. The following passage from that poem describes Newton's discovery of the composition of the white or colourless ray—

> 'Even light itself, which every thing displays,
> Shone undiscovered till his brighter mind
> Untwisted all the shining robe of day,
> And from the whitening undistinguished blaze,
> Collecting every ray into his kind,
> To the charmed eye educed the gorgeous train
> Of parent colours. First the flaming Red,' &c.
>
> ll. 102, *et seqq.*

An enumeration of the seven primitive rays follows.

218–220. *to give to light*, &c. There is some obscurity of meaning here. By the 'balmy treasures' are probably meant both the bloom and the fragrance, which were produced by the refreshing rain of the previous day. The lines ran originally—

> 'to give again,
> Transmuted soon by nature's chemistry
> The blooming blessings of the former day.'

227. Construe—'what dull and incurious people account as weeds.'

244. *their light slumbers gently fumed away.* Cp. Milton—
'Now Morn, her rosy steps in the eastern clime
Advancing, sowed the earth with orient pearl,
When Adam waked, so 'customed; for his sleep
Was aery light, from pure digestion bred,
And temperate vapours bland, which the only sound
Of leaves and fuming rills, Aurora's fan
Lightly dispersed,' &c.—*Par. Lost*, Bk. V. ll. 1–7.

270. *Such were those prime of days.* Thomson's description of the
age of primeval innocence may have been partly suggested by a passage
in Virgil's first Georgic, commencing (l. 125) 'Ante Jovem nulli subi-
gebant arva coloni'; but it bears a closer and fuller resemblance to
Ovid's beautiful lines on the golden age in the first book of the Meta-
morphoses.   Part of Dryden's translation of those lines may be given—

'The golden age was first, when men, yet new
No rule but uncorrupted reason knew. . . .
The mountain-trees in distant prospect please,
Ere yet the pine descended to the seas;
And happy mortals, unconcerned for more,
Confined their wishes to their native shore. . . .
Nor swords were forged; but void of care and crime,
The soft creation slept away their time. . . .
Content with food, which nature freely bred,
On wildings and on strawberries they fed. . . .
The flowers unsown in fields and meadows reigned,
And western winds immortal spring maintained. . .
From veins of valleys, milk and nectar broke,
And honey sweating through the pores of oak.'

Long though Thomson's account of the Age of primeval innocence
is, it was yet longer in the early editions by some twenty-eight lines.
In the edition of 1738 these lines still found a place; and, though it
was a proof of the growing refinement of his taste to withdraw them at
last, they are so characteristic, in a certain wild and even grotesque
luxuriance of imagination, that they may be reproduced here—

'This to the poets[1] gave the Golden Age,—
When, as they sung in elevated phrase,
The sailor-pine had not the nations yet
In commerce mixed; for every country teemed
With everything.   Spontaneous harvest waved
Still in a sea of yellow plenty round.

---

[1] Virgil and Ovid.

The forest was the vineyard, where, untaught
To climb, unpruned and wild, the juicy grape
Burst into floods of wine. The knotted oak
Shook from his boughs the long transparent streams
Of honey, creeping through the matted grass.
Th' uncultivated thorn a ruddy shower
Of fruitage shed on such as sat below
In blooming ease, and from brown labour free—
Save what the copious gathering grateful gave.
The rivers foamed with nectar; or diffuse,
Silent and soft the milky maze devolved.
Nor had the spongy full-expanded fleece
Yet drunk the Tyrian dye : the stately ram
Shone through the mead in native purple clad
Or milder saffron; and the dancing lamb
The vivid crimson to the sun disclosed.
Nothing had power to hurt : the savage soul,
Yet untransfused into the tiger's heart,
Burned not his bowels, nor his gamesome paw
Drove on the fleecy partners of his play;
While from the flowery brake the serpent rolled
His fairer spires, and played his pointless tongue.'

Some of this is grotesque enough to be ridiculous, but there is also much of that raciness which Johnson missed in the later editions. The warmth and variety of colouring should be noted.

271, 272. *whence the fabling poets took Their golden age.* Contrast Cowper—

'Would I had fallen upon those happier days
That poets celebrate,—those golden times
And those Arcadian scenes that Maro sings . . .
Vain wish! those days were never : airy dreams
Sat for the picture.'—*The Task*, Bk. IV.

279. *or else approving.* This can hardly be said of reason.

304, 305. *extinct each social feeling, fell And joyless inhumanity*, &c. '—social love is of quite another nature [from self-love] ; the just and free exercise of which, in a particular manner, renders one amiable and divine. The accomplished man I admire, the honest man I trust; but it is only the truly generous man I entirely love. Humanity is the very smile and consummation of virtue; it is the image of that fair perfection in the supreme Being, which while he was infinitely happy in himself, moved him to create a world of beings to make them so.' *Letter to Aaron Hill*, April, 18, 1726.

313, 314. Cp. the lines in Burns's *Brigs of Ayr*—which revealed to Carlyle 'a world of rain and ruin':

> 'Then down ye'll hurl . . . . . .
>
>   And dash the gumlie jaups up to the pouring skies.'

The criticism will apply more fitly to the lines of Thomson.

316, 317. These lines originally stood—

> 'The Seasons since, as hoar tradition tells,
>
>   Have kept their constant chase,' &c.

This explanation of the phenomenon of the Seasons, as due to the deluge, has no scientific value: it is purely fanciful.

319, 320. *fruits and blossoms blushed . . . on the selfsame bough.* So Milton—

> 'trees loaden with fairest fruit,
>
> Blossoms and fruits at once of golden hue.'
>
> > *Par. Lost*, Bk. IV. ll. 147, 8.

334. Originally—'The fleeting shadow of a Winter's sun.'

341. *And worse.* In respect that he acts in a manner contrary to his better knowledge and better nature. He is therefore more cruel; and is ungrateful in addition.

350–352. Cp. Milton's Comus—

> 'did Nature pour her bounties forth
>
> With such a full and unwithdrawing hand,
>
> Covering the earth with odours, fruits, and flocks.'
>
> > ll. 710–13.

361, 362. *the plain ox . . . that guileless animal.* 'The meik pluch ox.'—Dunbar.

367. *The clowns he feeds.* I.e., with the harvest with which he toiled to clothe the land, by preparing the furrows for the seed, and by harrowing and otherwise dressing the ground after sowing was over.

368. *the riot of the Autumnal feast.* Such as the Lady describes in Comus—

> 'Methought it was the sound
>
> Of riot and ill-managed merriment,
>
> Such as the jocund flute or gamesome pipe
>
> Stirs up among the loose unlettered hinds
>
> When, for their teeming flocks and granges full,
>
> In wanton dance they praise the bounteous Pan,' &c.
>
> > ll. 171–6.

372. *the numbers of the Samion Sage.* The doctrine of the transmigration of souls was taught by Pythagoras, and as a consequence abstention from animal food was required. The supposed transmigration was both into human bodies and the bodies of brutes. Pythagoras himself

professed to recollect having passed through former stages of existence. It is also said that he pretended to recognise in the cries of a dog that was being beaten the voice of a friend whose soul he believed to be imprisoned in the body of that animal. Pythagoras was born about 570 B.C. in the isle of Samos; travelled a great deal in the East in search of knowledge; made important discoveries in geometry, music, and astronomy; settled at Crotona in Italy, where, besides founding a philosophical sect, he organised a political order, which, at first successful, was afterwards suppressed: and died, it is generally supposed, at Metapontum, 504 B.C. (See Liberty, Part III. l. 32.)

Thomson's line of argument, commencing at line 271, and running not always clearly through the hundred following lines, seems to be that the wickedness of mankind, after the age of primeval innocence was past, was punished by the Flood, which brought about a great climatic change still visible in the succession of the Seasons. ' Great Spring before greened all the year.' This climatic change acting upon vitiated human nature—which had become ' fired with hot ravin ' and ' ensanguined '—has enfeebled the health of mankind, and greatly shortened the term of human life. And yet there is a remedy for the imperfections of ill-health and shortness of life, in a return to vegetable diet—

> ' the food of man
> While yet he lived in innocence, and told
> A length of golden years, unfleshed in blood.'

It is, however, now too late in the history of the world to propose a universal return to vegetable food. The attempt of Pythagoras more than two thousand years ago did not succeed; there is less likelihood of success now. (See *Par. Lost*, Bk. IV. ll. 331, *et seqq.*)

373. *High Heaven forbids.* Here Thomson throws up the argument: it is the will of Heaven, for wise ends, that we remain in our present state of imperfection.

376, 377. Besides, he seems to add, the slaughter of the lower animals may mean their admission into a higher life! There seems to be here a theory of evolution of a peculiar kind—the evolution of the indestructible spirit or principle of life in every animate individual into a higher state of existence.—These lines were added in the later editions. A passage in his Liberty, Part III, well illustrates Thomson's adaptation of the Pythagorean doctrine of metempsychosis—

> ' He even into his tender system took
> Whatever shares the brotherhood of life:
> He taught that life's indissoluble flame
> From brute to man, and man to brute again,

> For ever shifting, runs th' eternal round ;
> Thence tried against the blood polluted meal,
> And limbs yet quivering with some kindred soul
> To turn the human heart. *Delightful truth,*
> *Had he beheld the living chain ascend,*
> *And not a circling form, but raising whole!'*—ll. 61–70.

With this compare Blake's theory as set forth in Night, one of the Songs of Innocence (published 1789).

378–465. These exquisite lines, descriptive of an angling excursion, were a happy afterthought. They were not yet ready for the edition of 1738. The scene is apparently the poet's native Teviotdale, and the brooks and streams of the description, their undulating currents and dusky pools, still entice the angler to the moors and glens of the Cheviots. The whole passage is clearly a recollection of a day's fishing on the Upper Jed, or some one or other of its tributaries, which the poet enjoyed, let us say, when he was free from college in the long vacation in the early part of his student life. He has returned from his first experience of a town life with a new zest for the beauty and abandon of country life ; and he carries with him, in addition to the ' fine tapering rod ' and ' the slender watery stores,' a pocket-copy of Virgil. The book may be unsportsmanlike, but it is rather for companionship than serious study. And, indeed, the whole excursion is planned rather as a device for surprising nature than a serious attempt to secure a big basket.

387.   ' Around the steel no tortured worm shall twine.'
            Gay's *Rural Sports,* Canto I. (published 1713).

391. *the weak helpless uncomplaining wretch.* The trout. Fishing with worm is discredited on two grounds—it is cruelty to both worm and fish. Fly-fishing is preferred : the fly is not swallowed, but fastens in the trout's mouth in some cartilage which is almost, or altogether, insensible to pain. It was chiefly for upholding the use of live-bait that Byron characterized Izaak Walton as cruel, and angling as a solitary vice (vide Don Juan, Canto XIII. st. cvi). ' They may talk,' says Lord Byron, ' about the beauties of nature, but the angler merely thinks of his dish of fish ; he has no leisure to take his eyes from off the streams, and a single *bite* is to him worth more than all the scenery around.' Thomson at least was no such angler. Neither indeed was Walton insensible to the scenery of the riverside. But there was a great advance in the humanity of Thomson upon that of Walton. Not only does Thomson deprecate the use of live-bait [1], but he ' softly disengages' the young

---

[1] When he was a minor he had perhaps no such scruples. See his poem, in heroic couplets, On a Country Life, first published in The Edinburgh Miscellany of 1720.

trout from his hook and returns them to the water. To circumvent the 'monarch of the brook,' however, is in his opinion fair sport. It is noticeable that this is the only form of sport he favours which can be said to expose him to a charge of cruelty. He approves of fox-hunting, and the destruction of beasts of prey generally; but his sympathies are with the flying hare (see Autumn, ll. 401-425), and the murdered deer (Autumn, ll. 426-457). His tenderness, indeed, to the peaceful lower creation is a principal feature of his character and his poetry. An advance upon his tenderness is, however, very perceptible in the teaching of Burns and Wordsworth. The latter has taught us

> 'Never to blend our pleasure or our pride
> With sorrow of the meanest thing that feels,'
>
> > *Hart-Leap Well*, Pt. II;

while the former can find it in his heart to say of the fox—

> 'The blood-stained roost, and sheep-cote spoil'd,
> > My heart forgets,
> While pitiless the tempest wild
> > Sore on you beats.'—*A Winter Night*.

420, 421. Some annotators see in these lines an acquaintance on the part of Thomson with the long Latin poem (in ten books, afterwards enlarged to sixteen) of The Country Farm, written by the Jesuit Vanière (*Jacobi Vanierii è Societate Jesu Praedium Rusticum*). The first edition of this elaborate work was published at Toulouse in 1706, and a copy may have found its way into Thomson's possession. This is indeed more likely than that any portion of it inspired a single idea or suggested a single expression in Thomson's description of angling. Natural benevolence, and not Vanière, taught Thomson to return the little fish to the water: besides, Vanière's action is prompted by a different motive from that which actuates Thomson; his motive is prudence, Thomson's pity. Vanière writes:—

> ' *Ne pereat gens tota*, vagae miserere juventae
> Pisciculumque vadis haerentem tolle ; *futurae*
> *Spem sobolis*, vivumque novae demitte paludi.'

Thomson has no such ulterior end in view. But—

> 'Him, piteous of his youth, and the short space
> He has enjoyed the vital light of heaven,
> Soft disengage, and back into the stream
> The speckled infant throw.'

423. *The monarch of the brook ;* or rather of the pool—'his old secure abode' (l. 433). Such a trout is called in Scotland 'a linn-lier.' Vanière's trout, like the more interesting linn-lier, also occupies 'uninhabited

waters,' and 'lacubus dominatur avitis.' The similarity between
Vanière's description and that of Thomson is of the slightest, and the
points at which they make their nearest approach to each other are such
as Thomson could discover for himself, and indeed could hardly avoid
in a detailed account of angling. It is more likely that Thomson was
indebted to Gay's *Rural Sports*, Canto I.

434. *flounces round the pool.* In his minor poem On a Country Life
(1720) we find in a description of the capture of a pike—

> 'And, being struck, in vain he flies at last;
>
> He rages, storms, and flounces through the stream.'

444. And, in angler's phrase, the trout are no longer 'taking.'

452. *sounding culver.* A. S. *culfre,* a pigeon. The rock-pigeon, the
original of all varieties of the domestic dove, is probably meant. When
startled into flight, the pigeon makes a noisy flapping, or clapping, with
its wings, but when fairly launched in the air it can glide noiselessly
along on 'liquid wing.'

454. *the classic page.* Such as Virgil's. Even Walton made
provision of 'a book' as he 'loitered long days by Shawford brook,'
and 'angled on.' Thomson's admiration of Virgil is repeated in
Winter (ll. 530-532).

457, 458. *catch thyself the landscape,* &c. I. e. laying aside the book,
conjure up in your own imagination, the 'rural scenes' through which
'the classic page' has just been 'leading your fancy.' 'The landscape' is clearly *not* the scene around him. Thomson seems here to
distinguish for a moment between fancy and imagination, allotting to
the latter faculty a more sustained creative power, and a larger and
freer range.

459-465. These lines describe a further stage in the indulgence of the
imaginative mood, the condition, namely, of reverie. The mind escapes
into a solitude filled with a succession of tranquillizing images, where it
is free from the cares and passions of waking life, and enjoys the consciousness of being—or rather of beginning to be—at peace with the
whole world.

466, 467. At these lines the poet takes leave of the angler, and enters
upon a new subject—a description of the beauty and fragrance of Spring
vegetation. The loveliness of the living and fragrant landscape, he says
in effect, demands description, but will tax the highest descriptive talent
to do it justice. Yet (l. 479) he will try.

470, 471. *with that matchless skill . . . as appears.* 'That' and 'as'
are not true correlatives. But the appearance of 'as' is explained by
restoring a line which the poet struck out of the later editions. The
passage ran originally—

'Or can he [Imagination] mix them with that matchless skill,
  And lay them on *so* delicately fine,
  And lose them in each other, *as* appears
  In every bud that blows?'

The construction, though the line be restored, is loose and even slovenly, and the grammar faulty.

482–487. These lines appear in no edition till after 1738. Amanda was a Miss Young, one of the daughters of Captain Gilbert Young, a gentleman belonging to Dumfriesshire. Thomson made her acquaintance, probably at Richmond, about the year 1740, through her brother-in-law, James Robertson, who was then surgeon to the Household at Kew, and with whom Thomson had been in friendly relation so early 1726. Thomson was deeply in love with her. No fewer than seven of his minor poems are addressed to her, and all of them display the sincerity of his passion. A letter of his, directed to Miss Young from Hagley, of date August 29th, 1743, has also been published: it is interesting in many ways: in the course of it he says—'You mix with all my thoughts, even the most studious, and, instead of disturbing, as give them greater harmony and spirit. . . . . You so fill my mind with all ideas of beauty, so satisfy my soul with the purest and most sincere delight, I should feel the want of little else.' Amanda has been described by Robertson as 'a fine, sensible woman'; by Ramsay of Ochtertyre as 'not a striking beauty, but gentle-mannered and elegant-minded, worthy the love of a man of taste and virtue.' 'Thomson,' says Robertson, 'was never wealthy enough to marry'; and, says Ramsay (*Scotland and Scotsmen in the Eighteenth Century*, from the Ochtertyre MSS.), 'it was Mrs. Young, a coarse, vulgar woman, who constantly opposed the poet's pretensions to her daughter, saying to her one day, "What! would you marry Thomson? He will make ballads, and you will sing them!"' Amanda afterwards became the wife of Admiral Campbell.

484, 485. *Come with those downcast eyes sedate . . . Those looks demure.*
Cp.—

    'Come, pensive nun, devout and pure,
    Sober, steadfast, and demure, ...
    With even step and musing gait, . .
       .   .   .   . thine eyes . .
    With a sad leaden downward cast.'
                Il Penseroso, ll. 31–43.

497. *In fair profusion decks.* In the early editions, 'profusely climbs,' followed by the following passage—

             'Turgent in every pore
   The gummy moisture shines, new lustre lends,

> And feeds the Spirit that diffusive round
> Refreshes all the dale.'

499. *Arabia cannot boast.* Cp. Milton—

> 'Sabëan odours from the spicy shore
> Of Araby the Blest.'—*Par. Lost*, Bk. IV. ll. 162, 163.

501. *Breathes through the sense.* Enters the nostrils.

505. *undisguised by mimic art.* Growing wild—having their forms unaltered by domestication. Contrast, for example, the wild daisy with the garden daisy.

512, 513. *they soaring dare The purple heath.* This is a flight out of Spring into Autumn.

516. *its alleys green.* 'I know each lane and every alley green.'— *Comus*, l. 311.

517-524. The scene is perhaps laid in Wiltshire (see Introductory Note to Spring). It is characteristic of Thomson's love of uncultivated nature and a wide landscape, that he is no sooner in the flower-garden than his eyes are beyond its enclosing walls, sweeping the distant horizon. Contrast Cowper's love of nature—not less genuine, but quieter and more fastidious. To him a garden was 'a blest seclusion,' and when he walked abroad it was to see 'nature in her cultivated trim.' (See The Task, Bk. III.) His description of an English landscape may be profitably compared with Thomson's :—

> 'Far beyond, and overthwart the stream,
> That, as with molten glass, inlays the vale,
> The sloping land recedes into the clouds ;
> Displaying on its varied side the grace
> Of hedge-row beauties numberless, square tower,
> Tall spire, from which the sound of cheerful bells
> Just undulates upon the listening ear,
> Groves, heaths, and smoking villages remote.'
>
> *The Task*, Bk. I. ll. 169-176.

529. Here begins a poetical catalogue of garden flowers. It is worth noting that Thomson was early familiar with gardens and gardening work. His paternal grandfather, at least one uncle—also on the father's side—and some of his cousins, all followed the occupation of a gardener. It was one of those cousins that latterly kept the poet's own garden at Richmond in proper trim.—Crocus, Gr. κρόκος, from its saffron colour. Violet, dimin. of Fr. *viole*, 'a gilliflower'—according to Cotgrave, Gr. ἴον, a violet. Polyanthus, Gr. πολύ-, many, and ἄνθος, flower. Anemone, lit. wind-flower, from Gr. ἄνεμος, wind. Auricula, lit. the lobe of the ear, used to name the 'bear's ear' flower, a double dimin., from Lat. *auris*, the ear. Ranunculus, lit. a little frog, a double dimin., from Lat. *rana*, a frog.

tulip, originally from Pers. or Hind. *dulband*, a turban, through Turk. *tulbend*, and last from Fr. *tulippe* or *tulipan*, a tulip, a turban-like flower (early forms of turban in English are turbant (Par. Regained), tulibant, and tulipant). Hyacinth, Gr. ὑάκινθος (according to Prof. Skeat, not our hyacinth, but) an iris, larkspur. Jonquil, from Fr. *jonquille*, named from its rushlike leaves (Lat. *juncus*, a rush). Narcissus, Gr. νάρκισσος, a flower so called from its narcotic property (Gr. ναρκάω, I grow numb). Carnation, named from its flesh colour, Lat. *carn-* stem of *caro*, flesh. Pink, named from the *peaked* edges of the petals.

540. *the father-dust.* The fertilising pollen.

541. *while they break.* 'Break' is printed in the early editions in small capitals, as if it were a technical term of gardening. It means 'blossom' or 'burst into colour.' Cp. 'daybreak.'

549. *the fabled fountain.* For the story of Narcissus, who, falling in love with his own shadow in the water, pined and died on the fountain-brink, see Ovid's Metam. Bk. III.

> 'As his own bright image he surveyed
> He fell in love with the fantastic shade;
> And o'er the fair resemblance hung unmoved,
> Nor knew, fond youth! it was himself he loved.
>
> . . . .
>
> For him the Naiads and the Dryads mourn, . .
> And now the sister-nymphs prepare his urn;
> When, looking for his corpse, they only found
> A rising stalk with yellow blossoms crown'd.'
>
> Addison's translation.

555-570. It has been remarked that, while Cowper's gloomy views of religion drove him for relief and solace to the study of nature, Thomson's love of nature inspired him with a cheerful religious sentiment and a robust belief in the bounty and benevolence of deity. Here he traces the beauty of vegetable nature to the benevolence of God. In the remaining part of the poem he traces the joy of animal life to the same source.

566-570. These lines furnish an explanatory commentary on lines 78-82 *supra.*

578. *From the first note the hollow cuckoo sings.* In the well-known and much-admired Ode to the Cuckoo by Michael Bruce (born 1746) the cuckoo is correctly described as 'attendant on the spring.'

585. *the long-forgotten strain.* Referring to the silence of the birds during winter.

600. *listening Philomela.* The nightingale (literally the night-singer) is mostly silent by day.

609-612. *The jay, the rook, the daw,* &c. Cp. Cowper—
   'Ten thousand warblers cheer the day, and one
    The livelong night; nor these alone . . . .
    But cawing rooks, and kites that swim sublime
    In still repeated circles, screaming loud,
    The jay, the pie, and e'en the boding owl,
    That hails the rising moon, have charms for me.'
                      The Task, Bk. I. ll. 197–203.
The jay is named from its showy plumage (Fr. *gai*, gay). It dwells in
woods, and seldom flies into the open country. Indeed it is rarely seen,
though its note—which, when the bird is alarmed, is extremely harsh—
is often enough heard. It is a smaller bird and more predatory than
the magpie, and has a much shorter tail, broadening at the tip. By the
jay, however, Thomson probably means the magpie, which is much
commoner in Scotland, and often called the jay-pyot (pied). See
Summer, ll. 224, 225.—The daw, or jackdaw, is named from its cry;
it is a lively and noisy bird, almost impudently familiar. It haunts
steeples, ruined castles, and such inaccessible places.—The stockdove
is the ringdove, or cushat.

624. *approvance.* Approval.

627. After this line in the earlier editions—
    'And, throwing out the last efforts of love.'

652. In the earlier editions—
    'But hurry, hurry through the busy air.'

694. *The white-winged plover.* See note, line 24 *supra.*

699. *pious fraud!* A deceit prompted by their love for their young.
Cp. *pius Aeneas.*

701, 702. *the muse . . . Her brothers of the grove.* See Castle of
Indolence, Canto II. st. xxxiii:
        Philomelus—'in russet brown bedight
        As is his sister of the copses green.'

710. *this barbarous act forbear.* Cp. Shenstone—
    'I have found out a gift for my fair,
      I have found where the wood-pigeons breed;
    But let me that plunder forbear,
      She will say 'twas a barbarous deed.'
                Pastoral Ballad, Pt. II. (date 1743).

714. *Her ruined care.* Her young, stolen from the nest. The
objects of her defeated care.

719. The pause after the word 'robbed' is peculiarly effective. The
strain suddenly modulates into the minor key. This is a favourite
pause of Tennyson's. The picture of Philomela mourning in the

poplar shade for the loss of her young is copied from Virgil's Fourth Georgic.

724. *Sole-sitting.* Originally 'sad-sitting.' Wordsworth's use of this compound is well-known—

> 'Lady of the mere,
> Sole-sitting by the shores of old romance.'
> *Poems on the Naming of Places*, IV.

at every dying fall. Cp. Shakespeare—

> 'That strain again! it had a dying fall.'
> *Twelfth Night*, Act I. sc. i. l. 4.

729. *weighing . . . their wings.* In the sense of balancing themselves.

738. *Nature's common.* The air. Cp. Burns—

> 'Commoners of air
> We wander out, we know not where.'
> *Epistle to Davie.*

739. *Wing.* Fly. Construe—'Nature's common, the air, their range and pasture as far as they can see or fly.'

752. *The acquitted parents.* In the first text 'the *exonered* parents'— a Scotticism for 'exonerated.'

754–764. These lines graphically describe a striking scene. In the original version (scarcely less vigorous, but cancelled, probably because of the somewhat ridiculous image of the last line) the passage stood :—

> 'High from the summit of a craggy cliff
> Hung o'er the green sea, *grudging* at its base,
> The royal eagle draws his young, resolved
> To try them at the sun. Strong-pounced, and bright
> As burnished day, they up the blue sky wind,
> Leaving dull sight below, and with fixed gaze
> Drink in their native noon : the father-king
> Claps his glad pinions, and approves the birth.'

The colouring of the first draught should be noted.

765–787. Probably—at least in part—a recollection of Marlborough in Wiltshire. (See Lady Hertford's verses in the Introduction to Spring, *supra.*)

766–769. *Whose lofty elms . . . Invite the rook who . . . ceaseless caws.*

> ' The building rook 'ill caw from the windy tall elm-tree.'
> Tennyson.

779. *with oary feet.* The expression is Milton's : Par. Lost. Bk. VII. l. 440.

806. *balmy breathing near.* 'Redolent in view,' in the early editions. Much of this description is copied from the Third Georgic, from l. 215 onwards.

815. *exciting gale.* In the first version, 'informing gale.' 'Notas auras' in the Third Georgic, l. 251.

818, 819. *Such is the force,* &c. Cp. the courser of Adonis in Shakespeare; and Virgil's description in the Third Georgic, ll. 250-254.

825. Following this line, appeared in the earlier editions—

'How the red lioness, her whelps forgot
Amid the thoughtless fury of her heart;
The lank rapacious wolf, the unshapely bear;
The spotted tiger, fellest of the fell;
And all the terrors of the Libyan swain,
By this new flame their native warmth sublimed,
Roam the resounding waste in fiercer bands.'

830. *the British fair.* 'British' and 'Britons' seem to have been commoner expressions in the last century for the United Kingdom and its inhabitants than they are now. Cp. Rule, Britannia—' Britons never will be slaves.' In Goldsmith's Traveller it is Britons that are 'the lords of human kind.' 'English' and 'Englishmen' have almost superseded the words.

832. The same scene is described in similar language in Liberty, l. 320 of Part III.

852-854. *boundless spirit all,* &c. Cp. Pope—

'All are but parts of one stupendous whole,
Whose body nature is, and God the soul.'

Essay on Man, Ep. I. ll. 267, 268. (Published 1732-4.)

860. Instead of this line the earlier editions had—

'His grandeur in the heavens: the sun and moon,
Whether that fires the day or, falling, this
Pours out a lucid softness o'er the night,
Are but a beam from him. The glittering stars,
By the deep ear of meditation heard,
Still in their midnight watches sing of him.
He nods a calm. The tempest blows his wrath,
Roots up the forest, and o'erturns the main.
The thunder is his voice; and the red flash
His speedy sword of justice. At his touch
The mountains flame. He shakes the solid earth,
And rocks the nations. Nor in these alone,—
In every common instance God is seen;
And to the man who casts his mental eye
Abroad, unnoticed wonders rise. But chief
In thee, boon Spring, and in thy softer scenes.'

Then followed l. 861 of the present text.

864. *undesigning hearts.* I.e. actuated by instinct.

874. *flowing Spring.* A repetition of the idea contained in 'bounteous' in l. 873.

875–880. See note to ll. 304, 305, *supra.*

890. *these green days.* Of Spring.

892. *young-eyed.* This beautiful compound is Shakespeare's—'the young-eyed cherubins' (Merchant of Venice, Act V. Sc. i.).

901. *the present Deity.* The phrase occurs in Dryden's Alexander's Feast—' A present deity! they shout around.'

902. A noble image, seldom absent from the religious thought of Thomson. After this line in the earlier text came a passage which anticipates something of the teaching, and even reminds one of the style of Wordsworth :—

> ' 'Tis harmony, that world-attuning power,
> By which all beings are adjusted, each
> To all around, impelling and impelled
> In endless circulation, that inspires
> This universal smile. *Thus the glad skies,*
> *The wide-rejoicing earth, the woods, the streams,*
> *With every life they hold, down to the flower*
> *That paints the lowly vale, or insect-wing*
> *Waved o'er the shepherd's slumber, touch the mind*
> *To nature tuned, with a light-flying hand*
> *Invisible;* quick-urging through the nerves
> The glittering spirits in a flood of day.'

These are lines of the utmost significance to the student of Wordsworth considered in historical relation to his predecessors. They were followed by the passage commencing at l. 963 of the present text, to which they were joined by the word 'Hence'—'Hence from the virgin's cheek,' &c. The intervening lines (from 903–962) were inserted after the year 1738, and constitute a compliment to Lord Lyttelton, no small part of which is the description of his lordship's Worcestershire seat. Indeed it was not till the autumn of 1743 that Thomson saw Hagley Park. He was then engaged in the preparation of a corrected and enlarged edition of The Seasons, and the invitations to Hagley Park came at a time singularly favourable to the poetical fame of the place and its inhabitants. The poet's letter of acceptance is of date July 14, 1743, and part of it is in the following terms :—

' Hagley is the place in England I most desire to see; I imagine it to be greatly delightful in itself, and I know it to be so to the highest degree by the company it is animated with. Some reasons prevent me waiting upon you immediately, but, if you will be so good as to let me know how long you design to stay in the country, nothing shall hinder me from passing three weeks or a month with you before you leave it. As this will fall in autumn I shall like it the better, for I think that season of the year the most pleasing and the most poetical. The spirits are not then dissipated with the gaiety of spring, and the glaring light of summer, but composed into a serious and tempered joy. The year is perfect. In the meantime I will go on with correcting The Seasons, and hope to carry down [from London] more than one of them with me. The Muses whom you obligingly say I shall bring along with me, I shall find with you—the muses of the great simple country, not the little fine-lady muses of Richmond Hill. I have lived so long in the noise (or at least its distant din) of the town, that I begin to forget what retirement is.'

905. *O Lyttelton, the friend !* Here 'the' is a superlative. Cp. similar use of *ille* in Latin. Burns has 'O Henderson, the man, the brother !'

George, eldest son of Sir Thomas Lyttelton of Hagley Park, in Worcestershire, was born in 1709, and, after studying at Eton and Oxford, and travelling in France and Italy, entered political life as a Tory in 1730. He had already made some name as an author. His poem of Blenheim Palace was published when he was only nineteen. He afterwards published The Progress of Love, 1732; Letters from a Persian in England, 1735; The Conversion of St. Paul, written in 1746, to confirm the wavering Christianity of Thomson; Dialogues of the Dead, 1760–1765; and a History of King Henry II, 1767. He also wrote a Monody on the death of his wife, who died at the age of twenty-eight some five years after marriage; and the Prologue to Thomson's posthumous tragedy, Coriolanus. The Monody is written with much tenderness; and the Prologue—when spoken by Quin—brought tears to the eyes of a large audience. Of his friendship for Thomson and other men of letters he gave many convincing proofs. To him both Thomson and Fielding indeed owed the ease and independence of the latter part of their lives. In politics he was a vigorous opponent of Walpole. When Walpole was at last ousted from office, Lyttelton, who had previously been principal Secretary to Frederic, Prince of Wales, was, in 1744, made one of the lords of the Treasury. In 1755 he was Chancellor of the Exchequer, and was raised to the peerage on a change of administration in 1757. He died in 1773.

907, 908. *Hagley Park . . . thy British Tempè.* Lyttelton had himself compared the park surrounding Blenheim, in his poem on that historic house, to the vale of Tempe. Tempe was the name of a singularly beautiful valley in the north of Thessaly between Olympus and Ossa. Xenophon's is one of many famous descriptions of its pastoral beauty and fertility.—Thomson has described Hagley Park in prose : 'After a disagreeable stage-coach journey . . . . I am come to the most agreeable place and company in the world. The park, where we pass a great part of our time, is thoroughly delightful, quite enchanting. It consists of several little hills, finely tufted with wood, and rising softly one above another, from which are seen a great variety of at once beautiful and grand extensive prospects; but I am most charmed with its sweet embowered retirements, and particularly with a winding dale that runs through the middle of it. This dale is overhung with deep woods, and enlivened by a stream that, now gushing from mossy rocks, now falling in cascades, and now spreading into a calm length of water, forms the most natural and pleasing scene imaginable. At the source of this water, composed of some pretty rills, that purl from beneath the roots of oaks, there is as fine a retired seat as lover's heart could wish. . . . . Nor is the society here inferior to the scene. . . . This is the truly happy life, the union of retirement and choice society. It gives an idea of that which the patriarchal or golden age is supposed to have been, when every family was a little state of itself, governed by the mild laws of reason, benevolence and love.' (See Spring, l. 256).—*From a Letter to Miss Young* (Amanda), *dated Aug.* 29, 1743.

925. *conducted by historic truth.* Both Thomson and Lyttelton were great readers of history. Witness Liberty, which may fairly be called a historical poem ; witness also the hundred lines of Winter commencing l. 431. Lyttelton's Dialogues and Reign of Henry II give proof of his researches in history.

930. Lyttelton's political honesty cannot be impeached. He was a virtuous politician—a phenomenon rare in his day.

935. *Lucinda.* See note to l. 904 *supra*. Mrs. Lyttelton's maiden name was Lucy Fortescue, of Filleigh in Devonshire. A large number of Lord Lyttelton's poetical compositions consist of Verses to Lucy. His Monody in nineteen irregular stanzas, written to soothe his grief for her loss, is probably his best as it is his tenderest composition. The first line of her epitaph at Hagley describes her as—'Made to engage all hearts and charm all eyes.'

949-961. See note to ll. 517–524 *supra*.

953. *embosomed soft in trees.* Cp. Milton, describing Windsor:—
> 'Towers and battlements it sees
>   Bosomed high in tufted trees.'—*L'Allegro.*

960. Hereford is the march county between Worcester and Wales.

962. Having described 'the sacred feelings of the heart' (l. 903), the

poet now proceeds to describe ‘ the infusive force of Spring ’ (l. 867) on
the animal nature of man.

993, 994. The Sirens of classical story are here referred to. They had
the power of charming by their songs all that listened to them. Their
charms were fatal. The mermaid, or lorelei, is the modern form of
the siren.

1011. *bends into a dusky vault.* Cp. Shakespeare :—‘ This brave
o’erhanging firmament . . . why, it appears no other thing to me than
a foul and pestilent congregation of vapours.’—*Hamlet*, Act II. Sc. ii.

1016, 1017. *Sad amid the social band . . . inattentive.* Cp. Burns :—
    ‘ Yestreen when to the stentit string
      The dance gaed thro’ the lightit ha’,
      To thee my fancy took its wing—
        I sat but neither heard nor saw.’—*Mary Morison.*

1017, 1018. *From the tongue Th’ unfinished period falls.* Cp. Horace :—
    ‘ Cur facunda parum decoro
      Inter verba cadit lingua silentio ? ’—*Car.* IV. i.

1034. *the chambers of the fleecy east.* Blake (*b.* 1757, *d.* 1827) has—
    ‘ The chambers of the East,
    The chambers of the sun, that now
      From ancient melody has ceast.’

In Winter, l. 15, Thomson speaks of ‘ the lucid chambers of the South.’

1036. *Leads on the gentle hours.* An echo of Milton—
      ‘ The hours in dance
    Led on the eternal spring.’
             Par. Lost, Bk. IV. ll. 267, 268.

1060–1072. Cp. Horace :—
    ‘ Nocturnis ego somniis
      Jam captam teneo, jam volucrem sequor
      Te per gramina Martii
      Campi, te per aquas, dura, volubiles.’
             Car. I, i. ll. 37–40.

1069. In the early text—‘ Wild as a Bacchanal she spreads her arms.’

1082. *the yellow-tingeing plague.* Jealousy.

1113. *gentler stars.* A happier fortune.

1115. *tie of human laws.* The marriage laws of the country.

1116. *Unnatural oft.* The reference is to the ‘ tie ’ of the preceding
line. The poet alludes to ‘ marriages of convenience,’ made for the sake
of wealth, or rank.

1122. *Preventing.* Anticipating : the word is taken in its literal
meaning.

SUMMER.

INTRODUCTORY NOTE.

Encouraged by the success of Winter, which, published in March, 1726, was in its second edition by the middle of June following, Thomson enthusiastically set about the composition of Summer, and had indeed made a good start with his new subject when the proofs of the second edition of Winter were passing through his hands. The second of the Seasons seems to have been entirely written in London, and to have been the work of the summer and autumn months of 1726. The poet was then maintaining himself by teaching in the Academy of a Mr. Watts, in Little Tower Street. Writing to Aaron Hill, from Oldman's Coffee House, on the 24th of May, 'I go,' he says, 'on Saturday next, *to reside* at Mr. Watts' Academy in Little Tower Street, in quality of tutor to a young gentleman there.' And on the 20th of October following he begs Hill, 'if your business will allow me one line,' to direct the one line to him 'at the Academy in Little Tower Street.' During the composition of Summer he was gradually losing that feeling of loneliness which threatened to chill his youthful ambition in England before Winter brought friends around him, and to which he refers with some bitterness in a letter, written 11th August, 1726, to his countryman and fellow-adventurer in England, David Malloch. 'Let me, however,' he says, in criticism of some verses of Malloch's, 'mention that comprehensive compound epithet, *all-shunned,* as a beauty I have had too good reason to relish. Thank Heaven there was one exception' (meaning Malloch). His principal literary friends and correspondents of the year 1726 were Malloch and Hill. Part of his correspondence with them has happily been preserved, and from it we have interesting glimpses of the progress of the poem. 'Shall I languish out a whole summer in the same city with you,' he asks Hill, in a letter of 11th June, 'and not once be re-inspired with your company. Such a happiness would much brighten my description of that Season—from which, to fill out this letter, I venture to transcribe the following lines.' (The lines referred to are from 506 to 515.) Two days thereafter he writes to Malloch, with whom in the early part of his career he was in the habit of exchanging verses—'If my beginning of Summer please you, I am sure it is good. I

have writ more, which I'll send you in due time.' He had, it would
appear, already drawn out the plan of his poem, according to which it
was his design to describe the various phenomena of Summer as these
follow each other in the order of nature within the limits of one typical
day. By the 2nd of August he is able to inform Malloch 'that he has
now raised the sun to nine or ten o'clock, touched lightly on the drooping
of flowers in the forenoon heat, given a group of natural images, made
an incursion into the insect kingdom, and rounded off that part of his
subject with some suitable reflections.' On the 11th of August he again
communicates with Malloch, who had apparently suggested to him a
change of plan—probably because he found Thomson's plan for
Summer resemble too closely his own plan for a poem on a similar
subject upon which he was then engaged. The letter is pretty long, and
of particular interest in several ways: it contains some simple but
extremely generous criticism of Malloch's submitted verses, and the
following remonstrance—'Why did you not object against my method
with regard to Summer when I first gave you an account of it? I told
you then expressly that I resolved to contract the Season into a day: the
uniform appearances of nature in Summer easily allow of it. But, not
to dispute which of the schemes is most preferable, I am so far advanced,
having writ three parts of four, that I cannot without the most painful
labour alter mine. Let me tell you besides that we entirely agree from
the noonday retreat to the evening. I have already written of shade and
gloom, and woodland spirits, &c. exactly as you hint, more than a
week ago. . . I design towards the end of my poem to take one short
glance of cornfields ripe for the sickle as the limit of my performance.'
Later in the year, probably in October—though the date is not given—
he sends to Malloch another parcel of Summer verses, accompanied by a
letter from which we learn that the parcel contains the panegyric on
England and the English (commencing at line 1442), and that 'what remains of my poem is a description of thunder and the evening. Thunder
I have writ, and am just now agreeably engaged with the evening.'

The poem upon which Malloch was at work in the country—at
Twyford, on the Hampshire Downs, a seat of the Duke of Montrose, in
whose family he was tutor—while Thomson was busy in London with
Summer, was afterwards published with the title (which a later and
more important poet has appropriated) of The Excursion. It is in
blank verse, consists of two cantos, and runs altogether to somewhere

about one thousand lines. The second canto is astronomical. The first, so far as it goes, though it comprises a period of two days, reads like a dwarfed and fainter version of Summer. It describes the face of nature under the various lights of dawn, sunrise, noon, evening, and night. It includes a general prospect of the globe, more particularly a geographical survey of the deserts of Tartary and the midlands, or rather Mediterranean shores, of Europe; and ends with a display of earthquake and volcanic fireworks. While writing their poems the young Scotsmen kept up an active correspondence of mutual criticism and encouragement.

Summer was published by John Millan, a bookseller at Charing Cross, some time in the first half of 1727. In the same year Thomson wrote Verses to the Memory of Sir Isaac Newton, published in June; and Britannia, which, however, was not published till January, 1729. A third edition of Summer, 'with additions [1],' was issued in 1730, the price 1s. 6d. a copy: the poem then comprised 1205 lines; and this was still the extent of the poem in the edition of The Seasons issued in 1738. In the final edition published in the author's lifetime—that of 1746—the poem was enlarged to 1805 lines. The principal additions to the text of 1738 were the passage racily descriptive of the washing and shearing of sheep; the lines in memory of Miss Stanley; much of that long digression in which the poet expatiates on the phenomena of tropical summer; and the view of the Thames Valley. From its first appearance in 1727 to the publication of the settled text in 1746 the poem underwent at the hand of its author so many alterations that at last it looked almost like a new production. The minuter verbal changes were innumerable, ideas were expanded, transpositions made, new matter thrown in, old matter struck out, and, if greater clearness of expression was secured by these processes, it was sometimes at the expense of force and picturesqueness of effect. The whole poem, in short, was stirred about, without any very sensible gain of coherence among its parts.

Thomson's original intention was to dedicate Summer to Lord Binning, who had engaged him in the summer of 1725 as a tutor to his son; but his lordship generously waived the honour, advising the author to bestow it upon some one who could better advance his interests; and the poet accordingly fixed upon the Right Honourable Mr. Dodington, then a lord of the Treasury, himself a dabbler in verse, and known to be ambitious of enacting the part of a Mæcenas. To Dodington, who has

1 One of the additions was the haymaking scene, ll. 352–370.

appropriately been called the last of the Patrons, the poem was inscribed at first in a prose address, which was, in the third and subsequent
editions, displaced by the tributary lines incorporated with the text near
the commencement of the poem.   The prose dedication is chiefly
remarkable for the warmth and frankness of its professions. There is
good reason to doubt their sincerity, and in truth Dodington little
deserved them.   ' What reader,' says the extravagant poet, ' need be told
of those great abilities in the management of public affairs, and those
amiable accomplishments in private life, which you so eminently possess ?
The general voice is loud in the praise of so many virtues, though
posterity alone will do them justice. But may you, sir, live long
to illustrate your own fame by your own actions, and by them be trans-
mitted to future times as the British Maecenas ! Your example has
recommended poetry, with the greatest grace, to the admiration of those
who are engaged in the highest and most active scenes of life ; and this,
though confessedly the least considerable of those exalted qualities that
dignify your character, must be particularly pleasing to me, whose only
hope of being introduced to your regard is through the recommendation
of an art in which you are a master.   But I forget what I have been
declaring above, and must therefore turn my eyes to the following sheets.
I am not ignorant, that, when offered to your perusal, they are put into the
hands of one of the finest, and consequently the most indulgent judges of
this age ; but, as there is no mediocrity in poetry, so there should be no
limits to its ambition. I venture directly on the trial of my fame. If
what I here present you has any merit to gain your approbation, I am
not afraid of its success ; and if it fails of your notice, I give it up to its
just fate.'

The Argument of the enlarged poem as given in the edition of 1746
is as follows :—' The subject proposed. Invocation. Address to Mr.
Dodington. An introductory reflection on the motion of the heavenly
bodies—whence the succession of the seasons. As the face of Nature in
this season is almost uniform, the progress of the poem is a description of a summer's day. The dawn. Sun rising. Hymn to the sun.
Forenoon. Summer insects described. Haymaking. Sheep-shearing.
Noon-day. A woodland retreat. Group of herds and flocks. A solemn
grove—how it affects a contemplative mind. A cataract, and rude
scene. View of summer in the Torrid Zone.) Storm of thunder and
lightning. A tale. The storm over. A serene afternoon. Bathing.

The hour of walking. Transition to the prospect of a rich well-cultivated country; which introduces a panegyric on Great Britain. Sunset. Evening. Night. Summer meteors. A comet. The whole concluding with the praise of Philosophy.'

The most poetical passages of Summer are the descriptions of dawn and sunrise ; the dogs wakened by the wasp; the field of hay-makers ; noontide ; the horse stung by the gadfly ; the sheep-shearing scene ; the solitary bather ; and the transition from evening to the darkness of summer night. The long digression to the imagined fervours and phenomena of tropical summer contains many magnificent lines, but one is glad when it is ended, and the poet returns from his wide geographical wanderings in torrid tracts to the June aspects and associations of temperate climes. The tale of young Celadon and his Amelia is somewhat conventionally treated, but is effective in its way, and marked by a restraint of pathos almost classical. The episode of Damon and Musidora, which has been generally regarded as a characteristic example of Thomson's bad taste in the treatment of the passion of love, is presented with much of the warmth of colouring and breadth of handling which we find in pagan poetry and the works of the old masters. It has been much altered from the original draught : Damon, as he appears in the early editions, professes insensibility to female charms, and, instead of Musidora alone, three [1] nymphs of different types of loveliness are represented as bathing in the pool.

Thomson's Summer, Gay's Fables, Malloch's Ballad of William and Margaret, and Spence's Essay on the Odyssey were the chief publications in London of the year 1727. It was in his Essay on the Odyssey that Spence made favourable allusion to the new poet, the author of Winter, published just the year before.

Lines 1, 2. The first edition opened less melodiously, and less picturesquely :

> 'From southern climes, where unremitting day
> Burns overhead, illustrious Summer comes.'

[1] In Millar's edition of the Seasons, published in 1738, W. Kent's illustration of Summer represents Time sitting aloft with his chin in his hand and his scythe across his knee, looking at the arrival of Summer in his place in the Zodiac. Below are *four* nymphs bathing in a pool, or reclining on its brink, while a swain, with his hand on a cumbrous quarto, ventures to take a half-length look from behind a small tree.

T

3. *and felt through Nature's depth.* The words disturb the figure, by submitting a feeling for a person. Cp. the first line of Spring.

12. *haunted stream.* Haunted by nymphs or naiads, or by fairies, or by legendary associations. Cp. Horace's *fabulosus Hydaspes.* Cp. also Milton's lines—

> (*a*) ' Such sights as youthful poets dream
>   On summer eves by haunted stream ';

L'Allegro, ll. 129, 130;

and, in regard to the general meaning of ll. 9–13—

> (*b*)   ' When the sun begins to fling
>   His flaring beams, me, goddess, bring
>   To archèd walks of twilight groves,
>   And shadows brown, that Sylvan loves,
>   Of pine, or monumental oak,
>   Where the rude axe with heavèd stroke
>   Was never heard the nymphs to daunt
>   Or fright them from their hallowed haunt.
>   There, in close covert, by some brook,
>   Where no profaner eye may look,
>   Hide me from day's garish eye.'

Il Penseroso, ll. 131–141.

14. *the glories of the circling year* ; i. e. the grandest phenomena of the whole year, viz. the glories of Summer.

15. *Come, Inspiration!* ' I thank you heartily for your hint about personizing of Inspiration ; it strikes me.'—*Letter to Malloch*, 11th Aug., 1726.

15, 16. *from thy hermit seat, By mortal seldom found.* Inspiration here means the muse of poetry. Burns has—

> ' The muse nae poet ever fand her
>   Till by himsel' he learnt to wander
>   Adown some trotting burn's meander
>   And no' think lang' (i. e. *not become weary*).

17, 18, *raptured glance Shot on surrounding heaven.* Cp. Shakespeare—

> ' The poet's eye in a fine frenzy rolling
> Doth glance from heaven to earth, from earth to heaven.'

Midsummer Night's Dream, Act V. sc. i.

21–31. First appeared in the second edition, taking the place of the prose dedication.

21. *my youthful muse's early friend.* When Thomson wrote these words it was hardly possible for him to have known Dodington for more

than a year. The whole passage which they introduce, down to l. 31, is charged with the grossest flattery. If the lines were meant ironically they would fit perfectly. Dodington throughout the whole of his career— however Thomson may have been anticipating it in 1726–7—had neither the 'genius and wisdom,' nor ' the gay social sense chastised by decency,' nor the 'unblemished honour,' nor the 'active zeal for Britain's glory, liberty, and man,' with which, in addition to ' all the human graces,' the poet accredits him. Thomson was either desperately determined on a patron, or, which is more likely, singularly charitable in his estimate of character.—George Bubb, who afterwards (in his 29th year) took the surname of Dodington, and ultimately (in his 70th) became Lord Melcombe, was born in the year 1691. He was the son of Jeremias Bubb who has been variously designated an apothecary and an Irish adventurer; was educated at Oxford, and, through the influence of his mother's family, began his political life in 1715 as the representative of the borough of Winchelsea. In 1720, by the death of his maternal uncle, he fell heir to the fine estate of Eastbury, in Dorsetshire. It was on this occasion that he changed his name. He was member for Bridgewater from 1722 to 1754. In 1724 he became a lord of the Treasury, and was holding the office when Thomson first knew him, in 1726 or 1727, and dedicated to him his poem of Summer on its publication in the latter of these years. In politics he was a place-hunter, shifting from side to side with undisguised meanness. As he commanded five or six votes in the House of Commons he could generally make interest for himself with parties by the offer of his influence. His worthiest action as a politician was his defence of the unfortunate Admiral Byng. In 1761, under Lord Bute's administration, he received at last the title for which he had so long shuffled and shifted. He died the year after. He was a good scholar, had a reputation for wit, wrote passable verses, and posed as a patron of letters. He has been called the last of 'the patrons.' Young, Thomson, Fielding, Glover, and Lyttelton all made court to him. He was vain, pompous, affected, and unscrupulous; fond of surrounding himself with showy splendour, and of arraying his large person in embroidery and brocade; coarse in the execution of his rehearsed jokes, and in the display of his premeditated wit; and by no means restrained, even in the society of ladies, by any very refined sense of decency. His Diary gives a full disclosure of his vanity and selfishness. Two years after his death, Foote figured him in the burlesque drama, The Patron, as Sir Thomas Lofty.

After the dedication of Summer to Dodington, Thomson was an occasional guest at Eastbury, and, as his correspondence reveals, was apparently for some years on intimate terms with his patron, and highly satisfied with the intimacy. His published letters to Dodington were written in 1730 and 1731, during his visit to the Continent. He says in one of them : 'Should you inquire after my muse, all that I can answer is, that I believe she did not cross the channel with me. I know not whether your gardener at Eastbury has heard anything of her among the woods there; she has not thought fit to visit me while I have been in this once poetic land [Italy], nor do I feel the least presage that she will.' (Dated ' Nov. 28th, 1731.') Thomson spent part of the autumn of 1735 at Eastbury, and was still on the most friendly footing with his patron of the year 1727.

32–42. There is probably a reference here to the two texts of Scripture : (1) ' Let there be lights in the firmament of the heaven to divide the day from the night, and let them be for signs, and for seasons, and for days and years ' (Gen. i. 14) ; and (2) ' While the earth remaineth, seedtime and harvest, and cold and heat, and summer and winter, and day and night shall not cease ' (Gen. viii. 22).

43, 44. *the alternate Twins are fired. . . Cancer reddens.* Thomson's plan for Summer is thus stated in a letter to Malloch : 'I resolve(d) to contract the season into a day : the uniform appearances of nature in summer easily allow of it.' (Aug. 11th, 1726.) The typical day is a day in Midsummer. The sun is at the northern tropic (of Cancer) on the 22nd of June. (See Notes, Spring, ll. 26, 27.) ' Alternate' is for ' both,' ' the one and the other' ; it is, of course, redundant, the idea of ' two ' being in the word ' twins.' The sun is in the sign Gemini from 21st May till the solstice.

46. *observant.* The idea here is that of a sentinel set to watch and give warning. Cp.—but note also the difference—

> ' Ere the blabbing eastern scout,
> The nice Morn on the Indian steep,
> From her cabined loop-hole peep,
> And to the tell-tale sun descry
> Our concealed solemnity.'—*Comus*, ll. 138–142.

48. *dappled.* Prof. Skeat gives the following interesting note on this word : 'Dapple, a spot on an animal (Scand.). Icel. *depill*, a spot, dot. . . . The original sense is "a little pool," from Norweg. *dapi*, a pool. Allied to our " dub," and to " deep " and " dip." ' In the first edition ' streaky' was used.

52–56. The landscape here depicted in the twilight of a calm summer morning is the creation of genuine art, utterly faithful in its copy of the natural scene. Cp. the lines of the Marquis of Montrose—

> ' The misty mount, the smoking lake,
> The rock's resounding echo,

> The whistling winds, the woods that shake
> Shall all with me sing *hey-ho,*' &c.
>
> *An Excellent New Ballad,* Pt. II. st. 12.

57, 58. *the fearful hare Limps awkward.* This also is part of a summer morning scene. The Scottish word 'hirple' well expresses the awkward limping here noted. See Burns—

> 'The rising sun ower Galston muir
> Wi' glorious light was glintin',
> The hare was hirplin' down the fur,
> The laverocks—they were chantin'.'
>
> *Holy Fair.*

65, 66. *from the crowded fold in order drives His flock.* The touch of minute fidelity in the phrase 'in order' is apt to be overlooked. Cowper gives the same idea—an idea that suggests the repose of pastoral life—due prominence:

> 'The sheepfold here
> Pours out its fleecy tenants o'er the glebe.
> And first, progressive as a stream they seek
> The middle field; but, scattered by degrees
> Each to his choice, soon whiten all the land.'
>
> *The Task,* Bk. I. ll. 282–6.

67–80. Thomson's knowledge of the beauties and benefits of early rising had little influence on his practice, at least after he left Scotland. His favourite 'hour' for 'meditation' and 'song' was the midnight and not the morning hour. (Contrast this passage with ll. 204–6 of *Winter.*)

72. *losing half*; i. e. twelve of the four-and-twenty hours of each day! A liberal proportion.

81–96. This description of sunrise may be compared with Malloch's: the quotation will serve as a specimen of Malloch's style:

> 'But see, the flushed horizon flames intense
> With vivid red, in rich profusion streamed
> O'er heaven's pure arch. At once the clouds assume
> Their gayest liveries; these with silvery beams
> Fringed lovely, splendid those with liquid gold:
> And speak their sovereign's state. He comes, behold!
> Fountain of light and colour, warmth and life!
> The king of glory! Round his head divine,
> Diffusive showers of radiance circling flow,
> As o'er the Indian wave up-rising fair
> He looks abroad on nature, and invests,
> Where'er his universal eye surveys,

Her ample bosom, earth, air, sea and sky,
In one bright robe, with heavenly tinctures gay.'
                                        The Excursion, Canto I.

These lines are cold and commonplace beside Thomson's, which yet they
resemble in certain phrases and tricks of style. Very much the same
features of sunrise are noted, but Malloch's representation wants the breadth
and colouring of Thomson's. It should be remembered that Thomson
was at work upon Summer while Malloch was busy with The Excursion,
and that they submitted their verses in MS. to each other from time
to time in the course of composition, for mutual encouragement and
criticism.

82. *Rejoicing in the east.* A recollection of the nineteenth Psalm:
' In them [the heavens] hath he set a tabernacle for the sun, which is as
a bridegroom coming out of his chamber, and rejoiceth as a strong man
to run a race.' (Verses 4, 5.)

88. *the shining day.* ' Full lowns the shynand day.'—*Hardyknute.*
This (supposed) ' fragment of an old heroic ballad ' was published in
1724 in Ramsay's Tea-Table Miscellany, where Thomson may have seen
it. His romantic views of nature are certainly those of the old Scots
ballads.

89, 90. *wandering streams High-gleaming from afar.* The scene is
apparently Cheviot side.

91. *Of all material beings first and best.* Light, however, is not a
material substance, but a mode of motion. In Thomson's day it was
regarded as matter by ' natural philosophers ' who, because of its extreme
rarity, ranked it as one of the ' imponderables.' Cp. Milton—

        ' Hail, holy Light! offspring of heaven firstborn.'
                                        Par. Lost, Bk. III.

94. *Unessential gloom.* Hiding the existence of objects within it.

97–103. *'Tis by thy secret strong attractive force*, &c. The attraction
of gravitation, the discovery of Newton, by which the solar system
exists. See for a glowing poetical eulogium of Sir Isaac Newton the
Verses which Thomson inscribed to his memory (published in June,
1727). Natural Philosophy was a favourite study of Thomson's.
He had contracted a liking for it at Edinburgh University, and it
remained to the end of his life a subject of great interest to him. In the
verses to the memory of Newton, he asks, apostrophising ' the Sons
of Light '—

        ' Have ye not listened while he bound the Suns
        And Planets to their spheres ?   .   .   .
            .   .   .   .
            .   .   .   .   Our solar round

> First gazing through, he, by the blended power
> Of *gravitation* and *projection*, saw
> The whole in silent harmony revolve.

> The heavens are all his own; from the wild rule
> Of whirling *vortices* and circling *spheres*
> To their first great simplicity restored.'

100. *utmost Saturn.* This planet was thought to be the outermost member of the solar system in Thomson's day. Since then two additional planets of greater distance from the sun have been discovered—Uranus in 1781, and Neptune in 1846. Neptune takes more than five times the number of years required by Saturn to complete one revolution round the sun.

101. *Mercury* is the nearest planet to the sun, and the smallest, the Planetoids excepted. It is seldom distinctly visible to the unaided eye, partly because of its small size, and partly from the circumstance—to which Thomson here refers—that it is never above the horizon more than two hours after sunset or the same time before sunrise. (For a detailed poetical description of the planets as popularly known in Thomson's time, see Malloch's Excursion, Canto II.)

104. *Informer of the planetary train.* The sun. 'Inform' is used in its poetical sense of 'animate.' The idea is repeated in the next line —'quickening,' i. e. 'animating.' Cp. 'the quick and the dead.' See also l. 109, 'inhaling spirit.'

106. *brute . . . mass.* Dead matter.

107. *the green abodes of life.* The idea is fanciful. Saturn, at least, was believed in Thomson's day to be incapable of supporting life, as we understand it, through excessive cold: Malloch describes it as—

> 'An endless desert, where extreme of cold
> Eternal sits, as in his native seat,
> On wintry hills of never-thawing ice.'

> *Excursion*, Canto II.

109, 110. *from the unfettered mind . . . down to the daily race.* From angelic beings, or even archangels, to ephemeral insects.

112–135. These lines are a splendid improvement upon the first text. Thomson's imagination rises here with commanding force and ease 'to the highth of his great argument.'

113. *Parent of Seasons.* See l. 2—'child of the sun.' The antecedent of 'who' is 'the vegetable world' in the preceding line.

114. *thy throne.* The orb or sphere of the sun—as distinct from the personified Power of Influence which lodges in it.

115. *the bright ecliptic road.* The sun's *apparent* path round the

earth; more correctly, the great circle which the earth's centre describes among the fixed stars in its yearly revolution round the sun. It is the middle line of the zodiacal belt, *bright* with constellations. 'Ecliptic,' because it is the line in which eclipses occur. Gr. ἐκλείπειν, to leave out.

117, 118. *nations circled gay with . . . . tribes of foodful earth.* The various human communities surrounded with their farms and cultivated fields.

119, 120. This is not idolatry of the sun; but a poetical way of expressing the hope of having fine weather to ripen the crops, or thankfulness for having had it. Harvest-home is thus, in Milton's words, a 'praising of bounteous Pan.'

121–123. The imagery is classical. Cp., e. g., Horace—
          'Jam Cytherea choros ducit Venus . . . .
               Junctaeque Nymphis Gratiae decentes,' &c.—*Car.* i. 4.

122. *rosy-fingered Hours.* Said of the morning by Homer—
          'The Lady of the Light, the rosy-fingered Morn.'
                                             Chapman's Translation.

124. *light-footed Dews.* Referring to the silence with which dew is formed. 'Of bloom ethereal' is apparently 'of pearly, or crystalline, lustre.' Malloch has 'the silver-footed dews' in The Hermit, Canto I.

126–129. The same idea of bounty is expressed in similar words in Spring, ll. 180–184.

133–159. To attribute to the influence of the sun the formation of the various minerals, notably of the precious stones, is purely fanciful. George Stephenson, indeed, called coal 'bottled sunshine,' but Thomson makes no explicit reference to coal. (See Par. Lost. III. 608–612.)

136–139. Iron in its various forms—tools, weapons of war, parts of the structure of buildings, bridges, ships, &c.—is here chiefly alluded to. Metal in the form of money, as wages, the price of commodities, &c. is probably included.

140. *impregned by thee.* Milton has the word—
                         'As Jupiter
          On Juno smiles, when he impregns the clouds
          That shed May flowers.'—*Par. Lost*, Bk. IV. ll. 499–501.

142. *Diamond.* Another form of 'adamant.' Gr. α, priv., δαμάειν, to tame. From its hardness.

143. *collected light, compact.* Solidified light. See below, l. 149, where sapphire is called 'solid ether.' For the idea, cp. Malloch—
          'The sparkling gem   .   .   .   .   .   .
               .   .   .   .
          From thy unfailing source of splendour draw(s).'
                                                  Excursion, II.

145. 146. *Dares, as it sparkles,* &c. See Winter—' sparkling gems and radiant eyes '—l. 642.

147. *ruby.* From its red colour. Lat. *ruber,* red.

149. *sapphire.* Persian, *saffir.*

150. *tinct.* Older form of ' tint.' Spenser uses ' tinct ' as a participle = 'tinged.' Lat. *tinctus,* dyed. ' Taint' and ' stain ' are cognates.

151. *amethyst.* Gr. ἀ, priv., and μεθύειν, to be drunken. As an amulet this stone was supposed to prevent intoxication.

152. *topaz.* Gr. τόπαζος; from its brightness. Allied probably to the Sanskrit *tap,* to shine ; whence ' taper.'

154. *gives it.* Presents or exposes it. The meaning is—' in the first freshness of the spring season.'

155. *emerald.* Old Fr. *esmeraude*; Gr. σμάραγδος, emerald. 'Your hint of the sapphire, emerald, ruby strike my imagination . . . . and shall not be neglected.'—*Letter to Malloch*, 2 Aug. 1726.

156. *thick.* In numerous flashes. *Opal.* Gr. ὀπάλλιος, opal.

159. *As the site varies.* As you keep turning it in your hand.

161. *Assumes a mimic life.* Inanimate nature—the stream, the precipice, the desert, ruins, and the deep—seem to grow animate, and to feel the joy of life.

162, 163. *In brighter mazes . . . Plays.* In some of the earlier editions (that of 1738 for example)—' In brisker measures . . . frisks.'

165, 166. *The desert joys Wildly through all his melancholy bounds.* This description of the effect of sunshine upon the desert is a magnificent stroke of the imagination.

176. *Light Himself, in uncreated light . . . dwells.* Cp. Milton—

> ' God is Light,
> And never but in unapproachèd light
> Dwelt from eternity—dwelt then in thee,
> Bright effluence of bright essence increate!'
>
> *Par. Lost*, III. 3-6.

184. *spheres.* Meaning 'orbits.'

185-190. Cp. Milton—

> ' Nor think, though men were none,
> That heaven would want spectators, God want praise.
>
> *Par. Lost*, IV. 675-676.

195. *to translate.* To describe in verse.

206. *coolness to the shade retires.* ' A calm retreat, where breathing Coolness has her seat.'—Malloch.

210. *darts.* ' Rains ' in the first edition.

212. *Who can unpitying see the flowery race,* &c. There is a touch here of the tenderness of Burns for the daisy.

216. *the lofty follower of the sun.* The sunflower. Dr. A. T. Thomson has a note on the poetical fiction of the succeeding lines :—
'The plant neither turns its flower to the sun, nor can it close its petals in the manner described. . . . If we examine a bed of sunflowers at any period of the day we shall find them looking in every direction.'

220. *the swain retreats.* The shepherd (of l. 63) returns. It is noon. Burns has the same use of ' retreats '—

<blockquote>

' The miry beasts retreating frae the pleugh.'
Cotter's Saturday Night.
</blockquote>

223. *cottage then expecting food.* Milk for the cottage household.

224, 225. *the daw, the rook, and magpie.* See note, Spring, l. 609.

228–236. The whole scene here depicted, one of idyllic truth and beauty, finely suggests the lazy noontide of a long summer day. The position of the village is charmingly imagined.

232. *vacant greyhound.* In the first text ' employless.'

237. *noisy summer-race.* Suggested by the wasp. Flies and ephemera.

238. *Live in her lay.* They live also in the lay of Gray—

<blockquote>

' Hark ! how through the peopled air

The busy murmur glows !

The insect youth are on the wing

Eager to   .   .   .   .   .

      .   . float amid the liquid noon.'—*Ode on Spring.*
</blockquote>

The different kinds referred to include in Thomson's description the dragon-fly, may-fly, day-fly, house-fly, &c.

269. *spider.* Shortened from 'spinther,' to ' spither,' and then ' spider.' From ' spin.'

270. *mixture abhorred !* The mixture of cunning and ferocity.

276. *with rapid glide.* The noun ' glide ' is now seldom used.

289–317. This passage, slightly altered, was transferred from Spring to its present place as a part of Summer.

293. *the living cloud.* A fanciful idea : it is not now believed that pestilence arises from living insects, which exist in the ' reek of rotten fens.'

305. *floating verdure.* The green scum.

318–341. A specimen of Thomson's ' preaching ' style—in which he seldom indulges. It reads like a page from Young.

343. *convolved.* A favourite word of Thomson's. See Spring, l. 839.

348. *A season's glitter !* Following this, in the first edition, came—

<blockquote>

'In soft-circling robes,

Which the hard hand of industry has wrought,
</blockquote>

The human insects glow ; by Hunger fed,
    And cheered by toiling Thirst, they roll about,' &c.
—meaning that they are maintained by the toil of starving workers. Cp.
Goldsmith—
    'The robe that wraps his limbs in silken sloth
    Has robbed the neighbouring fields of half their growth.'
                                                    Deserted Village.
See also Burns—
                'The simple rustic hind
        Whose toil upholds the glittering show.'—*A Winter Night.*

350, 351. *Oblivion . . . . strikes them from the book of life* ; i. e. from
the memory of men.

352–432. These descriptions, of haymaking and of sheep-shearing, are
in Thomson's happiest style. They did not appear in the first edition
of Summer. They were as felicitous afterthoughts as the angling scene
in Spring. The former appeared before, the latter after, the edition
of 1738.

355. *Blown by prevailing suns.* The participle is here used in a
peculiar way. We say 'Roses blow,' but never 'the sun blows roses.'—
'Maid' in this line, along with 'youth' two lines above, stands in
apposition to 'village,' i. e. 'the village community,' of l. 352.

361. *the tedded grain.* 'Grain' has here the peculiar meaning of
'seeded grass.' To 'ted' is to spread mown grass, to turn and toss it
for drying. From Icelandic *teðja*, to spread manure ; *tað*, manure.
In Lowland Scottish 'to taith.'

363. *breathing harvest.* The hay-crop, exhaling its fragrant moisture
in process of drying.

365. *the green-appearing ground.* After the hay is made it is raked
into heaps, and by means of cords or light sledges drawn into still
larger heaps, and hay-ricking, or the piling of the hay into haycocks,
or hay-colls, commences.

367. *thick.* Numerous—its common meaning with Thomson.

369. The cause is surely here put for the effect. It may mean disturbing or enlivening the air.

382. This line beautifully realizes the scene—quick exertion of their
legs and slow progress of their 'woolly sides' through the deep water.

386. *sordid stream.* Muddied water of the deep pool, whither the
trout used to come to play—hence, in preceding line, 'lively haunt.'
Sordid is, of course, used in its primitive sense. Not only is much of
Thomson's diction Latin, but he employs the Latin words in their original
meaning.

389. *swelling treasures.* Their wool, 'swelling' as it dries in the sun.

390. *around the hills.* The scene is in Teviotdale, most pastoral of Scottish counties.

395. *Wattled pen.* Enclosure made of hurdles. Milton has 'hurdled cotes.' From A.-S. *watel*, a hurdle, something woven of pliant twigs and rods. Allied to Lat. *vitilis*, flexible.

398. Women make up the packs of wool.

407. *vagrant.* So named in anticipation of his wandering propensity. Hence the need of the 'cipher.'

410, 411. *the sturdy boy holds by the twisted horns,* &c. A much admired picture.

415. *What softness in its melancholy face.* Blake too has noted the 'soft face' of the sheep.

420. *to pay his annual care.* His rent for his farm.

423, 424. *A simple scene! yet hence Britannia sees Her solid grandeur rise.* Cp. Burns—

'From scenes like these old Scotia's grandeur springs.'
Cotter's Saturday Night.

Wool had long been the staple article of trade in England. One hundred years ago the native-grown wool supplied almost all that was needed for the home manufacture of woollen cloth. The Woolsack, the seat of the Lord Chancellor in the House of Lords since the reign of Elizabeth, is a memorial of the times when wool was the chief source of the national wealth.—See Spring, l. 75.

428, 429. *her dreadful thunder hence Rides o'er the waves.* Her men-of-war. Cp. Campbell—

'With thunder from her native oak
She quells the floods below.'
Ye Mariners of England.

429. *now, ev'n now.* Written after 1738; probably the war of Great Britain against France in connection with the Austrian succession is referred to. It began in 1741.

431. (*Britannia*) *rules the circling deep.* About the time he wrote this line he composed (1740)—for the Masque of Alfred—the famous national song, 'Britannia, rule the waves!' On internal evidence the song is Thomson's. Malloch, in an edition of his works published in 1759, retained, in his 'enlargement' of Alfred in that edition, a song 'part' of which, he allows, was written by Thomson. This could only have been the song of 'Rule, Britannia.' The other part was written (in 1751) by Lord Bolingbroke—as a footnote informs us.

435. *a dazzling deluge.* Of hot sunshine.

443. *the cheerful sound.* In all editions, down to 1738, 'the *sandy* sound' (of sharpening scythe).

447. After this line came, in the first edition—
> 'The desert singes; and the stubborn rock,
> Split to the centre, sweats at every pore.'

In a later edition, and retained in 1738, 'singes' was altered to 'reddens.'
Ultimately the two lines were struck out.

460, 461. *beneath the whole collected shade . . . Or in the gelid caverns.*
> 'O qui me gelidis in vallibus Haemi
> Sistat, et ingenti ramorum protegat umbra !'
> > Virgil, *Georgic* II. 487,488.

471. *Ashes . . . resounding o'er the steep.* Through which the wind is blowing.

475. *Laves.* This pause is not uncommon in Thomson's blank verse; e. g.
> Of him the shepherd in the peaceful dale
> Chants.—*Britannia,* ll. 136, 137.

Tennyson uses it with fine effect.

481–484. This variety of the brook's course has been inimitably described by Burns in Halloween—
> 'Whyles owre a linn the burnie plays
> As through the glen it wimpl't;
> Whyles round a rocky scaur it strays,
> Whyles in a wiel it dimpl't;
> Whyles glittered to the nightly rays
> Wi' bickerin' dancin' dazzle;
> Whyles cookit underneath the braes
> Below the spreading hazel.'

493–497. A very similar scene has been charmingly rendered (partly in prose) by Heine in The Tour in the Harz (1824). The metrical part begins—
> 'König ist der Hirtenknabe.'

The features of the scene and situation are in both poets the same—down to the wallet of bread and cheese. For l. 497 the later editions read—
> 'There, listening every noise, his watchful dog.'

506–515. This passage was composed so early as the beginning of June, 1726. On the 11th of that month Thomson transcribed it in a letter to Aaron Hill.

516–563. This passage of forty-eight lines, almost as they stand, was ready before the 11th August, 1726. In a letter of that date to Malloch, Thomson thus refers to them : ' I have already written of shade and gloom, and woodland spirits, &c., exactly as you hint more than a week ago.'

518. *forming ... a woodland quire.* Quire, for choir, here signifies the place frequented by song-birds, not the song-birds themselves. So Shakespeare—

> 'Yellow leaves, or none or few, do hang
> Upon those boughs which shake against the cold,
> Bare, ruined choirs, where late the sweet birds sang.'
> *Sonnet* lxxiii.

526, 527. *to save the fall of Virtue,* &c. Cp. Milton's Comus—

> ' If virtue feeble were
> Heaven itself would stoop to her.'—ll. 1022, 1023.

528, 529. *In waking whispers and repeated dreams To hint pure thought.* Cp. Milton—

> ' A thousand liveried angels lackey her [the soul],
> Driving far off each thing of sin and guilt,
> And in clear dream and solemn vision
> Tell her of things that no gross ear can hear,' &c.
> *Comus,* ll. 455-8.

531. *To prompt the poet.* The same idea occurs in Burns's Vision, where it is the leading feature of Duan Second :—

> ' Some fire the soldier on to dare,
> Some rouse the patriot up to bare
> Corruption's heart ;
> Some teach the bard, a darling care,
> The tuneful art.
>
> .   .   .   .   .
>
> Of these am I—Coila my name,' &c.

552-563. This passage will bear comparison with the exquisite harmony and solemn imagery of Milton's well-known lines—

> ' Millions of spiritual creatures walk the earth
> Unseen, both when we wake and when we sleep ;
> All these with ceaseless praise his works behold
> Both day and night. How often from the steep
> Of echoing hill or thicket have we heard
> Celestial voices to the midnight air,
> Sole, or responsive each to other's note,
> Singing their great Creator ! Oft in bands
> While they keep watch, or nightly rounding walk,
> With heavenly touch of instrumental sounds
> In full harmonic number joined, their songs
> Divide the night, and lift our thoughts to heaven.'
> *Par. Lost,* Bk. IV. ll. 677-688.

564. *And art thou, Stanley, of that sacred band ?* On this line

Thomson has the following footnote :—' A young lady well known to the author, who died at the age of eighteen, in the year 1738.'—Her epitaph, in Holyrood Church, Southampton, informs the reader that Elizabeth Stanley, daughter of George and Sarah Stanley, joined to the greatest beauty, modesty, and gentleness of female nature ' all the fortitude, elevation, and vigour of mind that ever exalted the most heroical man.' The epitaph includes twenty-four lines of verse written by Thomson, and terminating thus—

'Yes, we must follow soon, will glad obey;
When a few suns have rolled their cares away,
Tired with vain life, will close the willing eye :
'Tis the great birthright of mankind to die !
Blest be the bark that wafts us to the shore
Where death-divided friends shall part no more !
   To join thee there, here with thy dust repose,
   Is all the hope thy hapless mother knows.'

The mother of Miss Stanley was an early friend of Thomson. She was the daughter of Sir Hans Sloane, who, in the year (1727) of the publication of Summer, succeeded Sir Isaac Newton in the presidentship of the Royal Society, and who is now chiefly known for his noble bequest of books and MSS. which proved the nucleus of the British Museum.—This address to the shade of Miss Stanley was not ready for the edition of 1738.

582. *kills not the buds of virtue.* ' In Eden every *bud* is blown.' —David Gray.

592–606. The original lines, nine in number, of which these fifteen are an expansion, described the waterfall with more force and felicity of language, if with less fluency—

'In one big glut, as sinks the shelving ground,
The impetuous torrent, tumbling down the steep,
Thunders, and shakes the astonished country round.
Now a blue watery sheet ; anon, dispersed,
A hoary mist ; then, gathered in again,
A darted stream aslant the hollow rock,
This way and that tormented, dashing thick
From steep to steep, with wild infracted course,
And restless roaring to the humble vale.'

606. Five lines, afterwards dropped, introduced in the first edition the passage beginning here.

616. *Mournfully hoarse.* Thomson imports the grief into the note of the stock-dove. It sounds equally mournful when the bird is well pleased.

628. *Woodbine.* Honeysuckle, and so in the original. The working bee is neuter, or undeveloped female. The only male bees are the drones.

629-1102. These lines, 474 in number, are a far digression from the subject proper—which is the description of a typical summer day, such as we have in Britain. The poet visits in imagination the various countries of historical or geographical note in the torrid zone—Negroland, Bengal, Mexico, the Sahara, Abyssinia, Nubia, Egypt, Southern India, Siam, Brazil, Peru, Morocco, Arabia, the Cape, &c., the favourite region being Africa. Their flora and fauna, physical features, peculiarities of climate, &c., are dwelt upon in considerable detail. At last the vagrant muse (l. 1101) is happily recalled to England. In this long digression there are many magnificent lines, but Thomson's descriptive power is freshest when it is employed on scenes of which he has direct experience. Perhaps the most effective touch is at ll. 977-9; where, after describing the destruction of a caravan in the desert by the deadly simoom, he suddenly transports us to either extremity of the caravan route, to the towns most interested in the fate of the overdue caravan—

> 'In Cairo's crowded streets
> The impatient merchant, wondering, waits in vain,
> And Mecca saddens at the long delay.'

It may be noted here that the alterations in the first and subsequent texts, before the poem at last settled into the shape in which we now have it—the expansions, additions, distributions, subtractions, and substitutions—are much too numerous to be indicated, and it would serve no very useful purpose to indicate them all. These alterations upon the original text increase from l. 629 onward : those of them which are thought to be of real interest will be noted.

636, 637. *Rising direct, . . . chases . . . The short-lived twilight.* Cp. Coleridge's description—

> 'At one stride comes the dark.'—*Ancient Mariner.*

641. *the general breeze.* Thomson has a footnote on this expression :—'Which blows constantly between the tropics from the east, or the collateral points, the north-east and south-east : caused by the pressure of the rarefied air on that before it, according to the diurnal motion of the sun from east to west.'

645. *double seasons.* Thomson has the following note:—'In all climates between the tropics, the sun, as he passes and repasses in his annual motion, is twice a year vertical, which produces this effect.'

652. *boundless . . . immensity of shade.* Cp. Cowper's 'boundless contiguity of shade' (*The Task*, Bk. II. l. 2).

663. *Pomòna.* The Roman goddess of fruit-trees. From *pomum*, fruit.—*Citron*, a species of fruit-tree in India and other warm countries, belonging to the genus *citrus*, to which also belong the orange, lime, lemon, &c. The rind of the citron is more valuable than the pulp, having a delicious flavour and fragrance. A cooling beverage is made from it.

664. *the lemon and the piercing lime.* From the Persian *límú*, a lemon, or lime, or citron. A cooling beverage is made from these fruits, which is administered in febrile complaints, and is an agreeable drink in hot weather. The lime is much smaller than the lemon, and extremely acid. Both are natives of India and the East. The Crusaders are said to have brought the lemon into Europe.

665. *orange.* Persian *náranj* : the initial letter was lost in Italian ; in French *orange*, as if from *or*, gold—from the colour ; but in Spanish the initial is preserved, *naranja*, an orange.

667. *tamarind.* Literally, the Indian palm. From the Arabic, *tamr*, a ripe date, and *Hind*, India. It is a leguminous spreading tree 30 or 40 feet high ; the pods are brown, full of seeds, and about six inches long. The pulp in which the seeds lie is of a reddish black, sweet and acidulous. A sherbet is made from it, and is used in inflammatory and feverish disorders.

669. *the massy locust.* The reference must, from the use of 'massy,' be to the West Indian locust-tree, which grows to a gigantic height. All trees of the locust order are leguminous.

671. *the Indian fig.* The banyan-tree, remarkable for its rooting branches, which become stems, capable of supporting a vast extent of shade. Hundreds of stems are not uncommon, and there are cases where thousands have been counted up-bearing the branches of a single tree.

674. *the verdant cedar.* The cedar is an evergreen, with a dark shadow. Gr. κέδρος ; perhaps allied to Heb. *kadar*, to be dark.

675. *palmettos lift their graceful shade.* The palmetto is the dwarf or cabbage palm, a native of North America, found farther north than any other species of palm. It rises about 40 or 50 feet, and is crowned with a tuft of large palmated leaves, from one foot to five feet in length and having a long foot-stalk.

677, 678. *cocoa's milky bowl.* The juice of the nut was variously known as milk and wine. Cp. Goldsmith's ' palmy wine.' Cocoa is derived by Professor Skeat from Spanish *coco*, a bugbear, an ugly mask to frighten children ; hence applied to the cocoa-nut on account of the monkey-like face at the base of the nut. The original sense of *coco* was skull, head ; allied to Fr. *coque*, shell, from Lat. *concha*, a marine shell. *Freshening* for ' refreshing.'

U

679. *bounteous.* Not 'plentiful,' but 'bliss-bestowing.' Fr. *bonté*, Lat. *bonitas*, goodness.

680. *Bacchus.* The Greek and Roman noisy or riotous god of wine.

681. *the full pomegranate*; i.e. filled with juice. Literally, the grained or seeded apple, or fruit; from Lat. *pomum*, fruit, apple, and *granatum*, seeded—*granum*, a grain. Thomson's description of its 'slender twigs' is accurate; one writer states that 'in cultivation it is a low tree with *twiggy* branches.'

682, 683. *creeping through the woods, the gelid race Of berries.* Thomson has apparently come home for an instant, and appears to refer to the wild strawberry—the only 'creeping' berry that is ripe in summer. He seems to forget—he would not ignore—the cultivated strawberry, of which Dr. Boteler (as quoted by Izaak Walton) said, 'Doubtless God could have made a better berry, but doubtless God never did.'

685. *thou best anana.* The pine-apple, most delicious of all fruits. It is indigenous to tropical America. It had been introduced into the gardens of the wealthy in England only some forty or fifty years when Thomson thus sang its praises. The Dutch brought it to Europe.

688, 689. The sensuous nature of Thomson is well revealed in these lines.

692. *savanna.* A prairie, or meadow-plain; Spanish *sabana*, a sheet for a bed; from Gr. σάβανον, a linen cloth.

696, 697. *showers .... Exuberant Spring.* Less figuratively 'scatters a luxuriant verdure.'

700. *streaming dews.* If this means—as, taken with 'torrent rains,' it seems to mean—'dews falling copiously,' it is incorrect, since dew does not fall. It may, however, mean 'drops of dew already formed running together in streams.'

705. *fattening seas.* Fertilising waters. The Amazon is meant.

707. *his train.* The tail of the crocodile.

710. By 'behemoth,' Thomson signifies the hippopotamus. See Job, chap. xl. vv. 15–24, for a description which suggested that of the text.

717. *Niger's . . . stream.* The explorer of the Niger, Mungo Park, Thomson's countryman, was not yet born when Thomson wrote this line.

718. *the Ganges . . . . sacred wave.* The river, from its source in 'the cow's mouth' to its union with the bay, is regarded by the natives of Bengal, and indeed of India, with a feeling of reverence. They make pilgrimages from far and near to worship the river, and bathe in its holy waters.

724. Alluding to the great age the elephant sometimes attains.

728. *mine . . . . . his steps.* The wild elephant is sometimes taken in the way these words suggest. Holes are dug in the track the animal is known to frequent; they are lightly covered over with a roof of sticks or boards concealed under a natural appearance of turf, and the elephant tumbling into one of these pits is soon a captive.

729. *his towery grandeur.* Cp. Milton's reference to elephants 'endorsed with towers of archers' in *Par. Regained*, Bk. III. ll. 329, 330.

742. *Montezuma's realm.* Mexico, conquered by Cortes early in the sixteenth century. A peculiar art of the ancient kingdom of Mexico was the weaving of feathers into a kind of costly cloth. The art perished with the unhappy natives. See Milton—

> 'In spirit perhaps he also saw
> Rich Mexico, the seat of Montezume,
> And Cusco in Peru, the richer seat
> Of Atabalipa.'—*Par. Lost*, Bk. XI. ll. 406-409.

744. *Philomel.* The nightingale.

746. *sober-suited.* 'In russet brown bedight.'—*Castle of Indolence*, Canto II. st. xxxiii.

750. *vale of Sennar.* This region, situated in the south of Nubia, extends on both sides of the Bahr-el-Azrek (Blue Nile).

751, 752. *the secret bounds Of jealous Abyssinia boldly pierce.* When these words were penned, the future explorer of Abyssinia, James Bruce, was still a young boy in his home in Stirlingshire, or at school at Harrow. It was the Portuguese Jesuit missionaries, who, in the sixteenth and seventeenth centuries, introduced Popery into Abyssinia. But Christianity had been introduced as early as the fourth century.— 'Jealous,' as having guarded for centuries the supposed source of the Nile. But see Par. Lost, IV. 280-284; and Rasselas, chap. i.

753, 758. A reflection on the Portuguese traders and the Jesuit missionaries.

759. *like the harmless bee.* Cowper employs the same simile:—

> 'He travels and expatiates, as the bee
> From flower to flower, so he from land to land,' &c.
> > *The Task*, Bk. IV. ll. 107, 108.

764. *more than Alpine mountains.* 'Abyssinia,' says Prof. Hughes, 'consists of an alternation of plateaus and high mountain-chains . . . . the external features of the country are those of an Alpine region.'

767. *sun-redoubling valley.* A valley that by the reflection of the sun's rays from its sides doubles the heat of the sun. An awkward compound.

773, 774. *draw Ethereal soul;* i. e. inhale pure life-giving air.

778. ' The rivers bring down some grains of gold, which gives room to suspect the mountains are full of it.'—M. Legrand.

795. *upper seas.* Rain-clouds—'the big stores of steaming oceans' in l. 794. Cp. the Scriptural phrase—'the waters above the firmament.'

801, 802. *the whole precipitated mass,* &c. See Winter, ll. 154, 155, for almost the same language:—

> ' Hurls the whole precipitated air
> Down in a torrent.'

806. *From his two springs.* It is hardly necessary to point out that the problem of the source of the Nile was still far from solution in the time of Thomson, though here he seems to regard it as at last definitely settled. *Gojam :* a district south of Lake Dembea in Abyssinia, lying between the parallels 10° and 11° N. Lat.

806, 807. *From his two springs . . . . . . Pure-welling out.* In 1735— some time before these words were written—Johnson had published in London his translation from the French of ' A Voyage to Abyssinia, by Father Jerome Lobo, a Portuguese Jesuit, with a Continuation by Mr. (*sic*) Legrand,' which Thomson seems to have read. In the ' Continuation' we find : ' Father Peter Pays [Paez], a Portuguese Jesuit, was the first European who had a sight of the two springs which give rise to this celebrated stream. As I was looking round about me,' he says, ' with great attention, I discovered two round springs, one of which might be about 2 feet in diameter. The sight filled me with a pleasure which I know not how to express, when I considered that it was what Cyrus, Cambyses, Alexander, and Julius Cæsar had so ardently and so much in vain desired to behold.' This discovery was in ' Goiama,' and the date was 21st April, 1613. It is now 1891, and there is still some doubt whether the head of the Nile be yet discovered.

808. *fair Dambea.* The lake is about 60 miles long, and has a mean breadth of about 25 miles. It occupies the hollow of a very fertile plateau some 6000 feet above sea-level. Its beauty is much enhanced by several islands. The Blue Nile passes through the south end of it.

820, 821. *he pours his urn,* &c. A skilfully managed cadence. Reference is made to the cataracts of the Nile, and the annual inundation of Egypt.

822. *Niger.* It was not till 1796 that anything definite was known of this river. Park explored it.

826. ' Falling' on the Coromandel coast are the Mahanadi, the Godaveri, the Krishna, and the Cauveri, and numerous other rivers of less size. On the western, or Malabar coast of southern India, there are no rivers of note; unless the Nerbudda and the Tapti are meant.

827. *Menam's orient stream.* Orient, as being still farther east than

the rivers of Hindostan. Thomson gives the following note: 'The river that runs through Siam; on whose banks a vast multitude of those insects called fire-flies make a beautiful appearance in the night.'

829. *Indus' smiling banks*, &c. This description hardly answers the modern idea of the Indus. In the lower half of its long course it flows through a narrow and arid basin, with a decreasing volume of waters. But Thomson probably refers to the valley of Cashmere, 'with its roses the brightest that earth ever gave' (Moore.)

831. *pour untoiling harvest.* A rich deposit of mud from which, with little labour on the part of the agriculturist, abundant crops of millet, rice, &c. are produced.

832. *thy world, Columbus.* America, discovered on the 12th October, 1492. Christopher Columbus, the greatest of navigators, was born in Genoa, some say in 1436, others in 1446. He was in the service of Ferdinand and Isabella of Spain when he made the discovery. His expectation was to find a new route to India by sailing westward. The islands of the new world upon which he was blown were the Bahamas, which he believed to be—and named—the western isles of the Indies. He died in great poverty at Valladolid, in May, 1506, to the eternal disgrace of the ungrateful king Ferdinand. The continent was named by the Germans after Amerigo Vespucci whose account of the new world was the first to be published and become popular. Vespucci was a native of Florence, born there in 1451. He first visited the new world seven years after its discovery. It is right to say that his name was given to the new continent without his wish, and even to his surprise.

834. *The Orinoco.* In the wet season, as described by Dr. A. Russel Wallace, its waters unite with those of the Amazon, and the inhabitants of the submerged areas, where the basins unite, are forced to betake themselves for safety to the upper branches of the flood-invaded forests.

840. *The mighty Orellana.* The Amazon. Properly named from its first navigator Francisco de Orellana, who taking part in the great expedition of Gonzalo Pizarro, deserted his leader, and descended to the ocean in a brigantine. The Amazon is the largest of rivers, and occupies an area as large as Europe.

843. *sea-like Plata.* It is a broad fresh-water estuary, rather than a river, formed by the union of the Parana and the Uruguay.

854. *blameless Pan.* Simple shepherd-life. Pan was the Greek god of flocks and shepherds.

855. *Christian crimes.* Persecuting proselytism is not necessarily referred to. The satire lies in the contrast which the profession of Christian principles so often presents to the conduct of the individual who professes them.

859. 'So great is the volume of water which it [the Amazon] brings down, that its freshness is perceptible at a distance of more than 500 miles from the coast' (Prof. W. Hughes). 'The immense and turbid flood which the Rio de la Plata pours into the Atlantic is perceptible at a distance of more than a hundred miles to seaward, and forms a powerful current amidst the waters of the ocean.'—*Ibid.*

863. *Ceres void of pain.* Crops got without the trouble of cultivating the fields.

869. *fatal treasures.* As being the object of covetousness, and the occasion of strife and bloodshed.

870. [*hid*] *Deep in the bowels of the pitying earth.* Hidden deep underground as if to prevent strife about their possession. Cp. Milton—

> 'By him first
> Men also, and by his suggestion taught,
> Ransacked the centre, and with impious hands
> Rifled the bowels of their mother earth
> For treasures better hid.'—*Par. Lost*, Bk. I. ll. 684-688.

871. *Golconda. Potosi.* The former is a few miles from Hyderabad in the Nizam's dominions, and is proverbially famous for diamonds. They are not, however, got from mines at Golconda, but are brought thither to be cut and polished.—Potosi, in Bolivia, is the richest mining centre for silver in South America. There are thousands of mines in the top of the silver mountain, and hundreds of millions of pounds sterling have been taken out of them.

872. *the gentlest children of the sun.* The native Peruvians, a peaceful and inoffensive race of people, who fell an easy prey to the Spaniards under the Pizarros. They worshipped the sun, and called themselves his children.

890-893. Cp. Goldsmith—

> 'All the gentler morals, such as play
> Through life's more cultured walks, and charm the way,
> These, far dispersed, on timorous pinions fly
> To sport and flutter in a kinder sky.'—*The Traveller.*

898-938. This passage, before its expansion in the later editions, consisted of only some twenty lines in the first edition. It began—

> 'Here the green serpent gathers up his train
> In orbs immense, then darting out anew
> Progressive *rattles* through the withered brake,' &c.

905. *all other thirst*, i. e. thirsty animals.

908. *small close-lurking minister of fate.* The cerastes or horned viper is probably meant. It is exceedingly venomous.

916. *tiger darting fierce.* 'Tiger' is derived from Old Persian *tighri*, an arrow. The river Tigris, from the same root, is named from its swiftness.

921. *hyæna.* From Gr. ὕαινα, literally a 'sow-like' animal.

923. *Mauritania.* The old name for the extreme north-west of Africa, corresponding with the modern Morocco and Algiers. From *Mauri,* the Moors. It is to Mauretania that Horace refers as 'Jubae tellus . . . . leonum arida nutrix ' (Car. I. 22).

923, 924. *the tufted isles . . . . amid the Libyan wild.* Oases adorned with clumps of palm. Libya, a district of north Africa, west of Egypt. (See Liberty, ll. 247–251.)

925–938. This passage stood in the first text—

'In dire divan around their shaggy king
Majestic stalking o'er the burning sand
With planted step; while an obsequious crowd
Of grinning forms at humble distance wait.
These altogether joined from darksome caves,
Where o'er gnawed bones they slumbered out the day,
By supreme hunger smit, and thirst intense,
At once their mingling voices raise to heaven;
And, with imperious and repeated roars
Demanding food, the wilderness resounds
From Atlas eastward to the frighted Nile.'

939. *the first of joys,* i. e. the best.

939–949. Cp. Cowper's description of a similar situation, in Verses supposed to be written by Alexander Selkirk—

'I am out of humanity's reach,' &c.

949. *the wonted roar is up.* A recollection of Comus, l. 549—

'The wonted roar was up amidst the woods.'

952. *stooping Rome,* i. e. declining. The expression is repeated in Liberty, at l. 460 of Part III—where will be found a graphic sketch of the causes that led to the decline of the Republic, and the course of that decline.

954. *Cato . . . through Numidian wilds.* Numidia lay between Mauretania and Carthage. It was at Utica in Numidia, about twenty-seven Roman miles north-west of Carthage, that Cato the younger fell by his own hand, B. C. 46, at the age of forty-nine, rather than submit to Caesar. The contest between Caesar and the Pompeian party, to which Cato belonged, and the resultant tragedy of the death of Cato, are the subject of Addison's stately drama.

955, 956. Campania, a fertile, salubrious, and lovely district of Italy, lying along the Mediterranean immediately to the south-east of Latium ;

once a favourite summer retreat. The first inhabitants were variously called Ausones and Osci. But Ausonia was often applied to the whole of Italy.

959-1051. This long passage of nearly 100 lines on different subjects was interjected after 1738. It has no place in the edition of that year—though a line here and there may be found, but in a different connection, in the first edition of 1727.

964. *A suffocating wind.* The simoom.

977-979. ' A beautiful instance of the modifying and *investive* power of imagination may be seen . . . . in Thomson's description of the streets of Cairo, expecting the arrival of the caravan which had perished in the storm.'—Wordsworth (quoted in Prof. Knight's Life of Wordsworth, vol. ii, Appendix, p. 324).

984. *Typhon*; l. 986. *Ecnephia.* ' Names of particular storms or hurricanes, known only between the tropics.'—*Note by Thomson.* Pliny mentions ἐκνεφίας, a storm that breaks out of a cloud; Gr. ἐκ, out, and νέφος, cloud. On 'the old word *typhon* (not uncommon in old authors)' Prof. Skeat has a curious note. He derives it, of course, from ' τυφῶν, better τυφώς, a whirlwind,' and remarks on the 'close accidental coincidence' (of *typhon* and *typhoon*) ' in sense and form as being very remarkable.' *Typhoon* he describes as modern,—a Chinese word, meaning 'a great wind '; from *ta*, great, and *fang* or *fung*, wind. ' *Tyfoon* would be better.'

987. *cloudy speck.* ' Called by sailors the *ox-eye*, being in appearance at first no bigger.'—*Note by Thomson.* Cp. 'a little cloud out of the sea, like a man's hand' (1 Kings xviii. 44).

998. *Art is too slow.* Seamanship; or the furling of the sails.

1001. *the daring Gama.* ' Vasco da Gama, the first who sailed round Africa by the Cape of Good Hope to the East Indies.'—*Thomson's Note.*—Dom Vasco da Gama was of a good Portuguese family. With a small fleet of four vessels, manned by 160 men, he set sail from Lisbon in July, 1497, reached Table Bay (owing to stormy weather) so late as November, encountered terrific tempests in doubling the southern extremity of Africa, and at last—after quelling a mutiny among his terrified crew, and enduring unspeakable hardships—safely crossed the Indian Ocean to Calicut in India, where he arrived on the 20th May, 1498. He lived to enjoy the fame of this great feat twenty seven years. Courage and constancy were his most conspicuous moral qualities. He is one of the heroes of The Lusiad; and indeed the most striking part of the great epic of Camoens (*b.* 1524, *d.* 1579) is the passage descriptive of the giant Adamastor appearing to Gama as the Demon of the Storm, in the vain hope of turning him from his enterprise of doubling the Cape.

1010. *The Lusitanian Prince.* 'Don Henry, third son to John the First, King of Portugal. His strong genius to the discovery of new countries was the chief source of all the modern improvements in navigation.'—*Note by Thomson.* This prince is known as Enrique the Navigator. The good results of his encouragement to navigation and colonisation appeared chiefly in the reigns of Joam II, and Manoel. It was in Manoel's reign that da Gama discovered the new sea-route to the East Indies.

1015. *shark.* Perhaps from Lat. *carcharus*, a species of dog-fish ; Gr. κάρχαρος, rough, hard. ' To shirk ' = to act as a shark, to prowl about in a slinking manner.

1016. *steaming crowds.* The unhappy victims of the inhuman traffic in slaves, called ' that cruel trade ' a few lines below.

1020. *Guinea.* On the West Coast of Africa. A brave sailor, Sir John Hawkins, has the unenviable distinction of having commenced the deportation of negroes from Guinea to supply labour for the plantations of our American colonies.

1023–1025. A revolting scene, described in words too realistic. Heine has treated the same theme, *suo more*, in The Slave Ship.

1028. Cp. ' looks out the joyous spring ' (Winter, l. 16).

1040, 1041. *Carthagena. Vernon.* Under Walpole's administration, but against his judgment, an expedition was sent against the Spanish possessions in South America. Admiral Vernon was in command. He captured Portobello in 1739, but was baffled in his attack upon Carthagena by the disease of his men. Those unhealthy shores of South America had already proved fatal to Admiral Hosier, whose misfortunes as told in Glover's Ballad of Hosier's Ghost (written on receipt of the news of the capture of Portobello by Vernon) touched the public heart into a long-withheld sympathy. Thomson, in Britannia (ll. 34-40), had attempted anonymously to excite this sympathy in 1727.

1049, 1050. *on each other fixed . . . the blank assistants.* There is careless composition here, and some obscurity of meaning besides. Probably ' the blank assistants ' signifies the survivors who assisted in burying the bodies of their dead comrades ; and ' on each other fixed ' seems to mean ' with eyes fixed on each other.'

1054. *Nemesis.* The goddess of vengeance. As a common noun, the Greek νέμεσις signifies distribution, allotment, and hence retribution ; from νέμειν, to distribute.

1057. *locust-armies putrefying.* ' These are the causes supposed to be the first origin of the Plague, in Dr. Mead's eloquent book on that subject.'—*Note by Thomson.* The ' book ' when first published, in 1720, was a mere pamphlet.

1070. *uncouth verdure.* Unaccustomed, strange. From A.-Sax. *un-*, not ; *cúth*, known.

1078. *its cautious hinge*, &c. See Defoe's History of the Great Plague.

1070-1088. Instead of these lines, the original text (down to 1738) had the following :—

> 'And ranged at open noon by beasts of prey
> And birds of bloody beak. The sullen door
> No visit knows, nor hears the wailing voice
> Of fervent want. Even soul-attracted friends
> And relatives, endeared for many a year,
> Savaged by war, forget the social tie,
> The close engagement of the kindred heart,
> And, sick, in solitude successive die
> Untended and unmourned. While, to complete,' &c.

1090, 1091. *The grim guards . . . . a better death.* The reference is to the *cordon sanitaire.*—Better to be struck or shot down than to die of the plague.

1092-1102. The first draught of these lines formed part of a long passage, which, in the earlier editions, began at l. 1620 of the settled text.

1096. *the pillared flame.* But the fact is that flames do *not* shoot from volcanoes. The reflection of the red molten lava on the clouds of steam thrown up during an eruption produces the illusion.

1102. Here ends the long digression to tropical scenes and torrid summers. In the next line the poet is back in England.

1105-1116. A poetical, not a scientific, exposition of the cause or conditions of a storm of thunder and lightning. But Franklin's discovery of the nature of lightning was not made till after Thomson's death, namely, in 1752. It was then demonstrated that lightning and electricity are identical.—It may be noted that Malloch's explanation of the phenomenon of a thunderstorm is the same as Thomson's : he too speaks of—

> 'Sulphureous steam and nitrous, late exhaled
> From mine or unctuous soil,' &c.—*The Excursion,* Canto I.

1141-1143. The very sound of these lines suggests what they describe.

1149. Here in the earlier editions was introduced a description of a shepherd killed by lightning :—

> '[It] strikes the shepherd as he shuddering sits
> Presaging ruin 'mid the rocky clift.
> His inmost marrow feels the gliding flame ;
> He dies ; and, like a statue grimed with age,

His live dejected posture still remains,
His russet singed, and rent his hanging hat;
While, whining at his feet, his half-stunned dog,
Importunately kind and fearful pats
On his insensate master for relief.'

A striking picture, but in bad taste. It was withdrawn—chiefly perhaps because the theme was handled in the story of Celadon and Amelia (see below, ll. 1214-1222).

1151, 1152. Fuller and more effective in the first text :—

'A leaning shattered trunk stands scathed to heaven
The talk of future ages.'

There is tragedy here.

1153. *harmless look.* Said of naiads by Shakespeare (*The Tempest*, the masque scene).

1156-1168. This wild passage, somewhat bombastic, was substituted for the following less furious but more forcible lines of the first edition :—

'A little further burns
The guiltless cottage; and the haughty dome
Stoops to the base. In one immediate flash
The forest falls; or, flaming out, displays
The savage haunts, unpierced by day before.
Scarred is the mountain's brow; and from the cliff
Tumbles the smitten rock. The desert shakes,
And gleams, and grumbles through his deepest dens.'

1168. *Thule.* The Orkney and Shetland Islands. The area of the thunderstorm is thus Wales and all Scotland.

1170. *not always on the guilty head.* The vulgar creed even yet needs this correction.

1171-1222. The episode of Celadon and Amelia, gracefully and affectingly described, and giving relief to the main subject, as figures relieve a landscape, was possibly suggested by Pope's letter to Lady Mary Montagu, containing the tragic story of *two* lovers killed by lightning. The letter is of date Sept. 1st, 1717. Part of Pope's correspondence was published so early as 1726; the 'authorised' edition came out in 1737.

1174. Cp. Milton's description of Adam and Eve in Par. Lost, Bk. IV. ll. 296, 299.

1178. *informed.* Finer in the original edition—'alarmed.' See Spring, ll. 250-254.

1208, 1209. *the secret shaft That wastes at midnight.* 'The terror by night,' 'the arrow that flieth by day.'—Psalm xci. 5.

1215, 1216. In the first edition—

              'In a heap
Of pallid ashes fell the beauteous maid.'

1257-1268. This passage followed the episode of Damon and Musidora in the edition of 1738; and the passage beginning at l. 1269 of the settled text was joined to that ending at l. 1256 by the words—

    ''Twas then beneath a secret waving shade';

replaced, to suit the connection, by—

      'Close in the covert of a hazel copse.'

1269-1370. The story of Damon and Musidora first appeared in the edition of 1730, and was retained in the edition of 1738; but the first version has been so altered as to form in the final text an episode almost entirely different. In the first version Damon is represented as professing insensibility to the influence of female beauty. His profession is put to the test by his chance discovery of *three* nymphs bathing. They are Sacharissa, Amoret, and Musidora. The beauty of Musidora makes impression upon his obdurate heart: smitten by her charms, he falls deeply in love with her. Both versions have been objected to on the score of taste, more especially Musidora's frank avowal of her affection for Damon. The first version was doubtless suggested by the well-known Decision of Paris in classical story,—perhaps also by a passage (ll. 12-20 of Act I. sc. 2) in Allan Ramsay's Gentle Shepherd.

1271. After this line in the first draught came the following passage:—

    'Thoughtful and fixed in philosophic muse,—
    Damon, who still amid the savage woods
    And lonely lawns the force of beauty scorned,
    Firm, and to false philosophy devote.
    The brook ran babbling by, and, sighing weak,
    The breeze among the bending willows played,
    When Saccharissa to the cool retreat
    With Amoret and Musidora stole.'

Then followed—'Warm in their cheek' &c., at l. 1290. After l. 1292 came the description of the three nymphs,—in which Saccharissa is likened to Juno, Musidora to Minerva, and Amoret to Venus,—extending to l. 1303. Line 1304 began, 'Nor Paris panted stronger,' &c., and the text ran on, with some necessary changes, very much as we have it to l. 1332.

1275, 1276. *falsely he Of Musidora's cruelty.* As Roger complained of Jenny's cruelty in Allan Ramsay's Gentle Shepherd (Act I. sc. 1)—a pastoral comedy (published in 1725) which Thomson must have known.

1347. *the statue that enchants the world.* The Venus de Medici, in the Imperial Gallery at Florence.

1371–1437. All this was written after 1738, probably in 1744. (See a reference to time at ll. 1427–1428.)

1373–1376. Described with a more exalted figure, and richer melody of expression, in the Castle of Indolence :—

> 'Gay castles in the clouds that pass,
> For ever flushing round a summer sky.'
>
> Canto I, st. vi, ll. 3, 4.

1383. *pathetic*—for 'sympathetic.'

1387. *the vulgar never had a glimpse.* The love of natural scenery, of the beauty of this fair world, was a passion with Thomson. It is a feeling not so generally diffused as one is apt to imagine. Cowper, indeed, in the penultimate passage of The Winter Evening, declares that—

> 'The love of Nature's works
> Is an ingredient in the compound man,
> Infused at the creation of the kind,'

and that none are 'without some relish,'—that all retain, even in the depth of cities, an 'inborn inextinguishable thirst of rural scenes.' He allows, however, that the feeling requires to be educated, and that 'minds that have been formed and tutored' discern and taste the beauty of Nature 'with a relish more exact.' Thomson's highest honour is that he has taught 'the vulgar' to see both beauty and a spirit of divine benevolence in the arrangement of their dwelling-place, the earth. He has not only opened our eyes to the beauty of our natural surroundings, but set the soul of man in a freer filial relation to its Maker. The gifts of Nature express the fatherhood of God: this is his religious creed, and this is what he means by following Nature up to Nature's God.

1391. Supply 'which,' as a connective, after 'Virtue.'

1393. *portico of woods.* Reference is here made to the place, the Painted Porch (Στοὰ Ποικίλη), or Colonnade, in ancient Athens where Zeno—some three centuries before the Christian era—taught his peculiar philosophy (Stoicism).

1394. *Nature's vast Lyceum.* A Gymnasium outside the walls of ancient Athens, and just above the Ilissus, where Aristotle (*b.* 384 B. C.) walked and taught his disciples (the Peripatetics), bore the name of the Lyceum (τὸ Λύκειον) from its neighbourhood to the Temple of Apollo Lyceus—'Apollo the Light-Giver.' (For a poetical description of the Schools of ancient Athens, see Paradise Regained, Book IV, ll. 240–253. Note that Milton places the Lyceum *within* the city walls.)

1401. *Amanda.* Miss Young. See note, Spring, l. 482.

1403. *All is the same with thee.* Any path will be delightful in your company.

1408. *Thy hill, delightful Shene.* '"Shene": the old name of Rich-

mond, signifying in Saxon, *shining* or *splendour.'—Note by Thomson.*
Thomson, when he was in easy enough circumstances to own a country
residence,—some time in 1736,—fixed upon Richmond, and settled in a
neat garden-house in Kew-foot-lane, which looked down on the Thames,
and gave a wide view of landscape besides.   Amanda's sister, Mrs.
Robertson, was a near neighbour of the poet at Richmond.

1410. *huge Augusta.*   London.   See note, Spring, l. 107.

1411. *sister-hills.*   Highgate and Hampstead.

1412. Harrow-on-the-Hill, twelve miles north-west from London.
When Thomson wrote 'lofty Harrow' (1744?) he had not seen a
Scottish hill for about twenty years.   Harrow stands on a small
eminence.

1413. Windsor is about twenty-three miles up the river from London.
It has been a royal residence since the time of the Conqueror.   The
Castle stands on a plateau of natural chalk.

1419. *Harrington's retreat.*   Petersham, which gives the title of
Viscount to the Earls of Harrington.

1420. *Ham's embowering walks.*   A seat of the Earls of Dysart.
Ham House, near Twickenham, was built for Henry, Prince of Wales,
son of James I.   It is almost gloomy with elms.

1423. John Gay; born 1688, died 1732.   Author of The Shepherd's
Week (in six Pastorals, or Days), Trivia, The Beggar's Opera, the
ballad of Black-eyed Susan, and Fables.   Gay had an easy, graceful,
witty style, and a genuine lyrical vein.   For the last four or five years of
his life he was an inmate in the house of his patrons and friends, the
Duke and Duchess of Queensberry, and at Ham.

1424. *polished Cornbury.*   Son of the Earl of Clarendon, and the
author of some dramas written with more refinement of taste and style
than vigour of imagination.

1426, 1427. *the muses haunt In Twickenham's bowers.*   Pope, with
whom Thomson was on friendly and intimate terms—indeed Thomson
was of such a nature as to have no enemies—lived, as everybody knows,
at Twickenham, his residence from 1718 till his death, twenty-six years
after.   See Winter, l. 550, for another friendly reference to Pope:
'Twickenham' is there described as 'the Muses' hill.'   It is unnecessary
to say that Pope was the greatest English poet of his time—none of his
contemporaries denied it.   When Thomson made this complimentary
and 'right friendly' allusion to Pope, the latter was 'in his last sickness';
he died in May, 1744.

1428. *The healing god.*   Æsculapius was the god of the medical art;
Hygiea, the goddess of health.   Health, of course, is meant.

royal Hampton's pile.   The village of Hampton is some twelve miles from London, on the Middlesex side of the Thames. The Palace was built by Wolsey for himself. Henry VIII seized it; and it was, from time to time after that, a royal residence till the reign of William III. That king added to the building; and laid out the gardens (some 45 acres in area) in terraces, flower plots, and arcades, according to the Dutch taste in such matters. They are still very much as he left them.

1429. *Clermont's terraced height, and Esher's groves.* Claremont is a country-seat at Esher in Surrey, about fourteen or fifteen miles south-west from London; around it winds 'the silent Mole' on its way to the Thames. It was the residence of the Rt. Hon. Henry Pelham, who was First Lord of the Treasury from 1721 to 1743. Garth has a poem on Clairmont.

1434. *Achaia. Hesperia.* The former, 'the coast-land' (on the north side) of the Peloponnesus, was a narrow strip of country lying to the north of Arcadia, and sloping from the mountains to the sea. Thomson probably means any beautiful and secluded part of Greece. Hesperia, literally, 'the western land,' the Greek name for Italy; it was the Roman name for Spain. Thomson probably refers to the gardens that were watched by the Hesperides.

1435, 1436. *vale of bliss . . . On which the power of cultivation lies.* Cp. Wordsworth's well-known description of 'Yarrow vale':—

'And Yarrow winding through the pomp
Of cultivated nature.'

1442, 1443. *the Queen of Arts . . . Liberty.* This view of Liberty is dwelt upon and amplified at great length in the Poem on Liberty, Part V, l. 374 to the end. 'Liberty abroad walks' is an awkward inversion.

1449. *with golden waves.* Yellow corn-fields are meant.

1470. *the listed plain.* The battle-field enclosed for combats. From 'lists,' ground 'roped in' (*liciæ*, barriers; *licium*, a girdle) for tournaments.

1471-1478. Cp. Goldsmith's tribute of praise to the manhood of England in The Traveller, commencing—

'Stern o'er each bosom reason holds her state.'

1479-1579. This long passage of 101 lines, containing a list of England's worthies, was a gradual growth in the successive editions. The first edition (of 1727) included only More, Bacon, Barrow, Tillotson, Boyle, Locke, Newton, Shakespeare, and Milton. In the edition of 1738 we find the list enlarged with the additional names of Walsingham, Drake, Raleigh, Hampden, Philip Sidney, Russell, and Ashley (Lord Shaftesbury); while the names of Tillotson and Barrow are withdrawn. After 1738 were added Alfred, 'thy Edwards and thy Henrys,' Algernon Sidney ('the British Cassius'), Spenser, and Chaucer. It is noticeable that neither patriot nor poet of Scotland has the justice of a place on the roll. It is entirely English, although Thomson, by a figure, is supposed to be reading the roll to Britannia. The omission of Scottish names is the more remarkable as, when he sent a copy in MS. of the first draught of his panegyric to his countryman Malloch in the autumn of 1726, he took occasion to say in an accompanying letter, ' The English people are not a little vain of themselves and their country. *Britannia too includes our native country Scotland.*' Yet he did not admit a single Scottish name. It was both tardy and meagre justice to Scotland to allow her in Autumn (ll. 893-948), a ' bead-roll ' of fame for herself —of only three names, Wallace ; John, Duke of Argyle ; and Duncan Forbes, of Culloden. (But see note on ll. 877-948 of Autumn.)

1479. *Alfred,* surnamed the Great ; born 849, died 901. He cleared his country of the Danes ; built the first English navy ; made wise laws for the administration of justice—establishing, it is said, trial by jury ; and, besides encouraging husbandry, and the peaceful arts of life, translated useful Latin books into Anglo-Saxon for the good of his subjects, and practised original authorship as well, for the same noble purpose.

1484. Not *all* the Edwards, and not *all* the Henrys. Among the non-heroic Edwards and Henrys, who yet were ' dear to fame,' should be remembered the sixth Edward ; and the sixth Henry, the founder of Eton College—whom ' grateful science still adores.' Of the warlike Edwards, Edward III was the conqueror of France ; of the warlike Henrys, Henry V.

1486. *the terror of thy arms.* At Cressy, in 1346 ; and at Agincourt, in 1415.

1488. Sir Thomas More ; born 1480, martyred 1535. He was Lord Chancellor, after Wolsey, in 1529. The ' brutal tyrant ' was, of course, Henry VIII, whose divorce of Queen Catharine More refused to sanction.

1490. *useful rage.* The useful result of Henry's passion was the rupture with Rome, and the downfall of Popery in the State.

1491, 1492. For Cato, see note *supra,* l. 954. Aristides, surnamed ' the just,' the most upright and public-spirited of all the sons of ancient Athens. He fought at Marathon, Salamis, and Platæa. Utterly unselfish he died in poverty, B. C. 468. Cincinnatus, a hero of the times of the old Roman Republic. He lived on his farm, which he tilled with his own hand. When the State was in danger he was named Dictator (B. C. 458) ; accepted the office ; saved the Republic ; and, after a brief tenure of the Dictatorship, of sixteen days, quietly returned to his farm, and resumed his former mode of life.

1494. *Walsingham.* Born 1536 ; Secretary of State to Elizabeth. His ' wisdom ' was diplomatic duplicity.

1495. Sir Francis Drake ; circumnavigated the globe. 1577–9 ; was vice-admiral, under Lord Howard, when the Armada was defeated ; died in his ship during an expedition to the West Indies against the Spaniards, 1595. One of the boldest and bravest of 'the Sea Dogs' of Devonshire.

1498. Elizabeth's.

1499. Raleigh. Also of Devonshire ; born in 1552, the junior of Drake by some thirteen years. Worthy of all that is said of him in the text.

1502. 'The coward reign' was that of James I ; the 'vanquished foe' (l. 1504) was Spain. It was to ingratiate himself with the Spanish Court that James I commissioned the execution of Raleigh.

1507. The reference is to The History of the World, which Raleigh composed during his long captivity in the Tower.

1509, 1510. Elizabeth's and James's respectively.

1511. Sir Philip Sidney ; born 1554, died of a wound received at Zutphen in 1586 ; brave and chivalrous, and universally beloved and admired. He wrote poems in praise of 'Stella,' Arcadia, and A Defence of Poesie.

1514. John Hampden ; the first to resist the iniquitous tax of Ship-money ; fought in the civil war against Charles I ; and died of a wound received in the skirmish of Chalgrove Field, 1643.

1522, 1523. *let me strew the grave Where Russel lies.* An echo of Milton's line—

'To strew the laureate hearse where Lycid lies.'
Lycidas, l. 151.

This is Lord William Russell : born 1639 ; accused of taking a share in the plot to assassinate Charles II at the Rye House ; executed 1683. Cp. Campbell's lines :—

'Yours are Hampden's, Russell's glory,
Sidney's matchless shade is yours.'
Men of England.

1528. *the British Cassius.* Algernon Sidney.

1535. Bacon ; born 1561, died 1627 ; Lord Chancellor in 1618 ; author of the Novum Organum. Compared in this eulogium to Plato, Aristotle, and Cicero, for his speculative ability, powers of close, clear, and sustained reasoning, and lucid and eloquent style.

1551. Antony Ashley Cooper, third Earl of Shaftesbury ; born 1671, died 1713 ; the friend of Pope ; author of Characteristics.

1556. Robert Boyle ; son of the Earl of Cork ; born 1626 ; wrote on natural philosophy, and helped to form the Royal Society.

1558. John Locke ; born 1632, died 1704 ; wrote Essay on the

x

Human Understanding; the founder of the English School of Philosophy.

1560. Sir Isaac Newton; born 1642, died 1728; discovered the law of gravitation. See Note on Spring, line 207.

1566. *wild Shakespeare.* Cp. Milton's lines:—

> 'Sweetest Shakespeare, fancy's child,
> Warble(s) his native wood-notes wild.'
>
> *L'Allegro*, ll. 133, 134.

1568. *in thy Milton met.* Cp. the lines of Dryden:—

> 'Three poets in three distant ages born,
> Greece, Italy, and England did adorn;
> The first in loftiness of thought surpass'd,
> The next in majesty, in both the last;
> The force of nature could no further go,—
> To make the third she joined the former two.'

1569. *universal as his theme.* Paradise Lost is a misnomer; the scope of the poem is by no means confined to the Garden of Eden, or even the Earth, or even the Universe; but includes the Eternal Heavens or Empyrean, Chaos, and Hell—in short, all Space. Gray, in the Progress of Poesy, describes Milton as 'passing the flaming bounds of space and time.'

1573. *Spenser, fancy's pleasing son.* The author of the Faery Queene is sometimes called 'the poet of the poets,'—with great apparent truth.

1577. Chaucer; died in 1400; said to be Spenser's 'ancient master' in the line above, because of such chivalrous and romantic tales in the famous Canterbury collection as the Knight's, the Squire's, &c. Chaucer is the prince of story-tellers; and the most agreeable and effective, because the least obtrusive, of moralists. His satire, at the severest, is the satire of simple exposure. Notice that Thomson speaks disparagingly of his 'language': it was reserved to a later age to discover the melody and inimitable felicity of Chaucer's diction. 'Manners-painting' is an unhappy compound, which Burns adopted in his Vision—'I taught thy manners-painting strains.'

1588. *rose-bud moist with morning dew.*

> 'Her lips like roses wat wi' dew.'—Burns.

1592–1594. What Byron has called 'the mind, the music of the face.'

1595–1601. This apostrophe is followed by no direct statement; it is entirely exclamatory. Cp. the opening stanza of Gray's Ode on Eton College. Compare this description of Great Britain with Gaunt's impassioned outburst in the Second Act of King Richard II, beginning:—

> 'This royal throne of kings, this sceptred isle,' &c.;

and concluding :—

> 'England, bound in with the triumphant sea,
> Whose rocky shore beats back the envious siege
> Of watery Neptune   .   .   .   .
> That England, that was wont to conquer others!'

1602–1613. With a similar prayer Burns concludes the Cottar's Saturday Night :—

> 'Long may thy hardy sons of rustic toil
> Be blest with health, and peace, and sweet content!
> And oh, may Heaven their simple lives prevent
> From luxury's contagion, weak and vile!
> Then—howe'er crowns and coronets be rent—
> A virtuous populace may rise the while
> And stand a wall of fire around their much-loved isle.
>
> O Thou! who poured the patriotic tide
> That streamed through Wallace's undaunted heart . . . .
> Oh never, never Scotia's realm desert,
> But still the patriot, and the patriot-bard
> In bright succession raise, her ornament and guard!'

1616. *That first paternal virtue, Public Zeal.* See Liberty, Part V :—

> 'By those three virtues be the frame sustained
> Of British Freedom :—INDEPENDENT LIFE;
> INTEGRITY IN OFFICE; and, o'er all
> Supreme, A PASSION FOR THE COMMONWEAL.'—ll. 120–123.

And again at l. 222 :—

> 'Be not the noblest passion past unsung . . .
> DEVOTION TO THE PUBLIC.'

1619. After this line, in the edition of 1738, came a series of passages, amounting in all to 85 lines, which have been partly dropped, and partly transferred to an earlier part of the poem, and there, with many changes and additions, incorporated with it. The dropped passages include a description of a tropical forest on fire, with some telling lines :—

> 'Touched by the torch of noon, the gummy bark,
> Smouldering, begins to roll the dusky wreath';

and, notably, a realistic account of an unknown African city supposed to have been overwhelmed by a sand-storm :—

> 'Hence late exposed (if distant fame say true)
> A smothered city from the sandy wave
> Emergent rose,' &c.

The incorporated parts include glimpses of the 'rolling Niger,' the 'huge leaning elephant,' 'spicy Abyssinian vales,' &c.

† X 2

1626. *Amphitrite.* In Homer, Amphitrite is merely another name for the sea. She was, with the later poets, the Goddess of the Sea, the wife of Poseidon (Neptune), originally a Nereid.

1630–1646. The long summer day is now ended; and the poet appropriately enough, but rather abruptly, indulges in some reflections on the different feelings which a sense of the passage of time excites in different breasts. Mankind are divided into three classes—the dreaming or inactive, the selfish, and the benevolently active.

1654. *the face of things.* The expression recurs in Thomson. See Winter, line 57. It occurs in Milton, where he speaks of the moon 'with pleasing light shadowy' setting off 'the face of things.'—Par. Lost, Bk. V. ll. 42, 43.

1657. *the quail clamours for his running mate.* Clearly Thomson means the corn-crake, or land-rail. The bird is named from its cry—both quail (from *quack*) and crake, or rail. The crake is seldom seen on the wing, but runs with great rapidity. Cp. Burns's line—

> 'Mourn, clamorous craik, at close o' day!'
>
> *Elegy on Capt. Matthew Henderson.*

The description of summer gloaming ended here in the edition of 1738. The next six lines are an unhappy addition: the poet has already described 'the face of things' as 'closed' by the deepening darkness; now he introduces—what must have been invisible—'the whitening shower' of thistle-down.

1660. *Amusive.* The word recurs in The Seasons. It means 'in a way that amuses the observer.'

1662. *Her lowest sons.* The birds—such as linnets.

1664, 1665. Cp. Burns:—

> 'The shepherd steeks his faulding slap
> And o'er the moorlands whistles shrill.'
>
> *Meenie's ee.*

1660. *Unknowing what the joy-mixt anguish means.* See Spring l. 251.

1681. A passage beginning here in the first edition was transferred to Autumn, ll. 1151–1164.

1683. *The glow-worm.* Rare in the south of Scotland, but common in some parts of England. The female insect emits the stronger light.

1686. *Stygian.* Darkest. From *Styx*, the principal river in the infernal world.

1692. *one swimming scene.* What Gray, in the Elegy, calls 'the glimmering landscape.'

1698. After this line (but at an interval) came, in the first edition, a passage on the Aurora Borealis[1].

---

[1] It was reconstructed and transferred to Autumn, ll. 1108–1137.

1702–1729. Added after 1738.

1730. *Philosophy.* Natural philosophy, or science, is meant.

1735. *soothe the parted soul.* Cp. Addison's Vision of Mirza—
'Heavenly airs that are played to the departed souls of good men
upon their first arrival in Paradise, to wear out the impressions of the
last agonies.'

1758. Cp. the Bard's appeal in The Castle of Indolence, Canto II.
St. 51 :—

<blockquote>
'Had unambitious mortals minded nought . . . .
   Rude nature's state had been our state to-day,' &c.
</blockquote>

Cp. also the earlier stanzas of the same canto :—

<blockquote>
'Earth was till then a boundless forest wild ;
   Naught to be seen but savage wood, and skies,' &c.
</blockquote>

St. 14.

1789. This is mental Philosophy, or Psychology. The 'ideal kingdom'
is the world of mind, or ideas.

AUTUMN.

INTRODUCTORY NOTE.

Autumn was the last of The Seasons in the order of composition,—
following Spring at an interval of two years. The Hymn was written
at the same time, and the completion of the series was made the occasion
of a collected edition. The first edition of The Seasons accordingly made
its appearance in London in 1730, in a handsome quarto, for which most
of the leading men of the day were subscribers. Dodington, to whom
Summer had been dedicated, subscribed for twenty copies. It was a
famous year for Thomson. He was at the height of his fame, and at
a time of life when he could most keenly enjoy the pleasure of being
popular. The same year Sophonisba was produced at Drury Lane ; and,
though rather patronised than popular at the theatre, it ran to a fourth
edition at the printer's before the close of the year. Summer too, as a
separate poem, entered its third edition ; and a second edition of Autumn,
a slim octavo of 62 pp., published at one shilling [1], made its appearance

---

[1] With an engraving, 'representing [one of] the marble statues in the garden of
Versailles,' 1*s*. 6*d*.

before the year was out. The publisher was ' J. Millan, bookseller, near Whitehall.'

Part of Autumn, if not the whole of it, seems to have been written at Dodington's country seat at Eastbury, among the downs of Dorsetshire. Thomson was there in the autumn of 1729. Writing to his friend Malloch from Eastbury, on the 20th September, he says ; ' I wish for a walk with you upon the serene downs to talk of a thousand things . . . I have been in dead solitude here for some days by past. Mr. D[oding-ton] went to London to wait upon the king ; now he 's returned. Poor Stubbs [a poetaster and clergyman] kept me alive : he toils here in two parishes for £40 a year ! ' The solitude he speaks of was not unemployed. If he was not actually writing the poem, his mind at least was full of the subject. The poem itself will witness :—

> ' I court
> The inspiring breeze, and meditate the book
> Of nature ever open.   .   .   .   .
> And as I steal along the sunny wall
> Where Autumn basks with fruit empurpled deep
> My vacant theme still urges in my thought,' &c.
>
> ll. 668–674.

Autumn, unlike the other Seasons, was published without a prose dedication. It was, however, inscribed in fourteen lines of verse incorporated with the poem (ll. 9–22) to ' the Rt. Hon. Arthur Onslow, Esq., Speaker of the House of Commons.' It was to the same gentleman that Young, some twelve years later, dedicated the first book of his Night Thoughts. (See Note, l. 9, *infra.*)

Like that of the other Seasons, the text of Autumn underwent numerous alterations in the later editions. To it were transferred several passages which had originally appeared in more or less different form in Summer. These were the eulogium on the ' Caledonian Sons' of Britannia, beginning at l. 876 ; the description of the Northern Lights and of the effect of the phenomenon upon superstitious minds, beginning at l. 1108 ; and the picture of the horseman perishing in the morass to which in the darkness of night he has been allured by the will-o'-the wisp (ll. 1150–1164). Several verbal changes were made at the suggestion of Pope, and an occasional line or two of his composition received into the text. And three important additions of original matter were made to the poem subsequently to the edition of 1738,—viz. the introduction of the 'doctor of tremendous paunch' into the symposium of foxhunters, the vision of the infant rivers in their subterranean beds, and the compliment to Pitt and Cobham at Stowe. Altogether, the poem was enlarged from 1275 lines in 1730, the year of its publication, to 1372 lines in the edition of 1746—the last to receive the benefit of the author's revision.

The Argument, as amended for the later editions, is as follows :—

'The subject proposed. Addressed to Mr. Onslow. A prospect of the fields ready for harvest. Reflections in praise of Industry, raised by that view. Reaping. A Tale relative to it. A harvest storm. Shooting and hunting—their barbarity. A ludicrous account of fox-hunting. A view of an orchard. Wall-fruit. A vineyard. A description of fogs, frequent in the latter part of Autumn : whence a digression, inquiring into the rise of fountains and rivers. Birds of the Season considered, that now shift their habitation. The prodigious number of them that cover the northern and western isles of Scotland. Hence a view of that country. A prospect of the discoloured fading woods. After a gentle dusky day, moonlight. Autumnal meteors. Morning [1]; to which succeeds a calm pure sunshiny day, such as usually shuts up the Season. The harvest being gathered in, the country dissolved in joy. The whole concludes with a panegyric on a philosophical country life.'

Perhaps the best, or at least the best known, passages of Autumn are the beautiful pastoral story of Lavinia—which possibly owes part of its popularity to its suggestion of the Bible romance of Ruth ; and the richly humorous account of the festivities of foxhunting. But there is pathos as well as humour in the poem, and the 'poverty' of 'the triumph o'er the timid hare' is very touchingly accentuated. Numerous lovely glimpses of autumnal nature are scattered through the poem. Chief among these are the prospect of the harvest fields, near the commencement ; the orchard, at line 624 ; the moonlighted world, at line 1096 ; and the last fine day of the season, at line 1207. The grandest effort of the poet's imagination in the whole poem is his vision of the 'rivers in their infant beds '—a description which was not ready for the edition of 1738. The vision carries him, in one of those wide geographical ranges which he so much enjoyed, right round the globe.

Autumn, in its place in the collected Seasons, was by far the most

---

[1] A revelation of the morning—strangely omitted from the Argument—is the destruction of the bees overnight, by the fumes of sulphur, for the purpose of securing their honey.

important publication of its year. Indeed there was no other literary
work of any particular note, in either prose or verse, published in London
in 1730.

The poem of Autumn reveals to close observation a remarkable
struggle going on in the mind of Thomson between Nature and Art.
These terms, it is true, stand very much in need of definition, but the
distinction of the one from the other is made sufficiently apparent by the
contrast which the author of the Seasons offers to Pope. Autumn, the
last of the Seasons in the order of composition, shows traces of the
influence of the Artificial School, of which Pope was acknowledged
president, upon the genius of Thomson. The Scottish poet had now
been domiciled in England for five years, had lived all that time in
a literary atmosphere, and latterly had been admitted to the society and
friendship of Pope. When he came a stranger to London in 1725 the
Artificial School was paramount; his first poem, Winter, was written
before he really felt the influence of that School,—and exhibited, on
that very account, an independency of thought and style, which vital
contact with the influences of the Artificial School afterwards undoubtedly modified. The proof is in the Castle of Indolence. It was impossible that Thomson should give up his passion for Nature ; but it was
very possible, and a very certainty, that his relations to Nature as a
poet should admit of modification. There was much room for amend-
ment on his part in minor matters of expression : even his feelings might
profitably be tamed a little. He had strength enough and to spare,
but he lacked repose, and he was deficient in taste. In 1730, when
Autumn appeared, he had already begun to think that Nature, whom
he loved so well, might be more capable of a higher, i. e. a more refined,
love if she submitted to a little cultivation and trimming at the hands
of Art. And so, half convinced of this idea, he wrote :—

　　　‘All is the gift of Industry . . . .
　　His hardened fingers deck the gaudy Spring.’
　　　　　　　　　　　　　　　　　　ll. 141, 146.

There is a significant contrast between this and his unsuspicious faith in
the loveliness of uncultivated Nature—Nature ‘ magnificently rude ’—as
implied in the earlier poem of Winter. Again, at line 1059 he speaks
of ‘ forsaking the unimpassioned shades of nature,’ and ‘ drawing the
tragic scene.’ The influence of the maxim of Pope and his followers is
visible in the expression : ‘ the proper study of mankind is man ’ seems

to be here the avowed belief of Thomson. To all appearance the struggle for the mastery which was going on in his mind between Nature and Art, received a temporary check, in which, by the time the end of the poem was reached, the advantage lay with Nature :—

> 'Oh Nature all-sufficient! over all!
> Enrich me with the knowledge of thy works!
>
> . . . .
>
> From thee begin,
> Dwell all on thee, with thee conclude my song;
> And let me never *never* stray from thee!'

1–3. The emblem of Autumn with which the poem commences, while generally representative of the season, is wanting in both point and consistency. The expression 'nodding o'er the yellow plain' disturbs the figure, by presenting a view of ripe corn-fields, waving in the wind, where a continuation of the portrait of personified Autumn was expected. With the portrait itself the imagination has a difficulty in disposing of the extremely awkward crown of the sickle and the wheaten sheaf. Such a crown is, besides, suggestive rather of the completed than of the commencing harvest. That the latter idea is mainly intended is to be inferred from the scene of 'the nodding yellow plain,' and the advancing figure of Autumn 'coming jovial on.' Spenser's conception of Autumn is at once more distinct and more appropriate to the first appearance of the harvest season :—

> 'Upon his head a wreath, that was enrold,
> With ears of corn of every sort, he bore;
> And in his hand a sickle he did holde,
> To reape the ripened fruits the which the earth had yold.'
>
> *The Faery Queene,* Bk. VII, Canto VII, st. xxx.

The sickle is no longer in actual use among the insignia of Autumn : the reaping machine has almost universally displaced it in our country.

3. *jovial.* The word expresses the merriment of the old harvest field.

3, 4. *the Doric reed once more, Well pleased, I tune.* In plain prose— 'I proceed for the fourth time to write a poem on the congenial subject of nature and country life.' Though the season of Autumn is generally regarded as coming third in the order of nature, yet the poem of Autumn came last in the order of composition.—The Doric dialect was one of the three great branches of the ancient Greek tongue, and was characterised by broad and rough sounds, from which Æolic and Ionic (including Attic) were comparatively free. It was the speech of a pastoral or rustic people, originally inhabiting the mountains of Thessaly.—The reed, of course, is the shepherd's pipe.

4–8. Winter is here regarded as leading the procession of the Seasons, and as being, with Spring and Summer, mainly a period of preparation for Autumn—the consummation or crown of the year. 'Thou crownest the year with thy goodness . . . the valleys are covered over with corn.' Psalm lxv.

5. *Nitrous.* 'Laden with fertilizing salts.' Not merely, nor mainly, 'keen, piercing, and pulverising.' Thomson refers, more poetically than scientifically, to some imaginary ingredient which the frost imparts to the soil. See his reference to this active ingredient in operation upon the air, in Winter, ll. 693–696 :—

> 'Through the blue serene,
> For sight too fine, the ethereal nitre flies,
> Killing infectious damps, and the spent air
> Storing afresh with elemental life.'

He describes it in operation upon the soil in the same poem :—

> 'The frost-concocted glebe
> Draws in abundant vegetable soul,
> And gathers vigour for the coming year';

and at ll. 714–720, ventures upon a description of its substance :—

> 'Is not thy potent energy, unseen,
> Myriads of little salts, or hooked, or shaped
> Like double wedges, and diffused immense
> Through water, earth, and ether ?'

5, 6. [*Whate'er*] *the various-blossomed Spring Put in white promise forth.* See Spring for the anticipation of this idea :—

> 'One white-empurpled shower
> Of mingled blossoms; where the raptured eye
> Hurries from joy to joy, and, *hid beneath*
> *The fair profusion, yellow Autumn spies.*'
>
> ll. 110–113.

7. *Concocted strong.* 'Were secretly maturing with their heat.'

8. *swell my glorious theme.* In plain prose—'The results of this course of preparation afford me a magnificent subject.' The season of Autumn was Thomson's (as it was also Burns's) favourite time for poetical composition :—

> 'When Autumn's yellow lustre gilds the world
> And tempts the sickled swain into the field,
> .   .   .   .   through the tepid gleams
> Deep musing, then he best exerts his song.'
>
> *Autumn*, ll. 1322–1326.

See also a letter by Thomson to Lyttelton : ' I think that season of the year [Autumn] the most pleasing and the most poetical. The spirits are not then dissipated with the gaiety of Spring and the glaring light of Summer, but composed into a serious and tempered joy. The year is perfect.' (14th July, 1743.) In the Hymn on the Seasons he refers to '*inspiring* Autumn' (l. 96).

9. *Onslow.* Autumn was the only poem of the series which had no prose dedication. It was inscribed, in the fourteen lines of verse commencing at l. 9, to the Rt. Hon. Arthur Onslow, Speaker of the House of Commons. This gentleman, born in 1691, represented the burgh of Guildford, in Surrey, from 1719 to 1726. In the latter year he became member for the county, and honourably maintained this connection with Surrey throughout the reign of the second George. In 1727 he was chosen Speaker of the House of Commons by a large majority of votes, and continued to fill the Chair and guide the debates of Parliament, with dignity and impartiality, for the long period of thirty-four years. Thomson's compliment is by no means overcharged. Onslow's integrity was almost proverbial. Being significantly reminded on one occasion that it was Walpole's influence that placed him in the Chair of the House, he replied that, 'although he considered himself under obligations to Sir Robert Walpole, yet he had always a certain feeling about him, when he occupied the Speaker's Chair, that prevented him from being of any party whatever.' He retired in 1761, at the age of 70, on a well-earned pension of £3000 a year (which his son also was allowed to enjoy after him), and was followed into his retirement with the good wishes of both political parties. He died in 1768. In literary history he is known to have been a man of considerable learning, and the patron of Richardson and Young, and several others of less note than these.

The muse. The poet—meaning, of course, himself, the writer of the poem. For this use of 'Muse' see Milton's Lycidas :—

'So may some gentle Muse
With lucky words favour *my* destined urn,
And, as he passes, turn,
And bid fair peace be to my sable shroud.'—ll. 19–22.

11. *the public voice.* Parliament.

14. *Spread on thy front.* 'Can be seen in your very countenance.'

15. *listening senates.* Cp. Gray's Elegy :—

'The applause of listening senates to command . . .
Their lot forbade.'

Thomson repeats the phrase in Winter—in a passage added, after 1738, in compliment to Lord Chesterfield :—

'O let me hail thee on some glorious day

> When to the listening senate ardent crowd
> Britannia's sons to hear her pleaded cause.'—ll. 679–681.

16. *the maze of eloquence.* Not eloquence that bewilders the reason, but that astonishes or fills the mind with delight and wonder. The same phrase also occurs in the compliment to Lord Chesterfield in Winter, ll. 688, 689.

18. *pants for public virtue.* 'Eagerly longs to be of service to the state.' 'For' is here equivalent to 'for the performance of some action of.' In his Britannia, published in 1729, he had already shown that he panted 'for public virtue.'

22. *mix the patriot's with the poet's flame.* Nobly done, ten years later, in 'Britannia, rule the Waves '—next to 'God save the Queen' the most popular of our great national songs. See Summer, Note, l. 431.

23, 24. *the bright Virgin . . . And Libra.* The sun enters the sign of Virgo in the Zodiac on 21st August, and that of Libra (the Balance) on 21st September. The latter date is the time of the autumnal equinox; the year is then said to be 'weighed in equal scales.' See Spring, Note, ll. 26, 27.

25. *effulgence.* This noun is in the nominative case absolute.

26-28. *a serener blue . . . . . . happy world.* This is, indeed, an autumn sky. But the whole passage (ll. 23–42) is charged with the spirit of autumn, tranquil or 'tossing in a flood of corn.' It is difficult to say whether art or imagination most predominates in the description; not one essential feature of the autumnal world is omitted, and the phrases are most felicitous. Thomson is here in his most characteristic style.

35. *poise.* Old Fr. *peiser*, to weigh, Lat. *pensum.* The Old French form occurs in Langland's Vision of Piers Ploughman :—

> 'The pound that heo peysede a quatrun more peisede
> Then myn auncel [scales] dude when I weyede treuthe.'
>
> Passus Quintus.

and gives the breeze to blow. Burns has—

> 'And wings the blast to blaw.'

40. For 'heart-expanding' Pope is said to have proposed the far less suggestive 'heart-delighting.'

42. *Unbounded, tossing in a flood of corn.* A felicitous line, which Thomson had the courage to prefer to Pope's proposed emendation—

> 'O'er waving golden fields of ripened corn.'

43-150. This long passage of over one hundred lines, descriptive of the origin, development, and benefits of the industrial arts, may be regarded as an anticipation of much of the second canto of The Castle of Indolence. Cp. especially stanzas xvii, xix, xx, and, of the Bard's 'strain,' stanzas li and lx.

54. *corruption.* Vice which *breaks* and weakens the energies, by making self the sole object of its activity.

76. *to raise* [*His feeble force*]. 'To augment his own natural bodily strength by the use of those appliances known as "the mechanical powers."'

78. *the vaulted earth.* Probably 'the vaults, or natural cellars of the earth,' mines. It may mean 'the bulging *crust* of the globe'—as it used to be called by physiographers.

79, 80. The references here are to the smelting of iron, and the driving of mills by water- and wind-power.

86. *flowing lawn.* The manufactures from cotton have superseded to a very large extent the linen manufacture of Thomson's day.

88. *The generous glass.* The reference is not to the abundance of the wine, or the liberality with which it was poured, nor to its race, but to its liberalizing effect upon the heart and, probably, also the mind. Cp. Judges ix. 13—'wine, which cheereth God and man.' It is to this effect that Burns refers in the lines so often quoted to his reproach :—

> 'Freedom and whisky gang thegither—
> Tak aff your dram.'

97. *a public.* A community, or commonwealth, living under representative government.

103. *oppression.* For a description of the evils of oppression see Liberty, Pt. I, ll. 123–315.

106. *toiling millions.* An oft-quoted phrase in our own day. The imagery is from the hive and the industry of bees.

107, 108. From these lines one may infer Thomson's views on political questions. See, for a full statement of his political views, the concluding portion of the Fourth Part of Liberty.

114. *her tower-encircled head.* This was Pope's suggestion. Cp. Castle of Indolence, Canto II, st. li :—

> 'No cities e'er their towery fronts had raised.'—l. 6.

116. *twining woody haunts.* 'Constructing wattled huts.'

118. Here followed in the text of 1738, and earlier texts, these six lines :—

> ''Twas nought but labour, the whole dusky group
> Of clustering houses and of mingling men,
> Restless design, and execution strong.
> In every street the sounding hammer plied
> His massy task; while the corrosive steel
> In flying touches formed the fine machine.'

122. *gentle, deep, majestic, king of floods.* Cp. the beautiful description of the Thames by Denham in his Cooper's Hill :—

'Though deep yet clear, though gentle yet not dull;
  Strong without rage, without o'erflowing full.'

125. *the bellying sheet.* The sail. In nautical language the sheet is a rope—fastened to the corner of a sail.

130-3. The reference is to ship-building yards, and the launching of a man-of-war. 'Those who have ever witnessed the spectacle of the launching of a ship-of-the-line,' says the poet Campbell in his Specimens of the British Poets, 'will perhaps forgive me for adding this to the examples of the sublime objects of artificial life. Of that spectacle I can never forget the impression, and of having witnessed it reflected from the faces of ten thousand spectators. They seem yet before me. I sympathise with their deep and silent expectation, and with their final burst of enthusiasm. It was not a vulgar joy but an affecting national solemnity. When the vast bulwark sprang from her cradle, the calm water on which she majestically swung round, gave the imagination a contrast of the stormy element in which she was soon to ride. All the days of battle and nights of danger which she had to encounter, all the ends of the earth which she had to visit, and all that she had to do and to suffer for her country, rose in awful presentiment before the mind; and when the heart gave her a benediction, it was like one pronounced on a living being.'

134. By 'the pillared dome' is meant an Art Gallery.

136, 137. *the canvas smooth, With glowing life protuberant.* The objects depicted seeming to start, or stand out, from the flat canvas, as if they were real. In The Castle of Indolence, Part II, stanza xiii, Thomson has—'touch the kindling canvas into life.' Cp. Goldsmith's Traveller :—

'The canvas glowed, beyond ev'n nature warm.'

138. *the statue seemed to breathe.* Cp. Pope's descriptions of 'living sculpture' in The Temple of Fame :—

'The youths hang o'er their chariots, as they run,
  The fiery steeds seem starting from the stone.'—ll. 218, 219.

And—

'Gathering his flowing robe, he seemed to stand
  In act to speak.'—ll. 240, 241.

140. *art, imagination-flushed.* That is, 'the artist, inspired with some noble conception.'

141-143. In his praise of Industry Thomson seems here to forget his earlier love of uncultivated Nature. In l. 146 he is especially severe in characterizing Spring as 'gaudy,' and as requiring the 'hardened fingers' of the gardening art to 'deck' her and make her presentable.

Had his love of the rude magnificence of Nature given place to a love for Nature tamed by cultivation and trimmed by Art? And was this the result of his five years' residence in England surrounded by the influence of the artificial school? That his taste was being modified by that school is clearly exemplified by the style and form of The Castle of Indolence. In Winter he is rough, fresh and original,—a poet of nature's making; in the Castle of Indolence he is smooth, harmonious, reposeful—still a true poet in feeling and perception, but disciplined by art into more elaborate form and a more studied style of expression. There is homage to Pope in The Castle of Indolence, none in Winter. The history of Thomson's art was from blank verse to a most elaborate rhymed measure; for rhyme he had at first little but contempt—those who practised it were 'rhyming insects.' Contrast with his case that of Milton, the development of whose art of expression was from rhyme to the grander harmonies of blank verse, and to whom latterly rhyme was a mere 'jingling sound,' 'a troublesome bondage,' 'the invention of a barbarous age,' 'to all judicious ears, trivial and of no true musical delight.'

149, 150. *Those . . . stores That, waving round, recall me.* The corn-fields, from which he broke away (l. 42) to sing the praise of Industry and settled life.

152. *unperceived.* Because the light spreads so gradually.

154–156. *each by the lass he loves*, &c. The traditional customs of the old harvest-field, handed down from immemorial autumns, have only recently disappeared before the general introduction of the mechanical reaper. They were, of course, still prevalent on Scottish farms in the time of Burns. The latter poet, in an autobiographical letter to Dr. Moore (father of the hero of Corunna) of date August 2nd, 1787, describes an episode in the history of his own life, which charmingly illustrates the practice of the old harvest-field here referred to: 'You know,' writes Burns, 'our country custom of coupling a man and woman together as partners in the labours of harvest. In my fifteenth autumn, my partner was a bewitching creature a year younger than myself. . . . She was a bonnie, sweet, sonsie lass. . . . I did not know myself why I liked so much to loiter behind with her, when returning in the evening from our labours; why the tones of her voice made my heart-strings thrill like an Æolian harp, and particularly why my pulse beat such a furious *rantann* when I looked and fingered over her little hand to pick out the cruel nettle-stings and thistles.' See also Burns's poetical version of the incident— .

'I mind it weel in early date,
When I was beardless, young, and blate [bashful],

> When first amang the yellow corn
>> A man I reckoned was,
> And wi' the lave[1], ilk[2] merry morn,
>> Could rank my rig[3] and lass.'
>>>> *To the Guidwife of Wauchope.*

158–160. *the rural talk* &c. *Fly harmless, to deceive the tedious time.* As Burns has it, in the poem referred to above :—

> 'Wi' claivers and haivers [scandal and nonsense]
>> Wearing the day awa'.'

Cp. the old Scots lament, The Flowers of the Forest :—

> 'In hairst at the shearin'
>> Nae youngsters are jeerin'.'

162. *builds up the shocks.* Arranges, or sets up the sheaves into ' stooks '—as they are called in Scotland. 'Shock,' is from 'Shake,' a pile of sheaves tossed together. 'Sheaf' from 'shove,' a quantity of corn-stalks pushed, or put together, in one bundle.

166. *Spike after spike. Spica* (Lat.), an ear of corn.

167, 168. The instructions of Boaz to his reapers. See Book of Ruth.

176. Gleaning, with many another custom of the old harvest-field, has all but disappeared.

177–310. This is the story of Ruth and Boaz.

181–188. In the 1738 and previous editions, this passage stood thus :—

> 'She, with her widowed mother, feeble, old,
>> And poor, lived in a cottage lost far up
>> Amid the windings of a woody vale,
>> Safe from the cruel blasting arts of man.'

The present text is Pope's, with the exception of the last line. Pope had proposed for it—

> 'From the base pride of an indignant world,'

which Thomson rejected for his own.

192, 193. *the morning rose When the dew wets its leaves.* The same image occurs in Summer, l. 1588—'the red rosebud moist with morning dew.' See Note.

203, 204. *their best attire, Beyond the pomp of dress.* These words were not inserted till after 1738.

207–216. This passage is all but wholly Pope's undoubted improvement upon the original, which stood so late as 1738 as follows : —

> 'Thoughtless of beauty, she was Beauty's self
>> Recluse among the woods, if city dames

---

[1] *lave*, others, the rest.   [2] *ilk*, each.   [3] ridge of corn.

Will deign their faith. And thus she went, compelled
By strong necessity, with as serene
And pleased a look as patience can put on.'

215. *strong necessity's supreme command.* Cp. Burns—
'Ye ken, ye ken
That strong Necessity supreme is
'Mang sons o' men.'

220. *such as Arcadian song*, &c. 'Arcadian' is here equivalent to 'pastoral.' Such 'songs' as are found among the idyls of Theocritus are referred to—notably, perhaps, the idyl descriptive of the visit of Hercules to the farms of Augeas in Elis.

229. *He saw her charming.* A peculiar idiom; meaning, of course, 'that she was charming.'

233. *and its dread laugh.* Sc. 'would be incurred,' should 'his heart own a gleaner in the field.' The construction is unfinished.

238, 239. *where enlivening sense And more*, &c. Altered from—
'And harmonious shaped,
Where sense sincere and goodness seem to dwell.'

267. *O heavens!* Originally 'O yes!'

273. *sequestered.* Originally 'unsmiling.'

282. *It ill befits thee, oh! it ill befits.* Perilously like—
'O Sophonisba, Sophonisba O!'

288. *pittance.* Originally (according to Ducange) a dole of the value of a 'picta,' a small coin of the Counts of Poitiers—in Latin, 'Pictava.'

290–293. These lines were substituted after 1738 for—
'With harvest shining all these fields are thine,
And, if my wishes may presume so far,
Their master too—who then, indeed, were blest
To make the daughter of Acasto so.'

300. *she blushed consent.* Cp. Burns's ballad of Bonnie Jean—
'At length she blushed a sweet consent,
And love was aye atween them twa.'

301. *news.* Nom. case absolute.

311. I. e. by spoiling the harvest.

315. *soft-inclining fields.* The corn bending gently to the breeze.

322. *eddy in.* The verb is here used transitively : 'the mountains draw in eddies towards them the wildly-raging storm.'

327, 328. *The billowy plain floats wide*, &c. In the first text 'boils.' Cornfields swaying in the wind. They cannot evade the storm by yielding to it—being either whirled into the air, or threshed out by the storm where they stand.

330–338. This graphic description of the devastating power of what is

Y

known in Scotland as 'the Lammas Flood,' might almost pass for a paraphrase of these lines of Virgil :—

> 'Saepe etiam immensum caelo venit agmen aquarum,
> Et foedam glomerant tempestatem imbribus atris
> Collectae ex alto nubes ; ruit arduus aether,
> Et pluvia ingenti sata laeta boumque labores
> Diluit ; implentur fossae et cava flumina crescunt
> Cum sonitu.'—*Georgic* I, ll. 322-327.

333. *The mingling tempest weaves its gloom.* In the first text 'glomerating.' Cp. Winter—

> 'The weary clouds
> Slow-meeting, mingle into solid gloom.'—ll. 202, 203.

335. *sunk and flatted.* Beaten down by wind and rain ; 'laid,' as it is called in Scotland ; 'lodged.'

337, 338. *Red from the hills . . . streams Tumultuous roar.* Cp. Burns—

> 'Tumbling brown the burn comes down
> And roars from bank to brae.'

340. *Herds, flocks, and harvests,* &c. In short, what Thomson calls 'the mixed ruin of its banks o'erspread' in Winter, l. 95.

347. *with his labours.* The ruined crops.

350. This appeal, on the tenant farmer's behalf, is to the 'laird,' or landowner, to forego, in the circumstances, or at least to make reduction of, the year's rent. (See Somerville's The Chace, Bk. II, ll. 51-64.)

360. *the sportsman's joy.* Cp. Burns—

> 'The sportsman's joy, the murdering cry,
> The fluttering gory pinion.'
> *August Song to Peggy.*

361. *the winded horn.* 'Winded' = 'blown' ; from 'wind,' Lat. *ventus*; no connection with 'wind,' 'to turn round or twist,' though 'wound' is sometimes used—oddly enough—for past tense and past participle.

362. *the rural game.* Field sports. The subject had been treated by Gay in his Rural Sports (two Cantos, written in rhyming pentameter couplets), published in 1713. Somerville also wrote on this theme— The Chace (in four books of blank verse), published in 1735 ; and Field Sports, published in 1742.

363. *the spaniel.* Named from Spain, from which country it was brought to England. The variety of 'hound' here referred to is, of course, the pointer, or setter. When he scents the game he stops so suddenly, and remains so immovable, that even the forefoot, already raised, continues suspended in the air.

364, 365. *with open nose . . . draws full.* Here 'draws' signifies, of course, 'inhales.'

366, 367. *the latent prey . . . the circling covey.* Sc. partridges. The word 'covey' is the old French *covee*, a brood of partridges, from *cover* (*couver* in modern French) to sit, or hatch. Cp. Lat. *cubare*, to lie, or sit down.

370. This method of taking partridges, or quails, is now generally abandoned by sportsmen, though still practised by poachers. It will be remembered that Will Wimble's ingenious accomplishments included an improvement of the quail-pipe, by means of which quails were lured more effectually into the nets. (See Addison's Sir Roger de Coverley papers in The Spectator.) See also Gay's Fables :—

> 'The ranging dog the stubble tries,
> And searches every breeze that flies;
> The scent grows warm : with cautious fear
> He creeps, and points the covey near.
> The men, in silence, far behind,
> Conscious of game, the net unbind.'
>
> *The Setting-dog and the Partridge.*

372–378. Compare with this description of the shooting of partridges, Pope's lines on the pheasant, in Windsor Forest :—

> 'See! from the brake the whirring pheasant springs
> And mounts exulting on triumphant wings.
> Short is his joy: he feels the fiery wound,
> Flutters in blood, and panting beats the ground.
> Ah! what avail his glossy varying dyes,' &c.
>
> ll. 111–118 (published 1713).

379. *These are not subjects for the peaceful muse.* Thomson's sympathy, like that of Cowper, Burns, and Wordsworth, is with the hunted creature. (See Spring, Note, l. 391, where his tenderness for the harmless brute creation is noted as a leading feature of both his character and his poetry.)

385, 386. *This rage of pleasure,* &c. Construe—'this rage of pleasure which awakes the restless youth, impatient, with the gleaming morn.' The love of sport makes him an early riser.

390–400. Cp. Burns's Lines on Scaring some Water-fowl in Loch Turit :—

> 'The eagle, from the cliffy brow,
> Marking you his prey below,
> In his breast no pity dwells,
> Strong necessity compels.'

> But man, to whom alone is given
> A ray direct from pitying heaven,
> Glories in his heart humane—
> And creatures for his pleasure slain,' &c.

395. *the beamings of the gentle days.* August and September.

402. *Scared from the corn.* Originally 'shook from the corn.'

403. *the rushy fen.* Where the hare sometimes makes her 'seat' or 'form'; 'in the moist marsh, 'mong beds of rushes hid,' says Somerville in The Chace; also noted by Burns in his Lines on Seeing a Wounded Hare Limp by Me :—

> 'Seek, mangled wretch, some place of wonted rest,
> No more of rest, but now thy dying bed,
> The sheltering rushes whistling o'er thy head,
> The cold earth with thy bloody bosom prest.'

404. *stubble chapt.* The ends of the shorn, or cut, corn stalks. Akin to Gr. κόπτω, I cut.

406. *Of the same friendly hue the withered fern.* Cp. Somerville—

> 'The withered grass that clings
> Around her head, of the same russet hue,
> Almost deceived my sight, had not her eyes
> With life full-beaming her vain wiles betrayed.'
>   *The Chace*, Bk. II.

407. *fallow ground laid open.* This kind of ploughing is called 'stirring the land.' 'Fallow' is from A.-S. *fealu*, pale red; Lat. *pallidus*. Cp. 'fallow deer.'

414. *The scented dew.* Beagles, or harriers (the name is derived from 'hare'), hunt the hare, relying on their scent; coursing is by grey-hounds—formerly used to hunt the deer—and these rely on their sight.

415. *her early labyrinth.* Cp. Somerville—

> 'What artful labyrinths perplex their way!
> Ah! there she flies!'

and

> 'The puzzling pack unravel wile by wile,
> Maze within maze.'—*The Chace*, Bk. II.

417–419. 'As now in louder peals the loaded winds
> Bring in the gathering storm, her fears prevail,
> And o'er the plain, and o'er the mountain's ridge
> Away she flies.'—*The Chace*, Bk. II.

It is very evident that Somerville had made himself acquainted with Thomson's lines on the hare hunt before he wrote his own account of the sport, which occupies the first half of Book II of The Chace. He has copied Thomson's language, but not his denunciation and detestation of the 'barbarous game.' It is worthy of note that after relating with the relish of a true sportsman the incidents of the chase from the 'meet' to the 'death,' Somerville winds up, innocent of the faintest trace of pathos, with the words—'Thus the poor hare, a puny, dastard animal! but versed in subtle wiles, diverts the youthful train.' Thomson furnishes the contrast. Cowper is no less, but rather more, explicit—

> 'Detested sport!
> That owes its pleasures to another's pain;
> That feeds upon the sobs and dying shrieks
> Of harmless nature, dumb, but yet endued
> With eloquence that agonies inspire,
> Of silent tears and heart-distending sighs!
> Vain tears, alas! and sighs that never find
> A corresponding tone in jovial souls!
> Well—one at least is safe. One sheltered hare
> Has never heard the sanguinary yell
> Of cruel man, exulting in her woes,' &c.
>
> *The Task,* Bk. III (The Garden).

426–457. Thomson's stag-hunt was evidently inspired by Denham's, whose description will be found near the end of Cooper's Hill (published in 1642): there are not a few points of resemblance.

427. *the branching monarch.* The stag, or male of the red deer, is distinguished (among other ways) from the buck, or male of the fallow deer, by its round branching antlers: those of the buck are broad and palmated. Neither the hind, nor the doe, has horns. The horns of the stag continue to branch till the animal is about six years old, when it is called a hart; the branches, or tines, may then number ten or twelve, and, though there is seldom, if ever, an increase after that, they become thicker, stronger, and more deeply furrowed with age.

439. *The inhuman rout.* Of men, horses, and hounds. Thomson's sympathy with the stag is implied in the use of the adjective. Before the staghound—a courageous and powerful animal, in scent almost the match of the bloodhound, and nearly equal to the foxhound in fleetness —deer long used to be hunted with greyhounds. We read of Queen Elizabeth witnessing the sport of 'sixteen bucks, all having fair law (i.e. a fair start of so many yards), being pulled down with greyhounds.'

441–444. See Denham—

> 'Thence to the coverts, and the conscious groves,
> The scenes of his past triumphs, and his loves;
> Sadly surveying, where he ranged alone

Prince of the soil, and all the herd his own;
And, like a bold knight-errant, did proclaim
Combat to all, and bore away the dame;
And taught the woods to echo to the stream
His dreadful challenge, and his clashing beam' (*horn*).
                                                  Cooper's Hill.

445, 446. So Denham—
'Then to the stream, when neither friends, nor force,
Nor speed, nor art avail, he shapes his course;
Thinks not their rage so desp'rate as t'essay
An element more merciless than they.
But fearless they pursue, nor can the flood
Quench their dire thirst : alas! they thirst for blood.'
                                                  Cooper's Hill.

447, 448. So Denham—
'Then tries his friends; among the baser herd,
Where he so lately was obeyed and feared,
His safety seeks: the herd, unkindly wise,
Or chases him from thence, or from him flies.'
                                                  Cooper's Hill.

451. *fainting.* 'Wrenching' in the original.

452. *stands at bay.* Literally, 'at the baying of the hounds.' From the French *abois*; *être aux abois*, to be at bay.

454. *The big round tears run down his dappled face.* Cp. Shakespeare—

'A poor sequestered stag,
That from the hunter's aim had ta'en a hurt
Did come to languish; and, indeed, my lord,
The wretched animal heaved forth such groans
That their discharge did stretch his leathern coat
Almost to bursting; and the big round tears
Coursed one another down his innocent nose
In piteous chase.'—*As You Like It*, Act II, Sc. i.

458–463. See a detailed description of a lion-hunt in 'the magnificent manner of the Great Mogul and other Tartarian princes,' in the Second Book of Somerville's Chace.

469. *lighten.* Glance like lightning.

470–490. Thomson's sympathy does not cover the fox. See Spring, Note, l. 391.

477. *the shaking wilderness.* The quagmire (from 'quake'), or bog.

483. *snatch the mountains by their woody tops.* At first 'snatch the mountains by their tops.'

485. *swallowing up the space.* 'He seems in running to devour the way.'—Shakespeare.

490, 491. He is still a villain, and vermin; and his uncomplaining and heroic death wins from Thomson neither respect, admiration, nor sympathy. To be 'in at the death' is a great boast among fox-hunters.

494. *ghostly halls of grey renown.* The very size of those halls in old country mansion-houses makes them dim, and therefore ghostly-looking; and their many ancient associations and traditions concur to produce the same effect.

495. *woodland honours.* The trophies of the chase.

497. *drear walls, with antic figures fierce.* A line that impresses the imagination. The dim and ghostly walls of l. 494 have now the additional horror of old paintings, representing truculent warriors and hunters—ancient members of the family. 'Antic' is for 'antique.'

499. Hard-drinking—harder than the exertion of the chase itself.

500. Not in the 1738, or any previous edition. The Centaurs, or Bull-stickers, of ancient Thessaly, were savage monsters, half man and half horse, whose time was spent in hunting and fighting. Perhaps Thomson refers here to their battle with the Lapithae.

502–569. This scene could be ill spared from the poetical works of Thomson. To the student of his poetry only it reveals him in a new light as the possessor of a rich and genial vein of humour, which deepens as the foxhunters proceed from dining to drinking. Thomson himself has called the whole scene 'a ludicrous account'; and, while the subject itself presents phases of a humorous nature, it must be allowed that the humour lies chiefly in the style in which the subject is handled. Some critics (such as Heron) have objected to the entire passage as an unworthy production of a sedate and serious genius; but it is as genuine as any other passage characteristic of his prevailing mood—it is no less his than are the verses which display his views of nature, his philosophy, his pathos—and, while it enriches the poem with an unexpected variety of pleasantry, it enables us to form a fuller and more perfect conception of the character of the author. Thomson's hearty relish of fun and humour in his youth, and no inconsiderable part of his correspondence, fragmentary though it be, are sufficient to prepare one for some exhibition of humour in his poetry, and, if the exhibition comes rather unexpectedly at last, it is only because he has refused to indulge a vein which he undoubtedly possessed.

502. See Scott's Rob Roy, chap. v, last paragraph.

503. *the strong table groans.* Tables have usually groaned on festive occasions, since this was written; especially those of Sir Walter Scott.

504. *sirloin stretched immense [from side to side].* This exaggeration, with that of the groaning table, &c., is a feature of Thomson's humorous style—if, indeed, exaggeration be not a necessary feature of all humorous expression. Cp. Burns's Address to a Haggis :—

> 'The groaning trencher there ye fill,
> Your hurdies like a distant hill;
> Your pin wad help to mend a mill
>   In time o' need.'

505, 506. *with desperate knife,* &c. Cp. Burns, as above—

> 'His knife see rustic Labour dight
> An' cut you up wi' ready sleight,' &c.

510. *If stomach keen can intervals allow.* A parodied echo of Milton. It reads like a line from Phillips's Splendid Shilling.

513. *Produce the mighty bowl.* See Rob Roy, chap. vi.

516. *Maia.* The month of May—a Latinised form.

519. *brown October.* Ale, or strong beer, home-brewed (therefore 'honest,' l. 521) in October. The great brewing seasons are twice a year, in March and October. Thomson's own cellar at Richmond was well stocked with both wines and ales—as may be learned from the sale list of his effects.

523. 'To vie it with the vineyard's best produce'—in the 1738 edition.

524, 525. Here Thomson is probably expressing not his own, but the foxhunter's view of whist: at all events, he had a kindly word for the game in 1738 :—

> 'Perhaps awhile amusive thoughtful whisk
> Walks gentle round.'

528, 529. *romp-loving miss,* &c. See Winter, ll. 625–627.

531. *the dry divan [close in firm circle].* Somerville (in The Chace, Bk. II) has—

> 'Now sit in close *divan*
> The mighty chiefs;'

using the word in its appropriate sense of 'council.' 'Divan' is Persian, and has the various meanings of 'council-chamber,' 'sofa,' 'tribunal.'

535. *Indulged apart.* None were excused from deep-drinking. In the first text 'askew' held the place of 'apart.' See Scott's Rob Roy, chap. vi, the scene where Francis Osbaldistone escapes from the potations of the Hall.

549. A happy touch.

562. *The lubber power.* Drunkenness personified; a kind of English Silenus.

565–569. These five lines, humorously satirical of the convivial clergy of the day, were not added till after 1738. It may prove interesting here to quote from Macaulay's History of England the account he gives of the manners and mode of life practised by the English Country Gentleman of 1688 :—

'His chief pleasures were commonly derived from field-sports and from an unrefined sensuality. . . . His oaths, coarse jests, and scurrilous terms of abuse, were uttered with the broadest accent of his province. . . . His table was loaded with coarse plenty, and guests were cordially welcome to it ; but as the habit of drinking to excess was general in the class to which he belonged, and as his fortune did not enable him to intoxicate large assemblies daily with claret or canary, strong beer was the ordinary beverage. The quantity of beer consumed in those days was indeed enormous ; for beer then was to the middle and lower classes, not only all that beer now is, but all that wine, tea, and ardent spirits now are. . . . The ladies of the house, whose business it had commonly been to cook the repast, retired as soon as the dishes had been devoured, and left the gentlemen to their ale and tobacco. The coarse jollity of the afternoon was often prolonged till the revellers were laid under the table.'

570. *by this fierce sport*. In the first text, ' by this *red* sport.'

571. See Young's Love of Fame, Satire v, ll. 113–116.

579. This line was preceded in the earlier editions by the line—
' Made up of blushes, tenderness, and fears.'

590. *Float in the loose simplicity of dress.* Cp. Ben Jonson—
' Give me a look, give me a face,
That makes simplicity a grace;
Robes loosely flowing, hair as free ;
Such sweet neglect more taketh me
Than all the adulteries of art :
They strike mine eyes, but not my heart.'
The Silent Woman.

The idea here expressed was caught up by Herrick :—
' A sweet disorder in the dress—
A lawn about the shoulders thrown
Into a fine distraction, ...
A winning wave, deserving note,
In the tempestuous petticoat . . . .
Do more bewitch me than when art
Is too precise in every part.'

595. Meaning probably—' Disclosing a new charm in its every motion,' or ' disclosing all the charms of motion.' Dancing has been called ' the poetry of motion.'

597. *To train the foliage o'er the snowy lawn.* Cp. Cowper—

> 'Here the needle plies its busy task;
> The pattern grows, the well-depicted flower,
> Wrought patiently into the snowy lawn,
> Unfolds its bosom, buds, and leaves, and sprigs,' &c.
>
> *The Task*, Bk. IV. ll. 150-153.

598. *turn the tuneful page.* First editions give 'instructive page.' So Cowper, as above :—

> 'The poet's or historian's page by one
> Made vocal for the amusement of the rest.'

599, 600. *To lend new flavour to . . . Nature's dainties.* Thomson thus retains cookery in his list of a lady's accomplishments.

600–601. *in their race To rear their graces,* &c. To attend to the training and education of their children.

608. Such is Thomson's view of the woman's true kingdom. Like Milton's, it reveals no sympathy with what has come to be called 'woman's rights.'

612. *In close array.* Not in flowing garments, but in what Wordsworth calls ' woodland dress.'

614–617. Wordsworth has described the same scene in his fragment on Nutting, but he discovered, what escaped the robuster paganism of Thomson, ' a spirit in the woods ':—

> 'Then up I rose
> And dragged to earth both branch and bough with crash
> And merciless ravage; and the shady nook
> Of hazels, and the green and mossy bower,
> Deformed and sullied, patiently gave up
> Their quiet being . . . . . .
> —I felt a sense of pain when I beheld
> The silent trees and the intruding sky.
> Then, dearest maiden, move along these shades
> In gentleness of heart; with gentle hand
> Touch—for there is a spirit in the woods.'

620. *an ardent brown.* A shining or glossy brown

623. *these neglecting.* Unconscious, or at least not vain, of her personal charms.

625. *the busy joy-resounding fields.* The harvest fields.

627, 628. *taste . . . . The breath of orchard.* See Spring, l. 107— ' taste the smell of dairy.'—' Orchard,' literally ' wort-yard,' a ' herb-garden.'

633. *the gentle race.* Of pears.

638–642. It is worth noting that the very sound of these lines is

suggestive of the appearance, taste, and perfume of the fruit which they
describe. The same appropriateness of language is noticeable in the
description of 'juicy pears lying in soft profusion' (ll. 630–632
supra).

644, 645. *Thy native theme, ... Phillips, Pomona's bard.* John Phillips,
son of Archdeacon Phillips of Salop, and of Bampton, Oxfordshire,
was born on December 30, 1676. He was educated at Winchester,
and Christ Church, Oxford; and wrote The Splendid Shilling (1703) a
burlesque imitation of the style of Milton; Blenheim (1705); and (in
1706) a poem on Cider, in two books, of about 1500 lines in all,
composed in imitation of Virgil's Georgics, and remarkable as being a
pretty exhaustive and trustworthy treatise on apple-growing and cider-
making. He is said to have been a man of singular modesty and
amiability in private life. He died in 1708, in the 32nd year of his age.
His three principal poems are in blank verse—for which he is here
complimented by Thomson, as 'nobly daring to sing in rhyme-unfettered
verse' first after the example of Milton. The poem on Cider (Gr. σίκερα,
strong drink) opens thus :—

> 'What soil the apple loves, what care is due
> To orchats, timeliest when to press the fruits,
> Thy gift, Pomona! in Miltonic verse,
> Adventurous, I presume to sing, of verse
> Nor skilled, nor studious; but my native soil
> Invites me, and the theme, as yet unsung.'

And it concludes with the prophecy that ' Silurian cider '
> 'Shall please all tastes and triumph o'er the vine.'

648. The Silures inhabited South Wales generally. The English
county (on the Welsh March) of Hereford is specially referred to. In
his poem Phillips gives the palm to Hereford over Devon for cider.

651. *to cool the summer hours—*
> 'When dusty Summer bakes the crumbling clods
> How pleasant is't beneath the twisted arch
> Of a retreating bower in midday's reign
> To ply the sweet carouse, ...
> Secured of feverish heats.'—*Cider*, Bk. II.

653. *sheds equal.* The time of the autumnal equinox, the 22nd of
September, has now arrived.

654. *lose me.* Let me lose myself, let me wander.

655. *Dodington, thy seat.* (See Summer, Note, l. 21.) Eastbury, in
Dorsetshire, where Thomson was an occasional guest. See his
correspondence for the years 1731 and 1735.

660. *thy lofty dome.* Eastbury House was one of the many mansions

which John Vanbrugh (1666–1726), dramatist and architect, was commissioned to design after the erection, from plans which he furnished, in 1702, of Castle Howard, the seat of the Earl of Carlisle, in Yorkshire. Vanbrugh the architect is best known as the designer of Blenheim House. His style, both in the construction of dramas and of houses, may be characterised as solid and weighty. A modern critic neatly says that 'he was no poet, but *a heavy observer.*' After Dodington's death no tenant could be found for Eastbury House, though its owner offered a premium to any one who would occupy it. The taste for 'solid magnificence' (see Thomson's letter to Dodington of date December 27, 1730), which, in architecture, both Dodington and Thomson affected, had undergone a change.

665. 'These numbers free, Pierian Eastbury ! I owe to thee.'—Young, in Love of Fame, Sat. v.

666. After this line in the earlier editions of Autumn came—
      'They twine the bay for thee. Here oft alone,
       Fired by the thirst of thy applause, I court,' &c.
The compliment to Young was an afterthought, due probably to the publication of Night Thoughts in 1742–1744.

667. *virtuous Young.* Before the appearance of Night Thoughts, a poem in nine books of blank verse, written partly in emulation of Thomson, Young, though he had produced much, had given the world nothing that was really of superior and lasting merit. Thomson's opinion of him in 1726, when he was busy with The Universal Passion, may be inferred from the following passage which occurs in a letter to Malloch, of date August 2, 1726; the reference is to a poem which Young afterwards omitted from his collected works in 1741 : 'I have not seen these reflections on the Doctor's Installment, but hear they are as wretched as their subject. The Doctor's very buckram has run short on this occasion; his affected sublimity even fails him, and down he comes with no small velocity.' Edward Young was born in 1681, did not publish till his thirty-second year, entered the Church when on the borders of fifty, was over sixty when he began his one famous poem, and died—a proud, gloomy, disappointed man—in 1765, aged eighty-four years. Like many other authors of the day he paid court to 'the Patron'—Dodington. To him he inscribed the second satire of The Love of Fame.

673–679. These lines present the author in a characteristic attitude of sensuous ease and lazy meditation. Apparently he composed part of Autumn while luxuriating as Dodington's guest at Eastbury. (See his letter to Dodington, dated from Rome, November 28, 1731, for a reference to the gardens at Eastbury.) *Peach* : from old Fr. *pesche,*

Lat. *persicum*; from being the fruit of a *Persian* tree. *Plum*: from 'prune,' Lat. *prunum*, Gr. προῦνον. 'With a fine blueish mist of animals clouded'—omitted by Thomson from the last revision of the text. *Nectarine*: so called from being as sweet as 'nectar'; Gr. νέκταρ, the wine of the gods. *Fig*: Fr. *figue*, Lat. *ficus. Vine*: Fr. *vigne*, Lat. *vinea*, a vineyard, then a vine; Gr. οἴνη, a vine—named from its *wind*ing growth.

683–706. A short digression to the vineyards of France.

691, 692. Referring to the two varieties of black and white grapes.

693. The bloom.

697. *to cull the autumnal prime.* To gather the firstfruits, the first ripe clusters.

702. *the raised nations.* Excited, or invigorated. The former is a common meaning of 'raised' in Lowland Scotch.

703–706. *Claret*: Fr., from Lat. *clarus*, clear; a clarified wine. The name was originally applied to a light-red wine; with us it is a general name for the red wines of Bordeaux. *Burgundy*: this wine is from the vineyards of the Côte d'Or, between Chalons and Dijon. Both the red and the white wines of Burgundy rank among the finest in the world. Chambertin is one of the most famous of the red wines of Burgundy. *Champagne*: named from the ancient province, which means a 'plain'; Lat. *campus*. Perhaps the best varieties are Sillery, a white, and Verzenay, a red champagne.

708. Autumn is the 'season of mists' as well as of 'mellow fruitfulness.'—Keats.

713. Such as the Cheviots, in his daily view during boyhood. The Cheviot shepherd appears at l. 727 *infra*.

714. After the word 'division' came in the 1738 edition—

> 'While aloft
> His piny top is, lessening, lost in air:
> No more his thousand prospects fill,' &c.

723, 724. *Whence glaring oft . . . . He frights the nations.* Cp. Milton, Par. Lost, Bk. I. ll. 594–599, commencing, 'As when the sun new-risen.'

725. *beyond the life.* Larger than life; magnified shadows. The phenomenon here referred to is not uncommon in the Scottish highlands and uplands in misty weather. Among the Harz mountains of Germany it is popularly known as the Spectre of the Brocken. It is the magnified shadow of objects thrown by the light of sunrise or sunset against a veil of mist.

732. *the Hebrew bard.* Moses, in the first chapter of Genesis. Milton invokes the 'Heavenly Muse'—

> 'That, on the secret top
> Of Oreb, or of Sinai, didst inspire
> That shepherd who first taught the chosen seed
> In the beginning how the heavens and earth
> Rose out of chaos.'—*Par. Lost*, Bk. I. ll. 6–10.

733. *Light, uncollected.* That is 'ungathered in the sun.' The sun made its appearance in the heavens on the fourth day of Creation, while light was created on the first. *Chaos*, 'confusion,' is opposed to 'Order,' *cosmos*, in the next line.

736–835. By far the larger portion of this long passage of a hundred lines was written after 1738, for the purpose of negativing the theory of the origin of rivers advanced in the earlier text. That theory sought to explain the origin of rivers by postulating a system of attraction of oceanic waters upwards through the pores of the earth. It is stated, as the accepted view of 'some sages,' in the present text, ll. 743–756. Milton may be regarded as one of those 'sages,' for it is by porous attraction that he secures the irrigation of Paradise, having previously placed that lovely garden on 'the champaign head of a steep wilderness.' Southward, he tells us, through the low-lying district of Eden (*not* the garden)—

> 'Went a river large,
> Nor changed his course, but through the shaggy hill
> Passed underneath ingulfed ; for God had thrown
> That mountain, as his garden mould, high raised
> Upon the rapid current, which, through veins
> Of porous earth with kindly thirst updrawn
> Rose a fresh fountain, and with many a rill
> Watered the garden.'—*Par. Lost*, Bk. IV. ll. 223–230.

The correct theory of the origin of streams is briefly stated in the seven lines with which the passage opens. The fanciful theory, which just reverses the natural arrangement, after being vividly stated as already said (ll. 743–756), is then dismissed as a 'vain amusive dream,' and shown to be absurd, impossible, ruinous in the most comprehensive sense, and—unnecessary ! But if Thomson's scientific speculations and arguments are amusing, his poetical view of the globe's great rivers 'in their infant beds' is a noble effort of the imagination, expressed with something of the sonorous and stately measure of Milton.

742. After this line, in the edition of 1738, came the following scepticism of the established theory :—

> 'But is this equal to the vast effect ?
> Is thus the Volga filled ? the rapid Rhine ?
> The broad Euphrates ? all the unnumbered floods

That large refresh the fair-divided earth,
And, in the rage of Summer, never cease
To send a thundering torrent to the main?
   What though the sun draws from the steaming deep
More than the rivers pour? How much again
O'er the vext surge, in bitter-driving showers,
Frequent returns, let the wet sailor say:
And on the thirsty down, far from the burst
Of springs, how much, to their reviving fields
And feeding flocks, let lonely shepherds sing.
But sure 'tis no weak variable cause
That keeps at once ten thousand thousand floods
Wide-wandering o'er the world, so fresh and clear,
For ever flowing and for ever full.
And thus some sages deep-exploring teach
That where the hoarse innumerable wave
Eternal lashes,' &c.—(See text, l. 744.)

756–835. These lines were incorporated with the text after 1738 : in the
edition of that year appeared the following lines, which they displaced :—

'The vital stream
Hence, in its subterranean passage, gains
From the washed mineral that restoring power
And salutary virtue, which anew
Strings every nerve, calls up the kindling soul
Into the healthful cheek and joyous eye:
And whence the royal maid, Amelia, blooms
With new-flushed graces; yet reserved to bless
Beyond a crown some happy prince; and shine
In all her mother's matchless virtues drest
The Carolina of another land.'

772. *Deucalion's watery times.* The Flood. According to the
classical legend of ancient Greece, Deucalion, and Pyrrha his wife,
were, on account of their piety, the only human beings saved when
Zeus destroyed the world with a nine days' flood. They escaped
drowning in a ship. Cp. the story of Noah and his ark.

777. The ' pervading genius' of this line is the imagination.

778. Cp. Gray (of Milton) :—

'He that rode sublime
Upon the seraph-wings of Ecstasy
The secrets of the abyss to spy.'—*Progress of Poesy*, III. 2.

783, 784. *Imaüs . . . the roving Tartar's sullen bounds.* A
recollection of Milton :—

'As when a vulture on Imaus bred,
Whose snowy ridge the roving Tartar bounds,' &c.
Par. Lost, Bk. III. ll. 431, 432.

Taurus. A mountain range in Asia Minor. *Imaus.* The Himá-
layas, between India and Tartary. *Hemus* (l. 785), a range of hills
crossing Turkey in Europe eastward to the Black Sea: Haemus, Imaus,
and Himálaya are probably all from the same origin—Sanskrit *hima*;
Gr. χειμών; Lat. *hiems*, winter, the snowy season.

790, 791. *Caucasus.* A range of very high mountains stretching over
700 miles from the Black Sea eastwards to the Caspian. The Caspian is
an enormous salt-water lake in the south-west of Asia, about 900 miles
long, into which flow the Volga and the Araxes. The Euxine is the
Black Sea, called Euxine euphemistically by the ancient Greeks: εὔξεινος,
hospitable.

792. *Riphean rocks.* The rocks of the Ural mountains. Thomson's
own note is, 'The Muscovites call the Riphaean mountains Weliki
Camenypoys, that is, *the great stony girdle*; because they suppose
them to encompass the whole earth.'

795. Sc. the Obi, Irtish, Yenisei, Lena, &c.

798. *Atlas, propping heaven, as poets feign.* The Greek myth is to the
effect that one of the Titans (who had made war against Zeus), Atlas by
name, was punished after defeat by being condemned to bear heaven on
his head and hands. Later legends make Atlas a man who was
transformed into a mountain. Homer refers to the Greek myth; Ovid
has described the transformation in the Fourth Book of the Meta-
morphoses.

801. *cloud-compelling.* A Homeric epithet of Zeus.

802. Jebel-Kumra, or Mountains of the Moon, supposed in Thomson's
day to lie under the Equator across Central Africa. His note states that
they 'surround almost all Monomotapa.'

841. *to their wintry slumbers they retire.* The idea that swallows,
like bats, become torpid in winter, is still pretty popular. Thomson,
though he presents the theory of hibernation, clearly prefers the true
theory of migration.

850. *plains, won from the raging deep* [*by diligence amazing*].
Holland—' a new creation rescued from his [Ocean's] reign ' (Goldsmith).
The reference is, of course, to the dikes. Cp. The Traveller—

'Onwards, methinks, and diligently slow,
The firm connected bulwark seems to grow,
Spreads its long arms amidst the watery roar,
Scoops out an empire, and usurps the shore.'

853. *the stork-assembly.* These birds, belonging to the family of

herons and bitterns, though widely diffused over Europe, have always been extremely rare in England—rare even before the drainage of the fen regions. They are common in Holland, where great care is taken to protect them. The people place boxes for their nests, and it is reckoned a fortunate thing for the occupants of a house if the box which they have placed on the roof is tenanted. They are of great service in devouring reptiles, and in clearing the streets of offal, &c. Thomson accurately describes their 'consultations,' preliminary exercises, and arrangements previous to their departure for the winter. During these 'consultations' they make a great noise by the clattering of their long and strong mandibles.

861. The period closing here beautifully rounds off the description of their flight, conveying to the mind a sense of the aerial perspective in which the 'figured flight' is vanishing. They migrate in August or September.

864, 865. *Thule.* The Orkney and Shetland islands. *Hebrides.* The Western Isles off the coast of Scotland. *Pours in among the stormy Hebrides.* Cp. Thomson's description of the same scene in his Britannia:—

'Loud the northern main
Howls through the fractured Caledonian isles.'—ll. 88, 89.

866. *transmigrations.* Of solan geese, and other sea-birds.

871. *plain harmless native.* The crofter of the Western Isles; an accurate description.

872. *herd diminutive of many hues.* The Highland breed of cattle is distinguished by their small size, long horns, shaggy appearance, and variety of colour—black, red, umber, and yellowish-white.

874. *The shepherd's seagirt reign.* The 'shepherd of the Hebride Isles' is also introduced in The Castle of Indolence, Canto I, st. xxx.

875. *clinging, gathers his ovarious food.* The eggs (Lat. *ova*) of sea-fowl, from their nests in the cliff crevices and shelves. In The Pirate, Sir Walter Scott refers to 'those midnight excursions upon the face of the giddy cliffs [overhanging the roost of Sumburgh in the Shetland islands] to secure the eggs or the young of the sea-fowl'—'desperate sports,' he says, 'to which the "dreadful trade of the samphire-gatherer" is like a walk upon level ground.' (See The Pirate, chap. ii, and note.)

876. *sweeps the fishy shore.* With their nets; or, it may be, with oars.

877. *The plumage ... to form the bed [of luxury].* Eider-down. Even Ailsa rock, so far south as the Ayrshire coast, used to supply quantities of these feathers. Writing to his uncle, who lived opposite

z

Ailsa, Burns asks 'if the fowling for this season [the date is 4th May, 1788] be commenced yet, as I want three or four stones of feathers, and I hope you will bespeak them for me.'

878-949. This passage is devoted to an account of Scotland and its people. It is an expansion of the following thirteen half-hearted lines which originally appeared in Summer in connexion with the description of England and the English (see Summer, ll. 1442-1619) :—

> 'And should I northward turn my filial eye
> Beyond the Tweed, pure parent-stream, to where
> The hyperborean ocean furious foams
> O'er Orca or Berubium's highest peak,
> Rapt I might sing [1] thy Caledonian sons,
> A gallant, warlike, unsubmitting race!
> Nor less in Learning versed, soon as he took
> Before the Gothic rage his western flight;
> Wise in the council, at the banquet gay;
> The pride of honour burning in their breasts,
> And glory, not to their own realms confined,
> But into foreign countries shooting far
> As over Europe bursts the boreal morn.'

(See Summer, Note, ll. 1479-1579.)

881. *the waving main.* In the earlier editions, '*gelid* main'—which, though less picturesque, helps better to explain 'the keen sky' and 'soul acute' of the next two lines.

884. [*forests huge,*] *Incult, robust,* &c. Caledonia, 'land of brown heath and *shaggy woods,*' included such well-known historical forests of natural growth ('incult') as Athole, Birnam, Braemar, Rothiemurchus, Torwood, Cadzow, &c.

886. *extensive.* Such as Loch Lomond, covering an area of 45 square miles. *Watery wealth.* Fish of various kinds.

887. *her fertile vales.* Such as the '*carses*' of Stirling and Gowrie; but Thomson specially refers to the *dales* of the Lowlands—Tweeddale, Clydesdale, Teviotdale, Nithsdale, &c.

890, 891. These lines do not appear in the edition of 1738. Ednam, the birthplace of Thomson, in the north-east corner of Roxburghshire, is only a few miles distant from the Tweed. A couple of months after his

---

[1] One might ask, 'And why not, then?' But Thomson was himself ashamed of the meagre sketch, out of all due proportion to the long and noble panegyric of England and her worthies—and withdrew it altogether from its original place in the poem of Summer. He made some amends in Autumn. Thomson's patriotism is not arraigned here, but his slackness in expressing it to an English auditory.

birth, his father was ordained minister of Southdean on the Jed, and here the boyhood and youth-time of Thomson were spent—in a pastoral rather than ' sylvan ' region, however.   But the reference is probably to the ancient forest of Jedwood, through which the Jed flows on its way to Teviot, the chief tributary of Tweed.   He early began to write verse, his compositions being on homely country subjects—hence the reference to his ' Doric reed.'

893. *Orca.* Orkney. *Berubium.* Duncansbay Head, in the north of Caithness-shire, is the Berubium of Ptolemy.

895-897. *visited By learning*, &c.   Rome was sacked by the barbarians in 410. The last occupant of the throne of the Cæsars was overthrown by Odoacer in 476. It was in 563 that Columba came to Iona on his mission of Christianizing the Picts. Thomson's reference may be to the appearance of the Culdees in Scotland, which, according to tradition, was about the middle of the ninth century.

900. *Wallace.* Sir William Wallace, the hero of the Scottish wars with Edward I of England in the end of the thirteenth, and beginning of the fourteenth century. He was, after many brave but unsuccessful efforts to secure the independence of his country, meanly betrayed into the hands of King Edward, who barbarously ordered his execution in London in 1305.

902. *generous.* Probably in the sense of 'national,' or 'worthy of a noble race.'

905. *for every land.* As mercenary soldiers in France, Germany, &c. The ubiquity of the travelled Scot is proverbial.

909. The aurora borealis—no uncommon phenomenon of a Scottish winter.

911, 912. *luxury . . . Of blessing thousands.* Goldsmith speaks of the 'luxury of doing good,' in The Traveller, l. 22.

914-916. *to give A double harvest,* &c. This had been done for England by Walpole's policy of peace, about the time (1730) when this poem was published. ' His time of power,' says Green in The History of the English People, ' was a time of great material prosperity. . . . The rise of manufactures was accompanied by a sudden increase of commerce, which was due mainly to a rapid development of our colonies. . . . With peace and security, the value of land, and with it the rental of every country gentleman, tripled ; while the introduction of winter roots, of artificial grasses, of the system of a rotation of crops, changed the whole character of agriculture, and spread wealth through the farming classes.' (See the last thirty-four lines of Allan Ramsay's Prospect of Plenty.)   Lord Townshend introduced the turnip in 1730. In 1732 drill husbandry was introduced.

919. *To form the lucid lawn.* The linen manufacture is now an important part of the industry of the people. The chief centres are at Dundee and Dunfermline.

921-923. *Batavian fleets Defraud us of the . . . swarms,* &c. The herring fisheries of Scotland are now the most important of the fisheries of Great Britain. But it is only comparatively recently that they have been established and developed. Towards the close of the 17th century, and for many years after, the herring harvests of the Scottish firths were gathered by Dutch fishermen, whose fleets of boats were no unfamiliar sight in the Forth and other estuaries[1]. The unfortunate Darien Company had the development of the sea-fisheries of Scotland as one of their schemes. In 1720 a joint-stock company was formed to prosecute the herring fishery in Scotland. It held out a Prospect of Plenty to the country, and the Prospect was duly celebrated in a curious poem (1720) by Allan Ramsay; but the North Sea Scheme, like that of the more famous South Sea, collapsed. The fostering care of some patriotic statesman was still wanted in 1730, when Thomson put his question, and asked the Duke of Argyle to answer it.

927. *as in name.* By the treaty of Union, of 1707, the name of Great Britain was applied to the United Kingdoms of England and Scotland.

929. *Argyle.* John, Duke of Argyle and Greenwich. 'This nobleman,' says Sir Walter Scott, 'was very dear to his countrymen, who were justly proud of his military and political talents, and grateful for the ready zeal with which he asserted the rights of his native country.' (See, for a fuller and very favourable estimate of his character, The Heart of Midlothian, chap. xxxiv.) It was of him Pope wrote :—

> 'Argyle, the state's whole thunder born to wield,
>   And shake alike the senate and the field.'

He was born in 1678; served under Marlborough in Flanders, distinguishing himself at Ramillies, Oudenarde, Malplaquet, &c.; was appointed Commander of the Forces in Scotland, where he quelled the disturbances connected with the Rebellion of 1715; and was raised to the English peerage in 1718, with the title of Duke of Greenwich. He died in 1743. He is known in Scotland as 'The good Duke of Argyle,' —a designation which he merited from the kindliness of his disposition,

---

[1] In 1689 Dutch vessels,—'busses' as they were called,—engaged in the herring traffic, were mistaken for a French fleet in the Firth of Forth, and alarmed the inhabitants of Edinburgh. Allan Ramsay, in 1721, wrote of the Dutch fishermen—

> 'Lang have they plied that trade like busy bees
>   And sucked the profit of the Pictland seas.'

On the Prospect of Plenty.

and his many private acts of beneficence. There can be no doubt that Thomson's was the popular estimate of his character.

938. The village of Malplaquet in French Flanders, where Marlborough gained a great victory over Marshal Villars in 1709, lies on one side of the open gap (Trouée) between the forests of Taisnière and Lanière on the road to Mons. A great deal of the fighting was in Taisnière forest. This battle was the bloodiest in the whole of Marlborough's wars.—Six lines, of no great merit, have been dropt here from the edition of 1738.

944. *Forbes.* Duncan Forbes, of Culloden, Lord President of the Scottish Court of Session. Born in 1685, he was trained for the bar, and rose to be Lord Advocate in 1725. Ten years later he was raised to the Scottish bench, and in 1737 became Lord President. He died in 1747. He was one of the many personal friends of Thomson, who was also on terms of great intimacy with his son. His rapid rise to place and power was owing partly to his own talents and partly to his political and family connection with the Duke of Argyle. He is remembered in Scotland for his clemency and generosity (exhibited so particularly as almost to compromise his loyalty) in behalf of the Jacobite rebels of 1715 and 1745. The later years of his life were largely devoted to the improvement of Scottish methods of agriculture and the advancement of Scottish trade.

967. *low-thoughted.* Applied by Milton to 'care,' in Comus, l. 6.

968. *soothe the throbbing passions into peace.* In Spring, l. 463—

'Soothe every gust of passion into peace.'

970-1005. The substance of these lines had already been beautifully expressed by the poet in prose. Writing from Barnet, near London, in September, 1725, Thomson, who was then just commencing his poem of Winter, remarks in a letter to his friend and confidant, Dr. William Cranstoun, of Ancrum—a village about three miles from Jedburgh— 'Now I imagine you seized with a fine romantic kind of a melancholy on the fading of the year ; now I figure you wandering, philosophical and pensive, amidst the brown withered groves, while the leaves rustle under your feet, the sun gives a farewell parting gleam, and the birds—

"Stir the faint note, and but attempt to sing."

Then again, when the heavens wear a more gloomy aspect, the winds whistle, and the waters spout, I see you in the well-known *cleugh* [1] beneath the solemn arch of tall thick-embowering trees, listening to the amusing lull of the many steep moss-grown cascades, while deep, divine

---

[1] A glen, or chasm between two rocks.

Contemplation, the genius of the place, prompts each swelling awful thought. I am sure you would not resign your place in that scene at an easy rate. None ever enjoyed it to the height that you do ; and you are worthy of it. There I walk in spirit, and disport in its beloved gloom. This country I am in is not very entertaining ; no variety but that of woods, and them we have in abundance. But where is the living stream, the airy mountain, or the hanging rock ?' &c.

983. *aimed from some inhuman eye.* Cp. Burns—

> 'Inhuman man ! curse on thy barbarous art,
>   And blasted be thy murder-aiming eye !'
>
> > > > > > *The Wounded Hare.*

994. The peculiarly effective pause after 'sob' should be noted here.

1005. *philosophic Melancholy comes!* Appropriately to the fading year. Cp. Burns—

> 'Come, Autumn, sae pensive, in yellow and gray,
>   And soothe me,' &c.

1020–1022. A noble sentiment, characteristic of Thomson.

1025. *wonder.* Admiration.

1030–1036. The feeling for the supernatural (as expressed here, and in Summer, at l. 538, and elsewhere in his poetry) is a feature of Thomson's genius—to which, surely, Collins must have been looking when he figured Thomson as a Druid in the well-known Ode :

> 'O vales and wild woods (shall he say),
>   In yonder grave your Druid lies !'

1037–1081. These forty-five lines were not added till after 1738.

1042. *paradise of Stowe.* 'The seat of the Lord Viscount Cobham.' (*Note by Thomson.*) It is not now the attractive place it was in Thomson's time.

1048. *Pitt.* The elder, Earl of Chatham. He was born in 1708, and was therefore only twenty-two when Thomson published Autumn. The compliment to him was added after he began to make a name for himself as a statesman. It was not till 1735 that Pitt entered Parliament. He took the side of Frederick, Prince of Wales, and offered a determined resistance to Walpole. As Thomson died in 1748, he could only speak of Pitt as 'the early boast' of his country.

1050. *that temple.* The Temple of Virtue in Stowe Gardens. So at the Leasowes Shenstone had Damon's Bower, and there he wrote, 'towards the close of the year 1748,' to his friend 'William Lyttleton, Esq.'—

> 'Yes, there, my friend ! forlorn and sad,
>   I grave your Thomson's name ;

And there, his lyre, which Fate forbade
To sound your growing fame.'

1062. *draw the tragic scene [with juster hand]*. Thomson's first tragedy, Sophonisba, was produced at Drury Lane in Feb. 1729–30. It was rather a failure on the stage, though it passed through four editions in 1730. Agamemnon appeared in 1738, Edward and Eleanora in 1739; then came Tancred and Sigismunda (1745), and the posthumous Coriolanus.

1072. *Cobham*. The proprietor of Stowe, Sir Richard Temple, afterwards Lord Cobham. He it was that laid out the walks and gardens, planted the groves, and erected the statues and temples at Stowe,—a ' chief out of war,' to use Pope's phrase.

1072, 1073. *thy verdant files Of ordered trees shouldst ... range*. The arrangement greatly affected about the beginning and middle of last century was in the figure of the quadrum, or the quincunx, that is by fours, or perfect squares; or by fives, like the spots on the side of a die :·: In the Second Georgic Virgil describes the former arrangement :—

> ' Nec secius omnis in unguem
> Arboribus positis secto via limite quadret :
> Ut saepe ingenti bello cum longa cohortes
> Explicuit legio, et campo stetit agmen aperto,
> Directaeque acies,' &c.—ll. 277–281.

Pope, in his Satires and Epistles of Horace Imitated, refers to the quincunx :—

> ' My retreat the best companions grace,
> *Chiefs out of war*, and statesmen out of place;
> There St. John mingles with my friendly bowl
> The feast of reason and the flow of soul;
> And he, whose lightning pierced the Iberian lines
> Now forms my quincunx, and now ranks my vines.'
>
> Bk. II, Sat. I, ll. 125–130.

1093. *optic tube describes*. Cp. Par. Lost, Bk. I, ll. 288, 290.

1096. *through the passing cloud she seems to stoop*. ' Seems to descend,' that is, ' nearer to the earth.' Milton also notices the illusion—

> ' Oft, as if her head she bow'd,
> Stooping through a fleecy cloud.'
>
> *Il Penseroso*, ll. 71, 72.

See also Comus, l. 333.

1098. *the pale deluge*. Cp. ' the dazzling deluge' of sunshine in Summer, l. 435. Blake, in his lines to The Evening Star, has—' Wash the dusk with silver.'

1101, 1102. The effect of full moon is finely caught in these lines.

1106, 1107. *near extinct her deadened orb appears, And scarce appears.* This is the phenomenon, referred to in 'the grand old ballad of Sir Patrick Spens,' of 'the new moon with the old moon in her arms.'

1109-1114. This is a description of the Aurora, or Northern Lights, not of a meteoric shower. Cp. Burns, in his fragmentary Vision at Lincluden (1794) :—

> 'The cauld blae north was streaming forth
>   Her lights wi' hissing eerie din ;
> Athwart the lift they start and shift
>   Like Fortune's favours, tint as win.'

1115-1137. The first draught of this passage appeared in the first edition of Summer (1727). (See Summer, Note, l. 1698.)

1118. *Thronged with aërial spears,* &c. It recalls Milton's awful line—

> 'With dreadful faces thronged and fiery arms.'
>   *Par. Lost,* Bk. XII, l. 644.

1122, 1123. Cp. Chaucer's The Squieres Tale, ll. 204-261. Also Milton's Par. Lost, Bk. I, ll. 598, 599.

1132. That is, that the last day has arrived.

1134. *inspect sage.* Wise insight.

1136. *yet unfixed.* That is, 'till now unexplained, and unsettled.' This is very much the condition of affairs yet. That the phenomenon of the Aurora is due to electricity is generally believed, but how is still an open question.

1141-1144. The same idea has already been brought forward in this poem, ll. 730-735.

1148, 1149. See Comus, ll. 337-340, for 'the taper of some clay habitation,' &c.

1151-1164. This passage, in a somewhat different form, appeared originally in the first edition of Summer (1727). (See Summer, Note, l. 1681.)

1157-1159. Compare with this the more pathetic picture of the shepherd's wife and children, in Winter, ll. 310-317.

1183. *Convolved.* A favourite word of Thomson. See Spring, l. 836. The smoking of bees in order to secure their honey is now rarely practised. It is both more humane and more profitable to abstract honeycomb from the hive without destroying the bees.

1187. *the blooming waste.* The heather (in bloom in August and September), from which a richer honey is made than from garden flowers,

1190, 1191. *Nature groan . . . . awaiting renovation.* See St. Paul's Epistle to the Romans for this reference, chap. viii, 19-23.

1204. *Palermo.* The capital city and chief seaport of Sicily.

1211, 1212. Construe 'Save what brushes the filmy thread of eva-porated dew from the plain.' Thomson's closeness and delicacy of observation is revealed in these lines: they refer to a phenomenon of tranquil autumnal morning which few have observed. As 'the filmy thread of dew,' which has got somehow into the air, falls on one's face, one is apt to imagine that it is about to rain; but the sky all round is a sunny blue; neither is there wind to blow the dew from the hanging corn-ears.

1214, 1215. The high and wide skies of Autumn, on days of 'utter peace,' are like the creation of a new heaven.

1219. The corn-yard, or stack-y rd, securely enclosed.

1221. The festival of harvest-home:—
> 'Merriment
> Such as the jocund flute, or gamesome pipe
> Stirs up among the loose unlettered hinds
> When, for their . . . . granges full
> In wanton dance they praise the bounteous Pan.'
> *Comus*, ll. 172–176.

1222. 'The loud laugh that spoke the vacant mind.'—Goldsmith's *Deserted Village.*

1236. *The happiest he who far from public rage*, &c. Cp. Horace—
> 'Beatus ille, qui procul negotiis,
> Ut prisca gens mortalium,
> Paterna rura bobus exercet suis
> Solutus omni fenore,' &c.—*Epodon Carm.* I, 2.

1263, 1264. See *supra*, ll. 4, 5.

1267. *the chide of streams.* A beautiful expression. Shakespeare has it,—'Never did I hear such gallant chiding' (Midsummer Night's Dream, Act IV, Sc. i.), where it is said by Hippolyt in her eulogium of the Spartan breed of hounds.

1273–1277. Cp. Cowper's Task, Bk. IV, the concluding passage—'Hail therefore,' &c.

1287, 1288. This is very severe, for Thomson, on lawyers. See also ll. 1291–1294 *infra.*

1304. *who, from the world escaped.* Like Cowper, in his Olney retreat.

1317. *frigid Tempe.* See Spring, Note, l. 908.

1318. *Hemus.* See *supra*, Note, l. 784.

1326. *then [in Autumn] he best exerts his song.* See *supra*, Note, l. 670.

1339. His own affection for his sisters would serve to illustrate the line.

1341, 1342. *the little strong embrace Of prattling children twined around his neck.* Thomson must have had a child's arm round his neck, to describe ' the little *strong* embrace ' so accurately.

1348-1351. See the Age of Innocence fully described in Spring, ll. 241-270.

1353. *the knowledge of thy works.* He enumerates more particularly, in the succeeding lines, astronomy, geology, botany, natural history, and psychology. His love of the study of natural science is abundantly evident from his poetry. It was probably instilled into his mind at Edinburgh University, where the Baconian and Newtonian impulse was felt more powerfully in the first half of the 18th century than it seems to have been felt at the English Universities. (See Sir A. Grant's Hist. of Edinburgh University, vol. i, pp. 263 *et seqq.*)

1368. An allusion to his natural indolence. It was the alternative that was in store for Thomson—not vast and varied scientific knowledge ; but a place ' by the lowly brook '—' in lowly dale fast by a river's side ' —and a dream of a Castle of Indolence.

WINTER.

INTRODUCTORY NOTE.

Winter, placed last—agreeably to the natural order—in the col-lected Seasons, comes first in the order of composition, and perhaps of merit and popularity as well. It was entirely written in England. Thomson arrived in London in March, 1725. Disappointed in the immediate object of his journey, whatever it was—probably a situation in the service of the Government—he was forced by the slenderness of his purse to accept the office of tutor to a small boy of five, and mean-while prepare for a less precarious and more honourable means of maintenance. Writing in July to an intimate friend in Scotland, he says ' —' I am pretty much at ease in the country, ten miles from London, teaching Lord Binning's son[1] to read—a low task, you know, not so suitable to my temper ; but I must learn that necessary lesson of suiting my mind and temper to my state. I hope I shall not pass my time here without improvement—the great design of my coming hither —and then, in due time, I resolve through God's assistance to consum-mate my original study of divinity ; for you know the business of a

---

[1] Afterwards seventh Earl of Haddington.

tutor is only precarious and for the present.' The place referred to in this letter as ten miles from London was East Barnet; and here Thomson continued (with an occasional flying visit to London) to reside till the end of the year, by which time he seems to have finished together the first draught, at least, if not the full composition, of Winter, and his engagement as tutor in Lord Binning's family. He cannot be said to have begun the poem till the end of Autumn, when he was prompted to the work by the nature—one might say the necessity—of his situation. The subject had been determined for him by a variety of causes. He writes bravely enough on the manner in which he found and first began to work at his subject, but his mind was undoubtedly then disposed to a gloomier view of life than was habitual to him, and to less cheerful subjects of contemplation than had engaged his attention in the preceding Spring. He had not been in England more than six weeks when he received the sad news of the death of his mother, to whom he was tenderly attached; at Barnet he had run into debt, and was feeling as a strange sensation the first pressure of poverty; the 'melancholy' natural to his spirits 'on the fading of the year,' was of a deeper shade in the October of 1725 [1] than he had ever known it, or perhaps was ever again to know; and the influence of a poem by Robert Riccaltoun, every whit as lugubrious as The Grave of Blair, had filled his imagination with a gloom only too congenial with his circumstances, and cherished rather than chidden away by the desponding young poet. In the autumn of 1725, in another letter to his intimate friend (Dr. Cranstoun, of Ancrum) he writes: 'I am just now painting [Nature] in her most lugubrious dress for my own amusement, describing Winter as it presents itself. . . . After this introduction I say—

> "Nor can I, O departing Summer! choose
> But consecrate one pitying line to you;
> Sing your last tempered days, and sunny calms,
> That cheer the spirits and serene the soul."

Then terrible floods, and high winds, that usually happen about this time of the year, and have already happened here (I wish you have not felt them too dreadfully)—the first produced the enclosed lines; the last are not completed. Mr. Riccaltoun's poem on Winter, which I still have, first put the design into my head : in it are some masterly strokes that awakened me. Being only a present amusement it is ten to one

[1] 'This country I am in is not very entertaining; no variety but that of woods.'

but I drop it whenever another fancy comes across.' Riccaltoun's
poem, from this interesting connection, acquires an importance of some
historical value. It has been identified, on evidence that is almost
conclusive, with a set of some fifty-eight verses in the heroic couplet
'by a Scotch clergyman,' printed in 1726 in Savage's Miscellany, and
again, in 1740, in The Gentleman's Magazine for May, under the title
of 'A Winter's Day.' Thomson's copy of the poem was probably got
in MS. from the author's own hand; but it may have been a cutting
from an Edinburgh periodical of date anterior to 1726. Riccaltoun was
a young farmer at Earlshaugh, some four miles from the manse of
Southdean, when Thomson was a schoolboy; and, having a taste for
the classics, for he was college-bred, and taking a fancy to the minister's
son, he gave him help with his Latin lessons and exercises. He afterwards became minister of the parish of Hobkirk, near Jedburgh. The
influence of the following quotations from Riccaltoun's verses will
readily be traced in Thomson's poem :—

> 'Now, gloomy soul, look out! now comes thy turn!
> With thee, behold all ravaged Nature mourn;
> Hail the dim empire of thy darling night
> That spreads slow-shadowing o'er the vanquished light.
> Look out with joy! The ruler of the day,
> Faint as thy hopes, emits a glimmering ray;
> Already exiled to the utmost sky,
> Hither oblique he turns his clouded eye.
> Lo, from the limits of the wintry pole
> Mountainous clouds in rude confusion roll;
> In dismal pomp now hovering in their way,
> To a sick twilight they reduce the day.'—ll. 1-12.

> 'Let no intrusive joy my dead repose
> Disturb;   .   .   .   .   .   .
> In this moss-covered cavern hopeless laid
> On the cold cliff I lean my aching head
> And, pleased with winter's waste, unpitying see
> All Nature in an agony with me.
> Rough rugged rocks, wet marshes, ruined tours,
> Bare trees, brown brakes, bleak heaths, and rushy moors,
> Dead floods, huge cataracts, to my pleasèd eyes
> (Now I can smile!) in wild disorder rise;

And now, their various dreadfulness combined,
Black melancholy comes to doze my mind.'—ll. 33-44.

'But hark! a sudden howl invades my ear—
The phantoms of the dreadful hour are near;
Shadows from each dark cavern now combine,
And stalk around, and mix their yells with mine!'—ll. 51-54.

Thomson's chief, if not his only, literary correspondent during the composition of Winter was his former college companion at Edinburgh, David Malloch (or Mallet as he strangely preferred to be called), who in 1725, and for several years afterwards, was tutor to the two sons of the Duke of Montrose [1]. Spence, in his Anecdotes, &c.,has preserved a rumour that Thomson went down to live at Twyford, in Hants, a country seat of the Duke of Montrose, on the invitation of Malloch, and that while there he submitted to Malloch's judgment the MS. of Winter; that the friends had some difficulty in finding a publisher for it; and that, when it appeared at last, the Dedication was the composition of Malloch.

The publisher of Winter was John Millan, who gave the author three guineas for it; and the poem was issued in folio in March, 1726. Presently it began to be talked about in the London coffee-houses as a genuine poem on a new and original subject—the person who was first to discover its merits being the Rev. Robert Whatley. Almost as soon as Whatley, Aaron Hill [2] began to sound its praise; and there was a recommendation of it by Spence in his Essay on Pope's Odyssey, published in 1727. The rate of its success may be estimated from the facts that the second edition was called for in the following June, and that the fifth edition was out before the end of 1728. It brought Thomson the friendship of—among others—Lady Hertford, Mrs. Stanley, Dr. Rundle, and Sir C. Talbot.

Malloch may have written the prose Dedication, which was addressed to the Right Hon. Sir Spencer Compton, Speaker of the House of Commons, but Thomson unfortunately homologated it in a paraphrase of its extravagant statements to which he gave a permanent place in the

---

[1] See a curious poem 'To Mr. David Malloch on his Departure from Scotland,' by Allan Ramsay :—
                'The task assigned thee 's great and good
                    To cultivate two Grahams,' &c.
[2] 'You have given me fame,' was the acknowledgment of Thomson in a letter to Hill on May 24, 1726.

text of the poem. The prose Dedication was prefixed to the first five
editions of Winter : it ran as follows—

' Sir,—The Author of the following poem begs leave to inscribe this
his first performance to your name and patronage : unknown himself,
and only introduced by the Muse, he yet ventures to approach you with
a modest cheerfulness ; for, whoever attempts to excel in any generous
art, though he comes alone and unregarded by the world, may hope for
your notice and esteem. Happy if I can in any degree merit this good
fortune. As every ornament and grace of polite learning is yours, your
single approbation will be my fame.

' I dare not indulge my heart by dwelling on your public character,—
on that exalted honour and integrity which distinguish you in that
august assembly where you preside, that unshaken loyalty to your
sovereign, that disinterested concern for his people which shine out
united in all your behaviour and finish the patriot. I am conscious of
my want of strength and skill for so delicate an undertaking ; and yet,
as the shepherd in his cottage may feel and acknowledge the influence
of the sun, with as lively a gratitude as the great man in his palace,
even I may be allowed to publish my sense of those blessings which,
from so many powerful virtues, are derived to the nation they adorn.

' I conclude with saying that your fine discernment and humanity
in your private capacity are so conspicuous that if this address is
not received with some indulgence, it will be a severe conviction
that what I have written has not the least share of merit. I am,' &c.

This is fulsome. The fulsomeness, conscious or ignorant of its nature,
Thomson unhappily adopted ; but it is also stilted, insincere, and im-
pudent. The audacity of the concluding sentence was foreign to the
character of Thomson.

The second, third, and fourth editions of Winter contained a preface
of Thomson's own composition, which one might describe as the
poet's apology for poesy, or rather his vindication of poetry. It is
pervaded by a nobility of sentiment and an independence of tone, which
are in marked contrast to the effrontery and servility of Malloch's
Dedication. It begins—

' I am neither ignorant, nor concerned, how much one may suffer, in
the opinion of several persons of great gravity and character, by the
study and pursuit of poetry. Although there may seem to be some
appearance of reason for the present contempt of it, as managed by the

most part of our modern writers, yet that any man should seriously declare against that divine art is really amazing. It is declaring against the most charming power of imagination, the most exalting force of thought, the most affecting touch of sentiment; in a word, against the very soul of all learning and politeness. It is affronting the universal taste of mankind, and declaring against what has charmed the listening world from Moses down to Milton. . . . It is even declaring against the sublimest passages of the inspired writings themselves, and what seems to be the peculiar language of heaven.' Then follows some well-directed satire, and the poet continues: 'That there are frequent and notorious abuses of Poetry is as true as that the best things are most liable to that misfortune; but . . . let poetry once more be restored to her ancient truth and purity; let her be inspired from heaven, and, in return, her incense ascend thither; let her exchange her low, venal, trifling subjects for such as are fair, useful, and magnificent . . . and poets [shall] yet become the delight and wonder of mankind. But this happy period is not to be expected till some long-wished, illustrious man, of equal power and beneficence, rise on the wintry world of letters—one of a genuine and unbounded greatness and generosity of mankind, who, far above all the pomp and pride of fortune, scorns the little addressful flatterer, discountenances all the reigning fopperies of a tasteless age, and . . . stretching his views into late futurity, has the true interest of virtue, learning and mankind entirely at heart—a character so nobly desirable that, to an honest heart it is almost incredible so few should have the ambition to deserve it. Nothing can have a better influence towards the revival of poetry than the choosing of great and serious subjects.' There are some more satirical remarks on 'the little glittering prettinesses' of the fashionable verse of the day, from which the poet turns with a noble scorn—'A genius,' he says, 'fired with the charms of truth and nature is tuned to a sublimer pitch, and scorns to associate with such subjects.' He goes on to recommend to poets and readers of poetry a return to the study of Nature, too long neglected; and exclaims, after a brief survey of the grander phenomena of Nature,—'But there is no thinking of these things without breaking out into poetry.' He next refers to the example of 'the best poets, both ancient and modern.' Whence did they derive their inspiration? 'They have been passionately fond of retirement and solitude: the wild romantic country was their delight.' There are two or three

unavoidable compliments—to ‘Mr. Hill,’ ‘Mira,’ and ‘Mr. Malloch’;
and the Preface concludes with the announcement that the reforms, in
poetical composition and in poetical taste, which he has just been
urging, he will endeavour himself to practise ‘in the other Seasons,’
which it is his ‘purpose’ to describe.

Winter, which is the shortest poem of the series of The Seasons, was
very considerably shorter still when it first appeared. So late as the
edition of 1738 it consisted of only 787 lines; it was finally enlarged to
1069. The principal additions were a paraphrase (ll. 126-145) of a
part of the First Georgic of Virgil; a description (ll. 414-423) of
avalanches; an enlargement of the list of Greek and Roman Worthies;
the lament for Hammond (ll. 555-571); a eulogy of Chesterfield; an
extension of the view of life and Winter within the Arctic circle; and a
eulogistic outline of the career of the Czar Peter. Numerous verbal
alterations were made in the text after 1738, some of them at the
suggestion of Pope; and several lines were dropped. The geographical
range of the poem is only inferior to that of Summer. The best scenes
are Scottish. Holland, France, Italy, and Switzerland furnish impressive
Winter scenes; Siberia and Lapland are graphically presented; and a
glimpse is given, in a flight beyond Iceland and Greenland, of the
white terrors at the Pole. The historical range is a remarkable,
and a not very harmonious feature of the poem. Long winter evenings
are, no doubt, conducive to retirement and study; and the history
of the world's great leaders, in the spheres of thought and action,
may naturally enough form part of one's winter reading; but the
subject, thanks very much to Pope, is treated at unconscionable length,
and receives a prominence relatively to the other parts of the poem
which is quite disproportionate, and (some may be pardoned for
thinking) of the nature of an excrescence.

Perhaps the most poetical passages are those that describe a wet day
at the farm; a river in flood; the visit of the redbreast; a shepherd
perishing in the snow-drift, with the pathetic picture of his wife and
children becoming concerned about his absence; ‘the goblin-story’
told by village fires; the still, freezing night; and the Siberian bear
‘with dangling ice all horrid.’ The clearness and completeness of
these descriptions strike the imagination at once, and the singular
appropriateness of the language imprints them on the memory.

It is to be regretted that in his list of winter sports Thomson did not include a description of the Scots game of curling, 'the roaring play' of Burns.

The argument as amended for the final text runs as follows:—' The subject proposed. Address to the Earl of Wilmington. First approach of Winter. According to the natural course of the Season, various storms described—rain, wind, snow. The driving of the snows—a man perishing among them; whence reflections on the wants and miseries of human life. The wolves descending from the Alps and Apennines. A Winter evening described—as spent by philosophers; by the country people; in the city. Frost. A view of Winter within the Polar circle. A thaw. The whole concluding with moral reflections on a future state.'

Gulliver's Travels, by Swift, Butler's Sermons, and Dyer's Grongar Hill, were, with Thomson's Winter, the principal London publications of the year 1726. Addison, Defoe, Bentley, and Theobald also published works in the same year.

A curious story connected with the Dedication may be added. Lord Wilmington, then Sir Spencer Compton, and Speaker of the Commons, took no notice of the honour which had been done him till the first edition was almost exhausted. The neglect displeased Thomson, and roused the satire of Hill and Malloch against the indifference of patrons. Hill's reproaches were communicated to the Speaker, and were so far effective that the compliment of the Dedication was at last acknowledged by a fee of twenty guineas. Thomson's account of his interview with his patron, and the way in which it was more immediately brought about, is contained in a letter to Hill:—' On Saturday morning [June 4, 1726] I was with Sir Spencer Compton. A certain gentleman, without my desire, spoke to him concerning me; his answer was that I had never come near him. Then the gentleman put the question if he desired that I should wait on him; he returned he did. On this the gentleman gave me an introductory letter to him. He received me in what they commonly call a civil manner, asked me some commonplace questions, and made me a present of twenty guineas. I am very ready to own that the present was larger than my performance [he means, not the poem, but the Dedication as a piece of complimentary composition—usually attributed to Malloch!] deserved; and shall ascribe it to his generosity rather than the merit of the Address.' Meanwhile both Hill and Malloch had written verses to the praise of Thomson and

A a

the censure of the Speaker, which were intended to be prefixed to the second edition of Winter then in the press. Thomson either did not wish to lose the praise or did not wish to offend his friends by withdrawing the verses, and they were accordingly printed with but slight modification of the censure—certainly not enough 'to clear Sir Spencer.' Thomson's correspondence shows very amusingly the dilemma he was in.

---

1. The year has lost its autumnal look, and now assumes a wintry aspect. More figuratively, the reign of autumn is over; it is now Winter's turn to rule. 'The varied year' means 'the year that has varied, or changed its appearance,' and not 'the year that is varied by the succession of the seasons.' The idea contained in 'varied' is repeated at l. 43 in the word 'inverted.' It simply means 'altered,' or 'so altered as to exhibit a complete contrast.'

2. *rising.* Ascending from the horizon.

3. *Vapours, and clouds, and storms.* See ll. 54-56, *infra*.

6. *Congenial horrors.* Some trace the congeniality, avowed here so boldly, to the peculiar circumstances—of disappointment, loneliness, bereavement, and even poverty—in which Thomson was placed when he began the poem. They imagine him making choice of a subject of 'glooms' and 'horrors' much in the same mood as that which made Burns exclaim—

> 'Come, Winter, with thine angry howl,
>   And, raging, bend the naked tree;
> Thy *gloom* will soothe my cheerless soul,
>   When Nature all is sad like me!'—*Meenie's ee.*

They perhaps overlook the fact (stated in the immediately succeeding lines) that Winter-time had always been a pleasure to him: it was equally congenial to his cheerful, careless, robust boyhood. He could say with Burns—

> 'O Nature, a' thy shows and forms
> To feeling, pensive hearts ha'e charms;
> Whether the summer kindly warms
>   Wi' life and light,
> Or winter howls in gusty storms
>   The long dark night.'
>   *Epistle to William Simson.*

Probably by 'congenial' Thomson simply means the horrors and glooms of the Cheviot winters, to which he had been accustomed from his infancy; he had grown up amongst them.

7. *my cheerful morn of life.* From the third month to the sixteenth year of his life, his home was the solitary manse of Southdean in Roxburghshire, not more than five miles, as the crow flies, from Carter Fell, one of the summits of the Cheviots.

9. *sung of Nature.* Delighted in rural scenes. But there may be a reference to his boyish exercises in verse, which were probably on subjects connected for the most part with country life.

12–14. All this he could do at the door, or from the parlour window, of his father's manse. The Jed sweeps round the manse garden, and is a sufficiently 'big torrent' when in flood.

14. *the grim evening sky.* 'Red,' meaning 'lurid,' in the early editions, as late as that of 1738.

15. *the lucid chambers of the south.* A beautiful phrase, partly scriptural. See the Book of Job: '[He is mighty in strength] which maketh . . . the chambers of the south.' (chap. ix. 9). Cp. William Blake's To the Muses :—

> 'Whether on Ida's shady brow,
>   Or in the chambers of the East,
> The chambers of the sun, that now
>   From ancient melody have ceased,' &c.

See Spring, l. 1034.

17. *first essay.* The poem of Winter, though it comes last in the collected Seasons, was the first written of the series. It was published in 1726; Summer came next, in 1727; then Spring, in 1728; and Autumn, with the Hymn, last of all, published, in its due place in the natural order, with the other Seasons, in 1730.

18. *Wilmington.* Sir Spencer Compton, created Baron Wilmington in January, 1728; Earl, in May, 1730. He was born probably in the year 1673; and began his long parliamentary career in 1698 as the Member for Eye. A son of the Earl of Northampton, he belonged to a Tory family, but joined the Whigs, and was rewarded with a long succession of honourable appointments. The new Parliament of 1715 elected him their Speaker; he was then the representative for Sussex. In 1722 he was again chosen Speaker, and filled the chair till the dissolution of Parliament in July, 1727. He held at the same time the office of Paymaster-General; and was made a Knight of the Bath in 1725. In 1727 he might have been Prime Minister instead of Walpole, but confessed to the King 'his inability to undertake the duties of so arduous a post.' He had made a similar confession when he filled the office of Speaker, declaring that 'he had neither memory to retain,

judgment to collect, nor skill to guide the debates of the Commons.'
Public opinion took him at his word : he was generally regarded as a
mere cipher, and treated as such by the caricaturists and satirical writers
of his time. Yet he was not without dignity, especially on State
occasions, and secured some respect by the solemnity of his manner and
the impressive tones of his voice. His talents, however, were but
mediocre, and he lacked both tact and decision. His peerage came to
him rather as a solatium for the premiership he could not fill, than as a
reward for his services. He died unmarried in 1743, and the title lapsed.
His estates went to his brother, the Earl of Northampton. Thomson's
eulogy of him (ll. 28–40) is a remarkable instance either of gross
flattery or of crass ignorance.

renews her song. The expression means that Thomson repeats to
Lord Wilmington the dedication he had addressed to him when Sir
Spencer Compton four years previously. The dedication of the first
edition of Winter was in prose, and, according to Joseph Spence, was
written by Malloch. The passage, from l. 17 to l. 40, is the new
dedication, introduced into the text of Winter, in 1730, when the first
edition of the collected Seasons was published; the prose dedication,
which had appeared in the first five editions of Winter—all published
before the end of 1728—was, of course, no longer necessary. (See
Introductory Note to Winter.)

19. *Since,* i.e. since 1726. The date is now 1730. In the interval
he had completed The Seasons.

20. *Skimmed the gay Spring.* 'The Muse,' or his own poetical
imagination, is here presented under the metaphor of a swallow.

21. *Attempted through the Summer blaze to rise.* Summer is certainly
the most laboured of the series.

26. Well illustrated by the passage ending l. 105, *infra.*

28, 29. *Thrice happy, could she fill thy judging ear,* &c. 'Happy, if
I can in any degree merit this good fortune [*your notice and esteem*].
As every ornament and grace of polite learning is yours, your single
approbation will be my fame.'—*Prose Dedication* (1726).

30. For this line the editions from 1730 to 1738 give the following
three :—

> 'For thee the graces smoothe; thy softer thoughts
> The Muses tune ; nor art thou skilled alone
> In awful schemes, the management of states.'

32–38. 'I dare not indulge my heart, by dwelling on your public
character ; on that exalted honour and integrity which distinguish you in
that august assembly where you preside ; that unshaken loyalty to your
sovereign, that disinterested concern for his people, which shine out

united in all your behaviour, and finish the patriot.'—*Prose Dedication.* If Malloch wrote the prose dedication (it is little to his honour) Thomson unfortunately appropriated its sentiments in this outrageous panegyric. The verses are a scarcely disguised paraphrase of Malloch's sycophantic sentences.

41–44. In all editions up to 1738 these lines read—

<blockquote>
'When Scorpio gives to Capricorn the sway,
And fierce Aquarius fouls the inverted year,
Retiring to the verge of heaven, the sun,' &c.;
</blockquote>

in plain English, 'In mid-winter, the sun,' &c.

42. This method of marking time is a survival from the days of Chaucer. (See the opening verses of the Prologue to the Canterbury Tales.) Thomson is the latest poet of note in our literary history to maintain the traditional method. The sun enters the zodiacal sign of the Archer (*Sagittarius*) on the 21st November, and quits it, to enter the sign of the Horned Goat (*Capricornus*), on the shortest day, the 21st of December; the next sign (*Aquarius*, the Water-carrier) is entered on the 21st January. (See Spring, Note, ll. 26, 27.)

43. *the inverted year.* Cp. Cowper's Task (published 1785)—

<blockquote>
'O winter! ruler of the inverted year.'—Bk. IV. l. 120.
</blockquote>

Horace has the whole line in the first Book of his Satires (v. 36)—

<blockquote>
'Quae [*formica parvula*], simul inversum contristat Aquarius annum,' &c.
</blockquote>

See Note, l. 1, *supra.* 'To invert the year' is explained in some verses by Malloch, quoted by Thomson in a letter Sept. or Oct. 1726—'to bring wild Winter into Summer's place.'

48. *clothed in cloudy storm.* In 1738 and previous editions,—'at dull distance seen.'

49, 50. Cp. Burns—

<blockquote>
'Phoebus gi'es a short-lived glower,
Far south the lift.'—*A Winter Night.*
</blockquote>

57. *the face of things.* A common expression with Thomson and his imitators; Malloch, for example (referring to lightning),—

<blockquote>
'Now the face of things
Disclosing; swallowed now in tenfold night.'
</blockquote>

The Excursion, Bk. I.

64. *Fresh from the plough.* In the earlier editions (till 1738), 'Red from,' &c. Land may either be 'stirred' by the plough in November, or it may be ploughed to prepare a seed-bed for the winter wheat.

65. *crop the wholesome root.* Turnips, thrown down on the new ploughed land for sheep. But turnips did not become a common crop, even on English farms, till the success of Lord Townshend's experiments, in 1730, was seen. See Autumn, Note, ll. 913-915.

66-71. These lines were probably written at Barnet, near London. 'This country I am in is not very entertaining; no variety but that of woods, and them we have in abundance; but where is the living stream, the airy mountain, or the hanging rock?'—*Letter from Thomson to Dr. William Cranstoun, at Ancrum, near Jedburgh, September*, 1725. It is evident that when he wrote them his imagination was among Cheviot scenery and the horrors of a Cheviot winter.

71. 'That haunts the imagination.' *Listening* seems to be re- dundant.

73. *Wrapt in black glooms.* Better in the earlier text (till 1738)— 'Striding the gloomy blast,' an image perhaps suggested by Shake- speare—

> 'Pity, like a naked new-born babe,
> Striding the blast,' &c.—*Macbeth*, Act I. Sc. vii.

First, joyless rains obscure. Here begins a description of a Winter rain-storm and its effects; it continues to l. 110. A description of a Winter wind-storm and its effects follows—to l. 222; to be in turn succeeded by a description of a snowstorm and its effects, ending at l. 321.

74. *with vapour foul.* 'Foul' replaces 'vile' in the earlier text. As an adjective, it qualifies 'vapour'—not 'skies.'

85. *with meaning low.* 'Lowing for the shelter of their stalls and for the food there provided for them.' The form in the earlier text is 'lowe.'

86. Cp. Cowper's Task, Bk. V, ll. 27-30.

89-93. The scene here depicted is a cosy cottage interior, forming with its group of rustics, talking and laughing beside a bright fire, a complete contrast to the misery of the poultry and the cheerless winter weather prevailing without. It is the condition of rustic life in winter-time so beautifully suggested by Horace, Car. I. 4—'jam stabulis gaudet pecus *et* arator igni.' Only, the Scottish poet leaves the cattle 'asking for their stalls' or 'ruminating' under a shed in the farmyard. Cp. for the hind's happy oblivion of the storm, Burns's description of Tam o' Shanter in the alehouse at Ayr:—

> 'Ae market-night
> Tam had got planted unco right
> Fast by an ingle, bleezing finely,
> Wi' reaming swats, that drank divinely. . . .
> The night drave on wi' sangs an' clatter,
> And aye the ale was growing better; . . .
> The souter tauld his queerest stories,
> The landlord's laugh was ready chorus:

The storm without might rair and rustle,
Tam didna mind the storm a whistle.'—ll. 37–52.

90. *taleful there.* Recounting by the fire such country stories and gossip as the Scots poet, Fergusson (1750–1774), suggests in his Farmer's Ingle.

94–105. This description—of a river in flood, or, as they say in Scotland, 'in spate'—is characteristic of Thomson's style when he is handling a congenial subject : it is bold, graphic, and instantly suggestive of the whole scene. Cp. Burns's Brigs of Ayr :—

' When heavy, dark, continued, a'-day rains
Wi' deepening deluges o'erflow the plains ;
When from the hills where springs the brawling Coil,
Or stately Lugar's mossy fountains boil, . . .
Aroused by blustering winds and spotting thowes,
In mony a torrent down the snaw-broo rowes ;
While crashing ice, borne on the roaring spate,
Sweeps dams, an' mills, an' brigs, a' to the gate,
And, from Glenbuck down to the Ratton-key,
Auld Ayr is just one lengthened tumbling sea,' &c.
ll. 88–100 (Clarendon Press ed.)

94-96. Construe—' The roused-up river, swelled with many a torrent and with the mixed ruin of its overspread banks, at last pours along widely over its brim.' *The mixed ruin of its banks* : such as mills and bridges and embankments (see Burns, as quoted above), &c. The river here described is doubtless the Tweed, or one of its tributaries.

98. *rude.* ' Chapt' in the early editions.

109, 110. Perhaps no poet had a keener or more appreciative sense of the sublime in Nature than Thomson. His genius, says John Wilson, 'loves to paint on a great scale, and to dash objects off sweepingly by bold strokes.' He sets Nature rather 'before your imagination' than before your eyes. He 'paints woods—not trees ; paints in a few wondrous lines rivers from source to sea.'

113. *powerful beings.* ' Subtile ' in the earlier text.

115. For this line the earlier text gives—

' Against the day of tempest perilous.'

118, 119. Added after 1738. The next line opened the passage, and ran—

' Late in the louring sky red fiery streaks.'

125. *a wan circle round her blunted horns.* In the earlier text— 'her sullied orb.' The ring, or halo, is often a prognostic of stormy weather. In Longfellow's Wreck of the Hesperus—

'Up and spake an old sailor
    Had sailed the Spanish main,
"I pray thee put into yonder port
    For I fear a hurricane;

Last night the moon had a golden ring,
    To-night no moon we see."'

126-145. The whole of this passage, except l. 127 and l. 130 (where, however, 'fluttering straw' was used for 'withered leaf'), was introduced after the edition of 1738. Much of it seems to be a recollection or a copy of the First Georgic of Virgil : cp. for example, with Thomson's text—

(*a*) 'Saepe etiam stellas vento impendente videbis
    Praecipites caelo labi, noctisque per umbram
    Flammarum longos a tergo albescere tractus:
    Saepe levem paleam et frondes volitare caducas,
    Aut summa nantes in aqua colludere plumas.'—ll. 365-369.

(*b*)   'Aut bucula caelum
    Suspiciens patulis captavit naribus auras.'—ll. 375, 376.

(*c*) 'Cum medio celeres revolant ex aequore mergi (*cormorants*)
    Clamoremque ferunt ad litora.'—ll. 361, 362.

(*d*)   'Notasque paludes
    Deserit atque altam supra volat ardea (*heron*) nubem.'
                                                    ll. 363, 364.

(*e*)   'E pastu decedens agmine magno
    Corvorum increpuit densis exercitus alis.'—ll. 381, 382.

(*f*) 'Ne nocturna quidem carpentes pensa puellae
    Nescivere hiemem,' &c.—ll. 390, 391.

134, 135. *Even.* Demonstr. of 'taper.' The housewife is spinning from a distaff. The flaws, or little gusts of air, that precede a wind-storm, making straws and leaves 'play' in 'eddies,' enter the spinster's cottage, and make her candle gutter, or run, and the flame on her hearth emit the crackling sound referred to.

140. *blackening train.* Burns has the same phrase in The Cotter's Saturday Night :—

'And blackening trains o' craws to their repose.'

142. *closing shelter.* Enclosed, snug.

143. *Assiduous in his bower the wailing owl.* 'Assiduous,' literally 'sitting at'; hence 'ceaseless'—as in l. 184, *infra.* Cp. Gray—

'From yonder ivy-mantled tower
The moping owl does to the moon complain.'—*Elegy.*

144. *cormorant.* Fr. *cormoran* ; Lat. *corvus marinus,* the sea-crow, —the *t* being excrescent. The Breton word for 'sea-crow' is *morvran,* from *mor,* sea, and *bran,* crow. (Prof. Skeat.) In Lat., *mergus* is the sea-crow.

153–155. In the original text—
  'Then issues forth the storm with mad control,
   And the thin fabric of the pillared air
   O'erturns at once.'

157. A daring hyberbole.

158. Adopted at the suggestion of Pope, as a substitute for—
  'Through the loud night that bids the waves arise.'

160–163. Originally—that is, in all editions till after that of 1738—
  'Seems, as it sparkles, all around to burn.
   Meantime, whole oceans, heaving to the clouds,
   And in broad billows rolling gathered seas,
  Surge over surge, burst in a general roar,' &c.

166. *inflated.* In the early text 'hilly'; while at l. 169 'full-blown' stood for ' wintry.'

175. Instead of this opening the earlier text gives—
  'Nor raging here alone unreined at sea,
   To land the tempest bears; and o'er the cliff
   Where screams the seamew, foaming unconfined,
   Fierce swallows up the long-resounding shore.
   The mountain growls; and all its sturdy sons,' &c.

178. The introduction of the lone wayfarer gives a distinctly human interest to the description.

182. *honours.* Foliage. 'December . . . silvis honorem excutit.'— Hor. *Ep.* XI, 5–6.

191–194. A feeling for the supernatural, probably of Scottish growth, was an essential feature of Thomson's genius. See Autumn, Note, ll. 1030–1036; Summer, ll. 538–564; and elsewhere. Burns refers to the abundance of tales and songs in rural Scotland 'concerning devils, ghosts, fairies, brownies, witches, warlocks, spunkies, kelpies, elf-candles, dead-lights, wraiths, apparitions, cantrips . . . and other trumpery;' and owned their effect upon his imagination to have been so strong that, to the end of his life, in his nocturnal rambles, he found himself 'keeping a sharp look-out in suspicious places.' (Letter to Dr. Moore, Aug. 2, 1787.) What was true of Burns and his day, was certainly not less true of Thomson and his. The expression of the feeling here heightens the horror of the scene—a plain with its awakened hamlets and country houses in the wild possession of the midnight wind.

198. Cp. Milton—

> 'How oft amidst
> Thick clouds and dark doth Heaven's all-ruling sire
> Choose to reside, his glory unobscured,
> And with the majesty of darkness round
> Covers his throne, from whence deep thunders roar,
> Mustering their rage, and Heaven resembles Hell!'
>
> *Par. Lost,* Bk. II. ll. 263-268.

199. 'Who walketh upon the wings of the wind.'—Psalm civ. 3.

200. *commands a calm.* See Mark, iv. 39.

204. *while the drowsy world lies lost in sleep.* Thomson's favourite time for reflection and the composition of poetry was at midnight.

208. *meddling senses.* Distracting the contemplative soul.

217-222. The cheerfully serious piety of Thomson, his strong sense of the filial relation of man to the Great Father of us all, are well exhibited in his Prayer. The Scottish Church lost a great man in Thomson. Probably the gain was all the greater to English literature.

218. With Socrates, Thomson believed that a perfect knowledge of virtue meant the practice of virtue.

220, 221. See Matthew, iv. 4: 'Man shall not live by bread alone,' &c.

221. *conscious peace.* Peace of conscience: an enlightened or rational consciousness of peace of mind.

228. *And the sky saddens with the gathered storm.* Cp. Summer, l. 979—

> 'And Mecca saddens at the long delay.'

232. Originally—'Sudden the fields,' which artistically suggests the transformation to a white world. Unfortunately Thomson preferred in the later editions to be instructive, and substituted 'cherished,' i.e. 'protected' by the snow.

235. *Low the woods,* &c. Cp. Horace's 'Silvae laborantes.'—*Car.* I. 9.

239. *one wild ... waste.* A favourite form of phrase with Thomson. Thus l. 270, *infra,* 'one wide waft'; Britannia, l. 230, 'one wide flash'; and elsewhere.

240-245. Cp. Pope—

> 'Is thine alone the seed that strews the plain?
> The birds of heaven shall vindicate their grain.
> Thine the full harvest of the golden year?
> Part pays, and justly, the deserving steer.'
>
> *Essay on Man,* III, ll. 37-40 (published 1732-4).

240. *the labourer-ox.* Milton has—'the laboured ox,' coming with loose traces from the furrow (*Comus,* l. 291). See Spring, Note, l. 35.

241, 242. *demands The fruit of all his toil.* Has a rightful claim, in the period of his enforced idleness, on part of the produce of his own Spring and Autumn toil.

244. *The winnowing store.* The barn. After the sheaves were threshed by the flail—an ordinary winter task in the old farm-towns, and performed in the barn—next came the slow process of winnowing, which was done by throwing up the grain by means of shovels or sieves, while a current of air passing over the threshing-floor, between two opposite doors, blew away the chaff. While these operations of threshing and winnowing went on in winter time in the barn, the doorways were besieged by fowls, pigeons, wild birds, &c., which picked up and fought for the stray corn. Winnowing by shovel was displaced by winnowing with *fanners,* the invention in 1737 of a farmer called Andrew Rodger, who, curiously enough, belonged to Thomson's native county of Roxburgh. Even the fanners are now regarded as old-world implements. (It is right to notice that Knight, in his Pict. Hist. of England, gives the credit of the invention to the Dutch, and refers the introduction of it into England to the year 1710.)

   claim the little boon. Cp. Burns—

          'I doubtna, whyles, but thou may thieve?
          What then, poor beastie? thou maun live;
          A daimen icker in a thrave[1]
                'S a sma' request.
          I'll get a blessing wi' the lave
                And never miss 't.'—*To a Field-Mouse.*

245–256. The picture of the redbreast helping himself to the table crumbs is a charming vignette which, for clearness and accuracy of drawing, Thomson has nowhere surpassed. The simplicity of the language admirably befits the subject. Note 'askance' and 'slender.'

246. *sacred to the household gods.* Dear to domestic tradition; a favourite or pet of the household. See the nursery ballad The Babes in the Wood; also Webster's Vittoria Corombona (The White Devil)—

          'Call for the robin-redbreast and the wren,
                Since o'er shady groves they hover,
                And with leaves and flowers do cover
          The friendless bodies of unburied men.'

257–260. *The hare . . . . the garden seeks.* So Burns—

          'And hunger'd maukin 's ta'en her way
                To kailyards green,
          While faithless snaws ilk step betray
                Where she has been.'—*The Vision,* I, ll. 3–6.

---

[1] A few stray ears from every other shock.

261–263. *The bleating kind Eye the bleak heaven,* &c. Cp. Scott—
          ' In meek despondency they eye
          The withered sward and wintry sky.'
                              Marmion, Canto I. Introduction.

266. *Baffle the raging year.* To 'baffle' is to 'foil,' with, in the
original, a sense of disgrace. ' Baugh,' a word still in use among the
Scottish peasantry, is cognate, and signifies ' dull,' ' deficient in smoothness or briskness '; ice is said to become ' baugh' when the frost gives
way,—the edge or sharpness is taken off.

267. *food at will.* So that they may have it when they wish.

267, 268. *lodge them below the storm, And watch them strict.* Place
them where they will not be exposed to the winter wind, in the valley, or
on the lee-side of the hill ; and take care that in the sheltered place they
do not suffer from the danger peculiar to such a shelter—the danger of
being snowed up, or smothered with drifted snow.

271. *In one wide waft.* A vast blanket of snow, thrown upon them,
and burying them under its thick and weighty folds.

273. *whelms.* Take in composition with ' o'er ' in l. 269 ; and construe—' And the billowy tempest o'erwhelms the hapless flocks,' &c.
But probably Thomson uses the word as equivalent to the Scottish term
' whummles,' meaning 'tumbles up ' or ' overturns ': in this case the
construction is—' And the whirlwind's wing whelms (i. e. overturns) the
billowy tempest over the hapless flocks,' &c. (See Prof. Skeat's interesting note on ' Whelm ' in his Eng. Etym. Dict.)

277. The full fury of the winter wind sweeps up the surface-snow in
blinding drift.

278. *his own loose-revolving fields.* Fields familiar to him, that now
seem to be moving as the whirlwind catches up the loose surface-snow
and blows it in drift around him.

279. *Disastered.* ' Ill-starred,' ' unfortunate,' ' overtaken with calamity.'
Cp. with ' disaster,' ' consider,' ' influence,' &c.—words of astrological
origin.

      other hills—than those which the same landscape in summer
presents to his view ; snow-clad hills, and heaps of driven snow.

280. *joyless*—as being ' unknown,' ' strange' to him: he is bewildered.

285. *flouncing.* An imitative word ; allied to ' flounder.'

286. *thoughts of home.* The anxiety of his wife and children,
concerned about his long delay: their destitution, if he should perish,
&c.

291. *tufted cottage.* The reference is probably to the turf chimney-
top, or ridge, of his thatched cottage, just peering above the snow.

292. *middle waste.* A Latinism, meaning the middle of the waste.

299. *beyond the power of frost.* Into which, therefore, a fall would mean death by drowning.

302. *the still unfrozen spring.* 'Still' here signifies 'always': cp. Shakespeare's 'still-vext Bermoothës,' in The Tempest. For 'spring,' the earlier text (as late as 1738) gives 'eye': the common country name for such a spring in a marsh is still 'well-ee,' so named from its round shape and its brightness.

307. *bitterness of death.* That is, as a personal suffering; the phrase is scriptural—'surely (said Agag) the bitterness of death is past' (1 Sam. xv. 32).

308. *tender anguish.* The absence of his wife, and children, and 'friends' (Scots for 'relatives'), as explained in l. 310. (Contrast ll. 346–348, *infra.*)

311–315. This contrasting scene in the tragedy of the shepherd perishing in the snowstorm is all the more effective that it is suddenly introduced. There is pathos of a peculiarly tender kind in the picture of the little children calling from the doorway into the darkness for their father.

311. *officious.* In its literal sense of 'dutiful.' Thomson has it again in Lines to the Memory of Lord Talbot—'the officious muse,' l. 296.

311, 312. Cp. Gray's Elegy (published 1751)—

'No more the blazing hearth shall burn,
  Or busy housewife ply her evening care;
No children run to lisp their sire's return,
  Or climb his knees the envied kiss to share.'—ll. 21-24.

(Cp. also Goldsmith's description of the Swiss peasant's home, in The Traveller.)

313. *little children, peeping out.* Cp. a similar 'situation' in Longfellow's Twilight:—

'In the fisherman's cottage
    There shines a ruddier light,
  And a little face at the window
    Peers out into the night,' &c.—*By the Seaside.*

321. *Stretched out.* Pope's alteration for 'unstretched.'

bleaching. Becoming covered with the falling and drifting snow.

322–358. The transition here is natural, and the reflections are creditable to the heart of Thomson. It is ignorance of the sufferings of their fellow-beings, and not heartlessness, that makes so many people selfish.

334, 335. *the cup Of . . . . grief.* Matthew xxvi. 42.

339, 340. *the fiercer tortures of the mind,* &c. Cp. Gray's Ode on a Distant Prospect of Eton College—

> 'These shall the fury Passions tear,
>   The vultures of the mind ; . . .

> .   .   .   .   .

> Keen Remorse with blood defiled,
>   And moody Madness laughing wild.'

341. *Whence,* i. e. by reason of which.

345. *honest.* Honourable.   The 'passions' here alluded to are antithetic to those enumerated in l. 340, *supra.*

347. A line followed here in the earlier editions, which Thomson dropt after 1738:

> 'Like wailing pensive ghosts awaiting theirs.'

348. *point the parting anguish.* Render more acute the agony of dying.

349, 350. *the thousand nameless ills,* &c. Cp. Shakespeare—

> 'The thousand natural shocks
>   That flesh is heir to.'—*Hamlet,* Act. III, Sc. i.

354, 355. So Cowper, in The Task—

> 'It seems the part of wisdom, and no sin
>   Against the law of love, to measure lots
>   With less distinguished than ourselves ; that thus
>   We may with patience bear our moderate ills,
>   And sympathise with others suffering more.'
>   *The Winter Evening.*

357, 358. Construe—' And the social passions would work into clear perfection, [a process of] gradual bliss, still refining.' See Castle of Indolence, II, st. 61.

359. *the generous band.* 'The generous few,' in the first editions. The reference is to the Jail Committee of 1729, appointed to inquire into the condition of the prisons. The state of the Fleet Prison, a receptacle for debtors from the 12th century, and of the Marshalsea, was at this time, and indeed all through the 18th century, notorious. They were proved to have been the scene of great atrocities and brutalities. The evils arose from the extortion of the keepers, and from the practice of the Warden—as the head official of the Fleet was called—subletting the prison. (See an account of the Fleet Prison in Dickens's The Pickwick Papers. By Act 5 and 6 Vict. both the Fleet and the Marshalsea were at last abolished.) The work of the Jail Committee may be said to have been continued and extended by the philanthropical exertions of John Howard (1726 ?-1790) ; and Mrs. Elizabeth Fry (*née* Gurney),

'the female Howard' (1780–1845). (See Howard's An Account of the
Lazarettos, &c., published in 1789.) For a description of the state of
the prisons of England at the time when the Jail Committee of 1729–1730
was appointed, Knight's Pop. Hist., vol. vi, may be consulted.

367. *little tyrants.* The jailors, who used instruments of torture upon
their unhappy victims.

375. After this line, instead of the six lines in the final text, appeared
in the earlier editions, down to that of 1738, the following passage :—

> 'Hail, patriot band! who, scorning secret scorn,
> When justice and when mercy led the way,
> Dragged the detected monsters into light,
> Wrenched from their hand oppression's iron rod,
> And bade the cruel feel the pains they gave.
> Yet stop not here, let all the land rejoice
> And make the blessing unconfined as great.
> [Much still untouched remains ;' &c.]

384. *The toils of law.* Not the labours—but the net, or snare, of law.
See Autumn, ll. 1291–1294, where Thomson returns to his early attack
upon the abuse of law by pettifoggers—

> 'Let these
> Ensnare the wretched in the toils of law,' &c.

'Toils,' Fr. *toiles*, snares for wild beasts; in the singular, *toile*, cloth ;
from Lat. *tela* (for *texla*) a web ; *texo*, I weave.

388. Here followed, so late as the edition of 1738, a series of twenty-
one lines, which in the later editions Thomson partly dropped, and
partly, with but slight verbal alterations, elsewhere incorporated with
the text of Winter. The series commenced—

> 'Yet more outrageous is the season still,
> A deeper horror, in Siberian wilds.'

Then followed the three lines which will be found in the description of
'the wild stupendous scene' at the pole, ll. 895–897, *infra.* Next came
the graphic picture of the bear 'with dangling ice all horrid,' to be found
at ll. 827–833, *infra.* And the remaining nine lines of the series ran
thus :—

> 'While tempted vigorous o'er the marble waste,
> On sleds reclined, the furry Russian sits ;
> And, by his reindeer drawn, behind him throws
> A shining kingdom in a winter's day.
>   Or from the cloudy Alps and Apennine,
> Capt with gray mists and everlasting snows ;
> Where Nature in stupendous ruin lies,
> And from the leaning rock, on either side,

Gush out those streams that classic song renowns :
　[Cruel as death,' &c.]

389-413. This account of the ferocity of the wolf is scarcely overcharged. The animal is still a common winter horror in various parts of Europe. In severe winters it descends in hungry packs from the forests of the Apennines, Alps, and Pyrenees, and is greatly dreaded by the villagers and country people of the adjacent regions. Many terrible stories have been told of the pursuit of travellers by wolves in Russia, France, and Spain. It is only when severely pressed by hunger that wolves dare to attack man—in general they are cowardly and sneaking; but their ravages among sheep, and even cattle of full growth, and horses, are a serious yearly loss to those countries which they infest. They used to be plentiful in the British Isles, and in Saxon England January used to be known as the Wolf-month. When they disappeared from England is not well known, but they continued to plunder field and fold in Scotland down to the time of the Union of the Crowns. Cameron of Lochiel is said to have slain the last Scottish wolf in 1680.

405, 406. *Even beauty*, &c. A fanciful idea, common in one shape or another in many mediæval romances. Thus royalty, chastity, and other eminent qualities besides beauty, were believed to be respected by the lion. Cp. Shakespeare, I King Henry IV, Act II. sc. iv ; Milton's Comus, ll. 441-452 ; Spenser's Faery Queene, &c.

407. *undistinguished*. In no way favoured or respected over others.

413. Thus adding a new and real horror to churchyard superstitions. The subject is viewed from the standpoint of the superstitious peasant.

　Mixed with foul shades.
　　' Those thick and gloomy shadows damp
　　Oft seen in charnel vaults and sepulchres
　　Lingering and sitting.'—*Comus*, ll. 470-472.

414-423. This passage does not appear in the earlier editions. It was introduced after the edition of 1738.

The most easterly of the Cantons of Switzerland bears the French name of Grisons, and the German name of Graübundten—both given to the district for the same reason, the circumstance of the inhabitants wearing a dress of *gray* homespun. The bund, or states, into which the inhabitants of the different valleys of this hilly region formed themselves so early as the 14th century, were for mutual defence and protection, from the exactions of the numerous resident nobility. The country is an assemblage of hills and valleys of very various climate and fertility, and lying in the basin of the head-waters of the Danube, the Rhine, and the Ticino. The famous long and lovely valley of the Engadine is in this canton. The people are largely engaged in pastoral and sylvan industries—the chief exports being cattle, cheese, and timber. The country has long been subject to the terror of avalanches—the devastating descent of large masses of snow from the mountain cliffs and slopes *to the valleys*. Just the year after Thomson's death, an event which occurred in 1748, a village of Grisons, Rueras, in the Tarvich valley, was enveloped and pushed from its place by an avalanche during the night ; so quietly was this done that the inhabitants continued to sleep, and only wondered when they awoke why daylight was so long in dawning. Unfortunately many of them perished before they were dug out.

424-616. This long passage is a remarkable feature of the poem. It deals mainly with the manner and circumstances in which Thomson, if he had been free to choose, would have preferred to spend the months of winter. Nearly one half of it appeared for the first time subsequently to 1738.

431-433. *There studious let me sit*, &c. Cp. Malloch—

> 'From thought to thought in vision led,
> He holds high converse with the dead ;
> Sages or Poets. See, they rise !
> And shadowy skim before his eyes. . . .
> Lo! Socrates, the seer of heaven
> To whom its moral will was given.
> Fathers and friends of humankind,
> They formed the nation, or refined,
> With all that mends the head and heart
> Enlightening truth, adorning art.'—*A Fragment*.

It is impossible to say whether Malloch is the debtor or the creditor : the pieces are undoubtedly related. There was a brisk commerce of literary ideas, and a constant interchange of literary work between Thomson and Malloch from 1725 to 1727, and probably both before and after those dates.

　　Cp. Southey, in his library :—

> 'My days among the dead are past;
> Around me I behold,
> Where'er these casual eyes are cast,
> The mighty minds of old.'

437. *The long-lived volume*. The reference is probably to Plutarch's famous Parallel Lives, of forty-six Greeks and Romans arranged in pairs for the purpose of comparison, each pair—the one a Greek, the other a Roman—constituting a *biblion*. The work has been exceedingly

popular in ancient, mediæval, and modern times. Of the thirteen
Greeks in Thomson's list, from Socrates to Philopœmen, Plutarch
includes ten, viz. Solon, Lycurgus, Aristides, Cimon, Timoleon,
Pelopidas, Phocion, Agis, Aratus, and Philopœmen; and of the
eleven Romans in Thomson's list, from Numa to Marcus Brutus,
Plutarch includes five, viz. Numa, Camillus, Tullius Cicero, Cato the
Younger, and Marcus Brutus.

438. *The sacred shades.* The venerated spirits of great men, long
since dead, but famous to all future time.

439–528. This long passage of ninety lines is an expansion of the
original text, which appeared in all the earlier editions down to and
including that of 1738, and consisted of only some twenty lines.
Those twenty lines named or referred to only nine of the distinguished
men of ancient Greece and Rome. The expansion seems to have been
suggested, and, to the extent of nearly one-half, actually made by Pope.
The original text ran as follows:—

> 'First Socrates,
> Whose simple question to the folded heart
> Stole unperceived, and from the maze of thought
> Evolved the secret truth,—a god-like man!
> Solon the next, who built his commonweal
> On equity's wide base. Lycurgus then,
> Severely good; and him of rugged Rome,
> Numa, who softened her rapacious sons;
> Cimon, sweet-souled; and Aristides, just;
> With that attempered hero, mild and firm,
> Who wept the brother, while the tyrant bled;
> Unconquered Cato, virtuous in extreme;
> Scipio, the human warrior, gently brave,
> Who soon the race of spotless glory ran,
> And, warm in youth, to the poetic shade
> With friendship and philosophy retired;
> And, equal to the best, the Theban twain
> Who single raised their country into fame.
> Thousands behind, the boast of Greece and Rome,
> Whom virtue owns, the tribute of a verse
> Demand;—but who can count the stars of heaven?'

439. *Socrates.* A great Athenian philosopher, born B.C. 469. It was
not till B.C. 406 that he filled any political office. In that year he was
a member of the Senate of the Five Hundred, and had the great moral
courage to refuse to put to the vote a question which he regarded as
unconstitutional: he refused also to obey the order of the Thirty

Tyrants for the apprehension of Leon of Salamis. He incurred the hatred of the Tyrants, who passed a law, levelled specially at him, forbidding the teaching of oratory; and he incurred the enmity of the democracy by his friendship for the haughty Alcibiades and the cynical Critias. He was accused of introducing the worship of new divinities and of corrupting young people by his novel doctrines, religious and political. During his trial he behaved with a manly independence and superiority of manner which irritated his judges; refused to say or do anything that would conciliate them; and accepted his sentence of death with equanimity, and even cheerfulness. Thirty days after sentence he drank the cup of hemlock juice, and died with composure, being then in his 70th year. His teaching was carried on wherever he could find a listener—in the street, the workshop, or the field. His method was peculiar : it was not the conveyance of ready-made knowledge by direct instruction, but the development, by a series of questions, of the knowledge that was already in the mind of his disciple. His objects in undertaking at his own hand the post of public teacher of the youth and manhood of Athens were to awaken the sense of moral responsibility, and to guide the impulse after self-knowledge. He directed his own conduct by a divine voice, which, even from his childhood, he had been always hearing: it put a restraint upon words he was about to speak, upon actions he was about to perform. This warning voice is commonly spoken of as the Daimon or guiding spirit of Socrates. Thomson regards it as simply an enlightened and sensitive conscience. With Socrates knowledge was virtue. (See Note, ll. 209-216, *supra*[1].)

446. *Solon.* A famous lawgiver of Athens, one of the Seven Sages, born about 638 B.C. When he was 44 years of age he was chosen archon, and in virtue of his office was invested with supreme power to institute all necessary measures for the safety and prosperity of the State. He remodelled the constitution, basing his laws, as Thomson says, 'on equity's wide base.' He secured by the promise of the citizens a trial of at least ten years for his laws. He is said to have spoken of his laws, as 'by no means the best that could have been framed, but as the best the Athenians would have received.' Among his laws and institutions may be noted—a graduated income-tax, a deliberative assembly of representative members, the liability of people to support their aged parents if in their youth they had been taught some trade or profession by the parents, &c.

450. *the laurelled field of finer arts.* The sphere of poetry, painting, sculpture, &c. in which the ancient Greeks excelled. The laurel, sacred to the Muses, was bestowed on those who excelled in the arts.

[1] See Thomson's Liberty, Part II. ll. 222-235.

452. *smiling Greece.* Their approving and delighted countrymen.

453. *Lycurgus.* From Athens Thomson now turns for a while to Sparta. Lycurgus, who flourished about the middle of the eighth century B.C., was the originator of the famous Spartan laws, the result of which was to make Sparta a nation of soldiers. The city was a camp, every man a soldier. The interest of the State was supreme, and the citizen existed only for it. The education of the Spartan was undertaken by the State: from his childhood each male was inured to a system of severe discipline; there was no home life, the meals were common, and life was spent in barracks; commerce was discouraged by the introduction of iron money; agriculture was left to slaves or Helots, and despised; in short the Spartans were warriors, and nothing else. These laws laid the foundation of the military supremacy of Sparta.

456. *at Thermopylae he glorious fell.* This was Leonidas, king of Sparta. He was captain of the three hundred who kept the passage at Thermopylae against the host of Persian invaders. In the desperate battle in front of the pass he was among the first to fall, B.C. 480. Thermopylae (the Hot Gates—so named from the hot springs in the middle of the pass) lay between Mount Oeta and the marshy edge of the Malic Gulf, and was the only pass by which an enemy could penetrate into southern Greece from the north. The Western Gate was so narrow that there was only room for a single chariot between the mountain and the marsh. (See Liberty, II. l. 179.)

459. *Aristides.* The poet now returns to Athens. Aristides, surnamed The Just, had for his rival the 'haughty' Themistocles. He was ostracised about the year 482 B.C., but returned from his banishment to apprise Themistocles of the position of the Persian fleet. The result of his communication was the great naval victory for Greece of the battle of Salamis, B.C. 480. After the battle Aristides was recalled, and reinstated in popular favour. He continued to do noble service for Athens till his death, probably in 468 B.C., but died so poor that the property he left was insufficient to bury him.

466. *Cimon.* Son of Miltiades, the hero of Marathon. He was the great Athenian ruler in the interval between the death of Aristides and the rise of Pericles. It was at the time of the Persian invasion of Greece (480 B.C.) that he first distinguished himself. After the victory at Platæa he was brought forward by Aristides. He gained many subsequent victories over the Persians. Wealthy with Persian spoil he expended his riches freely for the gratification of the Athenians and the security of Athens. He kept a free table, and threw open to all and sundry his beautiful gardens and pleasure grounds. With part of the Persian treasure he increased the fortification of the citadel, and laid the

foundation of the long walls from Athens to the Piræus. He was of a frank and affable disposition, and in early life too much inclined to habits of conviviality.

472. *in unequal times.* Either in times inferior in glory to those just referred to, or, more probably, in times unworthy of the great men now to be named.

474. *Timoleon.* A native of Corinth. His brother Timophanes having formed the design of making himself tyrant of their native city, Timoleon, in his passion for the liberty of the State, slew him with his own hand. He almost immediately thereafter conducted an expedition to Sicily to repel the Carthaginians, and restore order in the island. This was in 344 B.C. The history of his successes reads like a romance. He died at Syracuse in 377 B.C., and was buried in the market-place at the public expense.

476. *the Theban pair.* Epaminondas, the hero of Leuctra and Mantinea—two great victories over the Spartans, the last fatal to himself (362 B.C.); and Pelopidas, his friend, who also aided in raising Thebes over Sparta and Athens to the supremacy of Greece.

481. *Phocion the Good.* An Athenian general and statesman, born about the year 402 B.C. When Demosthenes and others were urging opposition to Philip of Macedon, Phocion counselled peace : his opposition to the war-party brought about his condemnation, and he drank the hemlock, in 317 B.C., at the age of 85. He is to be commended for his private qualities ; his public virtue was at least above suspicion.

488. *Agis.* The fourth of the name, kings of Sparta. Agis IV reigned from 244 to 240 B.C. He attempted a re-establishment of the laws of Lycurgus, but was opposed by his colleague Leonidas (the Second) and the wealthy citizens, thrown into prison, and afterwards put to death.

490. *The two Achæan heroes.* Aratus and Philopœmen. They were in succession the chiefs of the Achaian League—a confederation of the states of Achaia, in the north of the Peloponnesus, which had for its object the union of Greece. Aratus was more successful as a diplomatist than as a general. In a dissension, however, with Philip of Macedon, who was bent on the conquest of Greece, he was put to death by poison, 213 B.C. Philopœmen was appointed General of the League in 208 B.C. He was a successful general, frequently defeating the Spartans ; but in 183 B.C., on an enterprise to punish the Messenians for their revolt from the League, he was taken prisoner, and compelled to drink poison. He is regarded as ' the last of the Greeks.' In the intervals of warfare, it is said, he withdrew to the cultivation of his farm.

498. *Of rougher front.* The Romans.

499. *those virtuous times.* Of the early kings, and of the early republic.

502. Romulus was the founder of Rome; Numa Pompilius, his successor, gave the Romans their religion.

504. *Servius, the king.* Servius Tullius, sixth king of Rome. He is famous less for military achievement than for his foundation of all the civil rights and institutions of ancient Rome.

507. *The public father who the private quelled.* Thomson's note here is—'Marcus Junius Brutus'; but this is clearly a mistake. Marcus is referred to at l. 524, *infra.* Lucius is meant. After the rape of Lucretia, Lucius Junius Brutus roused the Romans against the Tarquins, and on their expulsion he became first consul of the Republic. On his two sons joining in an attempt to restore the Tarquins he ordered them to be put to death.

510. *Camillus.* Marcus Furius Camillus. After many military exploits to the glory of Rome, he was driven into banishment on a charge of unfair division of the spoils of Veii; but when, in 390 B.C., the Gauls took Rome and threatened its destruction, the Romans in the Capitol made him Dictator in his absence, and sent for him as the only possible saviour of the State. He accordingly returned; and, with a hastily gathered army, attacked and completely routed the Gauls. The victory won for him the title of the Second Romulus. He was five times Dictator, and continued fighting and defeating Volscians, Gauls, and other enemies of Rome, till his 80th year, when he died of the plague, 365 B.C.

511. *Fabricius.* Like Cincinnatus, a favourite representative of the integrity and simplicity of the heroic times of ancient Rome. Pyrrhus, king of Epirus, was invading Italy, 280 B.C., and Fabricius was the Roman legate appointed to treat with him. Pyrrhus, to win him to his side, alternately offered money and intimidation, but in vain; the inflexible Roman was to be conquered neither by gold nor coercion. He lived poor, on the produce of his hereditary farm; and, after doing noble service as general and legislator for his country, died poor— leaving his dowerless daughters to the bounty of the Senate.

512. *Cincinnatus.* This is Thomson's favourite Roman hero: he has several references to him. (See Spring, ll. 58–65.) In Liberty, Part III. ll. 143–147, he is alluded to as—

> 'ready, a rough swain, to guide the plough;
> Or else, the purple o'er his shoulder thrown
> In long majestic flow, to rule the state
> With wisdom's purest eye; or, clad in steel,
> To drive the steady battle on the foe.'

He was twice called from his farm, which he cultivated with his own hands, to assume the dictatorship in times of great emergency ; in 458 B.C., and again, when he was 80, in 439. On the first occasion, he saved the Roman army, routed the enemy, and was back again at his farm, within sixteen days.

513. *Thy willing victim, Carthage.* Regulus. After winning many victories over the Carthaginians in Africa, he sustained a terrible defeat in a sanguinary battle in which 30,000 of his men were slain, and, being taken prisoner, remained a captive in Carthage for five years. He was then ordered to accompany an embassy which was sent to Rome with the object of securing peace, or at least an exchange of noble prisoners. He advised the Senate to enter into no negotiations, but to continue the war against Carthage at all hazards. The Senate took his passionately urged advice, and he prepared, as he had promised, to return to his captivity. His friends and relatives in vain implored him to remain in Rome. On his return to Carthage he was put to death with a refinement of cruelty hardly credible. Thomson elsewhere repeats the story of his heroic fulfilment of his promise:—

> 'Regulus the wavering Fathers 'firmed
> By dreadful counsel, never given before ;
> For Roman honour sued, and his own doom.
> Hence he sustained to dare a death prepared
> By Punic rage. On earth his manly look
> Relentless fixed, he from a last embrace,
> By chains polluted, put his wife aside,
> His little children climbing for a kiss ;
> Then dumb, through rows of weeping, wondering friends,
> A new illustrious exile pressed along.'
>
> *Liberty*, III. ll. 166-175.

517. *Scipio, the gentle chief.* Not the great Scipio, but the adopted son of *his* son. He is known as Scipio Africanus Minor. He served with distinction in Spain, and on the outbreak of the third Punic war, in 149 B.C., he went to Africa, and after the great glory of taking Carthage, 146 B.C., reduced Africa to the condition of a Roman province. The downfall of Carthage brought tears to his eyes. He was well read in Grecian literature, and consorted with such writers as Polybius the historian, Terentius the dramatist, Lucilius the poet, &c. His friendship for Lælius is celebrated in Cicero's dialogue De Amicitiâ.

521. *Tully.* Marcus Tullius Cicero, the great Roman orator and statesman, and an illustrious writer on many subjects—literary, political, and philosophical. His exposure and suppression of the dangerous

conspiracy of Catiline gained for him the title of 'Father of his country.'
Born in 106 B.C., he was consul in 63 B.C., and nearly twenty-one years
later was killed by the soldiers of Antony. He was then within a few
weeks of completing his 64th year.

522. *rushing Rome.* Rapidly declining Rome. The power of Rome
was not declining, but great encroachment was being made on consti-
tutional liberty.

523. *Unconquered Cato, virtuous in extreme.* The reference is
rather to Cato Uticensis than Cato Censor. Cato the younger was
born 95 B.C. He was conspicuous from early manhood for the stern-
ness of his character, and the purity of his morals. As a leader of the
aristocratic party he opposed Julius Cæsar and Pompey. Africa
submitted to Cæsar, except only Utica, in which Cato resolved to make
a stand ; but when he saw that the Romans in Utica were inclined to
submit he committed suicide rather than fall into the hands of the
conqueror. (See Addison's Cato—'Cæsar shall never say "I conquered Cato."'—Act IV. sc. iv. Also Pope's Temple of Fame—
'Unconquered Cato shews the wound he tore.'—l. 176.)

524. *unhappy Brutus.* Marcus Junius Brutus, a noble Roman who
joined the conspiracy of Cassius, and murdered his friend Julius Cæsar
in the belief that Cæsar's death was necessary for the preservation of the
Republic. He was afterwards defeated by Antony and Octavius at
Philippi, 42 B.C., and perished on the battle-field by his own hand.

532. *Phœbus.* The sun-god Apollo, who was also the god of
poetry.

the Mantuan swain. Virgil, born at Andes near Mantua on the
Mincius, 70 B.C. He is called a 'swain' from the nature of his Georgics
and Eclogues, which are on rural subjects. His great poem, the Æneid,
is one of the world's three great epics, and gives in language of singular
lucidity and sweetness a mythical account of the origin of the Roman
people. He died in the year 19 B.C.

533. *Homer.* The great Greek epic poet; author of the Iliad,
which describes the history of the siege of Troy; and the Odyssey,
which narrates the story of the return of Odysseus from the Trojan
wars.

534. *Parent of song.* In the Temple of Fame, Pope describes Homer
as the 'Father of verse.'

535. *The British muse.* The great English epic poet was, of course,
John Milton, born 1608, died 1674. He wrote Paradise Lost, Paradise
Regained, Comus, Lycidas, Samson Agonistes, &c. In the next line
'darkling'—a phrase employed by Milton himself—literally, 'in the
dark,' refers to the blindness which afflicted both Homer and Milton.

Thomson (l. 534, *supra*) ranks Milton on an equality with Homer: it
was Milton's ambition to rank with him—'blind Mæonides'—

> 'equalled with me in fate,
> So were I equalled with [him] in renown.'
> > *Par. Lost,* Bk. III. ll. 33, 34.

Dryden goes farther—

> 'Three poets, in three distant ages born,
> Greece, Italy, and England did adorn:
> The first in loftiness of thought surpassed;
> The next in majesty; in both the last.
> The force of nature could no farther go,
> To make the third she joined the other two.'

For a fuller criticism of Milton's genius by Thomson, see Summer,
ll. 1567–1571. See also Cowper's Table Talk, ll. 555–558.

536. *full up the middle steep to fame.* 'Right up the hill to the
very top.' The completeness of the achievement is indicated by 'full';
the directness of the ascent—proof of strength and energy of genius—by
'middle.' 'The middle steep' is, of course, a Latin idiom: so, l. 292
supra, 'the middle waste.'

537. *Nor absent are those shades,* &c. See l. 438, *supra.* The
reference here is to the three great Greek tragic poets, Æschylus (born
525 B.C.), Sophocles (born 495 B.C.), and Euripides (born 480 B.C.,
at Salamis and on the day of the battle).

537–540. In the earlier text the first and principal notice was given
to the lyrical poets (such as Pindar, Alcæus, Sappho, Anacreon), and
the great tragic dramatists were disposed of in a single line—

> 'Nor absent are those tuneful shades, I ween,
> Taught by the graces, whose enchanting touch
> Shakes every passion from the various string;
> Nor those, who solemnise the moral scene.'

538. *Pathetic drew the impassioned heart.* The expression is capable
of two meanings; either—'delineated in drama the pathetic tragedy of
human suffering,' or—'evoked by his dramas the profoundest feelings
(of pity or terror) of his audience.' In l. 537 the word 'touch' applies
equally to the pencil and the lyre, and in either application is quite in
accord with 'drew' of the following line.

541. *First of your kind.* First is here used in the sense of 'best.' In
this sense it is frequently used by Burns.

546, 547. For these two lines the earlier text gave—

> 'Save Lycidas, the friend, with sense refined.'

546. *a few chosen friends.* Thomson had many friends, and scarcely
an enemy—it would be hard to mention one. He was 'that right

friendly bard' to all his brethren. To Lyttelton he was 'one of the best and most beloved of my friends.' To Murdoch and Forbes he was 'honest-hearted Thomson'—tried, amiable, open. The 'few chosen friends' who were in the habit of visiting Thomson when he wrote these words at Richmond (where he settled in 1736) included Pope, Hammond, Collins, Dr. Armstrong, his neighbours the Robertsons, Mallet, occasionally Quin, and (as often as he thought he would be welcome) Millar the publisher. Thomson never 'chose' his friends; they were attracted to him, and though he had, in his heart, special favourites, he was of too genial and of too indolent a disposition not to make all welcome.

547. *my humble roof.* A neat garden-cottage in Kew-foot-lane, Richmond, looking down upon the Thames and commanding a good range of landscape. A cousin of his own kept his garden trim; he was fortunate in his housekeeper, a Mrs. Hobart; his rooms were adorned with a great many paintings and engravings—partly collected during his tour in Italy; his bookshelves were filled with foreign and classical books, and the works of standard English authors; and his cellar was well-stocked with wines, and Edinburgh ale.

550. Pope was some twelve years the senior of Thomson: he was a frequent visitor at Richmond; and at Twickenham there was a standing rule for the servants that Mr. Pope was always at home to Mr. Thomson. By *the muses' hill* (Parnassus) Thomson signifies the labours of poetical composition. Thomson's intimacy with Pope, however, dates from a time before the residence at Richmond.

553, 554. A beautiful compliment. *His own Homer*: the Translation of the Iliad, published 1715-1720; Translation of the Odyssey, published 1723-1725.

555-571. This passage was added to the text after the death of Hammond, in 1742. It is a very generous tribute to his memory, prompted and inspired by a friendship that was undoubtedly genuine. Hammond has been rather hardly dealt with by the critics: there is no real reason to set aside the judgment of Thomson as here expressed in his friend's favour. Thomson's anticipations of future greatness for young Hammond were probably well founded: in any case, whatever opinion one may hold of his love elegies, his character was of a kind to win the respect and affection of Thomson. There were two Hammonds known in a small way for their literary reputation; the one Anthony, the other, his second son, James. It was James Hammond whom Thomson knew. He was born in 1710; and, while still a youth, was equerry to George, Prince of Wales, afterwards George III. He has been judged entirely by his Love Elegies, which were written, on the model of Tibullus, before he was twenty-two, and were never intended for publication or print. They appeared after his death. They were inspired by an infatuation for a certain Delia—a Miss Dashwood, who rejected his addresses, and, it is said, drove him quite to the verge of insanity by her insensibility to all his appeals. Cibber, in his Lives, pronounces that he was a poet by love, not by nature; that he had warmth, but little poetry; that his verses 'are more the language of the heart than head.' In 1741 he became M.P. for Truro, and died at Stowe in the following year. It will be observed that Thomson's estimate of his character and abilities does not at all rest on his Elegies: he does not even speak of him as a poet, but only as a friend of poets, and a lover of poetry.

573. *pliant soul.* A paraphrase of the original text 'various turn'; and still further to be explained by the succeeding line.

575–577. In the edition of 1738, and previous years—

'With them would search if this unbounded frame
Of Nature rose from unproductive night,
Or sprung eternal from the Eternal Cause.'

Cp. Milton's inquiry into the origin of Light—

'Hail, holy Light, offspring of Heaven first-born!
Or of the Eternal co-eternal beam
May I express thee unblamed?'—*Par. Lost,* Bk. III. ll. 1–3.

581. Each part of creation, perfect in itself, would be seen to unite with other parts into a larger unity, still more wonderfully perfect. The word 'diffusive,' literally 'diffusing itself,' may be taken more prosaically as 'diffused.'

584. *to us it seems embroiled.* Originally, 'more seemingly perplexed.'

587. *historic muse.* 'Historic truth' in the earlier editions. Clio was the muse of history.

590. Plenty. Cp. Gray: 'To scatter plenty o'er a smiling land.'—*Elegy.*

591. *double suns.* Poetical for 'double crops.' Great attention was beginning to be paid to improved methods of agriculture when Thomson wrote thus. See Autumn, ll. 914–916, where the poet speaks hopefully of 'double harvest.'

594. The words are from Scripture, Luke xxiv. 32, 'Did not our heart burn within us?' &c.

595, 596. *That portion of divinity,* &c. A habitual idea with Thomson. See it repeated, and more fully unfolded in Autumn, ll. 910–913—

'Oh! is there not some patriot, in whose power,
That best, that God-like luxury, is placed
Of blessing thousands, thousands yet unborn,' &c.

597–603. *if doomed In powerless humble fortune*, &c. Cp. Gray, who had surely been reading these lines—

> 'Chill penury repressed their noble rage
> And froze the genial current of the soul.'

This is just Thomson's image, and it even recalls his words—'repress the ardent risings of the kindling soul.' Cp. further—

> 'Along the cool sequestered vale of life
> They kept the noiseless tenor of their way.'—*Elegy*.

605. *those scenes*. Of immortal life and the future state beyond death and the grave.

606–608. A favourite idea, and an essential part of Thomson's religious hope. See Spring, ll. 374–377, and Note; Liberty, III. ll. 68–70.

610. *play the shapes*. 'Play off,' or 'give play to.' This too was part of the pastime of Cowper's Winter Evening—

> 'Me oft has fancy ludicrous and wild
> Soothed,' &c.—ll. 285, 286.

And again—

> 'Discourse ensues   .   .   .
> Not such as with a frown forbids the play
> Of fancy,' &c.—ll. 174–176.

611. *frolic fancy*. Here 'frolic' is properly put to its original use as an adjective. So Milton—

> 'Ripe and frolic of his full-grown age.'—*Comus*, l. 59.

611–616. A happy discriminating description of wit and humour, as these are commonly understood. A less happy description appeared in the earlier editions, down to that of 1738:—

> 'And incessant form
> Unnumbered pictures, fleeting o'er the brain,
> Yet rapid still renewed, and poured immense
> Into the mind unbounded without space:
> The great, the new, the beautiful; or mixed
> Burlesque and odd, the risible and gay;
> Whence vivid wit, and humour, droll of face,
> Call laughter forth, deep-shaking every nerve.'

See Cowper's Table Talk, ll. 657, 658.

617–629. The scene shifts from the studious retirement of the scholar to the winter evening amusements of common country-folks. The scene is Scottish.

617. *the village rouses up the fire*. The villagers make preparation for a long and comfortable winter 'fore-night.'

618. *well attested and as well believed.* The language is humorously ironical.

619, 620. Cp. Fergusson—

'In rangles round, before the ingle's lowe,
  Fra guid-dame's mouth auld warld tales they hear,—
Of warlocks loupin' round the wirrikow;
  Of ghaists that win in glen and kirk-yard drear;
Whilk touzles a' their tap, and gars them shake wi' fear.'
      Farmer's Ingle, st. vii (published 1773).

621. *the sounding hall.* The roomy farmhouse kitchen. The 'hall' is the public room.

624. 'The loud laugh that speaks the vacant mind.'—Goldsmith's *Deserted Village.*

625–629. Cp. Autumn,—
          'Romp-loving miss
  Is hauled about in gallantry robust.'—ll. 528, 529.
  'The laugh, the slap, the jocund curse go round.'—l. 547.

627. *shook.* Racy of rustic dancing. Burns has—
    'I'll laugh, an' sing, an' shake my leg.'
          Epist. to Lapraik.

630–655. Winter evening in the city—the streets, the gaming-table, the ball-room, the theatre, &c.

630. *swarms intense.* Is full of busy eager crowds.

public haunt. Such as coffee-room, club-room, &c.

633. *Down the loose stream of . . . . joy.* In pursuit of fashionable immoral pleasures.

635. *The gaming fury.* A passion for gambling, or engaging in games of hazard, for high stakes; a fashionable vice of last century. (See Life of Fox the great statesman.)

640. *effuses.* In its etymological sense—'pours forth,' 'displays.'

641, 642. *beamed from*, &c. Expanded from the original text—
        'Rained from radiant eyes.'
Cp. Summer, ll. 145, 146.

645. *The fop light-fluttering*, &c. Thomson used to call one of his friends (Hammond) with good-humoured pleasantry 'a burnished butterfly.' Cp. Hamlet's description of the court-flutterer Osric— 'Dost know this water-fly?' (Act V. sc. ii.)

646–655. It is only in Winter that Thomson refers to the theatre as a place of amusement. Milton introduces it in both L'Allegro (l. 131) and Il Penseroso (l. 97)—but in the former, it is the Comic, in the latter the Tragic, drama that furnishes the entertainment. Thomson gives the preference to Tragedy, as better suited for the season—'a sad tale's best for winter,' says Shakespeare; but he provides Comedy too as a winter evening entertainment.

647. *Monimia.* The heroine of The Orphan (first produced in 1680), a tragedy by Thomas Otway.

648. *Belvidera.* The heroine of Otway's great tragedy Venice Preserved (1682).

653–655. These lines were added subsequently to 1738. 'Bevil' is one of the characters in Sir Richard Steele's The Conscious Lovers (produced in 1722, when the author was in his 52nd year: his first play, Grief à la Mode, was acted in 1702). A distinction is here implied between 'low' and 'genteel' comedy.

When Thomson first came up to London, in March, 1725, he was at once irresistibly attracted to the theatre. Apparently it was his first experience of the acted drama. He writes accordingly with all the freshness of inexperience, and with the delightful abandon of youth, on the subject of his first acquaintance with a pleasure forbidden in Scotland. The letter is to a young friend, a country doctor in Scotland :—

'The play-house is indeed a very fine entertainment, though not to the height I expected. A tragedy, I think, or a fine character in a comedy gives greater pleasure read than acted ; but your fools and persons of a very whimsical and humorous character are a delicious morsel on the stage ; they indeed exercise my risible faculty, and particularly your old friend Daniel, in Oroonoko [by Southerne, produced in 1696], diverted me infinitely : the grave-digger in Hamlet, Beau Clincher and his brother in the Trip to the Jubilee, pleased me extremely too. Mr. Booth has a very majestic appearance, a full, harmonious voice, and vastly exceeds them all in acting tragedy. The last Act in Cato he does to perfection, and you would think he expired with the *Oh! that ends it!* Mr. Wilks, I believe, has been a very fine actor for the [part of] the fine gentleman and the young hero, but his face now is wrinkled, his voice broken. . . . . . Mills and Johnstoun are pretty good actors. Dicky Norris, that little comical toothless devil, will turn his back and crack a very good jest yet : there are some others of them [that are] execrable. Mrs. Oldfield [admired by Pope for her rendering of Rowe's Jane Shore] has a smiling jolly face, acts very well in comedy. . . . Mrs. Porter excels in tragedy, has a short piercing voice, and enters most into her character ; and if she did not act well she could not be endured, being more disagreeable in her appearance than any of them. Mrs. Booth acts some things very well, and particularly Ophelia's madness in Hamlet inimitably ; but then she dances so deliciously, has such melting lascivious motions, air, and postures . . . . indeed, the women are generally the handsomest in the house, and better actors than the men—but perhaps their sex prejudices me in their favour.

'These are a few of the observations I have made hitherto at Drury Lane Theatre, to which I have paid five visits, but I have not been at the New House yet : my purse will not keep pace with my inclinations in this matter. Oh ! if I had Mass John [said by Lord Buchan to have been the Rev. Gabriel Wilson of Maxton, in the presbytery of Selkirk ; some thirty years older than Thomson] here, to see some of their 'top' fools ; he would shake the scenes with laughter.'—Letter to Dr. Wm. Cranstoun, Ancrum, April 3, 1725.

656-690. This complimentary apostrophe to Lord Chesterfield, not written till after 1738, is lugged into a place with which it has but a slender connection. Such as it is, the connection—to be found in the three preceding lines—was clearly manufactured for the compliment. (See Note, ll. 653-655, *supra.*) 'Whate'er can deck mankind or charm the heart' is delicately, or rather flimsily, hinted as the enviable attribute of Lord Chesterfield : Bevil suggests Chesterfield.

What is said here in praise of Lord Chesterfield must on the whole be allowed to be his due. The points touched upon in this eulogy are his elegance of manners, his intellectual accomplishments, his oratorical abilities, his statesmanlike qualities, and his patronage of literature. Philip Dormer Stanhope, fourth Earl of Chesterfield, was born in 1694. He was trained for a political career, and filled various important offices of State ; was in succession Ambassador to Holland, Lord-Lieutenant of Ireland, and Secretary of State. In 1748 he retired from political life. His death occurred in 1773. He is now chiefly remembered for the polish of his manners, his collision with Dr. Johnson, and his Letters to his Son. Johnson's Letter to Chesterfield was written 7th Feb., 1755. The Letters to his Son are written in good English and contain good sense. Nothing, however, that Chesterfield did could please the great moralist : 'they teach the manners of a dancing-master,' said Johnson, certainly savagely, and rather unjustly. Their morality, it must be allowed, is often of a Machiavellian cast.

In his Love of Fame, Satire II, Young also pays a compliment to the learning of Chesterfield :—

> '[He] titles knows, and indexes has seen,
> But leaves to Chesterfield what lies between.'—ll. 91, 92.

660. *Apollo's . . . fire.* Phœbus, the sun-god, and the god of poetry and beauty.

662. *the guardian, ornament,* &c. ' Et praesidium et dulce decus.'—Horace, I. 1.

675. *Attic point.* The keenness of Athenian wit. Athens was in Attica.

691, 692. These lines were added to the later editions (after 1738) to make the transition from Chesterfield to the subject proper easier and less abrupt.

693. This line in the earlier editions began—' Clear frost succeeds.'

694. *the ethereal nitre.* Frost, so called poetically from its penetrating nature. See Autumn, Note, ll. 4, 5. Cowper, in The Task, Bk. III, refers to 'the nitrous air of winter feeding a blue flame.'—ll. 32, 33. See also Savage's *Wanderer*, C. i., l. 56.

707. The benefit of frost to the soil is that it disintegrates the clods, and kills the germs of insect life destructive to vegetation. Cold is not the positive substance which Thomson seems, at least poetically, to consider it: it is the result of the absence of heat. ' Vegetable soul' means ' power to produce healthy vegetation.'

709, 710. There is a greater specific quantity of oxygen in the air in rosty weather, and more oxygen is consequently burned : the result is a brighter fire. ' The lively cheek of ruddy fire ' probably means that the sides of the flame are brighter. In rural Scotland the jambs or sides of the fire-place are sometimes called ' the cheeks o' the fire.' To sit at the cheek o' the fire is to sit by the hearth. Thomson, however, omits the necessary *the* for this interpretation.

710. *luculent.* Lat. *luculentus*, bright or clear ; from *lux*, light.

716. *the illusive fluid.* Quicksilver, the only metal that is fluid at ordinary winter temperatures. It freezes at 39° below zero.

718, 719. The crystals of which snow is composed are commonly in the form of six-pointed stars. But of this form there are, and have been figured, hundreds of varieties.

721. *Steamed eager,* &c. Sent forth as an invisible vapour of freezingly cold air. 'Steamed' qualifies 'gale' in l. 723.

722. *suffused.* This participle refers to the 'horizon' (in l. 721), which at evening is of a deep red because of 'the fierce rage of winter.'

724. *Breathes a blue film,* &c. Burns's description of the formation of 'infant ice' on a stream is not less delicately true :—

> ' The chilly frost, beneath the silver beam,
> Crept gently crusting o'er the glittering stream.'
>
> *The Brigs of Ayr,* ll. 39, 40 (Clarendon Press ed.).

Note the frequency of the letter *r* both here and in Thomson's description of the freezing ' stream '—not the pool.

725. *bickering.* The word is Celtic, and means ' skirmishing ' in ordinary English ; primarily, according to Prof. Skeat, it means ' to

keep pecking.' Applied to a stream it suggests the rapid tremulous movement of the current. Cp. Tennyson's Brook—

> '[I] sparkle out among the fern
> To bicker down a valley.'

727. *Rustles.* Cp. Burns, to whose ear the crisp sound of floating ice colliding suggested ' jingling '; but Thomson's ear was no less fine than Burns's—

> 'When thowes dissolve the snawy hoord,
> An' float the jinglin' icy boord,' &c.
>
> *Address to the Deil,* ll. 61, 62.

731. *The whole imprisoned river growls below.* In the original text ' detruded ' took the place of 'imprisoned,' and better explained the cause of the ' growling.' As the frost strengthens, the water shrinks, and there is a little free space between the ice and the water favourable to the production of a hollow sound.

732, 733. *Loud rings . . . . A double noise.* Sometimes described in Scotland as ' a hammer-clinking frost.' ' A double noise ' is not a twofold or duplicate noise, but a noise increased to twice its ordinary loudness. See l. 591, *supra*—' double suns,' meaning ' greatly increased crops.'

738. *full ethereal round.* The entire dome of the heavens, clear of cloud.

740. *all one cope.* One vast undimmed canopy.

742. *the rigid influence.* The hardening or stiffening power of frost.

746-751. Cp. Cowper's Task, Bk. V. ll. 110-121, for a similar effect of frost.

752. Introduced in the earlier editions by a line afterwards dropped :—

> ' The liquid kingdom all to solid turned.'

762-778. Instead of this excursion to Holland and Northern Europe Thomson in the earlier text, down to 1738, gives a British scene of sliders and skaters :—

> '[Swains] Fond o'er the river rush, and shuddering view
> The doubtful deeps below. Or where the lake
> And long canal the cerule plain extend,
> The city pours her thousands, swarming all,
> From every quarter : and, with him who slides,
> Or skating sweeps, swift as the winds, along
> In circling poise, or else disordered falls,
> His feet illuded sprawling to the sky,
> While the laugh rages round ; from end to end,
> Encreasing still, resounds the crowded scene.'

C c

768. *Batavia.* Holland, so called from the Batavi, the Roman name for the inhabitants of the island of Batavia at the mouth of the Rhine.

771. *The then gay land.* The Dutch being commonly a dull nation.

772. *the northern courts.* Those of Scandinavia and Russia.

782. Cp. Cowper—

> ' His slanting ray
> Slides ineffectual down the snowy vale.'
>
> *The Task,* Bk. V. ll. 6, 7.

789-793. Another of Thomson's many complaints against the practice of sport. See l. 257, and Note. (See Autumn, Note, l. 401.)

794-798. These lines originally ran—

> ' But what is this? these infant tempests, what?
> The mockery of Winter, should our eye
> Astonished shoot into the frigid zone;
> Where more than half the joyless year is night,
> And failing gradual life at last goes out.'

799. *There,* i. e. in the frigid zone, Siberia, to which political and criminal offenders are banished by the Czar. There used to be three grades of punishment—close confinement to the hard work of the mines, compulsory work of a less laborious kind, and simple exile with comparative freedom but under police surveillance. Thomson's exile, in l. 801, apparently belongs to the class of the comparatively free exile. The passage from l. 799 to l. 903 was added after 1738.

803. *heavy loaded groves.* A scarcely suitable description of pine-forests standing white with snow.

and solid floods. Such rivers, frozen over for many months, as Obi, Yenisei, Lena, &c.

805. *frozen main.* Arctic Ocean.

806. *cheerless towns.* Such as Tobolsk, Yakutsk, Petropaulovsk, &c.

807. *the caravan.* Company of travelling traders. The goods are transported for the most part on sledges.

808. *rich Cathay.* China. Commercial intercourse between Russia and China, through Siberia, began by treaty in 1689, renewed in 1727. Furs, cloth, and precious metals are bartered for tea. The gateway of the traffic is Kiachta, a Siberian town on the Chinese frontier.

812. *Fair ermines.* ' Ermine ' is said to be a corruption of ' Armenian,' from Armenia, in Asiatic Turkey.

813, *Sables.* From the Russian word *sobole*, the sable. Black sable furs were in greatest demand, and hence ' sable ' came to mean ' black.'

814. *freaked.* A rare word, coined from ' freckled,' and allied to ' flecked.' It means mottled, or spotted. Milton has—

> ' The white pink, and the pansy freaked with jet.'—*Lycidas,* 144.

818. *the branching elk.* The mature elk, or moose-deer, has antlers of a very broad blade, with from nine to as many as fourteen snags (or branches) on each horn. The weight of such antlers is great, and has been known to amount to 60 lbs. The neck of the elk is short and thick of necessity, to bear such a weight; and the creature goes on its knees to graze. It is about six feet high at the shoulder. Its timidity and inoffensiveness are remarkable, for it is strong as well as large.

821. *sounding bows.* Reference is made to the twanging bowstring, when the arrow is shot off.

826. The passage of ten lines ending here is almost a paraphrase of Virgil's Third Georgic, ll. 369–375.

827–833. A characteristic bit of description in Thomson's best style.

833. *Hardens his heart*, &c. The reference is to the bear's habit of hibernation—sleeping through the winter without food.

835. *Boötes* (Gr. βοώτης, the ox-driver). The constellation before the Great Bear, also called the Waggon, and the Plough, was named Boötes—which was fancied to represent and occupy the place of the driver of the Waggon. Arctos, as the whole group of stars known as the Great Bear, the Little Bear, and Boötes (Arcturus) is called, moves in a small circle round the pole, and therefore seems to move slowly—hence 'tardy' in the text.

836. *Caurus.* The north-west wind, which, being a stormy wind in Italy, is here used to designate a stormy wind.

836–838. *A boisterous race . . . Prolific swarm.* Cp. Milton—

    ' A multitude like which the populous north
    Poured never from her frozen loins to pass
    Rhene or the Danaw, when her barbarous sons
    Came like a deluge on the south, and spread
    Beneath Gibraltar to the Libyan sands.'

                Par. Lost, Bk. I, ll. 351–355.

Thomson pursues the subject in Liberty, Part III. ll. 512–543. There he describes the home-land of the Goths and Scythians, their training and early hardships, their incursions in the fifth and sixth centuries against the declining and falling empire of Rome, their destruction of ancient civilisation, and the long 'night of time that parted worlds'—the Dark Ages. He continues the subject in Part IV, and shows how at last a revival of learning and arts dawned on the Dark Ages.—The idea of a populous north was common from the sixteenth to the eighteenth century. In Liberty, III. l. 529, Thomson repeats the idea of the text—

    'And there a race of men prolific swarms.'

839. *lost mankind.* Lost manhood.

840. ' The wandering Scythian clans.'—Note by Thomson.

841. *enfeebled south.* Italy, Spain, &c., enervated by luxurious habits.

842. Established the feudal system.

843–886. The Lapps hardly deserve the praise here lavished upon them.

857. *marbled snow.* ' Glittering snow.' Milton speaks of the ' marble air.'

860. Referring to the Northern Lights, or the Aurora Borealis.

862. *radiant waste.* Either the starry expanse of sky; or, more probably, the snow-covered stretch of country, which by reflecting the light of the stars, may be said to double their lustre.

867. *dim Aurora.* This is not the Aurora Borealis, but the glimmer of the solar dawn.

870. *seen at last for ... months.* Owing to the inclination of the earth's axis, the extreme north polar regions are turned away from the sun during the months of winter, and are therefore then in ' the depth of polar night' (l. 863); while during the summer they are constantly turned towards the sun, and have then continual day. Those regions are ' the land of the midnight sun.'

875, 876. On these two lines, necessarily written after the publication (in 1738) of a certain book to be referred to shortly, Thomson has a couple of interesting notes: (*a*) ' M. de Maupertuis, in his book on The Figure of the Earth, after having described the beautiful lake and mountain of Niëmi, in Lapland, says: "From this height we had occasion several times to see those vapours rise from the lake which the people of the country call Haltios, and which they deem to be the guardian spirits of the mountains. We had been frightened with stories of bears that haunted this place, but saw none. It seemed rather a place of resort for fairies and genii than bears." '

(*b*) ' The same author observes: "I was surprised to see upon the banks of this river (the Tenglio) roses of as lively a red as any that are in our gardens." '

Pierre-Louis-Mareau de Maupertuis was born in 1698 at St. Malo. He abandoned the army, in which he held the rank of a captain of dragoons, for the purpose of devoting himself to the study of mathematics and astronomy. In 1723 he was admitted a member of the Royal Academy at Paris, and four years later became a Fellow of the Royal Society of London. He was commissioned by the Academy to proceed to the valley of Tornea to measure an arc of the meridian in Lapland. At the same time Commissioners were sent for a like purpose to Peru in the Southern hemisphere. In December, 1736, Maupertuis and his party, which included the Swedish astronomer Celsius, began their survey by measuring a base of 7407 toises [a toise, 6 pieds, being nearly 6.4 English feet] upon the frozen surface of Tornea. An account of this geodesical survey was published by Maupertuis in 1738—La Figure de la Terre, 8vo, Paris.

The Lapland village of Tornea is situated at the mouth of the river Tornea[1], at the head of the Gulf of Bothnia: the river in its lower course is the boundary between Sweden and Russia. At Tornea the midnight sun may be seen for almost a week at the time of the summer solstice.

Maupertuis, it may be added, defended the Newtonian theory of the earth's figure—that it is an oblate spheroid—against the theory of Descartes. He was vain even for a Frenchman, and had himself represented in the attitude of compressing the poles of the earth.

887. *Tornea's lake.* In the far north of Sweden, not far from the Norwegian frontier, and within the Arctic circle. The river issues from it.

888. *Hecla flaming.* The well-known volcano of Iceland.

891. *The muse . . . her solitary flight.* The poet's imagination among unpeopled snow-covered tracts of country and frozen seas.

893. *new seas beneath another sky.* Thomson's note here is—'The other hemisphere.' He means the north polar regions of the Western or New World hemisphere.

900, 901. These lines answer the question of ll. 113-115, *supra*.

902. *the Tartar's coast.* Siberia ; Northern Asia.

912. In the earlier text down to the edition of 1738, this line read—
    'Shake the firm pole, and make an ocean boil';
and was followed by the following six lines, dropped in the later editions :—
    'Whence heaped abrupt along the howling shore,
      And into various shapes (as fancy leans)
      Worked by the wave, the crystal pillars heave,
      Swells the blue portico, the Gothic dome
      Shoots fretted up, and birds and beasts and men
      Rise into mimic life, and sink by turns.
      The restless deep [itself can]not [resist],' &c.

918. *wavy rocks.* Waves frozen into rocks.

920-925. *Miserable they, Who . . . Take their last look,* &c. Cp. Burns—

---

[1] Campbell's reference to Tornea is due to Thomson:—
    'Cold as the rocks on Torneo's hoary brow.'
                         Pleasures of Hope, ii, l. 8.

'Clarinda, mistress of my soul,
   The measured time is run!
   The wretch beneath the dreary pole
   So marks his latest sun.'—*To Clarinda.*

925. *the Briton's fate.* The reference is to the expedition of Sir Hugh Willoughby, an Englishman, sent forth at the instance of commercial London in the year 1553, the last year of the reign of Edward VI, to find, if possible, a new sea route of trade to India and Eastern Asia. The route of traffic to India by the Cape, discovered by Vasco da Gama in 1498, was in the possession of Spain, and there was a great desire on the part of England to find and appropriate an independent route. Willoughby departed on his mission with three ships, and tried the North-East passage, round by the North Cape and the Northern shores of Russia and Siberia. Shortly after rounding the North Cape one of his ships was separated from the other two by a violent tempest, and entering the White Sea, arrived at Archangel. The commander of this vessel was Richard Chancellor ; the other two, under the leader of the expedition, sailed as far as Nova Zembla, whence they were driven back to the shores of Russian Lapland; and there the crews perished of cold. Their frozen bodies were subsequently found, much as Thomson has described them, in the mouth of the Arzina, east of the North Cape. Some other attempts to force the North-East passage were made ; but at last it was abandoned. The glory of discovering the passage was left to our own day: quite recently a Danish navigator, Nordenskjold, still living (1891), sailed completely round the Old World. The route, however, like the more famous North-West passage, is of interest only to geographers, of none to traders.

937. *the last of men.* The Samoyedes, inhabiting between Obi and Yenisei.

940. *wears its rudest form.* In the earlier text—'just begins to dawn.' The Samoyedes are a wretched race of men, untouched even by Russian civilisation.

944, 945. Cp. Goldsmith, of the Swiss—
   'Unknown to them, when sensual pleasures cloy,
   To fill the languid pause with finer joy ;
   Unknown those powers that raise the soul to flame,
   Catch every nerve, and vibrate through the frame ; . . .
   And love's and friendship's finely-pointed dart
   Fall blunted from each indurated heart.'—*The Traveller.*

947, 948. In the earlier text (from 1726 to 1738) these lines ran—
   'Till long-expected morning looks at length
   Faint on their fields (where Winter reigns alone),' &c.

950–987. This passage was added subsequently to 1738. It consists of a laudatory sketch—destitute of shading—of the life and character, and political work of Peter the Great of Russia. His death, in 1725, was a subject of general talk in England when Thomson was writing his Winter, but he deferred all reference to him in the earlier editions. The introduction here of his reforms in Russia is to the discredit of the Samoyedes, who are a 'gross race,' apparently incapable of 'active government.' The connection in the poem between the passage on the Samoyedes, and that on the Russians as civilised by the Czar Peter, is the contrast which the present state of the one people presents to that of the other.

952. *A people savage.* The Russians consist of several nationalities, but the prevailing element is Slavonian.

954. *from Gothic darkness.* Peter was, of course, a Slavonian; 'Gothic' is not used here in an ethnological sense, but as synonymous with 'barbaric.'

956–959. *His stubborn country tamed.* He introduced improved methods of engineering. drainage, agriculture; opened the Caspian Sea to Russian commerce, established a navy on the Black and Baltic seas, and disciplined his armies according to the military system of Western Europe by persistent warfare with the Swedes. He organised schools ; invited teachers of the arts from Austria, Italy, and Holland to Russia; commanded the young nobility of Russia to acquaint themselves by travel with the civilisation of Western and Southern Europe ; controlled and developed the press ; and caused translations of the most important works of foreign authors to be made and published. When, in 1698, he left England, whither he had been invited by William III, and where he took practical lessons (at Deptford) in the art of ship-building, &c., he carried with him to Russia, it is said, five hundred English artificers, engineers, surgeons, &c. to act as teachers of their respective arts and crafts to his own subjects.

960. *Ye shades,* &c. See l. 438, *supra.* Lycurgus, Solon, Servius, are here apostrophized.

967. *roaming every land.* He set out on his travels in 1697 (he was then in his 25th year) and visited Prussia, Hanover, Holland, England, and Austria.

in every port, e. g. Amsterdam, Saardam, Deptford, London, &c. A prime object of his policy was the establishment and maintenance of a Russian navy. To the art of ship-building he gave in his own person practical attention—working as a common ship-carpenter both at Saardam and at Deptford.

973. *cities rise amid the . . . waste.* Notably, his new capital,

St. Petersburg, founded in May, 1703, on an appropriated portion of Ingria, which was then a Swedish province.   In a few years it was the great commercial centre of the Baltic trade.

975. *flood to flood.*   By canals.   Volga and Don were so joined.

980. *Alexander of the north.*   Charles XII, King of Sweden.   The Swedes were at first successful in their encounters with the Russians, winning the great battle of Narva in 1700, but were at last defeated with overwhelming loss at Pultava, in 1709.

981. *Othman's shrinking sons.*   The Turks, or Osmanlis as they call themselves.   Peter's ambition was to possess the Black Sea.   Achmet III, the Sultan at this time (1710–1711), was dragged into war with the Russians by Charles XII, who was then residing in exile at Bender.

988. Thomson returns to his subject proper.   A temporary thaw and its effects and dangers are described in the following lines.

988–990.   These three lines stood originally, down to 1738—

> ' Muttering, the winds at eve with hoarser voice
> Blow blustering from the south.   The frost subdued
> Gradual resolves into a trickling thaw.'

' Muttering' and ' blustering' well describe the sound of the strong south wind, by which the snow is driven from the winter landscape, and the country flooded with *slush.*

resolves into a . . thaw.   Cp. Shakespeare's ' melt, thaw, and resolve itself into a dew ' in Hamlet's well-known soliloquy.

991. *Spotted, the mountains shine.*   With lingering patches of un-thawed snow.   Cp. Burns's—

> 'Aroused by blustering winds and spotting thowes.'
>
> *Brigs of Ayr.*

993. *Of bonds impatient.*   In the earlier text ' Impatient for the day.'   In the same line, for ' Sudden' the earlier text has ' Broke.'

1002. For ' deep' the original text gives ' main '—which, on the score of cadence, is to be preferred.

1004. *the bark with trembling wretches charged.*   In the earlier editions—' the bark, the wretch's last resort.'

1005–1008. *moors Beneath the shelter . . . While night,* &c.   Con-structed on Miltonic lines :—

> 'Moors by his side under the lee, while night
> Invests the sea, and wishèd morn delays.'
>
> *Par. Lost,* Bk. I. ll. 207, 208.

1014. *embroil the deep.*   Produce a scene of greater confusion. 'Embroil' is from Fr. *brouiller,* to jumble or confuse.   Cf. l. 247, *supra.*

1014–1016. *Leviathan And his unwieldy train . . . Tempest the*, &c. This too is a distinct echo of a passage in Paradise Lost, Bk. VII.—

> 'Part, huge of bulk,
> Wallowing unwieldy, enormous in their gait,
> Tempest the ocean. There leviathan, . . .
> Stretched like a promontory, sleeps or swims.'—ll. 410–414.

1016–1023. Campbell has caught up the situation, and elaborated it in his Pleasures of Hope, in the well-known passage descriptive of the hardships endured by 'the hardy Byron'; see Part I, ll. 102–120. See also, of the same Part of the poem, ll. 61–66, ending—

> 'And waft, across the waves' tumultuous roar,
> The wolf's long howl from Oonalaska's shore.'

1024. *'Tis done!* &c. The year is ended. In the earlier text the line ran—

> ''Tis done! Dread Winter has subdued the year.'

1025. *the conquered year.* 'The desert plains,' in the earlier editions.

1028–1045. Cp. Book of Job, chap. xiv. 1–15. (The Paraphrase by Michael Bruce is full of echoes from Thomson.)

1028. In the earlier editions, down to that of 1738—

> 'His solitary empire. Here, fond man!'

1029. *thy pictured life.* A Latin idiom; meaning 'the picture, or emblem of thy life.'

1033–1041. This reads like a part of Young's Night Thoughts. The reflections are in the same strain as those at l. 209, *supra*.

1055. *gall and bitterness.* An adaptation of a Scriptural phrase, see Acts viii. 23. 'Gall' is the Greek χολή, bile.

1058. *straining her.* In the earlier text 'prompting his.'

1061. *why licensed pain*, &c. The mystery of the existence of pain is here referred to. Thomson's conclusion is Longfellow's—

> 'It must be for some good
> By us not understood.'—*The Golden Legend.*

1065–1067. Enlarged from the earlier text, which ran—

> 'Yet a little while,
> And what you reckoned evil is no more.'

1069. Thus to the cheerful nature of Thomson, Winter ends with a promise of Spring.

A HYMN.

[The Hymn, which now consists of 118 lines, originally consisted of 121 : every alteration made on the text of 1738 is noted below.]

1. *These.* The seasons of the year.

2. *Are but the varied God.* Are manifestations of the power, bounty, beauty, benevolence, and other attributes, of the Deity. The idea is pantheistic. The material world in its various and varying forms is the expression of the divine mind appealing to the mind of man through the bodily senses. Cp. Pope's Essay on Man, Bk. I. ll. 267–274 (published two years subsequently to the Hymn),—'All are but parts,' &c.

4. *Thy beauty walks,* &c. In flowers and blossoms, universally diffused. Cp. Longfellow's poem on Flowers :—

'In the bright flowerets under us
Stands the revelation of his love.
Bright and glorious is that revelation
Written all over this great world of ours.'

Voices of the Night.

6. *the forest smiles.* In the earlier editions, down to that of 1738, 'the forests live.'

9. *refulgent.* See Summer, l. 2. In the earlier text the word used was 'severe'; and the metre was made up by beginning the next sentence with the word 'Prone.'

11. *dreadful.* Substituted for 'awful,' being more suggestive of the sound of thunder.

14, 15. For these two lines the edition of 1738, and all previous editions, give the following five lines—

'A yellow-floating pomp, thy bounty shines
In Autumn unconfined. Thrown from thy lap
Profuse o'er Nature, falls the lucid shower
Of beamy fruits ; and, in a radiant stream,
Into the stores of sterile winter pours.'

16. *awful.* Substituted for 'dreadful.' See Note, l. 11, *supra.* These slight alterations show the fineness of Thomson's ear for verbal melody. 'Awful' is a better sequence to 'Winter' than 'dreadful.'

18. *Majestic darkness.* Substituted for 'Horrible blackness.'

19. *adore.* Substituted for 'be low.'

23–26. In the edition of 1738, and previous editions—

'Yet so harmonious mixed, so fitly joined,
One following one in such enchanting sort,
Shade unperceived so softening into shade,
And all so forming such a perfect whole,' &c.

30. *the silent spheres.* The orbs of the stars. There is probably no reference here to the Ptolemaic, or pre-Copernican system of the starry universe, as set forth in Paradise Lost, and implied in many previous poems.

31. *the secret deep.* Not the sea, but the earth, where are the roots, 'the dark retreat of vegetation.'—Spring, ll. 79, 80.

steaming thence. Referring to the sap which in spring ascends from the roots in stem and stalk. See Spring, Note, ll. 79, 80.

40. *One general song.* Substituted for ' An universal hymn.'

40-88. These lines include the Hymn proper. They are modelled on the Psalm cxlviii of David. Coleridge's Hymn before Sunrise in the Vale of Chamouni (in Sibylline Leaves, published in 1817) is on the model of both.

41. *in your freshness breathes.* Substituted for 'teaches you to breathe.'

42-44. Such a passage as this, full of a fine feeling for the supernatural, and eminently characteristic of the religious sentiment of Thomson—which here and there anticipates the teaching of the great high priest of Nature, William Wordsworth—helps to explain, or at least to illustrate, the beautiful elegy which Collins wrote on the death of Thomson—' In yonder grave *a Druid* lies.'

44. *the brown shade.* Less felicitous than the original ' the brown void.'

45. *whose bolder note.* Cp. Psalm cxlviii. 7, 8 : ' Praise the Lord from the earth, ... stormy wind fulfilling His word.'

54. *stupendous.* Originally ' tremendous.'

56. *Soft roll.* Originally ' Roll up.'

57. *exalts.* Preferred to ' elates.'

58. *breath.* In the 1738 edition, 'hand.'

60. *Breathe your still song* [ye harvests!] *into the reaper's heart.* One of the most beautiful lines in Thomson's poetry—fraught with the heart-felt tranquillity of a typical autumn evening.

61. In the early editions (down to and inclusive of the edition of 1738)—' Homeward rejoicing with the joyous moon.'

62-65. Cp. Addison's well-known hymn—' The spacious firmament on high.'

66, 67. *Great source of day, best image here below,* &c. Cp. Milton, in the well-known Address to the Sun, Book IV. of Paradise Lost:—

> 'Thou that . . . .
> Look'st from thy sole dominion like the god
> Of this new world.'—ll. 32–34.

67, *pouring.* In the earlier text, 'darting.'

68. *the vital ocean.* The air enveloping the hemispheres.

71. *solemn.* Substituted for 'dreadful' in the earlier text.

75. For this line the earlier editions give—

> 'And yet again the golden age returns';

and add—

> 'Wildest of creatures! be not silent here,
> But, hymning horrid, let the desert roar.'

Line 75 of the finally settled text contains references, implied or expressed, to various Scriptural texts—to the second petition of the Lord's Prayer; to the doctrine of St. Paul, 'The creature itself also shall be delivered from .. bondage' (Rom. viii. 21); and to the prophecy of Isaiah, 'The wolf and the lamb shall feed together . . . They shall not hurt nor destroy in all my holy mountain' (Isaiah lxv. 25).

76. *boundless.* 'General' in the earlier text.

79. *sweet Philomela.* The nightingale. Philomela was one of the two daughters of King Pandion of Athens, and, being changed into a nightingale, gave her name to that bird. (See the story of Tereus in Ovid's Metam. Bk. VI.)

80. *teach the night His praise.* A condensation of the original text—

> 'Through the midnight hour,
> Trilling, prolong the wildly luscious note,
> That night as well as day may vouch his praise.'

81. *Ye chief.* Mankind.

82. *tongue.* 'Mouth' in the earlier editions.

84. *Assembled men.* 'Concourse of men' in the earlier editions.

84–86. *to the deep organ join,* &c. Cp. Milton's Il Penseroso—

> 'Let the pealing organ blow
> To the full-voiced quire below
> In service high and anthems clear.'—ll. 161–163.

at solemn pauses. 'At' for 'after.'

90. Originally 'To find a fane,' &c. See Note, ll. 42–44, *supra.*

91. *the virgin's lay.* Originally 'the virgin's chant.'

92. *The prompting seraph.* The muse of religious lyrical poetry. Cp. Milton's 'Heavenly Muse,' and 'Spirit,' in the opening lines of his great epic.

94. *the darling theme.* Praise to God; 'His praise' in ll. 48, 54, 69, 80.

'Gentle Thomson, as the Seasons roll,
   Taught them to sing their great Creator's praise
   And bear their poet's name from pole to pole'
         Michael Bruce, *Elegy written in Spring* (of 1766).

Young Michael Bruce, a Scots poet of great promise, was one of the most devoted of the followers of Thomson.

96. *Russets the plain.* Said, not of autumn but summer: referring to the effect of summer drought upon the grass. See Castle of Indolence, I. l. 16.

inspiring. In the original text 'delicious.' The reference here is to poetical inspiration. Thomson found the autumn season most conducive to poetical thought and composition. Cp. Shenstone's Verses to W. Lyttelton—

'Thomson, sweet descriptive bard,
   Inspiring Autumn sung.'—ll. 29, 30.

Autumn gleams. In fields of yellow corn—the reflected light from which is strong enough to illumine the evening.

97. *blackening.* 'Reddening' in the earlier text.

100–104. Cp. Horace—

'Pone me pigris ubi nulla campis
   Arbor aestiva recreatur aura,' &c.—*Car.* I. 22.

101. *distant.* 'Hostile' in the earlier text.

105–107. The same sentiment is more fully expressed in Paradise Lost:—

'Yet doubt not but in valley and in plain
   God is, as here, and will be found alike
   Present; and of his presence many a sign
   Still following thee, still compassing thee round
   With goodness and paternal love, his face
   Express, and of his steps the track divine.'
                     Bk. XI. ll. 349–354.

107–113. Substituted after 1738 for—

'Rolls the same kindred seasons round the world,
   In all apparent, wise and good in all;
   Since he sustains and animates the whole,' &c.

113. *their sons.* Their inhabitants.

114. *educing.* 'Educes' in the earlier editions. The line is Miltonic in sentiment. Cp. Par. Lost, Bk. VII. ll. 615, 616:—

'His evil
Thou usest, and from thence creat'st more good.'

See Winter, l. 1061, and Note.

115, 116. *and better still, In infinite progression.* Thomson's theory of spiritual evolution, often referred to in his poetry, was an essential part of his religious belief.

> ' Heirs of eternity, y-born to rise
> Through endless states of being, still more near
> To bliss approaching, and perfection clear.'
>> *Castle of Indolence*, II. st. lxi.

See also, and compare, Liberty, III. ll. 69, 70; Spring, ll. 375-377; Winter, ll. 357, 358, &c. In a letter to Dr. Cranstoun, of date Oct. 20, 1735, Thomson writes: ' This I think we may be sure of, that a future state must be better than this; and so on through the never-ceasing succession of future states, every one rising upon the last, an everlasting new display of infinite goodness.'

THE CASTLE OF INDOLENCE.

INTRODUCTORY NOTE.

The Castle of Indolence was published early in the summer of 1748, the last year of Thomson's life: his death occurred on the 27th of August, about four months after the publication of the poem. The work was the slow and leisurely composition of nearly fifteen years. Writing in the middle of April, 1748, to his friend, and successor in the office of Surveyor-General of the Leeward Islands, William Paterson, then resident at Barbadoes, the poet announces ' that after fourteen or fifteen years the Castle of Indolence comes abroad in a fortnight.' He goes on, ' It will certainly travel as far as Barbadoes. You have an apartment in·it as a night-pensioner [see l. 521, Canto I], which, you may remember, I fitted up for you during our delightful party at North Ham.' The composition of the Castle of Indolence thus covered more than the entire period of Thomson's residence at Richmond, where he lived in a garden-house in Kew-foot Lane, in comparative retirement and moderately luxurious ease from 1736 to the day of his death. The publisher was his old friend, ' good-natured and obliging Millar,' the bookseller, who had taken a house at Richmond to be near Thomson. The first edition was in quarto; the second, published in the same year, in octavo. The text of the latter has been faithfully followed in the present edition.

The origin of the poem is of amusing interest. Thomson's indolent habits, both of life and composition, were notorious —

'His ditty sweet
He loathed much to write, ne carèd to repeat;'
and they were often made the butt of the good-natured banter, and remonstrance, of his friends. He did not seek to deny the soft impeachment; but he ventured to retaliate upon his friends that they were equally inclined in their own way to ease and idleness, and took his revenge by gently caricaturing in a few disconnected stanzas the peculiar phases of their common failing. The poem grew out of those stanzas. In its finished state it may be regarded as an apology and a warning. The apology, mostly playfully urged, is for his own indolence; the warning is meant to discourage the indulgence of indolence in others. The warning is eloquent, with outbursts of true poetry, but—as is usually the fate of warnings—is likely to continue to be neglected for the more engaging charms of the apology. And yet there is much sympathetic writing on the pleasures of an industrious life very capable of inspiring and directing the energies of healthy youth.

The poem is allegorical, and was professedly written in imitation of The Faerie Queene. The Advertisement prefixed to the poem runs as follows :—' This poem being writ in the manner of Spenser, the obsolete words, and a simplicity of diction in some of the lines which borders on the ludicrous, were necessary to make the imitation more perfect. And the style of that admirable poet, as well as the measure in which he wrote, are, as it were, appropriated by custom to all allegorical poems writ in our language; just as in French the style of Marot, who lived under Francis the First, has been used in tales and familiar epistles by the politest writers of the age of Louis the Fourteenth.' Notwithstanding this explanation of his employment of the Spenserian stanza for The Castle of Indolence, Thomson's avoidance of the measure which Pope had so popularized and perfected is significant of the robustness of his genius in refusing, even in respect of verse-form, to own allegiance to the artificial school. Neither in The Seasons nor in The Castle of Indolence did he adopt the heroic couplet. It may have been that the popular taste was beginning to be cloyed with the monotonous sweetness and smoothness of Pope's art, which seemed incapable of further development; at all events the change of form accompanying the more important change of theme in poetical literature which Thomson instituted, and in which others followed his example, was relished from the very first. At the same time it must be owned that Thomson's ideas on the subject of

verse-forms had been greatly modified by the influence of the artificial
school during the period of his residence in England. When he sat
down in 1725 to write his Winter it was with a contempt for rhyme
only less pronounced than that of Milton in the later period of his life.
He lived to entertain worthier ideas of form; and few will doubt that
his poetical genius was improved by the discipline of art, and that it
shines on the whole to better advantage in the elaborate setting of the
Spenserian stanza than in the rough though rich accumulations of The
Seasons.   Thomson manages the Spenserian stanza with an easy grace
of art which is not constantly reminding you of the artist.   In his hands
the measure seems the natural expression of the sentiment.   There is
probably as much redundancy of phraseology in The Castle of
Indolence as in The Seasons; but there is an absence of tumidity:
the diction is more natural in the sense that it is less conventional.
The archaic and rustic words with which the poem is sprinkled help
to withdraw the imagination of the reader out of the work-a-day present
into an ideal world of the romantic past; but, it must be said, they are
not always correctly, nor even systematically, employed.   The poet
breaks away now and again for whole stanzas from the use of these old
forms; then, as if reminded of the omission, suddenly scatters a
handful.   The style shows more variety than The Seasons.   Now it is
serious, grave, even solemn; now it is cheerful, lively, and gay.   It
borders frequently on burlesque, mostly of a genially brisk and airy
character; once or twice it drops into downright inanity (see l. 383,
Canto II); there are, however, numerous descriptive passages of clear-
ringing and exalted melody sufficient in themselves to rank Thomson
as a genuine singer of commanding rank.   It might be possible to trace
in the poetry of Keats and Shelley the influence of those passages.

The poem is less popular than The Seasons, but it is the most
exquisite of all Thomson's works.   It consists of two Cantos: the first,
which might almost be entitled The Pleasures of Indolence, describes
the 'fatal valley gay,' the enchanting castle and its luxurious appointments, its wizard, and its willing inmates.   The second follows the
career of a certain Knight of Arts and Industry, who, with his friend
the bard Philomelus, invades the valley, snares the wizard, and offers
freedom to the captives—which they are all at first reluctant, and some
at last unable or unwilling, to accept.   These irreclaimable victims of
Indolence are punished by being hunted through the world by Beggary

and Scorn. They are compared to a strayed herd of the swine of Comus, driven by dogs and sticks through the miry thoroughfare of a provincial town; and with the unsavoury simile the poem rather abruptly ends.

The four medical stanzas at the end of the first canto were written by Dr. Armstrong, author of The Art of Preserving Health; and the description of the indolent bard 'more fat than bard beseems' (Canto I, st. lxviii) is the Hon. George, afterwards Lord, Lyttelton's portrait of Thomson himself.

In May, 1802, Wordsworth wrote a set of eight Spenserian stanzas in his pocket copy of The Castle of Indolence, which may briefly be noticed here. They are written in a style that is in wonderful harmony with that of Thomson, except that it is more diffuse. They offer two additional portraits to the series of the Castle inmates, representing more or less faithfully Wordsworth himself and his friend Coleridge. The latter is thus presented :—

> 'With him there often walked in friendly guise,
> Or lay upon the moss by brook or tree,
> A noticeable man with large gray eyes,
> And a pale face that seemed undoubtedly
> As if a blooming face it ought to be :
> Heavy his low-hung lip did oft appear,
> Depressed by weight of musing phantasie;
> Profound his forehead was, though not severe,
> Yet some did think that he had little business here.'

And the two together are thus described in the last stanza :—

> 'He would entice that other man to hear
> His music, and to view his imagery :
> And, sooth, these two did love each other dear
> As far as love in such a place could be ;
> There did they dwell, from earthly labour free,
> As happy spirits as were ever seen :
> If but a bird, to keep them company,
> Or butterfly sate down they were, I ween,
> As pleased as if the same had been a maiden queen.'

D d

CANTO I.

The short-lined quatrain of doggerel with which each of the two Cantos is introduced, and which briefly indicates its contents, is in imitation of 'my master Spenser' (Canto II, st. lii, l. 9). The first canto of the first Book of The Faerie Queene, for example, has for prelude—

> 'The Patrone of true Holinesse
> Foule Errour doth defeate:
> Hypocrisie, him to entrappe,
> Doth to his home entreate.'

The 'alas!' of the third line is in sorrow for the transitoriness of the pleasures of indolence. It is well named a Castle, for, though the description conveys rather the idea of a palace, the inmates were really captives with small chance of regaining their freedom.

The first stanza points the moral of the Allegory. The story commences at the second stanza.

1. *here.* Not in the Castle of Indolence, of course, but in this world.

2. *Do not complain of this,* i.e. of 'living by toil'—'thy hard estate.'

3. *emmet.* Doublet, 'ant'; from A.-S. *æmete*, shortened in Middle English into *amte*, whence 'ant.' The ant has long been proverbial for its industry. See Proverbs vi. 6.

4. *sentence of an ancient date.* Pronounced upon Adam on the occasion of his expulsion from the Garden of Eden :—' In the sweat of thy face shalt thou eat bread, till thou return unto the ground' (Gen. iii. 19).

7. *curse thy stars.* Thy ill fortune—an expression that has survived belief in the superstition of astrology. Cp. 'disaster,' 'consider,' 'influence,' &c.

8. *an heavier bale,* i.e. heavier than toil. For 'bale,' see Glossary.

9. Illustrated at some length in the last five stanzas of this Canto.

10, 11. Cp. the opening lines of Keats's Hyperion. And see Faery Queene, Bk. I, Canto I, st. xxxiv.

16. *with summer half imbrowned.* So in the Hymn on the Seasons—

> 'The summer ray
> Russets the plain.'—ll. 95, 96.

17. *A listless climate.* A warm enervating climate inducing listlessness.

22. *From poppies breathed.* Exhaled from poppies. The common poppy (*papaver somniferum*) yields the well-known opium, a powerful narcotic formed of the dried juice of its unripe capsules.

26. *as they bickered.* The original Celtic meaning of 'bicker' is 'to skirmish.' It comes from 'peak' or 'peck,' and signifies 'to keep on pecking'; applied to a stream it suggests the rapid tremulous movement of the current. Thomson uses it in the last sense in Winter, l. 725, in speaking of the frost 'arresting the bickering stream.'

27. *a lulling murmur made:* The sense here is aptly aided by the sound, and the monotony is produced by the repetition of the liquid *l*'s and *m*'s. For the same effect of monotony produced by the same cause of repetition, see l. 45 *infra.*

28–30. Cp. Spring, ll. 197–200—

> 'Full swell the woods : their every music wakes,
> Mixed in wild concert with the warbling brooks
> Increased, the distant bleatings of the hills,
> And hollow lows responsive from the vales.'

31. *vacant shepherds.* Free from care. Cp. Goldsmith's 'loud laugh that speaks the vacant mind.'—*Deserted Village.*

32. *Philomel.* Philomela, one of the two daughters of King Pandion of Athens, having been transformed into a nightingale, her name is poetically given to the bird.

33. *'plain.* For 'complain.' Referring to the low, soft, plaintive note of the wood-pigeon.

35. *a coil the grasshopper did keep.* A sharp grating sound with pleasant associations of sunshine and green fields, accentuating the repose and stillness of rural life. 'Coil,' which means 'noise' or 'bustle,' is Celtic—*goil*, rage, battle. The word recurs in Shakespeare —in Hamlet's soliloquy, 'this mortal coil'; in Romeo and Juliet, 'Here's a coil,' &c.

38 and 41. See l. 11, *supra.*

39. *shadowy forms were seen to move.* See Autumn, ll. 1029–1033—

> 'Oh bear me then to vast embowering shades . . .
> Where angel-forms athwart the solemn dusk
> Tremendous sweep, or seem to sweep, along.'

42, 43. *blackening pines, aye waving . . . Sent forth a sleepy horror.* The 'horror' was from the 'blackening pines,' the sleep was induced by the monotony of the 'waving.' Cp. Genesis xv. 12, 'A deep sleep fell upon Abram ; and, lo, an horror of great darkness fell upon him.' Cp. also—

> 'Through every joint a gentle horror creeps,
> And round you the consenting audience sleeps.'
> Thomson's *Soporific Doctor.*

D d 2

45. The distant undertone and monotone of the sea is finely brought out in this alliterative line. See Note, l. 27, *supra*.

46–49. These are lines of singular beauty, descriptive of the pleasures of day-dreaming.

55. *The landskip such.* Such was the landscape.

60. *unceasing.* Unfailing, constant. ·

61. The palm is the product of a summer climate. In poetry it may grow in the same soil with the pine, as in Milton's Eden [1], Shakespeare's Arden, the forests of the Faery Queene, &c.

62. *Was placed.* Was seated; placed himself.

　cruel fate. The 'labour harsh' in the next line.

65. *that pass there by.*

> 'The moon, sweet regent of the sky,
> 　Silvered the walls of Cumnor Hall,
> 　And many an oak that grew there by.'—Julius Mickle.

Milton has 'that passed that way' (Par. Lost, Bk. IV, l. 177) to express the same idea.

66. *chaunced to breathe.* Happened to rest—take breath from toil. Contrast this with its older meaning 'to exert' or 'exercise':—'I am not yet well breathed.'—*As You Like It*, Act I, sc. ii.

70. *syren melody.* Thus described in Comus :—

> 'I have oft heard
> My mother Circe with the Sirens three, . . .
> Who, as they sung, would take the prisoned soul,
> And lap it in Elysium : Scylla wept
> And chid her barking waves into attention,
> And fell Charybdis murmured soft applause.
> But they in pleasing slumber lulled the sense,
> And in sweet madness robbed it of itself.'

According to Homer the Sirens (Σειρῆνες) were sea-nymphs, who had the power of luring to destruction, by the charm of their songs, all who heard them. The island on which they lived was between Aeaea and the rock of Scylla, near the south-west shore of Italy. Homer says nothing about their number.

76. *her wintry tomb.* The chrysalis (aurelia), or gold-coloured sheath of butterflies, &c.

77. *What . . . bride can equal her array?* Cp. Thomson's Paraphrase of the latter part of the sixth chapter of Matthew :—

> 'What regal vestments can with them compare?
> What king so shining, and what queen so fair?'

---

[1] 'Cedar and pine and fir and branching palm,
　A sylvan scene.'—*Par. Lost*, Bk. IV, l. 139.

82–90. Cp. Thomson's Paraphrase of part of Matthew vi :—

> 'See the light tenants of the barren air!
> To them nor stores nor granaries belong,
> Nought but the woodland and the pleasing song. . .
> To Him they sing   .   .   .   .   .   .
> He hears   .   .   .   .
> And with inspiring bounty fills them all.'

83. *careless grove.* The grove where they have no cares. Cp. 'listless climate,' l. 17, *supra.*

84. *the flowering thorn.* So Burns, in Banks and Braes o' Bonnie Doon :—

> 'Thou'll break my heart, thou warbling bird,
> That wantons thro' the flowering thorn.'

85, 86. So Chaucer in the Prologue to the Canterbury Tales :—

> 'Smale fowles maken melodie, . . .
> So priketh hem nature in here corages.'—ll. 9, 11.

87, 88. *They neither plough, nor sow,* &c. Cp. Matthew vi. 26 : 'Behold the fowls of the air ; for they sow not, neither do they reap, nor gather into barns.'

fit for flail. Ready for threshing : the reference is to the sheaves.

nodding sheaves. Cp. Autumn, ll. 1, 2—

> 'Crowned with the sickle and the wheaten sheaf,
> While Autumn, nodding o'er the yellow plain,' &c.

drove. The tense here is present ; an archaic-looking form for 'drive.'

89, 90. *theirs each harvest,* &c. Cp. Pope's Essay on Man—

> 'Is thine alone the seed that strews the plain?
> The birds of heaven shall vindicate their grain.'
>
> Epist. III, ll. 37, 38.

91, 92. *the wretched thrall Of bitter-dropping sweat.* The slave of toil. 'In the sweat of thy face shalt thou eat bread' (Gen. iii. 19).

93. *cares that eat away the heart.* Cp. Milton's L'Allegro—

> 'Ever, against eating cares,
> Lap me in soft Lydian airs.'—ll. 135, 136.

95. *savage thirst of gain.* Cp. Virgil's 'auri sacra fames.'

96. *Interest.* Self-interest ; selfishness.

97. *Astræa left the plain.* In the golden age this star-lovely divinity lived on earth, and blessed mankind with her presence ; but when the golden age was over, she too, with other divinities that loved the simplicity of primitive man, at last reluctantly withdrew, shocked at the crimes and vices which were polluting the early world. She represented Justice.

97-99. Cp. Campbell's Pleasures of Hope—
> 'Murder bared her arm, and rampart War
> Yoked the red dragons of her iron car,
> [And] Peace and Mercy, banished from the plain,
> Sprung on the viewless winds to Heaven again.'

99. *for.* Instead of.

100. *cumbrous load of life.* Here compared to the stone which Sisyphus was condemned to roll up hill in the infernal world, and which, as soon as he had pushed it with great labour to the top, always rolled down again.

109. Thomson's own habit latterly was to rise at noon.

110. *To pass the joyless day.* Cp. Burns—'And pass the heartless day.'—*Winter, a Dirge.*

111. *upstart fortune.* Fortunate upstart.

113-116. Thomson seems to have cherished an ineradicable hatred and contempt for pettifogging lawyers. Cp. Autumn, l. 1287—
> 'Let this through cities work his eager way
> By legal outrage and established guile, . . .
>   Let these
> Ensnare the wretched in the toils of law,
> Fomenting discord and perplexing right,
> An iron race!'

Also Winter, l. 384—
> 'The toils of law,—what dark insidious men
> Have cumbrous added to perplex the truth
> And lengthen simple justice into trade—
> How glorious were the day that saw these broke!'

118. *No cocks . . . to rustic labour call.* Cp. Gray's Elegy—
> 'The cock's shrill clarion   .   .   .
> No more shall rouse them from their lowly bed.'

But see l. 690, *infra,*—'Gout here counts the crowing cocks.'

118-124. Cp. Cowper's Task, Bk. I, l. 225—
> 'Hidden as it is, and far remote
> From such unpleasing sounds as haunt the ear
> In village or in town,—the bay of curs,
> Incessant clinking hammers, grinding wheels,
> And infants clamorous, whether pleased or pained—
> Oft have I wished the peaceful covert mine.'

126. *Sybarite.* A voluptuary. Literally, an inhabitant of Sybaris, a Greek town in Lucania in southern Italy. The prosperity of the town induced in the inhabitants an indolent and luxurious habit of life.

133. *With milky blood the heart is over flown.* Cp. Shakespeare's Macbeth—

　'It [thy nature] is too full o' the milk of human kindness.'

　　　　　　　　　　　　　　　　　　　　Act I, Sc. v.

136. *What, what is virtue?* The repetition of 'what' more emphatically challenges any other answer to the question than that given by the sophist.

140. *a proud malignant worm!* The factitive object; supply 'making him.'

141. *But here, instead, soft gales of passion play.* See ll. 50–52, *supra.*

145. *The best of men.* 149. *Even those whom fame,* &c. Such as Scipio Africanus the younger, cited by Thomson himself at l. 152, *infra.* See Winter, ll. 517–520, and Note :—

　　　　　'Scipio, the gentle chief,　.　.　.　.
　　　　　[Who], warm in youth to the poetic shade
　　　　　With friendship and Philosophy retired.'

The 'friends' and 'philosophers,' to whose society he is represented as 'retiring' from warfare and politics, included Polybius, Laelius (his friendship with whom is the subject of Cicero's De Amicitia), Lucilius, and Terentius. (See Liberty, Part V, ll. 419–421.)

152. *the soft Cumæan shore.* The ancient town of Cumae stood on the coast of Campania, a few miles to the west of Neapolis (Naples), and not far from Cape Misenum. It was at Cajeta (Gaeta) on the border of Campania, but in Latium, where Scipio found retirement. Its bay is inferior only in beauty to that of Naples. Both Virgil and Horace have celebrated it.

154. The 'exercise' congenial with an indolent life is here made to include the composition of poetry, gardening, and angling. Compare the pastimes of Cowper in his Olney retirement—which chiefly consisted of gardening and 'the poet's toil.'

　　　　　'How various his employments whom the world
　　　　　　Calls idle!　.　.　.　.　.　.
　　　　　Friends, books, a garden, and perhaps his pen.'

　　　　　　　　　　　　　　　　　　The Task, Bk. III.

157. *deck the vernal year.* Have a fine display of flowers in Spring-time.

158. *with your watery gear.* In Spring 'thy slender watery stores,' —flies, rod, line, &c. (See Spring, ll. 383–386.)

159. *crimson-spotted fry.* 'The speckled captives' of Spring, l. 421.

163. *estate.* Here it means 'fortune' or 'possessions'; the original

meaning is 'condition of life,' and the word is used in this sense in l. 2, *supra.*

164. *beneath the sun.* 'Under the sun'—a recurring phrase in Ecclesiastes; see chap. viii. 15 : 'The days of his life which God giveth him under the sun.'

165. *comes blind unrelenting fate.* Cp. Milton's Lycidas—

'Comes the blind Fury with the abhorrèd shears
And slits the thin-spun life.'—ll. 75, 76.

165-169. This passage seems to present various recollections of Horace, e. g.—

'Linquenda tellus et domus . . .
Absumet heres Caecuba dignior
Servata centum clavibus et mero
Tinget pavimentum superbo.'—*Car.* II. 14.

'Jam te premet nox fabulaeque Manes
Et domus exilis Plutonia.'—*Car.* I. 4.

172, 173. *He ceased. But still,* &c. Cp. Milton's Par. Lost, Bk VIII. ll. 1-3 :—

'The angel ended, and in Adam's ear
So charming left his voice that he a while
Thought him still speaking, still stood fixed to hear.'

177-180. This in itself is an exquisite simile, charming the imagination with both picture and melody ; but it is, in respect of application, hardly in harmony with a throng entering pell-mell and pouring in heaps on heaps. True, Thomson describes this same throng as slipping along at the same time in silent ease ; but the mind refuses to blend two descriptions that are so contradictory. See l. 208, *infra.*

The simile suggests a scene in A Midsummer Night's Dream. The 'gleam' of l. 179 is, of course, the reflected light of summer-moons. The entrance of the fairy train into the natural world from their supernatural home is finely suggested by the concluding line of the stanza.

181. *the smooth demon.* The wizard, Indolence. His character is evidently modelled on that of Archimago in the Faery Queene, whose tongue was 'filed as smooth as glass,' and who 'of pleasing wordes had store' (I. i. xxxv). See Canto II, l. 281, *infra,* for confirmation of this idea.

195, 196. *the giant crew, Who sought,* &c. The Titans, or rather the Gigantes, who are often confounded with the Titans.

209. *A comely full-spread porter, swoln,* &c. Cp. with Morpheus in the Faery Queene, I. i. xl–xliv.

215. *black staff.* His rod, or wand of office.

his man. His servant. Cp. Shakespeare's Tempest :—
'Caliban
Has a new master ;—get a new man !'

221, 222. *each band . . . . Garters and buckles.* Of the inmates of the Castle.

223. *But ill.* 'But' is here an adverb, with an intensive force on 'ill.'

225. *performèd it.* The pronoun 'it' here represents the disengagement of the bands, buckles, &c.

229, 230. The downs of Hants and Dorset were well-known to Thomson. He was a frequent visitor at Eastbury House, and had lived at Twiford. 'When Evening *frowns*,' i. e. 'darkens.'

234. *and turned to sleep again.* So Morpheus in the Faery Queene (I. i. xliv).

240. *nepenthe.* A drug which lulled sorrow, or freed from sorrow. From Gr. νη-, negative, and πένθos, grief.

'Not that Nepenthes . . . .
Is of such power to stir up joy.'—*Comus*, ll. 675, 677.

241-243. *as Dan Homer sings.* For 'Dan' see Glossary. Homer refers to the pain-lulling property of a certain drug which when cast into wine brought oblivion of every sorrow. In the Odyssey he traces its origin to Egypt, 'where earth, the grain-bestower, yields abundance of herbs, many medicinal and many baneful,' and describes the use which was made of it by 'Helena, daughter of Zeus.' Milton also refers to this passage in the Odyssey :—

'Nepenthes, which the wife of Thone [Polydamna]
In Egypt gave to Jove-born Helena.'—*Comus*, ll. 675, 676.

242. *oblivion of . . earthly care.* Cp. 'And all their friends and native home forget.'—*Comus*, l. 76.

244. This line consists of two absolute clauses.

247. *through hall or glade.* In the Castle, or in the Castle grounds. 'Hall' is usually associated with 'bower'—both words signifying rooms in a house, the 'hall' the public room, and 'bower' a private room.

'I will tell you now
What never yet was heard in tale or song,
From old or modern bard, in hall or bower.'
Comus, ll. 43-45.

It is impossible that Thomson has mistaken the meaning of 'bower' by offering 'glade,' with its woodland bowers, as a translation.

249. *as likes him best.* The verb is impersonal, and is followed by a dative. Literally, ' As it is likest or most suitable for him.' So, 'if you like,' is 'if to you it be suitable or pleasing.'

250. *his neighbour's trade.* His neighbour's affairs, whether of business or pastime.

257. *blank area.* Empty by reason of their departure. The metaphor is a white page, having nothing printed on it.

261. 'So that one was almost constrained to think that one was dreaming.' The 'singular' use of 'you' is to be noticed here.

262. The beautiful simile beginning here is in the manner of Milton; see e.g. Par. Lost, Bk. IV, ll. 159-165, and ll. 183-191; only it is more loosely connected with the passage (in the preceding stanza) which it is meant to illustrate, than are any of Milton's with their context. Milton's 'as' is usually followed, though at a long interval, by a corre- lating 'so' which makes application of the simile to the scene or action described. There is here no such final application of the simile; the introductory 'as' is the sole connection, and it seems to introduce an afterthought. The simile is intended, of course, to illustrate the suddenness and completeness of the change from 'endless numbers swarming round' to 'solitude and perfect silence'; but the reader is less concerned with the thing illustrated than with the illustration, and his imagination is inclined rather to stay with the shepherd on that sunset-illumined isle 'placed far amid the melancholy main' than to return to the blank area of the Castle courtyard.

the Hebrid Isles. The Western islands of Scotland, from Lewis to Islay.

263. *amid the melancholy main.* A musical and suggestive phrase. Cp. Autumn, ll. 861-864:—

> 'Where the Northern Ocean in vast whirls
> Boils round the naked melancholy isles
> Of farthest Thulè, and the Atlantic surge
> Pours in among the stormy Hebrides.'

264. *Whether it be lone fancy him beguiles.* Cp. Wordsworth's Excursion—

> 'By creative feeling overborne,
> Or by predominance of thought oppressed.'—Bk. I.

268. *Phœbus dips his wain.* The sun sets. Cp. Milton's Comus—

> 'The gilded car of day
> His glowing axle doth allay
> In the steep Atlantic stream.'—ll. 95-97.

271. Here, after an apology to the very vice of Indolence which it is the object of his poem to expose (see also l. 3 of the quatrain which introduces this canto), Thomson commences a series of stanzas—ending

with stanza lv.—which might very well be entitled The Pleasures of Indolence. But for his having himself been a votary of Indolence, he thinks he could have done justice to the subject! It will hardly be denied that the indolent habit of Thomson well qualified him both to appreciate and to express, as he has done, the pleasures of an idle and easy life.

275. 'What never yet was heard in tale or song.'—Comus, l. 44.

276. *attempt such arduous string.* 'Essay a strain so difficult—a subject so much beyond my power.' The metaphor is taken from the art of the musician whose instrument is the harp.

277. *nightly days.* Days turned into nights by sleeping or idling through them. Thomson's normal hour of rising was noon.

279. *uprear my moulted wing.* Rouse my imagination which has not been exercised for a long time. The image is a falcon confined to a mew.

281. *imp of Jove.* For 'imp,' see Glossary. The nine Muses were the daughters of Zeus, or Jupiter, and Mnemosyne, or Memory.

282, 283. *Thou yet shalt sing,* &c. And so he has, in Rule Britannia. Cp. Milton's Epitaphium Damonis (l. 162)—

     'Ipse ego Dardanias Rutupina per aequora puppes
      Dicam . . . .'

284. There is no reference here to any intended translation from classical authors—for which, indeed, Thomson had not the necessary scholarship; but to a revival of the old approved methods and themes of poetry.

285–288. Thomson's dramas were Sophonisba (1730), Agamemnon (1738), Edward and Eleanora (1739), Tancred and Sigismunda (1745), and Coriolanus (1749—the year after his death). The Masque of Alfred (1740) may be added, for the sake of the lyric, Rule Britannia—though most of the piece was the composition of Malloch.

This stanza is interesting as containing a sketch of Thomson's literary plans. See, for a reference to other plans of a like nature, the concluding lines of his Autumn, and the Note.

285. *in tragic pall.* Cp. the 'inky cloak' in Hamlet. Lat. *palla,* a mantle. 'Thespis was succeeded [in representations of the tragic drama] by Æschylus, who erected a permanent stage, and was the inventor of the mask [*persona*], of the long flowing robe [*palla*], and of the high-heeled shoe or buskin [*cothurnus*], which tragedians wore; whence these words are put for a tragic style or for tragedy itself.'— Adam's Roman Antiquities.

289, 290. *no shrill . . . bell, Ne cursèd knocker.* Cp. Cowper's Task, Bk. IV—

> 'No powdered pert, proficient in the art
> Of sounding an alarm assaults these doors
> Till the street rings.'—ll. 145–147.

292. *expand.* Used transitively here in the first edition.

293. *The pride of Turkey*, &c. Carpets, introduced into Europe from the East, where the custom among Orientals of sitting cross-legged on the floor suggested their invention.

297. *each spacious room was one full-swelling bed.* 'The first canto,' says Johnson, 'opens a scene of lazy luxury that fills the imagination.' Much of 'the lazy luxury' is caught in this one line.

298–300. These lines remind one of the banquetting hall in the 'stately palace' of Comus—'set out with all manner of deliciousness: soft music, tables spread with all dainties.'

> 'See, here be all the pleasures
> That fancy can beget on youthful thoughts,   . .
> And first behold this cordial julep here
> That flames and dances in his crystal bounds
> With spirits of balm and fragrant syrups mixed.'
>   *Comus*, ll. 668–674.

Thomson's music is not provided till we come to l. 343 ; and then he devotes three stanzas to it.

300–302. Cp. Comus—

> 'Wherefore did Nature pour her bounties forth,
> Covering the earth with odours, fruits, and flocks,
> Thronging the seas with spawn innumerable,
> But all to please and sate the curious taste ?'—ll. 710–714.

303–306. . . *You need but wish* . . . A refinement of the well-known device to be found in fairy and Oriental tales of purveying a feast by the utterance of a few magical words. Even 'signs' are dispensed with in The Castle of Indolence, as being too fatiguing.

306. *thick the glasses played.* The light glanced on innumerable glasses. 'Thick' almost always signifies 'numerous' in The Seasons.

308. *ancient maiden.* The modern 'old maid'—popularly supposed to be the source of all the scandal that disturbs a neighbourhood.

309. *saintly spleen.* The ill-nature, or spite, of clerical bigotry; or, it might be, the interference of 'the unco guid'—as they are called in Scotland.

310. Poisoning one's pleasures, and making them 'pall,' by denouncing them as sinful. 'Pall' here is used 'causatively.' The use of 'our' is to be noted: Thomson frankly classes himself amongst the votaries of Indolence.

316. Tapestry—said to have been invented by the Saracens, and

early introduced into Europe as a decorative hanging for the walls of
rooms. The famous Bayeux tapestry contains embroidered representations of battle, and military movements, connected with the Norman
invasion and conquest of England. It belongs to the eleventh, at latest
the twelfth century, and is the oldest piece in existence. The Flemings
brought the highest decorative art to the weaving of tapestry. Even
Raphael furnished carefully prepared designs for the tapestry-weavers.
Historical and ideal sylvan and pastoral scenes were favourite subjects
of the tapestry designers.

317. *inwoven many a gentle tale.* The incidents of many a love
history, and pastoral romance, were represented.

318, 319. *the rural poets* [of old], &c. Theocritus, a native of
Syracuse, represented in his Idyls—which, for dramatic simplicity and
fidelity to nature have never been equalled—scenes in the ordinary life
of the people of Sicily. Virgil imitated him, but he wants the force
and naturalness of Theocritus. Cowper, in The Task, Bk. IV, refers to
'those Arcadian scenes that Maro sings.'

327. *the Chaldee land.* 'Ur of the Chaldees,' Gen. xi. 31. For
an account of Abram's wanderings see the immediately succeeding chap-
ters. *What time,* a Latinism, *quo tempore,* used also by Milton and
other poets.

328. The word 'nomad' (Gr. *νομάς*) exactly expresses the meaning
of this line—'roaming in search of pasture.' Cp.—

'From plain to plain they led their flocks,
In search of clearer spring and fresher field.'
Liberty, II, ll. 5, 6.

329. *engage.* 'Promise' (or 'pledge'—the original meaning, from
Fr. *gage,* Lat. *vas, vadis*); 'where water and pasture were most pro-
mising.' The secondary meaning of 'engage' is 'allure' or 'attract.'

333. *true golden age.* It is the indolence of the patriarchal age, its
large leisure, and immunity from the cares of city and political life, that
so charm Thomson, and that make the representations of that primitive
mode of life adorn the tapestried rooms of the Castle so appropriately.
As for 'the golden times' of the ancient poets (see a description of them
in Ovid's Metam. lib. i), in the words of Cowper—

'Those days were never; airy dreams
Sat for the picture; and the poet's hand,
Imparting substance to an empty shade,
Imposed a gay delirium for a truth.'—*The Task,* Bk. IV.

It is to be noted that it is not the golden age, nor the patriarchal age,
which Thomson has described in Spring, ll. 241–270, but the age of
innocence—what he calls 'those prime of days.'

334. *the pencil.* The word is used here in the old sense—a small hair-brush for painting with. Old Fr. *pincel*, from Lat. *penecillus*, a brush, or small tail; from *penis*, a tail. 'Sometimes' in this line signifies 'in some of the rooms'—the cool airy galleries.

336. Here autumn figures in a brown dress; but the colour is given to summer (l. 16, *supra*); and in an illustrated enumeration of the seasons, in The Hymn, ll. 95, 96, Thomson describes 'the summer ray as *russetting* the plain.'

341, 342. *Lorrain light-touched . . . savage Rosa . . learned Poussin.* These descriptive epithets are all well-chosen. Claude Gelée, named Lorraine from his birthplace, was born in 1600, and studied, and finally settled, at Rome. He died in 1682. 'His tints have such an agreeable sweetness and variety as to have been imperfectly imitated by the best subsequent artists, and were never equalled.' He studied Nature in the open fields, 'where he frequently continued from sunrise till the dusk of the evening, sketching whatever he thought beautiful or striking.' One critic describes his ' skies' as 'warm, and full of lustre,' with every object 'properly illumined'—the 'distances' admirable, and in every part ' a delightful union and harmony.' Another writes—'No one could paint with greater beauty, brilliancy and truth the effects of sunlight at various hours of the day, of wind on foliage, the dewy moisture of morning shadows, or the magical blending of faint and ever-fainter hues in the far horizon of an Italian sky.' In the National Gallery, London, are excellent specimens of Claude's art, of which may be mentioned ' Cephalus and Procris' and 'Embarkation of the Queen of Sheba.' Salvator Rosa was born in the vicinity of Naples in 1615. He settled in Rome when he was twenty-three, and died there in 1673. His fame, like that of Claude, rests on his landscapes. His subjects are ' generally representations of wild and savage scenes executed with a freedom and decision remarkably appropriate.' Nicolas Poussin, the most popular figure and landscape painter of his time, though a Frenchman—having been born at Andelys in Normandy, in 1594—owed his education in art, and the patronage he ultimately so abundantly received, to Italy. He was thirty before he acquired the means of visiting Rome. Here he settled; and died here in 1665. He was a most accomplished painter; Sir Joshua Reynolds said of him that 'no works of any modern have so much the air of antique painting as those of Poussin.' His designs are often pagan, not to say impure ; but his execution, says Hazlitt, ' supplies the want of decorum.' Poussin the elder better deserves the epithet 'learned' than his brother-in-law Gaspar Dughet, commonly referred to as Poussin the younger.

Thomson had a refined taste in pictures, and during his Italian tour made a collection of antique drawings and engravings from the old masters, which, to the number of some eighty, were sold with his other effects in the cottage at Kew-foot Lane, Richmond, in 1748, the year of his death. The walls of his cottage were also adorned with numerous pictures.

356. *the well-tuned instrument.* An Æolian harp, thus described in Chambers's Encyc.: ' It is formed by stretching eight or ten strings of catgut, all tuned in unison, over a wooden shell or box, made generally in a form sloping like a desk. The sounds produced by the rising and falling wind, in passing over the strings, are of a drowsy and lulling character . . . . the most suitable kind of music for The Castle of Indolence.' Thomson has an Ode on Æolus's Harp. See Collins's Ode on the Death of Thomson—stanza second.

358. *each mortal touch*, &c. The fingers of the most accomplished player.

359. *The god of winds.* Æolus. See Virgil's Aeneid, Bk. I, ll. 56–67, for a description of his cave-castle and his unruly subjects.

362. *up the lofty diapason.* ' Through all the notes of an octave.' From Gk. διὰ πασῶν (χορδῶν), through all the chords.

364. *Then let them down again into the soul.* Cp. Shakespeare's Twelfth Night—'That strain again! it had a dying fall,' &c. (Act I. sc. i).

365. *pleasing dole.* ' Sweet sorrow '—as Juliet says of lovers parting (Act II. sc. ii).

368. E.g. the hymn of the Angels on the night of the Nativity; or, Psalm cxxxvii. (See Thomson's Ode on Æolus's Harp.)

369. *Wild warbling.* Cp. Milton's L'Allegro—

' [If] sweetest Shakespeare, Fancy's child,
Warble his native wood-notes wild.'—ll. 133, 134.

Burns, in The Cotter's Saturday Night, has—' Dundee's wild-warbling measures.'

371. *Caliphs.* Fr. *calife*, from Arab. *khalîfa*, successor (of the prophet).

372. *Baghdad*; the scene of many of the stories of The Arabian Nights' Entertainments.

375. *the bard in waiting.* Thomson has the following note: ' The Arabian Caliphs had poets among the officers of their court, whose office it was to do what is here mentioned.' See Moore's Oriental Romance, Lalla Rookh—where 'the young poet of Cashmere' ' cheers the [long journey] with the Muses' lore.'

379, 380. Cp. George Peele's King David and Fair Bethsabe—

> ' I'll build a kingly bower
> Seated in hearing of a hundred streams . .
> That shall . . . .
> In oblique turnings wind the nimble waves
> And with their murmur summon easeful sleep
> To lay his golden sceptre on her brows.'

See also Faerie Queene, I. i. xli.

385. *demons of the tempest.*   See Winter, l. 193—'the demon of the night.'

388. *Morpheus sent his kindest dreams.*   Morpheus was the son of Sleep, and the god of Dreams—literally, ' the shaper' or ' creator' (of dreams), from Gr. μορφή, shape.   We learn from the next stanza that the dreams were sent by the hand of angel-forms.   So Spenser—

> ' And forth he cald out of deepe darknes dredd
> Legions of sprights . . . .
> Of those he chose out two . . . . . .
> The one of them he gave a message to. .
>
> He, making speedy way through spersed ayre,
> To Morpheus' house doth hastily repaire. . . .
>
> The God obayde ; and, calling forth straightway
> A diverse Dreame out of his prison darke
> Delivered it to him . . . .
> He, back returning by the Yvorie dore,
> Remounted up as light as chearefull Larke ;
> And on his litle winges the dreame he bore
> In hast unto his Lord.'—I. i. xxxviii–xliv.

390. *shadowy cast Elysian gleams.*   The Elysium here referred to is that of Virgil, the residence of the shades of the Blessed in the lower world,—' a pensive though a happy place.'   To the Elysium of Homer heroes passed without dying : it was no part of the regions of the dead, but situated on the west of the earth, near the ocean stream.

392. ' The light that never was on sea or land' (Wordsworth's Elegiac Stanzas on a Picture of Peele Castle in a Storm).

393. *Titian's pencil.*   Vecelli Tiziano (better known as Titian) ranks with Raphael, Leonardo da Vinci, and Michael Angelo, as one of the great Italian masters of painting.   He was born of a noble family at Capo del Cadore, among the Friulian mountains in the Venetian territory, in 1480.   He was educated at Venice, where he had Giorgione, famous as a colourist, for one of his instructors.   Titian lived to a great

age—96, and produced upwards of six hundred works. The splendour of his colouring, which is equally bold and true, is the great attribute of his style. 'The luxury of light did never so enrich a painter's canvas.' The best specimen of his art in the National Gallery is his Bacchus and Ariadne.

404. *Poured all th' Arabian heaven.* In visions of fair women (see ll. 395, 396, *supra*)—*houris,* or nymphs of Paradise. 'Arabian' = 'Mohammedan.'

409. *those fiends.* The bringers of horrible dreams, in contrast to the 'angel-seeming spirits' of l. 402.

413. *beetling.* Derived by Prof. Skeat from 'bite'—a beetling cliff resembling a projecting lower jaw. Cp. 'beetle-browed.'

415. *Ye guardian spirits.* Guardian angels—as distinct from 'the angel-seeming spirits' of l. 402 as from the 'fiends' of l. 409. See a description of the ministry of holy angels on earth in Spenser's Faerie Queene, Book II, Canto vii, stanzas i and ii, 'And is there care in heaven?' &c.

419. See Winter, l. 438, where begins a long enumeration of 'the sacred shades' of ancient Greece and Rome.

422. *Those long lost friends.* Such as his mother (see Thomson's Lines on his Mother's Death); Miss Stanley (see Summer, ll. 564–575, and see also the Epitaph—especially the concluding lines, given in the Note on Summer, l. 564); Hammond (see Winter, ll. 555–571); and Aikman the painter (see his Lines on the Death of Mr. Aikman, beginning—

'As those we love decay, we die in part').

The memory of dear departed friends is here fittingly introduced as a safeguard of virtue.

424. *Or are you sportive?—bid the morn of youth,* &c. The 'guardian spirits' of l. 415 are addressed. The memories of childhood and youth are summoned as a preservative against vice and vain imaginations, which come to an indolent life.

428–431. Recollections of his native Teviotdale.

433–436. Cp. Cowper's Task, Bk. IV:—

''Tis pleasant, through the loopholes of retreat
    To peep at such a world; to see the stir
    Of the great Babel, and not feel the crowd,' &c.—ll. 88–90.

437. *idly busy.* Cp. Goldsmith's Traveller—

'Thus idly busy rolls their world away.'

441. *greater waste.* Sc. 'of energy and time.'

447. In Scotland this proverb runs—'A penny hained 's a penny gained.'

E e

450. *Till it has quenched his fire, and banished his pot.* Till he becomes a confirmed miser, who at last denies himself both fire and food. Thomson had not only a great detestation of the mere money-grubbing spirit, but practised himself with his modest means a careless liberality. He was indifferent about money all his life.

451. *this low grub.* The afore-mentioned 'muckworm.' The contrast beginning here has been often pointed—not always for the purpose of conveying the same moral. (See ll. 163–169 *supra*, and Note).

455. Cp. the opening stanzas of Byron's Childe Harold.

456. Thomson is persistently severe upon lawyers. See l. 116 *supra*, and Note.

458, 459. Limbo, or limbus, the borders of hell. The imagery of these lines is taken from the second scene of the Parable of the Rich Man and Lazarus. 'Him' in the concluding line of course refers to the 'father's ghost.'

463. *in a Thespian rage.* The reference to ambitious authorship in stanza lii. is not confined to dramatic writers : the words quoted here probably signify 'in a frenzy' or 'in a tragic rage.' Thespis was the father of Greek tragedy, and the first to give it a strictly dramatic character : before his time (he flourished 535 B.C.), there was no actor; everything was undertaken by the chorus.

466. 'Losing the present in order to gain the future age.'

468. *when useless worldly store.* 'When fame is of no personal use to you.'

472, 473. *At every door,* &c. Cp. Cowper's Task, Bk. IV, ll. 144–147 :—

'No rattling wheels stop short before these gates,' &c.

See also l. 290 *supra*, and Note.

474–477. Calls, scandal, and invitations—the pastimes of the world of fashion.

478. *sons of party.* Party politicians. The whole of the stanza commencing here is a humorously ludicrous account of our English mode of government by party. 'We keep it going like an hour-glass ; when one side's quite run out we turn up the other and go on again' (Jerrold). Cp. Cowper's account, under a more dignified figure than Thomson's, in The Task, Bk. IV, ll. 57–62.

483. *Lucifer.* Thomson himself is careful to state in a note that by Lucifer he means 'the morning star.'

487. Thomson passes from the pursuit of politics to the game of war—'a game which, were their subjects wise, Kings would not play at.'—Cowper, The Task, Bk. V.

498. *those who at the helm appear.* Rulers, statesmen in office, &c.

501. Cp. Chaucer's line—

'And yit he seemede besier than he was.'—Prol., l. 322.

502. *tape-tied trash, and suits of fools.* Papers and documents, useless but looking very important; and applications and supplications that will never be granted.

506. *a man of special grave remark.* The original of this character-sketch was almost certainly William Paterson, Thomson's intimate friend, occasionally his amanuensis, his deputy, and successor in 1746, in the Surveyor-Generalship of the Leeward Islands, and the translator of the historian Paterculus. Not much more is known about Paterson, except that, as Murdoch says, 'he courted the tragic muse, and had taken for his subject the story of Arminius the German hero.' The Censor refused it licence, because it was in the handwriting of Edward and Eleanora! There is a long and interesting letter from Thomson (of date, middle of April, 1748, addressed to Paterson at Barbadoes) which reveals the intimacy between the two friends. The letter is sufficient to prove that Thomson *could* write beautiful prose; but it is too long to quote at length. Part of it runs :—

'Now that I am prating of myself, know that after fourteen or fifteen years The Castle of Indolence comes abroad in a fortnight. It will certainly travel as far as Barbadoes. You have an apartment in it as a night pensioner.' The description would suit Collins.

516. *Dan Sol.* The sun, the lord of day.

527. *the cerulean field.* The heavens—'the azure deep of air' of Gray (Progress of Poesy); 'the broad fields of the sky' of Milton (Comus, l. 979).

534. *One shyer still.* The prototype of this character was John Armstrong, son of a Roxburghshire minister, and M.D. (1732) of Edinburgh University. He went up to London, and first attracted notice by his verses. In 1744 appeared his Art of Preserving Health. He was a skilful physician, but his shy, caustic, indolent manner kept him out of a very lucrative practice. He died in 1779. Thomson was his senior by some nine years. In the letter to Paterson, referred to above, Thomson writes thus of Armstrong: 'Though the doctor increases in business he does not decrease in spleen; but there is a certain kind of spleen that is both humane and agreeable, like Jacques in the play: I sometimes, too, have a touch of it.'

541. *a wretch, who had not crept abroad* (for forty years). The 'wretch' of this stanza is said to have been a 'Henry Welby, Esquire, an eccentric solitaire of the period.'

551. *A joyous youth.* The original of this character was John Forbes, only son of Duncan Forbes of Culloden, President of the Court

of Session, Scotland. (See Autumn, Note, l. 944.) Writing to a friend (George Ross) in 1736, Nov. 6, ' Remember me,' says Thomson, ' to all friends, and above them all heartily to Mr. Forbes. Though my affection to him is not fanned by letters, yet it is as high as when I was his brother in the virtu, and played at chess with him in a post-chaise.' Again, on Jan. 12, 1737, he writes to Ross—' Forbes I hope is cheerful and in good health. . . . Remember me kindly to him with all the zealous truth of old friendship.' But the description would suit Hammond. See Winter, ll. 566–569.

558. See l. 289, *supra.*

568. *a burnished fly.* Thomson used good-humouredly to call Hammond, whom Dr. Robertson of Richmond knew as ' a very pleasant man,' ' a burnished butterfly.' Compare the simile, in its loose attachment to stanza lxiii, with that of stanza xxx.

577. *Another guest.* George, Lord Lyttelton. See Spring, Note, l. 905.

594. *Hagley Park.* The seat of Lord Lyttelton, in Worcestershire. See Spring, Note, l. 907. The following stanza, which is supposed to refer to the wife of the future Lord Lyttelton, is said to be by Thomson, but it has nothing to recommend it as his, except the rhymes and the compliment to the lady. It was never printed in Thomson's lifetime.

> ' One nymph there was, methought, in bloom of May,
> On whom the idle fiend glanced many a look
> In hopes to lead her down the slippery way
> To taste of pleasure's deep deceitful brook:
> No virtues yet her gentle mind forsook,
> No idle whims, no vapours filled her brain;
> But prudence for her youthful guide she took,
> And goodness, which no earthly vice could stain,
> Dwelt in her mind: she was ne proud, I ween, or vain.'

595. *th' Esopus of the age.* James Quin, the actor. He was of Irish descent; born in London in 1693, he began his career as a player in Dublin at the age of twenty-one; proceeded to London, where he made his mark, in 1716, in the character of Bajazet in Marlowe's Tragedy of Tamerlane; and from 1735 to 1741 was regarded as the first actor in England, delighting Drury Lane Theatre with his impersonations of Falstaff and Captain Macheath. On the appearance of Garrick he gradually ceased to be the popular favourite. He died in 1766. Quin's relations to Thomson were of the friendliest. About the year 1737 Thomson was arrested for a debt of some £70: Quin came to his relief, and insisted on the astonished debtor's acceptance of £100 as payment of the pleasure he had derived from Thomson's works. Quin was a frequent visitor at Thomson's cottage at Richmond, where, indeed,

his convivial habits rather scandalized the neighbourhood. He was one of the four intimate friends who attended the funeral of Thomson in 1748. When Thomson's posthumous play of Coriolanus was first acted in 1749, Quin, dressed in a suit of mourning, spoke the Prologue (which had been written by Lyttelton) with such genuine feeling and eloquence that, at the line 'Alas! I feel I am no actor here!' there was scarcely a dry eye in the theatre. It may be added that Shenstone thought Thomson's 'manner of speaking not unlike Quin's.'

The Æsopus, to whom Thomson compares Quin, was Clodius Æsopus, the greatest Roman actor of tragedy, the friend and contemporary of Cicero, and of Roscius—the greatest Roman actor of comedy.

604. This line, descriptive of his own disposition and habit of body, is the only part of stanza lxviii which Thomson composed. The rest was written by Lyttelton. Thomson's figure in youth was handsome.

613, 614. A gentle satire on the indolent lives of the clergy.

615. *oily man of God.* The original of this character was Thomson's old and intimate friend and countryman—afterwards his kindly biographer—the Rev. Patrick Murdoch. Murdoch was tutor to John Forbes, 'the joyous youth' of l. 551, and afterwards to the son of Admiral James Vernon of Great Thurlow. By the latter he was presented to the living of Stradishall in Suffolk in 1737–8. Writing on the 12th Jan., 1738, Thomson refers to 'Pettie's' settlement as follows: 'Pettie came here two or three days ago: I have not yet seen the round "man of God" to be. He is to be parsonified a few days hence. How a gown and cassock will become him! and with what a holy leer he will edify the devout females! There is no doubt of his having a call, for he is immediately to enter upon a tolerable living [£100 a year]! God grant him more, and as fat as himself! It rejoices me to see one worthy excellent man raised at least to an independency.' Murdoch was afterwards promoted to the living of Kettlebaston, and finally, in 1760, to the vicarage of Great Thurlow. It was here he wrote his Memoir of Thomson. He died in 1774.

622. A variety of the genus, the village politician, has been immortalised by Wilkie.

625. *on their brow sat every nation's cares.* The line comically recalls the sublime description of Milton :—

> 'Care
> Sat on his faded cheek, but under brows
> Of dauntless courage.'—*Par. Lost*, Bk. I, ll. 601–603

627, 628 The references are to tobacco-smoking and coffee-drinking.

628. *sage berry . . . Mocha bears.* Coffee-bean (Arab. *bunn*), not a berry. Mocha is in Arabia.

630. *mysterious as of old.* ' Ambiguously expressed, so as to apply equally well to contradictory results; ' or ' expressed definitely enough, but with an air of confidence in their infallibility that is, in the absence of knowledge, rather " mysterious." '

632. *Bevies of dainty dames.* Cp. Milton, ' A bevy of fair women, richly gay ' (Par. Lost, Bk. XI, l. 582). For ' bevies,' see Glossary.

638. To knit, and make up bouquets ; perhaps embroider.

640–648. See Young's Love of Fame, Sat. V—' The languid lady next appears,' &c.

644. *with tottering step and slow.* Goldsmith has ' With fainting steps and slow.'—Hermit.

648. *the vapoury god.* Sleep, with its opiate fumes. See ll. 21, 22, *supra.*

657. As foretold at l. 414, *supra.*

658–693. These thirty-six lines, forming the four concluding stanzas of Canto I, and consisting of an enumeration of the diseases which are fostered by an indolent life, were the composition of Thomson's friend, Dr. Armstrong (see Note, l. 534 *supra*). They afford a gloomy contrast to the rest of the Canto—which, but for them, might almost be entitled, The Pleasures of Indolence, over the motto ' *Dolce far niente.*' Armstrong's stanzas remind one of the lazar-house in the eleventh book of Paradise Lost, ll. 477–492.

660. *Lethargy.* From Gr. ληθαργία, drowsiness ; λήθη, oblivion.

668. *Hydropsy.* Dropsy—in O. F. *hydropisie* ; from Gr. ὕδωρ, water

672. *Hypochondria.* Melancholy. ' Named from the spleen (which was supposed to cause it) situate under the cartilage of the breast-bone : Gr. ὑπό, under ; and χόνδρος, cartilage of the breast-bone ' (Prof. Skeat). Cp. ' hipped '=' melancholy.' Armstrong could well write about the spleen, both as a physician, and a patient. (See Note, l. 534.)

689. *the Tertian.* Fr. *tertiane*, a tertian ague—recurring every third day ; Lat. *ter*, thrice.

690. *Gout :* Lat. *gutta*, a drop ; the disease having been supposed to be owing to defluxion of humours. See, for ' crowing cocks,' l. 118 *supra.*

692. *Apoplexy.* From Gr. ἀπό, off, and πλήσσω, I strike.

CANTO II.

1. *the sire of sin.* Indolence. Cp. the homely motto of Dr. Isaac Watts, 'Satan finds,' &c.

10. *the Muse.* The poet is indirectly meant. Milton is more direct —'So may some gentle muse,' Lycidas, l. 19.

11. *Parnassus.* A double-headed mountain mass a few miles north of Delphi in Greece, sacred to Apollo and the Muses, and 'an inspiring source of poetry and song.' Divested of its mythological imagery the question of this line is simply 'Are there no means of securing for the poor poet the profits arising from his poetry?'.

14. *a fell tribe.* The middleman—in the poet's case the publisher.

the Aonian hive. Aonia was part of Bœotia in which stood Mount Helicon, also sacred to the Muses. The Muses were sometimes called 'Aonides.' In the metaphor the poet is the bee, poetry the honey, the publisher the wasp.

16. *that noblest toil.* The making of poetry. Cowper, too, speaks of 'the poet's toil' in Bk. IV of The Task (l. 262).

18. *starve right merrily.* Poets have from time immemorial been notorious for their poverty. For the manner ('merrily') in which they bear their poverty, cp. Cowper's description of the English poor in Bk. IV of The Task (467, 468): 'this merry land, though lean and beggared.'

19–27. This stanza contains the poet's noble protest against the belief that money can confer happiness. So Goldsmith, in the midst of obscurity and poverty, could exclaim—

'Creation's heir, the world, the world is mine.'—*Traveller.*
And so Burns—

'What though, like commoners of air,
    We wander out, we know not where,
        But either house or hall?
    Yet Nature's charms, the hills and woods,
    The sweeping vales, an' foaming floods,
        Are free alike to all. . . .

It's no' in titles nor in rank,
    It's no' in wealth like Lon'on bank
        To purchase peace and rest,' &c.
                                            Epistle to Davie, ll. 43–59.

23, 24. *to trace the . . lawns by living stream at eve.* Cp. Milton—
'Such sights as youthful poets dream
    On summer eves by haunted stream,'
                                    L'Allegro, ll. 129, 130.

And Burns—

> 'The muse, nae poet ever fand her
> Till by himsel' he learnt to wander
> Adoun some trotting burn's meander.'
>
> *Epistle to William Simson*, ll. 85-87.

25. *finer fibres.* Brains; poetical powers.

26. *And I their toys to the great children leave.* Burns has the same sentiment—

> 'The warly race may drudge an' drive,
> Hog-shouther, jundie, stretch, an' strive :
> Let me fair Nature's face descrive,
>   And I, with pleasure,
> Shall let the busy grumbling hive
>   Bum owre their treasure.'
>
> *Epistle to W. Simson*, ll. 91-96.

27. *fancy.* The poetical faculty.

28. *a bolder song,* i.e. than her praise of Indolence, in Canto I. With the apostrophe to his Muse in this line, cp. that of l. 280 in Canto I.

30. This alliterative line is a good instance of Pope's maxim—'The sound should be an echo of the sense.'

31. The poem itself, The Castle of Indolence, was good evidence of the truth of this confession : it was some fourteen or more years on the way.

33. *imp of fame.* The Knight of Arts and Industry (see l. 58 *infra*).

34. *sons of softness.* The votaries of Indolence.

36. *the slumbering flame.* Of industry or enterprise.

38. *Selvaggio.* A savage; denizen of the woods (see l. 45 *infra*). The same character figures in Autumn, where he is called (l. 57) 'a sad barbarian,' (l. 59) 'a shivering wretch,' and (l. 69) 'the rugged savage.' Indeed the whole passage in Autumn, from l. 43 to l. 140, is the germ of this second Canto. It will be found extremely interesting to compare the finished picture with the first study.

43. *in November steeped,* i.e. in the rains of that wet or misty month (see l. 437 *infra*).

69. *Minerva pity of him took.* An archaic idiom for 'on him.' Minerva (connected with *mens*, mind), the embodiment of the thinking power. She was one of the three leading divinities of ancient Rome, and the goddess of wisdom and war, i.e. she 'guided men in the dangers of war where victory is gained by cunning, prudence, courage, and perseverance.'

70. *all the gods that love the rural wonne.* Such as Pan, Pales, Vertumnus, Silvanus, Ceres, &c. For 'wonne,' see Glossary.

71. *rule the crook.* One would have expected 'sway,' or 'rule with.'

72. The Muses; a country life naturally instilling poetical ideas into an intelligent mind.

73. *Of fertile genius.* Naturally possessed of great capacity for development.

76. *or use, or joy, or grace.* The first 'or' is equivalent to 'either.'

77, 78. His education was of that complete kind which develops the intellectual, moral, and physical powers.

84. *drew the roseate breath,* &c. Inhaled the morning air while it was yet flushed with the red splendours of sunrise.

88. Foot-racing is referred to.

89. *wheeled the chariot,* i. e. adroitly deflected its course while the horses were racing at full speed. This was a favourite Roman exercise ; see Horace (Car. I. 1) :—

  'Sunt quos . . . .

   . . . metaque fervidis

   Evitata rotis palmaque nobilis

   Terrarum dominos evehit ad Deos.'

92. *the ethereal round.* The heavens, with their various phenomena of stars, meteors, clouds, birds, &c.

94. It was usual, till lately, to speak of 'the three kingdoms of nature'—the animal, the vegetable, and the mineral.

95. *scanned the globe.* Studied the geography of the various states—political and physical.

98, 99. Studied mental and moral philosophy.

107. *Neptune's school.* The water of lake or river, as well as of sea. For Milton's limitation of Neptune's 'sway' see Comus, ll. 18–21.

110. Cp. Goldsmith's line in The Traveller—

  'The canvas glowed beyond e'en Nature warm.'

113. *Pygmalion's wife.* The original story is to the effect that Pygmalion, king of Cyprus, made in ivory the image of a maiden which was of such surpassing loveliness that he became enamoured of it, and prayed Aphrodite (Venus) to make it live. His prayer was granted, and he married the maiden.

114. *with varied fire.* With enthusiasm of a different sort.

117. *that well might wake Apollo's lyre.* Worthy to be sung with the accompaniment of the best music. Apollo was both the sun-god and the god of poetry and music.

142. *Egypt, Greece, and Rome.* For the history of the rise and progress

of the liberal arts and virtues in these countries, see Thomson's great but neglected and under-rated poem Liberty, Parts II and III.

143. *ruins grey.* Burns has 'ruined castles grey' in his Address to the Deil.

146. *made for Britain's coast.* See Liberty, Part IV, ll. 382–388; also ll. 626–642.

159. *the genius of the land.* The natural disposition of the people.

160–162. Compare this with the eulogy in Summer, ll. 1467–1478.

165, 166. *agriculture . . Fair Queen of Arts !* Thomson never wearies of crying up the rural industries and virtues. In Spring, it is 'the sacred plough,' which 'employed the kings and awful fathers of mankind' (ll. 58, 59); and at l. 66 he exclaims—

'Ye generous Britons, venerate the plough.'

177. *either Ind.* Both the East and the West Indies.

180. *Britannia's thunder.* So in Campbell's Ye Mariners of England :

'With thunders from her native oak
She quells the floods below.'

181, 182. The reference is to the revival of learning that began on the downfall of Constantinople in 1453. Propontis, now the Sea of Marmora.

185. *Castalie.* A spring on Parnassus sacred to Apollo and the Muses.

186. *Isis.* The Upper Thames—the Thames at Oxford. The reference in the line is to the fame of Oxford University for classical learning.

187. *old Cam soft-paces o'er the lea.* The reference here is to Cambridge University. Cp. Milton's Lycidas—

'Next Camus, reverend sire, went footing slow.'—l. 103.

187–189. These lines were evidently inspired by the pastoral spirit of Milton's Lycidas. See more especially of that poem, ll. 23-36; ll. 103, 104; and ll. 186–189.

190–192. Cp. Liberty, Part V, ll. 374–377—

'To softer prospect turn we now the view,
To laurelled Science, Arts, and Public Works,
That lend my *finished* fabric comely pride,
Grandeur, and grace,' &c.

194. *the coy sisters.* The Fine Arts—Sculpture, Painting, Poetry, Music, Architecture, &c.

202. *Mæcenas.* A noble Roman, the friend and patron of Horace, Virgil, &c. Bubb Dodington was ambitious of figuring as the Mæcenas of his time; he is commonly known as the last of *the* patrons—for the

most part a degrading class in English literature. (See Summer, Note, l. 29.)

204. *Unbroken spirits, cheer!* An exhortation to his brother-poets who have not allowed their ardour to cool because of national neglect.

207. *toil-created gains*, i. e. 'honestly earned.'

216. *vacant eve* [*of life*]. Free from business and other cares—excepting only 'the amusing care of rural industry' (l. 236). For the sentiment of the whole stanza ending here, see Liberty, Part IV, ll. 1177–1186.

217. *he chose a farm in Deva's vale.* The Latin name of Chester, on the Dee.

220. 'Blended the various duties of,' &c.

222. *sided by the guardians of the fold.* Accompanied by his sheep-dogs. The scene here depicted will remind the classical reader of the Idyl of Theocritus which describes, with a charm simply inimitable, the visit of Hercules to the farm of Augeas in Elis.

223. 'Made happy by his presence.' The fashionable habit of absenteeism—which has been rather increasing since Cowper (The Task, Bk. IV, ll. 587–590) and Burns (The Twa Dogs, ll. 173–176) lamented it—deprives our landlords of the happiness depicted in this and the following stanzas.

229–231. *the nodding car*, &c. The harvest-wain, loaded with sheaves, on its way to the stackyard. (See Autumn, ll. 1–3.) The scene here described is known as 'leading the field'—a pleasant part of the labours of harvest time, which Thomson strangely omitted to notice in his Autumn. (See that poem, ll. 151–176.)

233. *ruffian idleness.* The parent of War. Those who wage war are, agreeably with this view, called 'honourable ruffians' (l. 491, Canto I).

234. *this life.* Of rural industry. The origin of agriculture is also traced to heaven at l. 166 *supra*.

240–243. References to drainage, irrigation, reclamation, and plantation of the land.

246, 247. These lines are interesting as showing Thomson's ideas of the proper relation of Art to Nature.

248, 249. *In graceful dance . . . Pan, Pales . . . played.* Imitated probably from Milton, Par. Lost, Bk. IV, ll. 266–268 :—

> 'Universal Pan,
> Knit with the Graces and the Hours in dance
> ed on the eternal Spring.'

But the figure is a common one in the classical poets, e. g. Hor. Car. I. 4.

Pan, the great Greek god of flocks and shepherds; Pales, a Roman divinity of flocks and shepherds; Flora, the Roman goddess of flowers and spring; and Pomona, the Roman goddess of the fruit of trees—these are among 'the gods that love the rural wonne' referred to at l. 70 *ante*.

251. *A happy place.* Already so described (ll. 64, 65 *supra*).

261. The line does not contain a contradiction or correction of traditional report, but accepts it: 'as old Fame reports' is parenthetical; 'as' = 'so,' 'this.'

264. *To his . . . wish.* 'Up to,' 'agreeably to,' &c.   Cp. Burns—

> 'Bless him, thou God of love and truth,
>
>   Up to a parent's wish!'
>
> *Prayer for a Rev. Friend's Family.*

266, 267. Vice leads the van, bearing the standard; Corruption commands the rear. 'Arrière-ban,' lit. 'proclamation made in the rear' or 'to the rear.'

268. *mind yourselves.* The motto of selfishness.

276. *the noble colour.* The flush of righteous anger. This stanza (xxxi) may be compared with stanzas vii and viii of the noble fragmentary Scots ballad Hardyknute, with which Thomson must have been acquainted :—

> 'The little page flew swift as dart
>
>   Flung by his master's arm;
>
> Cum down, cum down, Lord Hardyknute,
>
>   And rid zour king frae harm.
>
> Then reid, reid grew his dark-brown cheiks,
>
>   Sae did his dark-brown brow;
>
> His luiks grew kene, as they were wont
>
>   In dangers great to do,' &c.

281. *That villain Archimage.* See Note, Canto I, l. 181 *supra*.

285. *the sisters three.* The Weird Sisters, or Sisters of Destiny; called Moiræ by the Greeks, Parcæ by the Romans; the Fates. They were—Clotho, who spun the thread of human life; Lachesis, who measured it; and Atropos the inevitable, who cut it.

289. *the bard, a little Druid wight [Of withered aspect . . . In russet brown bedight].* Cp. Milton's Comus, ll. 619-621—

> 'A certain shepherd lad
>
> Of small regard to see to, yet well skilled
>
> In every virtuous plant and healing herb.'

A druid was a priest of the ancient Britons. Here it means a poet who

loved nature and frequented woods. In this sense it is used of Thomson himself, in Collins's melodious lines to his memory :—
'In yonder grave a druid lies,' &c.

292. *his sister of the copses.* The nightingale ; Philomela.

293. *He crept along, unpromising of mien.* The description would have suited Thomson himself in his later years. He stooped in walking, was slovenly in his dress; was 'neither a *petit maître* nor a boor—he had simplicity without rudeness, and a cultivated manner without being courtly.' (Testimony of Dr. Robertson, Richmond.) This is the bard of Canto I, st. lxviii, reformed of his one vice.

295. Angels are meant.

303. *those wretched men, who* will *be slaves.* The line reminds one of the chorus of Thomson's Rule Britannia.

306. *Thrice happy he who,* &c. The persuasive poet, happier than the coercive statesman.

307-312. The knight on a red horse, emblematic of war ; the bard on a milk-white palfrey, emblematic of persuasion and peace.

325. *that fatal valley gay.* See its description fully set forth in Canto I, st. ii, and st. v.

336. *The frail good man.* The victim of Indolence.

345. *of this avail.* An archaic idiom ; 'take advantage of this.'

351. In purgatorial fires. Cp. Hamlet, Act I, sc. v, ll. 10-12.

352. 'Beneath a spacious palm.'—Canto I, l. 61.

367. *With magic dust their eyne,* &c. Cp. Comus—
'Thus I hurl
My dazzling spells into the spongy air,
Of power to cheat the eye with blear illusion. . . .
Her eye
Hath met the virtue of this magic dust.'—ll. 153-165.

380. *The wary retiarius.* Thomson has a note on this: 'A gladiator, who made use of a net which he threw over his adversary.' He carried the net (*rete*) in his right hand, and a three-pointed lance (*tridens*) in his left. If he missed his aim, by either flinging the net too short or too far, he at once took to flight, preparing his net the while for another cast. Meanwhile his adversary (*Secutor*) followed, and attempted to dispatch him with a sword, or a ball of lead. (See an account of the ancient gladiatorial shows in any book of Roman Antiquities.)

383. The weakest line in the poem—'bordering, indeed, on the ludicrous.'

385. *flounced to and fro.* See Spring, l. 434, and Note. Cp. Savage's Wanderer, Canto IV—
'Where [in the net] flounce, deceived, the expiring finny prey.'

387. *his . . . nail.* For the sing. form, cp. ' Dick, the shepherd, blows his *nail.*'—Shakespeare.

398. *Avernus.* A lake filling the crater of an extinct volcano, round (in circumference about a mile or more), very deep, and girt with high banks. It was near Cumæ, and the Cumæan Sibyl lived near it in a cave which had connection with the infernal world (see Æneid). The Cimmerians lived in the perpetual gloom of its banks.

405. *Touch soul with soul.* 'Speak from the heart, and touch their hearts with the sincerity of your appeal.'

410. *Till tinkling in clear symphony they rung.* A singularly expressive line, suggesting by its very sound the peculiar tones of a harp. Cp. Scott's Lay of the Last Minstrel—
> 'Till every string's according glee
> Was blended into harmony.'—Introd. Canto I.

415-567. The song of Philomelus, contained in these lines, matches at every point the Song of Indolence in the first Canto. It is as poetical, as powerful in its appeal, and is animated, of course, by a higher morality.

423. Cp. Pope's Essay on Man, Ep. I, ll. 267-280, ending with the line which so closely resembles this one—
> 'He fills, he bounds, connects, and equals all.'
See also Spring, l. 854.

426-429. The theory of spiritual evolution here briefly expressed was the firm belief of Thomson throughout his life. He makes numerous references to it. See Spring, Note, ll. 374-377 ; Liberty, III, ll. 68-70 ; The Hymn, Note, ll. 115, 116 ; and ll. 562, 563 *infra.*

432, 433. 'That cosmos excels chaos.'

443. *the brighter palm.* Because excellence in Art is of a superior kind to excellence in feats of bodily strength, &c., for which also the palm was given.

448. *o'er the nations shook her conquering dart.* The pilum. Cp. Milton, Par. Lost, Bk. XI, ll. 491, 492—
> 'Over them triumphant Death his dart
>   Shook.'

449.   'The laurell, meed of mightie conquerours
>   And poets sage.'—*Faerie Queene*, Bk. I, Canto I, st. ix.

456. *cities . . . their towery fronts.* 'Pheræ deckt with towers' (Chapman's Homer).

460. *Great Homer's song.* The Iliad. (See Winter, l. 533, and Note.)

462. *Sweet Maro's muse.* The poet Virgil. (See Winter, l. 532, and Note.) Virgil regarded Mantua, on an island in the Mincius, as his

birthplace, but he was born rather at the village of Andes in the neighbourhood.

463. the Mincian reeds. Milton's Lycidas—

'Thou honoured flood,

Smooth-sliding Mincius, crowned with vocal reeds.'—ll. 85, 86.

464. The wits of modern time. The poets after the Renaissance.

466. Paradise Lost would not have been written.

467. Stratford-on-Avon is in Warwickshire. Shakespeare would have been merely a happy and companionable peasant.

468. my master Spenser. Cp. Lydgate's 'My mayster Chaucer' in his Prol. to The Falls of Princes. The Castle of Indolence was written professedly in imitation of Spenser's style. (See Thomson's Advertisement prefixed to his Poem.) The Mulla was Spenser's poetical name for the Awbeg, a tributary of the Blackwater of county Cork. It was on the banks of the Mulla that Spenser read part of his Faerie Queene to Sir Walter Raleigh in 1589; the friends sat—

'Amongst the coolly shade

Of the green alders by the Mulla's shore.'

469. the sage historic muse. Clio.

471. starry lights of virtue. See a lengthened description of them in Winter, ll. 439–540.

535. The world is poised. The balance of power is preserved.

554. Resolve! and

557, 558. Let godlike reason . . . Speak the . . . word, &c. Cp. Young's Night Thoughts, I, ll. 30, 31—

'On Reason build Resolve,

That column of true majesty in man!'

Cp. also Burns's Epistle to Dr. Blacklock—

'Come, firm Resolve, take thou the van,

Thou stalk o' carl-hemp in man!'

562, 563. See Note, Canto II, ll. 426–429 *supra.*

580. this fleshly den. The body.

614. That lazar-house. See Canto I, st. lxxiii.

639. [Repentance] rejoices Heaven. See Parables of The Lost Sheep, Lost Piece of Money, &c. 'There is more joy in heaven over one sinner that repenteth,' &c.

653. dolorous mansion. Purgatory.

655. soft and pure as infant goodness. Cp. the Scripture story of Naaman the Syrian leper washing away his disease in the Jordan: 'And his flesh came again like unto the flesh of a little child, and he was clean' (2 Kings v. 14).

685. *their scornèd day of grace was past.* Cp. the Scots Paraphrase, X :—

> 'How long, ye scorners of the truth,
>   Scornful will ye remain? . . .
>
> The time will come when humbled low
>   In sorrow's evil day,
> Your voice by anguish shall be taught,
>   But taught too late to pray. . . .
>
> Prayers then extorted shall be vain,
>   The hour of mercy past.'

697. *Auster.* The south-west wind, bringing fogs and rains.

698. *Caurus.* The north-west wind; 'frosty Caurus' in Winter, l. 836.

703. *The first.* Beggary personified.

712. *The other.* Scorn personified.

721. *Brentford town, a town of mud.* The county town of Middlesex,
at the mouth of the Brent, a tributary of the Thames. There is a bridge
here over the Thames, leading to Kew. Thomson knew the town well,
but apparently did not admire it. From his description one might infer
—what is quite true—that the town is one long street.

GLOSSARY

OF

RARE OR OBSOLETE WORDS, AND ARCHAIC FORMS,

IN

THE CASTLE OF INDOLENCE.

Agen, again.

Apaid, recompensed; cf. Fr. *payer*, to pay, to satisfy.

Arrier-ban, probably a French corruption, from O. H. G. *hari*, army, and *ban*, proclamation: the order summoning to military service. See Murray's *New English Dictionary*.

Atween, between.

Backening, stepping back.

Bale, evil, destruction; A.-S. *bealu*.

Bate, abate; Fr. *battre*, to beat.

Bay, reddish-brown; O. Fr. *bai*; Lat. *badius*.

Bedight, fully prepared; A.-S. *dihtan*, to set in order; Lat. *dictare*.

Behoves, befits; A.-S. *behófian*.

Benempt, named.

Beseems, befits.

Bevies, flocks, companies; Fr. *bevée*, a flock.

Bicker, to skirmish; metaphorically of a 'brawling' stream.

Bides, awaits; endures.

Blazon, proclaim, blaze abroad; M. E. *blasen*. Often confused with F. *blason*, a coat of arms.

Blemished, of a livid colour; O. Fr. *blesmir*, to wound, stain.

Boon, bountiful, good; Fr. *bon*.

Breme, cruel, sharp.

Brewed, concocted, planned; A.-S. *bréowan*, to brew.

Cabals, intrigues, secrets; Heb. *qabbáláh*, mysterious doctrine.

Caitiff, a wretch, a captive; O.Fr. *caitif*; Lat. *captivus*.

Carking, causing anxiety; O.Fr. *karke*, dialect form of *charge*, load.

Carle, a sturdy rude fellow, a churl; A.-S. *ceorl*, a freeman, but of the lowest rank.

Casten, false form for 'casted.'

Catacombs, sepulchral vaults; orig. of the subterranean cemeteries lying around Rome.

Cates, dainties; Fr. *achat*, purchase. Cog. 'cater.'

Certes, certainly.

Chaunced, befell; O.Fr. *chaance*; Lat. *cadens, -tem*.

Clerks, scholars, the clergy; Lat. *clericus*, one of the clergy.

Contrite, thoroughly bruised and humbled; penitent; Lat. *terere*, to rub.

Crouchen, crouch.

Cunning, dexterous; A.-S. *cunnan*, to know.

Dainties, delicacies; O. Fr. *daintie*, agreeableness; Lat. *dignitas, -tatem*.

Dalliance, pleasant trifling; cog. 'dally,' and 'dwell.'

†

F f

Dan, Lord, a title of respect for monks, &c.; Lat. *dominus*; Fr. *dom*; O. Fr. *dans.*

Delves, digs; A.-S. *delfan.*

Delves, dales? given as 'deserts.'

Depeinten, depicted; Fr. *peint*; Lat. *pictus.*

Dispightful, despiteful.

Distaff, A.-S. *distæf*; properly 'a staff provided with flax to be spun off' (Skeat).

Draught, a drawing, or plan.

Drowsyhed, drowsihead, for drowsiness.

Eath, easy, easily.

Eftsoones, soon after, forthwith. Common in Spenser.

Eke, v., to join, to increase; A.-S. *écan*, to lengthen; cog. with Lat. *augere.*

Eke, conj., also.

Eld, old age.

Emmet, ant; A.-S. *æmete.*

Emongst, amongst.

Emove, move. 'Enmove' in Spenser.

Emprise, enterprise.

Estate, state or condition; property.

Eyne, pl. of eye.

Fain, glad; A.-S. *fægen*, glad.

Fand, found.

Fay, fairy; O. Fr. *fée.*

Fee, a grant of land, payment; A.-S. *feoh*, cattle.

Fell, cruel; O. Fr. *fel*, cruel.

Felly, in a cruel manner.

Fit, an attack, or a turn; A.-S. *fit*, a song, a struggle. Orig. sense 'a step.'

Fone, pl. of foe; A.-S. *fán.*

Fray, a contest; shortened form of 'affray.'

Fry, fish-spawn; a shoal of persons.

Gallow-tree, from A.-S. *galga*, cross, gibbet; *treó*, timber.

Gear, geer, weapons, clothing, property; A.-S. *gearwe.*

Gelid, cold, frozen: Lat. *gelidus.*

Genders, produces.

Glaive, sword; Lat. *gladius.*

Han, have.

Hight, is *or* was named; named: A.-S. *hátan*, to call, to be called. Cog. 'behest.'

Houghs, for 'hoes.'

Idless, for 'idleness.'

Immingle, to mingle thoroughly.

Imp, a graft or shoot, a child; A.-S. *impan*, pl. Never used jocularly by Spenser.

Inly, inwardly.

Issúed, with the accent on the last syllable; O. Fr. *issir*, Lat. *exire*, to go forth.

Jot, iota, the smallest letter in the Greek alphabet.

Junto, a secret alliance, a faction; Span. *junta*; Lat. *juncta.*

Keen, v., to sharpen.

Kest, for 'cast.'

Lacquey, a menial; Fr. *laquais.*

Lad, led. So in Spenser. A.-S. *lædan*, pret. *lædde.*

Lair, den, retreat; A.-S. *leger*, a bed.

Landskip, for landscape. So in Milton. '-scape' is our affix '-ship.'

Lank, slender; jointed; and so, flexible. Cog. 'link.'

Lazarhouse, a leprosy hospital; from Lazarus, the name of the beggar in the parable; contraction of the Heb. name 'Eleazar.' A lazaretto.

Leeches, physicians, healers; A.-S. *læce*, a healer.

Lees, dregs; Fr. *lie.*

Lenient, mild; Lat. *leniens*, soothing.

Libbard, leopard. Chaucer's form is 'libart.'

Lig, to lie ; M. E. *liggen, lien.*

Limber, flexible, supple ; from 'limp.'

Lithe, flexible.

Loathly,loathsome. So in Spenser.

Loll, to lounge about ; cog. 'lull.'

Loom, from A.-S. *ge-lóma,* a tool. Cog. 'heirloom.'

Losel, worthless fellow.

Lout, a lazy clown ; A.-S. *lútan,* to stoop. Cog. 'loiter.'

Louting, stooping, bowing. Still in use in Lowland Scots.

Lubbard, a lubber ; cog. 'lob,' 'lump,' &c. Cf. Milton's lubberfiend.

Lustyhed, pleasure, enjoyment ; the form in Chaucer is 'lustiheed' (Squieres Tale, l. 288).

Massy, massive.

Meed, reward.

Mell, mingle ; O. Fr. *mesler,* to mix. Cog. 'medley.'

Mew, lair ; from *mews.*

Moe, more. Older forms 'moo' and 'mo.' A.-S. *má.*

Moil, to drudge ; O. Fr. *moiler.*

Mold, mould.

Mote, might.

Muchel, much ; Scots 'meikle' or 'muckle.' Chaucer 'mochel.' A.-S. *mycel.*

Nathless, nevertheless.

Ne, nor.

Needments, necessaries.

Noisome, hurtful ; *noy* is a contraction of *annoy.*

Noursling, child, pupil.

Noyance, annoyance—found in Spenser ; *annoy.*

Painful, industrious, taking great pains.

Palfrey, O. Fr. *palefrei,* riding-horse ; Low Lat. *paraveredus,* an extra post-horse.

Palmer, pilgrim ; literally, one who bore a palm-branch in token of having visited the Holy Land.

Passen, pass ; 'I passen' is a wrong form.

Pell-mell, confusedly ; from Fr. *pelle,* a peel or fire-shovel, and *mesler,* to mix ; pêle-mêle.

Penurie, penury.

Perdie, weak form of Fr. *pardieu.*

Plain, complain ; Fr. *plaindre.*

Pleasaunce, pleasure.

Practised, made ; Gr. πράττω, I make or do.

Prankt, adorned : from 'prink,' a nasalised form of 'prick,' to trim so as to look spruce.

Pricked, spurred, rode.

Quilt, a coverlet ; Lat. *culcita,* a pillow. Cog. 'cushion.'

Rabblement, mob. From the noise of their chattering. Lowland Scots 'raible,' to chatter (Burns).

Rampant, rearing ; Fr. *ramper,* to creep up, to climb.

Refel, refute ; prove to be false ; from Lat. *fallere.*

Replevy, rescue ; O. Fr. *replevir,* to give back detained goods on a pledge.

Sable, black, dark ; O. Fr. *sable,* a black furred carnivore.

Saunter, stroll idly. Derivation unknown ; see Skeat.

Sear, withered, dried.

Sheen,adj.bright; subs.splendour.

Shook, for shaken.

Sicker, sure, secure.

Sir, familiarly 'sirrah' ; also a title of respect. Lat. *senior.*

Sleek, to make sleek.

Smackt, tasted, savoured.

Soot, sweet, sweetly. One of Chaucer's forms.

Sort, manner. 'Smiles in such a sort.'—Shakespeare.

Spill, Scots for 'spoil' ; to waste.

Spittles, hospitals.
Spred, spread.
Spright, sprite, spirit. Milton's form.
Stark, dead, stiff, rigid.
Store, a number, abundance.
Stounds, hard hours ; pangs.
Strook, struck. Used by Shelley.
Sublime, v., to elevate or ennoble.
Sweltry, older form of 'sultry.'
Swink, toil. Cf. Comus. A.-S. *swincan,* to labour.
Teem, to be prolific ; A.-S. *team,* a family. Cog. 'team.'
Thrall, slave, or bondman. O.N. *thræll.*
Tight, neat and trim.
Tinct, tint : Lat. *tinctum,* dyed.
Trade, matters whether of business or pastime.
Transmewed, transmuted; cog. 'mews' and 'moult': Lat. *mutare,* to change.
Traunce, trance ; Lat. *transire,* to go over.
Trippen, to trip.
Tromp, trump, form of which 'trumpet' is the diminutive.
Undone, ruined.
Unkempt, uncombed; Scots 'unkaim'd'; rude.
Vacant, idle ; Lat. *vacans, -tem.*
Vild, vile.
Vulgar, common ; Lat. *vulgaris.*
Wain, waggon ; A.-S. *wægn.*

Ween, suppose, think. A.-S. *wénan.*
Weet, know ; from 'wit.'
Welkin, sky. A.-S. *wolcen,* a cloud.
Well-a-day, for 'well away,' a corruption of A.-S. *wá lá wá* = woe lo ! woe.
Whenas, when.
Whilom, formerly; A.-S. *hwilum,* dat. pl. of *hwil,* time.
Wight, a being ; A.-S. *wiht.*
Wis, for **ywis,** certainly.
Wise, guise, manner, or way; A.-S. *wise.*
Withouten, without.
Wonne, dwelling ; A.-S. *wunian,* to dwell.
Wot, from 'weet,' *supra.*
Wroke, wreaked.
Y-, A.-S. *ge-,* sign of past participle.
Y-blent, blended.
Y-born, born.
Y-buried, buried.
Y-clad, clad.
Y-clept, named ; A.-S. *clepian,* to call.
Y-fere, in company ; M.E. *fere,* a companion ; *faran,* to go.
Y-hung, hung.
Y-molten, melted.
Yode, went.
Yore, long ago ; A.-S. *gedra,* = in years past.
Y-spring, spring.

THE END.

Books published during the twelve months ending June 1, 1909, or in the Press, or in preparation, are underlined.

ENGLISH

DICTIONARIES

CONCISE ETYMOLOGICAL DICTIONARY. ByW.W Skeat. New Edition, arranged alphabetically. 5s. 6d.

STUDENT'S DICTIONARY OF ANGLO-SAXON. B H. Sweet. 8s. 6d. net.

CONCISE DICTIONARY OF MIDDLE ENGLISH from 1150-1580. By A. L. Mayhew and W. W. Skeat. 7s. 6d.

GRAMMAR AND PHONETICS

THE KING'S ENGLISH: Abridged Edition. B H. W. F. and F. G. F. 1s. 6d. Complete Edition, 5s. net.

SENTENCE ANALYSIS. By one of the authors of *Th King's English.* 1s. 6d.

WRITING OF ENGLISH. By Philip J. Hartog, with the assistance of Mrs. A. H. Langdon. Second Edition. 2s. 6d.

PHONETIC TRANSCRIPTIONS OF ENGLISH PROSE. By D. Jones. 2s.

SOUNDS OF ENGLISH. By H. Sweet. 2s. 6d.

PRIMER OF PHONETICS. By H. Sweet. 3 Ed. 3s. 6d

PRIMER OF SPOKEN ENGLISH. By H. Sweet Second Edition, revised. 3s. 6d.

CHART OF ENGLISH SPEECH SOUNDS. With key-words and notes. By D. Jones. 4d. net.

DR. SWEET'S HISTORICAL GRAMMARS

PRIMER OF HISTORICAL ENGLISH GRAMMAR. 2s

SHORT HISTORICAL ENGLISH GRAMMAR. 4s. 6d

NEW ENGLISH GRAMMAR. 2 Ed. Part I, 10s. 6d Part II, 3s. 6d.

I

ANGLO-SAXON AND MIDDLE ENGLISH

DR. SWEET'S PRIMERS & READERS

FIRST STEPS IN ANGLO-SAXON. 2s. 6d.

ANGLO-SAXON PRIMER. 8 Ed., revised. 2s. 6d.

ANGLO-SAXON READER. 8 Ed., revised. 9s. 6d.

SECOND ANGLO-SAXON READER. 4s. 6d.

ANGLO-SAXON READING PRIMERS. 2 vols. Second Edition. 2s. each.

SECOND MIDDLE ENGLISH PRIMER. 2 Ed. 2s. 6d.

FIRST MIDDLE ENGLISH PRIMER. 2 Ed., rev. 2s. 6d.

PRIMER OF ENGLISH ETYMOLOGY. By W. W. SKEAT. Fourth Edition, revised. 1s. 6d.

PRIMER OF CLASSICAL AND ENGLISH ETYMO-LOGY. By W. W. SKEAT. 2s.

BOOK FOR THE BEGINNER IN ANGLO-SAXON. By J. EARLE. Fourth Edition, revised throughout. 2s. 6d.

EARLY ENGLISH
DR. SKEAT'S EDITIONS

CHAUCER: Prologue, Knightes Tale, Nonne Prestes Tale. R. Morris's Edition, re-edited. 2s. 6d. Separately, *Prologue*, 1s.

Man of Lawes Tale, Pardoneres Tale, Second Nonnes Tale, Chanouns Yemannes Tale. New Edition, revised. 4s. 6d.

Prioresses Tale, Sir Thopas, Monkes Tale, Clerkes Tale, Squieres Tale. Seventh Edition. 4s. 6d.

Hous of Fame. 2s.

Legend of Good Women. 6s.

Minor Poems. Second Edition, enlarged. 10s. 6d.

ENGLISH

LANGLAND: Piers the Plowman. Sixth Edition. 4s. 6d

LAY OF HAVELOK THE DANE. 4s. 6d.

PIERCE THE PLOUGHMAN'S CREDE. 2s.

PROVERBS OF ALFRED. 2s. 6d.

TALE OF GAMELYN. Second Edition. 1s. 6d.

WYCLIFFE'S BIBLE. Job, Psalms, Proverbs, Ecclesiastes, and Song of Solomon. 3s. 6d.

New Testament. 6s.

DREAM OF THE ROOD. Edited by A. S. Cook. 3s. 6d

ELIZABETHAN

BACON: Advancement of Learning. With woodcuts. By W. Aldis Wright. 3s. 6d.

HAKLUYT: Voyages of the Elizabethan Seamen. By E. J. Payne. With notes and maps by C. R. Beazley. With illustrations. 4s. 6d. Separately, *Voyages of Hawkins, Frobisher, and Drake*, 2s. 6d.; *Voyages of Gilbert and Drake*, 2s. 6d.

Select Narratives. Containing the Voyages of Gilbert, Hawkins, Drake, Frobisher, Raleigh, and others. With portraits. By E. J. Payne. First and second series. Second Ed. 5s. each.

HOOKER: Ecclesiastical Polity, Bk.I. By R. W. Church. 2s.

MARLOWE: Edward II. By O. W. Tancock. Third Edition. 2s. (boards) and 3s. (cloth).

MORE: Utopia. By J. Churton Collins. 2s.

NORTH: Translation of Plutarch's Lives of Coriolanus, Caesar, Brutus, and Antonius. By R. H. Carr. 3s. 6d. Separately, *Coriolanus*, and *Caesar*, 1s. 6d. each.

CLARENDON PRESS SCHOOL BOOKS

SHAKESPEARE: Select Plays.

By W. G. Clark and W. Aldis Wright.

Hamlet. 2s.	Merchant of Venice. 1s.
Macbeth. 1s. 6d.	Richard II. 1s. 6d.

By W. Aldis Wright.

As You Like It. 1s. 6d.	King John. 1s. 6d.
Coriolanus. 2s. 6d.	King Lear. 1s. 6d.
Henry VIII. 2s.	Midsummer Night's Dream. 1s. 6d.
Henry V. 2s.	Much Ado About Nothing. 1s. 6d.
Henry IV. Part I. 2s.	Richard III. 2s. 6d.
Julius Caesar. 2s.	Tempest. 1s. 6d.

Twelfth Night. 1s. 6d.

SCENES FROM OLD PLAY-BOOKS. By P. Simpson. 3s. 6d.

SELECT PLAYS OF SHAKESPEARE FOR SCHOOLS
(Merchant of Venice, Tempest, As You Like It, Henry V, Julius Caesar, Hamlet, Macbeth, Midsummer Night's Dream, Richard II). Slightly abridged, with introduction and notes, by G. S. Gordon. 3s. 6d.
In the press.

SIDNEY: Apologie for Poetry. By J. C. Collins. 2s. 6d.

SPENSER: Faery Queene, Books I, II. By G. W. Kitchin and A. L. Mayhew. 2s. 6d. each.

SEVENTEENTH CENTURY

BUNYAN: Pilgrim's Progress, Grace Abounding, and Imprisonment. By E. Venables. With portrait. Second Edition, revised by M. Peacock. 3s. 6d.

Holy War and the Heavenly Footman. By M. Peacock. 3s. 6d.

CLARENDON: History of the Rebellion, Book VI. By T. Arnold. Second Edition. 5s.

DRYDEN: Selections. Prose and verse. By G. E. Hadow. 2s. 6d.

Dramatic Poesy. By T. Arnold. Third Edition, revised by W. T. Arnold. 3s. 6d.

Selections. Including Oliver Cromwell, Astraea Redux, Annus Mirabilis, Absalom and Achitophel, Religio Laici, and The Hind and the Panther. By W. D. Christie. Fifth Edition, revised by C. H. Firth. 3s. 6d.

Select Essays. By W. P. Ker. Two vols. 8s. net.

4

ENGLISH

MILTON: Areopagitica. By J. W. HALES. 3s.

Comus. By R. C. BROWNE, 6d. By O. ELTON, 1s.

English Poems. By R. C. BROWNE. New Edition
revised by H. BRADLEY. Two vols. 6s. 6d. Separately: Vol. I
4s.; Vol. II, 3s.

Vol. I: Early Poems (L'Allegro, Il Penseroso, Arcades, Comus
Lycidas, &c.); Sonnets; Paradise Lost, I-VI.

Vol. II: Paradise Lost, VII-XII; Paradise Regained; Samson
Agonistes.

Il Penseroso. By O. ELTON. 4d.

Lycidas. By R. C. BROWNE, 3d. By O. ELTON, 6d.

L'Allegro. By O. ELTON. 4d.

Paradise Lost. Book I, by H. C. BEECHING, 1s. 6d.
Book II, by E. K. CHAMBERS, 1s. 6d. Together, 2s. 6d.

Samson Agonistes. By J. CHURTON COLLINS. 1s.

EIGHTEENTH CENTURY

ADDISON: Selections from the Spectator. By T. ARNOLD.
4s. 6d.

ADDISON and STEELE: The Coverley Papers from *The
Spectator*. By O. M. MYERS. 2s.

BURKE: Selections. By E. J. PAYNE. Second Edition.
Vol. I: Thoughts on the Present Discontents; the two Speeches on
America. With additions and corrections. 4s. 6d.
Vol. II: Reflections on the French Revolution. 5s.
Vol. III: Letters on the Regicide Peace. 5s.

BURNS: Selections. By J. LOGIE ROBERTSON. Second
Edition. 3s. 6d.

COWPER: Selections. By H. T. GRIFFITH.
Vol. I: Didactic Poems of 1782, with some Minor Pieces 1779-1783. 3s.
Vol. II: The Task, with Tirocinium and some Minor Poems 1784-
1799. Third Edition. 3s.

CLARENDON PRESS SCHOOL BOOKS

GOLDSMITH: Deserted Village. (Text only.) By G. BIRK-BECK HILL. 2d. Traveller. By G. BIRKBECK HILL. 1s. Selections. By AUSTIN DOBSON. 3s. 6d.

GRAY: Elegy, and Ode on Eton College. (Text only.) 2d. Selections. By EDMUND GOSSE. With additional notes for schools, by F. WATSON. 1s. 6d.

JOHNSON: Life of Milton. By C. H. FIRTH. 1s.6d.(boards) and 2s. 6d. (cloth).
Rasselas. By G. BIRKBECK HILL. 2s. and 4s. 6d.
Rasselas, and Lives of Dryden and Pope. By A. MILNES. Second Edition, revised. 4s. 6d. Separately, *Lives*, 2s. 6d.
Vanity of Human Wishes. By E. J. PAYNE. 3rd Ed. 4d.

LOCKE: Conduct of the Understanding. By T. FOWLER. Fifth Edition. 2s. 6d.

PARNELL: Hermit. 2d.

POPE: Essay on Man. By MARK PATTISON. 6th Ed. 1s. 6d. Satires and Epistles. By MARK PATTISON. 4th Ed. 2s. Rape of the Lock. By G. HOLDEN. 2s.

STEELE: Selections from the Tatler, Spectator, and Guardian. By AUSTIN DOBSON. With portrait. 7s. 6d.

SWIFT: Selections. By SIR HENRY CRAIK. Two vols. 7s. 6d. each.

THOMSON: Seasons and Castle of Indolence. By J. LOGIE ROBERTSON. 4s. 6d. Separately, *Castle of Indolence*, 1s. 6d.

NINETEENTH CENTURY

ARNOLD: Selected Poems. By H. B. GEORGE and A. M. LEIGH. 2s.
Merope, with the Electra of Sophocles translated by R. WHITELAW. By J. C. COLLINS. 3s. 6d.

BROWNING: Strafford. By H. B. GEORGE. 2s.

BYRON: Childe Harold. By H. F. TOZER. 3rd Ed. 3s. 6d.

CAMPBELL: Gertrude of Wyoming. By H. M. FITZ-GIBBON. Second Edition. 1s.

DE QUINCEY: Spanish Military Nun, and Revolt of the Tartars. By V. H. COLLINS. With 2 maps. 2s. Text only, 9d. (paper) and 1s. (cloth). *In the Press.*

6

ENGLISH

KEATS: Hyperion, Book I. By W. T. ARNOLD. 4d.
Odes. With 4 illustrations. By A. C. DOWNER. 3s. 6d. net.

KINGSLEY: Water Babies. Slightly abridged. With
notes and illustrations. By J. HORACE-SMITH and M. L. MILFORD. 2s. 6d.
Westward Ho! By A. D. INNES. 2s.

MACAULAY: History of England, Ch. III. By A. L.
BOWLEY. 2s. 6d. Text only, 9d. (paper), and 1s. (cloth). *Immediately.*

MACAULAY and THACKERAY: Essays on Addison.
With twelve essays by Addison. By G. E. HADOW. 2s.

SCOTT: Lady of the Lake. With map. By W. MINTO. 3s. 6d.

Lay of the Last Minstrel. By W. MINTO. Second
Edition. 1s. 6d. Separately, Canto I, with introduction and notes, 6d.

Lord of the Isles. By T. BAYNE. 2s. and 2s. 6d.

Marmion. By T. BAYNE. 3s. 6d.

Ivanhoe. By C. E. THEODOSIUS. 2s.

Legend of Montrose. By G. S. GORDON. With map. 2s.

Old Mortality. By H. B. GEORGE. 2s.

Quentin Durward. By P. F. WILLERT. 2s.

Rob Roy. By R. S. RAIT. 2s.

Talisman. By H. B. GEORGE. 2s.

Waverley. By A. D. INNES. *Immediately.*

Woodstock. By J. S. C. BRIDGE. 2s.

SHELLEY: Adonais. By W. M. ROSSETTI and A. O.
PRICKARD. Second Edition. 3s. 6d.

TENNYSON. English Idylls and other Poems, 2s. Lady
of Shalott and other Poems, 2s. Together in one vol., 3s. By B. C
MULLINER. *Immediately.*

Enid. By C. B. WHEELER. 1s. 6d.

WORDSWORTH: White Doe of Rylstone, &c. By
WILLIAM KNIGHT. 2s. 6d.

CLARENDON PRESS SCHOOL BOOKS

SELECT ENGLISH CLASSICS

Edited with introductions by A. T. QUILLER-COUCH.
Each 3d. (paper) and 4d. (cloth).

SELECTIONS FROM—

POETRY AND DRAMA

ARNOLD : Poems.

BLAKE : Poems.

BROWNING (R.) : Poems.

COLERIDGE : Poems.

COWPER : Poems.

CRABBE : Poems.

EARLY ENGLISH LYRICS (with glossarial notes).

EVERYMAN (complete, with glossarial notes).

GOLDSMITH : Traveller, and Deserted Village.

HOOD : Poems.

KEATS : Poems.

MARLOWE : Plays.

MARVELL : Poems.

MILTON : Minor Poems.

MILTON and WORDSWORTH : Sonnets.

ROBIN HOOD : Old Ballads.

SHAKESPEARE : Songs and Sonnets.

POETRY AND DRAMA (contd.)

SHELLEY : Poems.

TENNYSON : Poems.

WHITMAN : Poems.

WORDSWORTH : Poems.

PROSE

BOSWELL : Life of Johnson.

BUNYAN.

DEFOE.

HAZLITT.

LAMB.

NAPIER : Peninsular War.

WALPOLE : Letters.

WALTON : Lives, and Angler.

Together in cloth bindings.

BUNYAN, COWPER, CRABBE, and DEFOE. 1s. 3d.

BUNYAN and DEFOE. 8d.

OXFORD PLAIN TEXTS

Each 3d. (paper) and 4d. (cloth).

ARNOLD : Balder Dead, and Mycerinus. Sohrab and Rustum.

BYRON : Childe Harold, Cantos I, II, III, IV, 3d. or 4d. each. Together, cloth, I-II, 8d. ; I-IV, 1s. 3d.

COLERIDGE : Ancient Mariner, and Christabel.

GRAY : Elegy, and Odes.

KEATS : Isabella, and Eve of St. Agnes.

MILTON : Paradise Lost, Books I, II, V, VI, 3d. or 4d. each. *In the Press.*

Each 9d. (paper) and 1s. (cloth).

DE QUINCEY : Spanish Military Nun, and Revolt of the Tartars. *In the Press.*

MACAULAY : History of England, Ch III. *Immediately.*

SPENSER : Faerie Queene, Book I. *Immediately.*

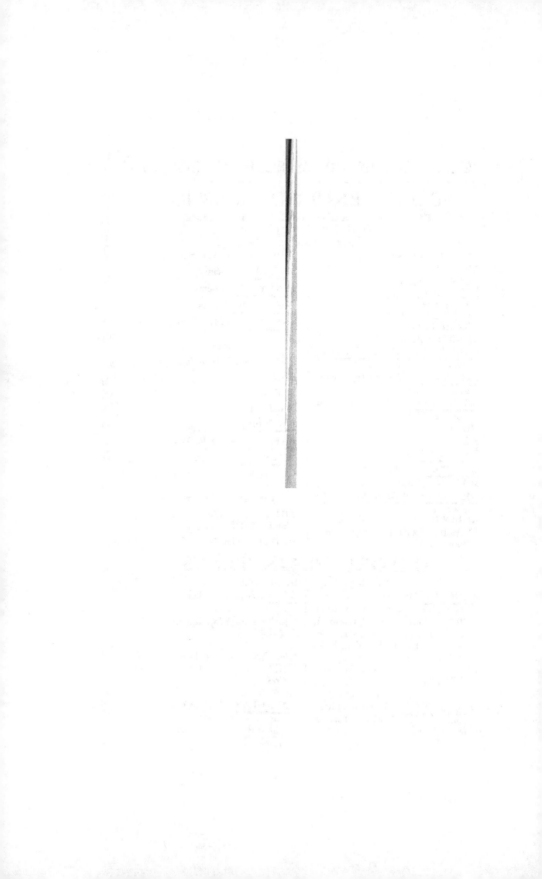

CPSIA information can be obtained
at www.ICGtesting.com
Printed in the USA
LVHW020924270121
677608LV00013B/339

9 781346 666860